WRITING
BRIEF EDITION

DISCARD

WRITING
BRIEF EDITION

Elizabeth Cowan
Texas A & M University

SCOTT, FORESMAN AND COMPANY
Glenview, Ill.

Dallas, Tex.
Oakland, N.J.
Palo Alto, Calif.
Tucker, Ga.
London, England

Acknowledgments for all copyrighted material used are given on pages 347–348, which are a legal extension of the copyright page.

Illustrations by Edward Malsberg and edward a. butler.

An Instructor's Manual is available. It may be obtained through a local Scott, Foresman representative or by writing to English Editor, College Division, Scott, Foresman and Company, 1900 E. Lake Avenue, Glenview, IL 60025.

Writing, **Brief Edition, was prepared with the assistance of Martha Weathers, Houston Community College.**

Library of Congress Cataloging in Publication Data:

Cowan, Elizabeth, 1940–
  Writing.

  Brief ed. of: Writing/Elizabeth Cowan.
Glenview, Ill.: Scott, Foresman, 1982.

  Includes index.
  1. English language—Rhetoric.   I. Cowan, Elizabeth.
Writing.   II. Title.
PE1408.C659 1983   808′.042   82–16930
ISBN 0–673–15735–0

Copyright © 1983 Scott, Foresman and Company.
All Rights Reserved.
Printed in the United States of America.
1 2 3 4 5 6 RRC 87 86 85 84 83 82

PREFACE

Writing, in its hardbound form, has met and continues to meet with enormous success. So why a brief edition of *Writing?* In effect, because of your requests.

I have received letters from many parts of the country which read, "When is there going to be a short edition?" "When will the book be out in paperback?" "We want to adopt your book, but we have only a one-semester course."

It turns out that what was needed was a brief edition of *Writing* that selected the essential parts of the text to make a shorter whole. And that is what has been done.

Writing, Brief Edition, is the *heart* of *Writing,* presented in a cohesive, smoothly flowing whole. Many parts of the text have been rewritten; all have been brought up to date. *Writing,* Brief Edition, provides the same lively, detailed instructions in the writing process, done with fewer extras than are found in the bigger book. Here is what *Writing,* Brief Edition, contains.

There are five major sections: *Creating, Shaping, Completing, Practical Applications,* and a *Handbook*. The first three of these follow the writing process from the first random word put down on paper; through the thesis formation/development stage; to the polished, revised, and edited final copy. The fourth section applies the concepts learned in the *Creating, Shaping,* and *Completing* stages to practical writing: research papers, essay examinations, and business writing. The final section supplies the necessary information about conventions of grammar, punctuation, usage, and mechanics in a concise handbook. Throughout the text you will find:

—lively conversation
—visual reinforcement of concepts
—an attractive and functional design format
—a "divide-and-conquer" plan that makes writing more manageable
—traditional and basic principles of writing placed in contemporary contexts
—every aspect of writing illustrated by both student and professional examples
—self-contained writing assignments, complete with how-to instructions for students and writing contexts for essays

Stage 1/Creating concentrates on how to get ideas for writing. Covering invention from Aristotle to modern times, Stage 1 provides step-by-step instructions in how to find something authentic and interesting to say in a piece of writing: how to know what you think about a subject. Specifically, this first section teaches three heuristics in depth (called *Creating Techniques* in this text): **looping, cubing,** and **classical invention.** Studying these approaches will not only provide writers with a number of ways to think about a subject but will also reinforce the fundamental concept: *Find something to say before attempting to write the essay itself.* After studying Stage 1, beginning writers will always have something beneficial to do when they sit down to write. It is the aim of this first section to teach invention heuristics that are directly related to the writing of essays, research papers, and kindred applications. That is why the techniques have not been referred to as *free writing* or *prewriting.* While there are warm-up exercises that are valuable to students for getting pen to paper, those exercises have not been included in this text. Instead, the *Creating Stage* includes heuristics that can lead directly to an essay or other piece of writing. There is a direct relationship between the writing students learn to do in this stage and the final copy of their assignment. You will find that there is no time wasted in the process; the activities from *Creating* through *Completing* are of a piece: they are time- and work-efficient.

Stage 2/Shaping begins with a down-to-earth discussion of current communication theory, emphasizing the crucial role that *audience* plays in any piece of writing. *Shaping* covers such crucial subjects as identifying and evaluating an audience, finding a good thesis, developing a thesis, forming the essay, recognizing and practicing various basic essay arrangements, writing first drafts, outlining, and rewriting. In *Shaping* you will find the essential concepts of structured, developed writing placed in a context that explains to students why such things are important. The writing assignments and application exercises reinforce these shaping concepts.

Stage 3/Completing covers all of the basics for revision and editing. *Revising for flow* concentrates on the paragraph: topic sentence and function paragraphs, transition words—ways to make writing coherent. *Revising for energy* concentrates on the sentence: sentence combining, sentence variety, parallelism, subordination, coordination, and repetition and balance. *Revising for punch* concentrates on the word: vague vs. specific, jargon vs. concrete, colorless vs. descriptive. Editing skills—correct spelling, punctuation, accepted usage, mechanics—are covered in detail for students as they finish a piece of work.

In the **Practical Applications** section of the text, students are taught how to apply the three stages of the writing process—*Creating, Shaping,* and *Completing*—to particular kinds of writing. There is a thorough chapter on the *Research Paper* with instruction in both the MLA and the APA styles of documentation. The chapter on the *Essay Examination* teaches students how to write good test answers in short time and contains student examples for study and practice. The chapter on *Business Writing* is complete with business letters, job applications, résumés—everything needed to refer to for entering and performing in the job market. Models and examples abound.

Finally, the **Handbook** is a compilation of information about parts of speech, diction and style, in-depth editing, spelling, punctuation, grammar, mechanics, and usage.

In addition to the five major divisions of the text, there are six mini-chapters scattered throughout the book: *Writing Assignments for Essays*. These assignments cover the following purposes for writing: personal experience, how-to, problem/solution, explanation, evaluation, and assertion-with-proof. Included with each assignment are contexts that students can use to determine their audience and purpose for writing, as well as rules and information appropriate to that particular kind of essay.

The book is filled with exercises for practice and discussion. Because the book has sprung from years of classroom teaching, it is practical as well as theoretical. Instructors using this text will have a coherent and sequential syllabus for teaching writing. Students using this book will have a step-by-step guide to writing that will stand them in good stead now—while they are writing in college—and later when they write outside of school.

An Instructor's Manual written especially for this Brief Edition is available. It contains teaching suggestions, answers to exercises, and sample graded essays.

I would like to thank Tom Gay and Cliff Mills for their roles in the development of *Writing* and Tom, again, for his crucial role in the early development of *Writing,* Brief Edition. To Amanda Clark, Jane Steinmann, Andrea Coens, and Lydia Webster go more acknowledgments than I have room to state. These people have shown a dedication to and support for the completion of this book which is unprecedented in my experience. I thank each of you.

I would also like to thank Edward P. J. Corbett, Donald Stewart, Paul Bryant, and Marilyn Cooper for their central roles in the development of *Writing;* they reviewed the text at every stage, encouraged, corrected, and revised. And to the reviewers for this Brief Edition, Jeffrey Gross, University of Mississippi; Walter Klarner, Johnson County Community College; Lucille Schultz, University of Maryland, and David Skwire, Cuyahoga Community College: I am grateful to you.

Without my friend and colleague, Martha Weathers, this book would not have been completed when it was. She cut, smoothed fuzzy edges, melded, refined, cleared out snarls, caught inconsistencies, and made almost magically a coherent whole. Her dependability, diligence, keen intellect, and hard-nosed scrutiny were always supported by her belief in what *Writing* accomplishes in the classroom. Without her, this Brief Edition would not be the book that it is.

Finally, to Tommie and Rachel Harper, Barbara and Wilson Walker, Frank, Sheri and Sarah Harper, Pearl Cowan, Blanch Ninesling, Frances Leach, Ernestine Hambrick, Hans and Marjorie Rutimann, Amilde Hadden, John Bradley, Perry Skates, Paul Franks, Sue Young Stewart, Ron Radke, Kathy Nigh, Pat Martin, Tom Waldrep, Rita Keneipp, and Jerele Don Neeld: thank you for being in my life.

Elizabeth Cowan
Possom Creek
Soddy-Daisy, Tenn.

FOR GREG

i carry your heart with me(i carry it in
my heart)i am never without it(anywhere
i go you go,my dear;and whatever is done
by only me is your doing,my darling)
                                                i fear
no fate(for you are my fate,my sweet)i want
no world(for beautiful you are my world, my true)
and it's you are whatever a moon has always meant
and whatever a sun will always sing is you

here is the deepest secret nobody knows
(here is the root of the root and the bud of the bud
and the sky of the sky of a tree called life;which grows
higher than soul can hope or mind can hide)
and this is the wonder that's keeping the stars apart

i carry your heart(i carry it in my heart)

                                                                             e. e. cummings

TABLE OF CONTENTS

BUILDING A CABIN, WRITING AN ESSAY   1

STAGE 1/CREATING

   Overview   7
   Purpose   8

CREATING AND WRITING   8

SIMPLE CREATING TECHNIQUES   9

   The Reporter's Formula   10
   Brainstorming   10
   Making a List   11

      APPLICATION   12

EXPANDED CREATING TECHNIQUES   13

   Looping   13

      APPLICATION   20

   Cubing   21
   Classical Invention   25

      APPLICATION   34

SUMMARY   34

      SUMMARY CHART   35
      APPLICATION   36

WRITING ASSIGNMENT
THE PERSONAL EXPERIENCE ESSAY 37

CONTEXTS 37
CREATING 38
WRITING THE ESSAY 38
FINAL CHECK 39

STAGE 2/SHAPING

Overview 41
Purpose 42

GOING PUBLIC: WRITING FOR AN AUDIENCE 42

The Difference Between Public and Private Writing 42

HOW COMMUNICATION HAPPENS 43

Speaking—"Person A" 43
Listening—"Person B" 44
Get It? 44

APPLICATION 45

WRITING TO COMMUNICATE 46

EARLY SHAPING 48

PRELIMINARY AGREEMENTS 48

Why Are You Writing? 49
To Whom Are You Writing? 49
Picture a Specific Audience 50
What Do You Want to Communicate in the Writing? 51

APPLICATION 52

WRITING ASSIGNMENT
THE HOW-TO ESSAY 53

CONTEXTS 53
CREATING 54
SPECIFIC AUDIENCE 54
FINAL CHECK 55

THE TRIAL DRAFT   56

How to Write the Trial Draft 57

BETWEEN EARLY AND LATE SHAPING   60

READER: THE READER IS A PERSON, NOT A WALL   60

APPLICATION 63

THESIS: THE THESIS IS A MAGIC STRING   66

Summary of Thesis 68

APPLICATION 68

FORM: THE MESSAGE CONTAINS THE FORM 70

Time Order 72
Spatial Order 73
General-Specific Order 74
Breakdown Order 75
Relationship Order 76
Mixed Forms 77
Review of Patterns of Organization 79

APPLICATION 79

WRITING ASSIGNMENT THE PROBLEM/SOLUTION ESSAY 81

CONTEXTS 82
CHOOSING A PROBLEM 83
CREATING 83
SHAPING 83
FINAL CHECK 84

LATE SHAPING   85

MAKE THE MOST OF YOUR INTRODUCTION 86

APPLICATION 87

STICK TO YOUR THESIS   89

APPLICATION 94

DEVELOP YOUR THESIS 96
    The Bare Bones Outline 97
    What Does Development Look Like? 99
    Examples and Illustrations 100
    Description 100
    Narration 101
    Details 101
    Comparison and Contrast 101
    Cause/Effect 102
    Analysis 102
    Analysis by Division 102
    Classification 103
    Definition 103

MAKE THE MOST OF YOUR CONCLUSION 105
    APPLICATION 107

THE PROMISE AND DELIVERY SYSTEM—WHAT SHAPING IS ALL ABOUT 108
    APPLICATION 108

WRITING ASSIGNMENT THE EXPLANATION ESSAY 110
    CONTEXTS 110
    CREATING 112
    SHAPING 112
    FINAL CHECK 112

STAGE 3/COMPLETING

    Overview 115
    Purpose 116

WHY COMPLETE? 116
    The Constructive Critical Eye 116
    What Completing Will Do 117

REVISING FOR FLOW: PARAGRAPHS 119

THE TOPIC SENTENCE PARAGRAPH 120

APPLICATION 122
Principle 1: Tell the Reader Clearly What the Paragraph Is About 123

APPLICATION 126
Principle 2: Make Sure That Every Sentence in the Topic Sentence Paragraph Is Related to the Topic Sentence 128

APPLICATION 129
Principle 3: Always Give the Reader Enough Information 130

APPLICATION 133
APPLICATION 137

THE FUNCTION PARAGRAPH 138

Make a Transition from One Part of the Writing to Another 139
Set Off Conversational Dialogue 140
Break Up Long Paragraphs or Make Paragraphs of About Equal Length 140
Accommodate the Author's Personal Writing Style 141
Emphasize a Point, Develop an Example, or Add Detail 142

APPLICATION 143

TRANSITIONS AND REMINDER SIGNS 145

Transitions 146
Giving What You Say a Sense of Wholeness 146
Transition Signal Words 149
Reminder Signs 150

APPLICATION 151

WRITING ASSIGNMENT THE EVALUATION ESSAY 152

CONTEXTS 153
CREATING 154
SHAPING 155
COMPLETING 155

REVISING FOR ENERGY: SENTENCES — 156

MAKING VARIETY HAPPEN IN YOUR SENTENCES — 156
APPLICATION 158

SENTENCE COMBINING — 159
APPLICATION 160

COMBINING FOR EMPHASIS — 161

Coordination 161
APPLICATION 163

Subordination 164
APPLICATION 165

GETTING ENERGY THROUGH STYLE — 165

Parallelism 166
APPLICATION 168

Balance and Repetition 169
APPLICATION 170

REVISING FOR PUNCH: WORDS — 172

EXACTNESS, SPECIFICS, PICTURES, AND IMAGES — 172

Replace Vague Words with Specific, Concrete Words 175
Cut Our Every Word You Don't Absolutely Need 176
Use Action Verbs 176

APPLICATION 177

DISSECTING YOUR PAPER — 179

FINAL CONSIDERATIONS — 182

Editing 182
Manuscript Form 183

WRITING ASSIGNMENT
THE ASSERTION-WITH-PROOF ESSAY
186

CONTEXTS 186

PRACTICAL APPLICATIONS

Overview 189
Purpose 190

WRITING THE RESEARCH PAPER   190

WATCHING A RESEARCH PAPER BEING WRITTEN   193

QUESTIONS TO ASK ABOUT YOUR RESEARCH PAPER   223

SOMETHING EXTRA: A LAGNIAPPE   224

Documentation: MLA Style 224
Documentation: APA Style 230
Outline 233
Paraphrase 234
Plagiarism 234
Reference Material 236

APPLICATION 241

WRITING ESSAY TESTS   243

THE CREATING STAGE   243

THE SHAPING STAGE   243

What to Do If You Think of a New Point While Writing 244

THE COMPLETING STAGE — 245

SUMMARY — 245
APPLICATION 246

WRITING FOR BUSINESS — 247

FEATURES OF BUSINESS WRITING — 247
Tone 247
Accessibility 247
Accuracy 248
Format 249
Appearance 250

BUSINESS LETTERS — 251
The "You" Attitude 251
Requests 251

JOB APPLICATIONS — 252
Audience 252
Conventions of the Job Application Letter 254
Creating 254
Shaping 256
Completing 259

RÉSUMÉS — 262

THE HANDBOOK

Overview 267

PARTS OF SPEECH — 268
Nouns 268
Pronouns 270
Verbs 273
Adjectives 278

    Adverbs 280
    Prepositions 281
    Conjunctions 283
    Interjections 284

SENTENCE ERRORS   284

    Syntax Errors 284
    Punctuation Errors 290

DICTION AND STYLE   293

    Problems of Diction and Style 293
    Errors in Diction and Style 296

PUNCTUATION   298

SPELLING   307

    Spelling Rules 310

MECHANICS   311

    Capitalization 311
    Abbreviations and Symbols 313
    Numbers 314
    Italics 314

A.B.C. GLOSSARY OF USAGE   315

INDEX   338

BUILDING A CABIN, WRITING AN ESSAY

Does it seem strange to begin a textbook on writing with an essay on building a cabin?

Actually, there's a definite connection. Writing essays—what you will be doing in this class—is similar in several ways to building a cabin. The steps you go through, from first having the idea to finally completing the project, are very much the same. Let's consider these stages, one at a time.

STAGE 1

Naturally, a cabin doesn't simply materialize out of thin air. A lot of planning and preparation happen before you can sit in a cheerful room and enjoy the view through the brand-new windows. That planning and preparation may actually have begun so far back that it would be hard now to know just when the idea of building a cabin first occurred. It may have been at age four, when you got some Lincoln Logs for a birthday present and started building pioneer cabins. It could have begun with staying in cabins at camp. The planning or dreaming or thinking-about-it could have continued with seeing cabins in television shows and in movies. And perhaps along the way there were occasional stories about people who lived in cabins.

No matter when and how the thought about building a cabin first appeared, having the idea is at the center of the first stage. First there is an idea of building. During this stage you merely think about it, collect ideas, gather impressions.

When we look at this initial stage closely, we find that it has several specific characteristics.

Stage 1 is Exploratory. You might buy cabin books, send off for floor plans, draw blueprints, build model cabins out of matchsticks, visit cabins, consider different locations to build on, save money for a cabin, collect pictures of cabins. You are just thinking of *all* the possibilities at this stage, and you want to range as far as you can.

Stage 1 is Tentative. In this stage you're merely collecting ideas; you've made no commitment. You have not decided where the cabin is going to be built. You are not committed to a particular kind of cabin. You haven't invested in land or materials, only thought about them. You're just considering a lot of possibilities. It's all tentative, and you are totally free to change your mind as often as you want.

Stage 1 is Enjoyable. You can dream your biggest dreams in this stage; it doesn't cost you a dime. You can say "I like this . . . I like that . . . I like the other" without having to choose among the contradictory ideas. You can experiment, change, adapt and be extravagant, wild, and impractical. The point is to collect as many ideas as possible—*and to have fun while you are doing it*.

OK; now what about writing?

There's a comparable *Stage 1* in writing, when you collect ideas on a subject much as you would collect ideas for building a cabin. Perhaps you begin with an assignment or a simple urge to write. You merely think about it from time to time, maybe while you're vacuuming the rug or washing the car, or maybe while you're walking to another class or standing in line in a cafeteria. Thoughts about the subject simply come up, and you explore what you think about it, what you know about it, and how you feel about it. Certainly, *Stage 1* in writing is *exploratory*.

You also get to experiment with the subject. You can try various approaches, arguing now for it, now against. You can pretend to be an amateur or an expert, an insider or a visitor, someone who is involved or someone who is merely an observer. And you can switch around as much as you like, seeing what works for you and what doesn't. The ideas are tentative.

But can it be *enjoyable* too? Why not? Humans naturally like to explore. And we enjoy operating without limits sometimes, free from commitments and accountabilities. So this stage is enjoyable almost automatically, simply because it is exploratory and tentative. But more than that, it is enjoyable because it gives us something to do to start writing. Rather than sitting there worrying, we're engaged in generating ideas, pursuing thoughts and insights. Eventually, there's the delightful surprise of bumping into a new way of thinking about a thing, a new way of looking at it, a fresh seeing, a forgotten memory, a strong sense of clarity. But that reward comes at the end. At the beginning it is the sense of moving, of being on your way. If you approach this stage by staying open and seeing what you can discover, you'll enjoy it. In fact, if it's not enjoyable, you are probably doing *Stage 1* all wrong.

STAGE 2

There comes a time in building a cabin when the dreaming stops and actual work begins. Here things get more serious. You don't have quite as much freedom as before because you must begin to make some firm decisions. You determine what kind of cabin you are going to build: log, A-frame, prefab, lean-to, or whatever. You start looking seriously for a site, and then you purchase one. You settle on a definite blueprint.

Stage 2 Requires Commitments. You make a series of decisions, plans, agreements, contracts. The project moves out of dreams and ideas into reality—*out of your mind and onto the ground.* Changes at this stage can cost something.

Stage 2 Requires Clear Plans. At this point in the work *you need to be as clear and certain as possible* about the plan of the cabin. Although it is still possible to change a window here and add a partition there, any major changes—say to the foundation or roof—will be very costly.

Stage 2 Requires Physical Work. After the plans, the land, the contracts, and the contractors have all been dealt with, *the physical work begins.* You clear the land, purchase materials, and start building. Down goes the foundation, up go the framing, roof, and walls.

What is the comparable *Stage 2* in writing?

Though the parallels are not exactly the same, there is a *Stage 2* in writing.

That's where you begin making definite choices and commit yourself to a particular purpose, a specific message, an orderly plan. Those *commitments* help you get the ideas out of your head and onto the paper. *Stage 2* moves from private to public writing. And while there was complete freedom in just collecting ideas for yourself, now some discipline needs to be imposed on that jumble of ideas if you want to make logical order of them for someone else.

To be sure, there is *physical work* involved. You can't "think" a piece of writing onto paper, or "talk" it there. You need to sit in one place with a pencil, pen, or typewriter, and keep putting down one word after another, one sentence after another, until the task is done. And serious changes at this point can lead to frustration. On the other hand, you have more leeway to change in *Stage 2* of writing than you would in cabin building. For example, if you don't like what you've written, all it costs you is your time and some paper. But it *does* cost something, and *clear plans can keep the cost to a minimum.*

STAGE 3

Finally, in cabin building there comes the finishing-up stage. Some people think this is the hardest part of building. (Prefab companies will sell their houses *much* more cheaply if the buyer agrees to do the finishing.) The frame, walls, cabinets, and countertops are all there. The rough work has been done; all the big pieces and major chunks are in the right places. Now it's time for the finishing touches.

Stage 3 Handles the Fine Details. It's time to sand, rub, paint, stain, varnish, install fixtures, clean glass, haul away building scraps, make a path to the door, put up curtains—in general, turn the shell into a livable cabin. All the major decisions have been implemented at this point. The size, shape, and type of cabin, as well as the location, have all been taken care of. But there are a thousand and one tiny details that have to be handled before the cabin is really finished.

And, yes, there is a *Stage 3* in writing.

Stage 3 completes the writing. It's the cleaning-up stage, the time to consider *fine details*. Are the words spelled right? Any grammatical errors? Is there enough information? Are the left margins even? Is anything left out? These picky, often tedious, time-consuming details do the same for the essay that they do for a cabin: they put on the finishing touches that make the essay presentable to other people. This stage completes the project, and nothing remains to be done. It's finished, ready for an appreciative world. Many people mistakenly think that *Stage 3* is the whole writing process. Although *Stage 3* activities *can* occur any time during the writing process, it makes the most sense to do them at the end. The kind of thinking that *Stage 3* requires actually works *against* your discovering what you want to say and how you want to say it because it is extremely structured and critical. Waiting until *Stage 3* to use this way of looking at your writing lets you have much more freedom in *Stages 1* and *2*.

Paying attention to the similarities between building a cabin and writing an essay can brighten matters more than you think. You don't need to be told that there are differences between building a cabin and writing an essay. It's the similarities, however, that are important. In fact, these similarities can help you learn to write more efficiently—and more enjoyably.

As soon as writing is broken down into stages the way building a cabin is, it becomes *manageable*. Obviously, if you were trying to vacuum your cabin (a *Stage 3* activity) while the roofers were sawing rafters overhead (a *Stage 2* activity), you surely wouldn't get much done; you'd just be frustrated. In the same way, it's ridiculous to worry about spelling while you are collecting ideas in *Stage 1*. Yet we are all prone to do exactly that—to *un*focus our attention and surrender our energy *by trying to handle all three stages at once*.

When you learn to deal with each stage in the writing process at the appropriate time, you will find that you not only accomplish the job but you also enjoy the feeling of satisfaction as you move through each stage. Just as in building a cabin you might decide to change a door after you had already begun to build the room, you may get new ideas (Creating, *Stage 1*) in the very middle of organizing your essay (Shaping, *Stage 2*). Because the stages of writing are recursive, you will discover that each stage is also distinct enough for you to concentrate on one thing at a time. You aren't a nervous wreck, then, from trying to do everything at once. In fact, you are calm and in control because you direct your attention and intention to one part of the process at a time. There's satisfaction *three* times instead of once, since you appreciate finishing each stage. Then there's the final sense of accomplishment when you give your writing to the persons for whom you wrote it.

Wouldn't it be great if, when you finished this book, you found that you could actually enjoy writing essays as much as you'd enjoy building a cabin?

STAGE 1/CREATING

HOW TO FIND SOMETHING TO SAY

OVERVIEW

Creating and Writing

Simple Creating Techniques

    Reporter's Formula
    Brainstorming
    Lists

Expanded Creating Techniques

    Looping
    Cubing
    Classical Invention

Summary

**WRITING ASSIGNMENT:
PERSONAL EXPERIENCE ESSAY**

PURPOSE	Set yourself up to have ideas on the subject
	Follow specific activities to get started on a writing assignment or task
	Tap your total resources by putting all thoughts on paper with no immediate evaluation of their significance or importance
	Discover what you know and think about a particular subject
	Decide exactly what you want to communicate to another person about a particular subject

CREATING AND WRITING

How often have you sat down to write, only to find that you couldn't think of a single thing to say? You wrote a line or two, scratched it out, crumpled up the paper, threw it away, and started the whole cycle all over again. The thoughts just wouldn't come.

This situation occurs for all writers at some time or other, but it occurs most frequently for people who are waiting for a "good idea." Somehow they developed the belief that it is possible to know what they want to say before they begin to write—but that's not usually the way ideas come. Since "good ideas" and fully developed subjects almost never pop into the writer's head—especially during those first minutes or hours—there tends to be a lot of sitting and staring, and even some despair that any thoughts will *ever* come.

Actually, not knowing what to write when you sit down is a perfectly natural reaction to the situation. The feeling is uncomfortable, but it is normal. And the uncertainty can actually be *beneficial*.

"Not knowing what to say can actually be beneficial?" you exclaim, as you watch the clock ticking on the wall.

Yes.

If you sit down and write the very first thing that pops into your mind, you will often get clichés or worn-out information, stuff everybody already knows. You won't really care about what you are saying, and readers won't be involved or interested.

Beginning to write *before* you know what to say and finding out as you go along are some of the best ways for you to think of something personal, fresh, and interesting on the subject, something out of your own experience, something that nobody but you might think of. It also allows you to find out what you think about a subject, to discover something about it, because often you see something quite differently after you write about it than you do before you write. In fact, often it turns out that just getting your thoughts down on paper produces clarity or insight that you wouldn't have otherwise.

"But this is Catch 22," you say. "I've got to write an essay on the topic and give it to someone else, and you say it's OK to start writing before I know what I'm going to tell the person! That will really go over big!"

Well, the way out of Catch 22 is to realize that the writing you do in this stage is *not* the essay; it is a collection of thoughts that will *lead* to the essay.

To CREATE:
To bring into existence: to cause, make; to produce through imaginative skill.

To INVENT:
To think up or imagine; to create or produce for the first time; to make.

To DISCOVER:
To obtain sight or knowledge of; unearth; (presupposes exploration, investigation, or chance encounter, and always implies the previous existence of what becomes known; implies finding rather than making).

> The dog that trots about finds the bone.
> —Spanish proverb

You don't have to worry at this point about whether your thoughts are good or bad; you are just exploring the subject to find something to say. What you put down now is very tentative and is really being written just for you yourself (and your own enjoyment). This stage, in fact, is very private—just you and your subject. You aren't trying to be clear for anyone else; you aren't thinking of committing yourself to any specific part of the subject. You are just writing whatever comes into your head on the subject—maybe a list, a dialogue, even a heap of disjointed thoughts, so that later, with an objective eye, you can read through your private writing and find something you really want to develop into an essay.

"But I've got a deadline," you lament. "I don't have time to waste on writing personal stuff that isn't an essay."

This is The Great Paradox:

Although such exploratory writing won't be an essay, it will perhaps be the most important piece of writing you do for the essay. A good *Creating* period will make the next two stages—*Shaping* and *Completing*—much easier, faster, and more productive. You will discover that you actually *save* time by spending it this way. It may seem strange now, but when you've tried it once or twice, you will see. The freer you are with your time at this stage, the more efficiently your time is spent on the other two stages. This is so because you will have a lot of material to use when you get to the point of deciding exactly what you want to say to a reader, and you will not have to stare at the sheet of paper, waiting for inspiration to strike. It's like already having all the groceries, measuring cups, knives, spoons, utensils, and the like, ready on the kitchen counter before you begin to cook dinner. There's something there for you to work with, and you really will save time.

The creating stage, as chaotic and unsure as it may seem, is not only efficient; it actually leads to a strong, interesting idea for your paper. You will always come up with something to say *if* you are willing to be in motion—curious, persistent, willing to explore. The *Creating Stage* is every bit as valuable as a careful revision or a final draft, and it is truly a major source of writing power.

SIMPLE CREATING TECHNIQUES

Actually, you have been using simple creating techniques for years. Remember sitting down to make a grocery list and as you wrote, thinking of a number of other items you needed that were nowhere in your thoughts when you began the list? And when you gave that oral book report in the fourth grade, your teacher probably told you to answer the 5 W's—*who, what, when, where,* and *why*—and you found that these worked like nudges to help you think of what to say.

Simple creating techniques are *thought-producing* techniques and, while useful in many situations other than writing, they are a particularly valuable way to begin to probe your mind when you have something to write. Let's review these simple creating techniques.

THE REPORTER'S FORMULA

Newspaper reporters use six simple questions as a method for discovering the essentials of events on which they are reporting. You can use these same questions to discover more about a subject on which you want to write.

RULES FOR THE REPORTER'S FORMULA

Rules: Take your subject and ask the following questions about it:

Who?	Where?	Why?
What?	When?	How?

Answering these questions could lead you to see a particular part of the subject that you know enough about—or are interested enough in—to use for the main idea in a piece of public writing. This is a particularly good creating technique to use when you have to write something in a hurry, such as an essay exam question or a newspaper article.

BRAINSTORMING

BRAINSTORM:
A sudden and violent disturbance in the brain; a sudden clever, whimsical, or foolish idea; a group of people freely calling out ideas on a subject; a session to explore a topic in order to produce as many ideas as possible.

Business leaders often employ a *brainstorming* session to discover ways to solve problems, create new products or services, or get a fresh approach to an old situation. Brainstorming is a group activity—ideas spoken by someone else stimulate you to have ideas of your own. It is this back and forth play that causes new thoughts to come. Brainstorming can work particularly well for you as a creating technique if you and several of your friends have the same topic or assignment to write on.

RULES FOR BRAINSTORMING

1. Do it as a group activity.
2. Call out every idea you have on the subject.
3. Be absolutely nonjudgmental. No idea should be made fun of or discarded. You and the others in the group must feel completely free to say whatever comes to mind and know that the idea won't be evaluated.
4. Jot down all the ideas as they are spoken so that you will have a list to use later.
5. Do your own evaluation of the ideas privately sometime after the brainstorming session.

You will probably have a long list of ideas when the brainstorming session is over. Now go through the list and mark out all the ideas that absolutely won't work or that you are just not interested in. Then, of the remaining ideas, pick the one or two that you can really see yourself writing on. Finally, run these ideas through one of the written creating techniques, and you will be well on your way to knowing what you want to say about this subject when you write.

MAKING A LIST

We all make lists in order not to forget. What about making lists in order to discover?

List-making can be a valuable first step in many writing situations, especially those that require you to recall or realize something you already know. For example, you might list the steps in a process—how to make a bookshelf—or list arguments for or against something.

As you settle down to write, a list can a) give you a definite purpose and activity to get you started; b) cause you to have associations and thereby to think of something you might not have thought of before; c) provide you with a framework for your thinking at that moment.

LIST:
An item-by-item printed or written entry of persons or things, often arranged in a particular order, and usually of a specified nature or category: a guest list; a shopping list; to itemize; to catalog.

SUGGESTIONS FOR LIST-MAKING

1. Put a title at the top of your list so you will stay on purpose and always know why you are making the list. ("Why I deserve a raise" or "Things our town could do for young adults.")
2. Write as fast as possible and use short words or phrases.
3. Don't be critical of any item on the list at this point; just collect as many things on the list as you possibly can in a limited time.

When you have finished the list, you can do several things: select the items on the list that seem to have the most promise for your writing; put the items on the list in some order—say, most important to least important; cross out items that you don't like; expand one or two items; add new items. The important thing is for the list to serve as a source of ideas for you as you begin to write your paper.

Elizabeth Cade is president of the local Chamber of Commerce. She must prepare a report to mail to the membership in which she outlines new directions for the organization for the coming year. She dreads this writing task because she isn't sure what she wants to say. She sits down and does a *Creating Stage*, and she finds that ideas emerge that give her confidence that she'll be able to get the report done. The following is what she wrote when doing the *Creating Stage:*

EXAMPLE:
Making a List

Simple Creating Techniques

What do I want the Chamber of Commerce to do next year?

1. Get new business and industry into our town.
2. Sponsor a series of symphony concerts for young people.
3. Have more meetings.
4. Get a government grant to set up a tutoring center for adults in the community.
5. Buy the old Mansard House and convert it into a library and reception hall for the organization.

That list seemed to be everything she could think of right off the bat, so she reread what she had written and had this dialogue with herself:

What does this list tell me?

- That I have long-range and short-range goals for the Chamber of Commerce.
- That I need to decide which of my goals I want the most.
- That I have lots of ideas on things to do but not many on where to get the money to do them.

So I'd better do some serious thinking on this before I start my report. Serious thinking about what?
About arranging goals into short- and long-term groups. About arranging goals in order of importance. About places to get money.
Great. So now you know exactly what you need to think about.
Right. And now that I have these ideas, I know what to develop before I get back to writing the actual report.

In this example you can see how Ms. Cade uses the creating stage to make lists of things she'd like to do and how she talks to herself, in writing, in order to organize her thoughts and direct her energies. And you can also quite clearly see that Elizabeth is actually discovering what she thinks as she goes along. She is spotting areas she needs to concentrate on and seeing problems that she hadn't thought of until she sat down to put words on paper. Her final report will be much better because she does a creating stage *before* she actually begins writing the report.

APPLICATION

Choose one of the writing situations below and do a simple creating stage similar to those described.

1. You are a student whose teacher has just assigned the term's first essay: a description of your home town. What would you write in the creating stage for this assignment?

Stage 1/Creating

2. You are looking for a job; the employment counselor tells you to write a short paper in which you describe all the jobs you have had in the past and what skills you developed on those jobs. What would you write in the creating stage for this assignment?
3. You have just been elected president of your hobby club or interest group, and your local newspaper would like you to write an article that points out to the general public what is so interesting about your group. What would you write in the creating stage for this assignment?

EXPANDED CREATING TECHNIQUES

You have just seen an example in which something as simple as making a list can be a creating activity in the writing process. Unfortunately, creating devices such as lists, dialogues, or brainstorming sessions don't always produce the best idea or enough ideas for a piece of writing. Because this is so, writers find it useful to have a whole catalog of creating techniques that they can choose from. These techniques, to be efficient and profitable, must result in more than motion for motion's sake. After all, if it were just motion we wanted, we would be as satisfied with seasickness as with an essay. The creating stage must lead somewhere; it must move the writer toward a structured, developed piece of writing. Even though the writing in the creating stage is for the writer's benefit and need not be finished (or addressed to any specific audience), still it must be *purposeful*. The purpose of the creating technique is to assist you in coming up with ideas for your writing.

The following three creating techniques are designed to help any writer come up with something to say for any writing task. The techniques are directed toward the writing of essays because that is probably the kind of writing you will be doing most frequently in this course. You will see in the **Applications** section, however, how the three creating techniques can be used for all kinds of writing, including term papers, memos, and letters. For now, however, you want simply to practice the three techniques so that you can experience how they help you form ideas on any subject. Become familiar with them. Make them a permanent part of your own personal repertory of ways to get ideas. With such a repertory you should never again have to worry about not having something to say.

REPERTORY: The stock of songs, plays, operas, readings, or other pieces that a player or company is prepared to perform; the range or number of skills, aptitudes, or special accomplishments of a particular person or group.

LOOPING

Looping is a writing activity in which you start with a subject and, without planning or consciously thinking, write anything that comes into your mind on the topic. This technique lets you explore a subject to see what you know or think about it without making any decisions about whether the ideas are good or bad, or whether they are important enough to do a paper on. The looping activity also gets other things that are on your mind out on paper so they don't block your mind as you work to come up with something to say on the subject.

(You might like to know that this technique is based on an approach Peter Elbow discusses in his book *Writing without Teachers;* in fact, you might enjoy reading his version.)

RULES FOR LOOPING
1. Begin with a specific topic.
2. Write nonstop for *x* amount of minutes.
3. Make no changes or corrections.
4. Write a center of gravity sentence for each loop before going on to the next one.

Begin with a Specific Topic. At the top of the page, put down the subject (topic) you are going to write on in the loop. This allows your mind to focus on one particular thing at the beginning. As you write, you may discover that your mind gets off the subject and you are writing about something else entirely. When this happens, go ahead and finish what you are writing about and then go back to the subject you listed at the top of the page and concentrate on *that* subject. Often what you write that is *off* the subject will be something that is *on* your mind, perhaps worrying you. Or what you write may look as if it were off the subject but is actually connected somehow. Either way, "off-the-subject" writing is valuable because either it gets whatever is on your mind (and in the way of your sticking to the subject) out onto paper, or it gives you an idea that you didn't at first think was connected to the topic. The aim of **looping,** however, is to come up with some idea on a specific subject for a paper. So staying on that subject as closely as possible is the best thing to do.

Write Nonstop for *X* Minutes. This rule is simple but crucial. (Give ten minutes to each loop when you are first learning the technique. As you progress, you may want to increase the amount of time you spend on each loop.) Part of the magic of this technique comes about because you *must* keep writing. Do not take your pencil or pen off the page. Keep it moving the whole ten minutes. You can write things like "I can't think of anything on this topic," or "This topic is dumb," or "I despise this looping activity." You may even draw circles or make chicken-scratch marks on the paper, but *you must keep the pen moving*. This is to keep your thoughts stirred up and your mind open to whatever ideas may occur on the topic.

Make No Corrections. Whether a writer follows this rule or breaks it will determine the success or failure of **looping.** It is just that simple. You absolutely cannot stop to think about whether a word is spelled right or whether a comma is in the wrong place. You cannot stop to make a judgment of whether a statement you have just written is stupid or smart. You cannot stop to decide whether you want to say something or don't. *Any kind of correcting or deliberating will cause the looping activity not to work.* (There is, of course, a time to correct your work; it isn't, however, during the *Creating Stage*.) The purpose of **looping** is to scare up ideas, and to do that you need to forge ahead, not pausing or polishing. So don't mark anything out; don't change anything. Just keep writing.

Write a Center of Gravity Sentence for Each Loop Before Going on to the Next One. Stop when you have finished each loop, *read* what you have written, and *decide* what main thing you seem to be talking about in that loop. What comes up again and again? What is the drift of that particular piece of writing? When you've read your writing and thought about it, express in a single sentence a statement that catches the "hot spot" or essence of what you said in that loop. This activity lets you see what seems to have the most potential at this point. The center of gravity sentence for each loop will give you a starting place for the next loop, a focus for the next piece of writing. The ultimate result is a zeroing in of your thoughts on the subject as you write. Do three loops to complete the creating activity.

To be sure that you understand how **looping** helps you have ideas on a subject, let's do a dry run. We will take a very unspecific subject, a very broad one, and see how the technique leads you to have something quite specific and focused to say about the topic. Just for the sake of setting up a writing context, let's pretend that Opportunity Savings and Loan is opening a new branch in your neighborhood and as part of the advertising is sponsoring a contest for the best completion of this caption: "When opportunity knocks . . ." You plan to enter but have *no* idea what you want to say. We'll run through the creating stage on the subject, *opportunity*.

PRACTICING LOOPING

To get ready to do a ten-minute loop writing on the subject of opportunity, you will need some clean paper (be sure you have plenty) and a pen that won't run out of ink (you may want to have a spare handy). Write the word *opportunity* at the top of the first sheet. Have a clock, watch, or timer so that you can be sure when the ten minutes are up. Be clear about the rules: **no stopping, no changing, no correcting.**

OK. Ready?

TOPIC:
Opportunity

Expanded Creating Techniques

Write the first ten-minute loop on OPPORTUNITY.

What happened during that ten minutes of writing? Did you write much on the subject itself? Did you find that your thoughts mostly rambled and didn't stay on the subject at all? Did you get bored? Did your hand hurt from writing?

Whatever you wrote about in this first loop is right! In the Creating Stage there is no wrong way; every word you write will contribute to your finding something to say. You will see later exactly why this is so.

Find the center of gravity in this first loop on OPPORTUNITY.

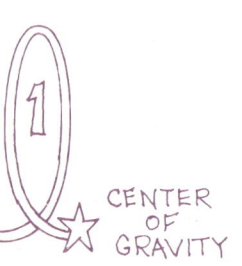

Reread it. Your writing probably moved in several directions and raised a number of different points. But if you *had* to write a single sentence that expressed the hot spot, or the center of gravity of this loop, what would you write? This center of gravity sentence may not be the thing you *wrote the most* about; it may instead be the thing you *like most* in the writing or the thing you find the *most interesting*. Or it might be the idea or subject that you *returned to* several times in the loop. Just make a decision. If you can't figure out the main topic in that loop writing, just make up what you *think* the main topic is.

Write this center of gravity sentence at the end of your first loop.

Now you are ready for the second loop. Copy the center of gravity sentence on the top of a fresh sheet of paper. The rules are the same: your pen can't stop on the page; you can't correct. And, remember, there is *nothing* that can go wrong at this stage.

All set?

Write the second ten-minute loop on OPPORTUNITY.

Is your hand hurting? Shake it and rest. Shift around in your chair. Take two or three good deep breaths.

Now, read over what you wrote this time. Did anything pop up that didn't surface last time? Anything absolutely new? Or did you write about the same thing you wrote about last time? This loop may be closely related to the first one, may be something that *grew out of* the first loop, or may be *completely different from* the first loop. Any of these outcomes is completely all right!

Find the center of gravity in the second loop on OPPORTUNITY.

Decide what the main thing was in this writing, and express that in a center of gravity sentence. Again, remember that the center of gravity sentence is whatever you think it is. It can be what you *wrote* about the most, what you *liked* the most, what seems *most interesting* to you. Anything you *think* is the main topic of the loop *is* the main topic.

Write one sentence expressing that.

Stage 1/Creating

Get ready to repeat the process one more time. Write your second center of gravity sentence at the top of a fresh piece of paper, set your watch for ten minutes, and begin.

Write the third ten-minute loop on OPPORTUNITY.

When you finish this third loop, read it.

Then write the center of gravity sentence at the bottom of the page.

Congratulations! You have finished the complete cycle. And you are probably tired. Get up and stretch.

Usually by the end of the third loop you have come up with an idea that could be developed into an essay, something you could share with another person. Something will have stirred you or excited you or interested you; it may have just barely cropped up in the loop writings, but there are strong odds that you do see *something* to use as a slightly more focused subject than the broad word *opportunity*. If so, you are ready at the end of the third loop to move on to the next step in the writing process, the *Shaping Stage,* in which you decide on a specific message to send to another person and put this message into organized, planned, orderly form. If an idea has not surfaced by the end of the third loop, you might try writing an extra loop or two, or you might switch to another creating technique to see if it will work better.

Debbi Pigg, one of our students, actually did enter a contest and wrote on *opportunity*. Here are the loops and the essay that Debbi wrote.	**STUDENT EXAMPLE:** Looping
This may be the start of a bad habit. I bought this new pen today so I could write neater and now I'm doing a looping with it. Oh, well, I'll just be careful of my pen. First of all, to get some things off my mind before I write on opportunity (which is a very dumb topic). Excuse me, but my pen's messing up. First of all, the coach of the football team resigned today and that's pretty sad because he's a human being and what will he do and where will he go from here. Also, I'm mad at my bestfriend because I was taking a nap and she turned the television on. Later I found out she wasn't even watching anything. Now, to zero in on opportunity. I have had opportunities to sing, to dance, to jog, to be me. I've had lots of opportunities throughout my life. I was brought up in a nice home with neat parents who never fought in front of me and who will be married for 25 years this August. I went to a great high school with a rotten football team, but that's o.k. because I guess I learned a lot about people while I was there. I learned a lot about boys anyway! Ha. In high school they were all nerds. Oh, well, what will be will be. I also went to a nice church and we had lots of kids and a fabulous choir director. We put on musicals and	LOOP 1

Expanded Creating Techniques

went all over the United States. I almost didn't take that opportunity, though, because I hated choir at first. I never did want to go to rehearsals. I really didn't want to spend my Saturdays all day practicing music and choreography. I'm glad I did, though. That was a neat opportunity my parents *made* me do.

Center of gravity sentence: *I've had lots of opportunities in my life, and some of them my parents made me take when I didn't want to.*

LOOP 2

Center of gravity sentence: *I've had lots of opportunities in my life, and some of them my parents made me take when I didn't want to.*

I really have . . . I guess I'm glad my parents made me do those things. In fact, I'm more than glad; I'm ecstatic. Really. I think my best opportunity is myself, though, how I am. I owe it to my parents for bringing me up the way they did, though. They instilled values and personality into me. But right now going to college, planning my biggest opportunity is about myself—IS myself. I guess that sounds conceited but . . . I'm thinking about something a former teacher of mine told me, that writing was an art and a writer didn't have to paint by number or follow drawn lines. Well, that's the way I feel about my opportunities to get out there and make something of my life. See, I'm the artist; I hold the brushes and the oils and my parents' training is the. . . . I have the opportunity to be anybody I want this person to be. Conceit, conceit, conceit. I better narrow this thing down further. I have grabbed opportunities and created opportunities by all the things I've done. One way that I've realized this and changed my attitude about myself in the world is by working in Colorado this summer cleaning cabins. I've always thought of myself as a city girl, but I've always loved the mountains, so when the opportunity came, I went to clean cabins. I look back on it now and think, man, what all different opportunities there were. I learned how to fly fish, how to flip gas refrigerators to make the frezon circulate. I think, most of all, I had the opportunity to learn that it's people who make a feeling, not a place. A place can bring back memories, but it can't make you feel things. I don't know, I thought I was just going to clean cabins, and I ended up learning lots about business.

Center of gravity sentence: *My biggest opportunity is MYSELF, and I proved this by working in Colorado this summer.*

LOOP 3

Center of gravity sentence: *My biggest opportunity is MYSELF, and I proved this by working in Colorado this summer.*

When I was a little girl, we used to go to Taylor Park, Colorado, for vacation, and we found this rickety place called Holt's Guest Ranch. I'll never know what made me love that place so much except maybe it was the childhood memories I feel there. Fishing with my dad. Dancing at family night. Anyway, Mr. and Mrs. Holt always hired two college girls to work with them.

Stage 1/Creating

I used to tag along behind them, and Mrs. Holt would always say, "Debbi, someday when you're in college, maybe you can come work for us." I had all my plans made when I was nine. . . . I realize as I write this that what looked like an opportunity last summer wasn't just a fluke or just good luck. I, myself, brought that opportunity about by keeping in touch with Mrs. Holt, even after they sold the ranch to the Speers who almost ruined it, and then when they bought it back. And, especially, I caused that opportunity to happen when I told Mrs. Holt last year to call me if they kept the cabins. I wonder how many things we call opportunities are really like this; we do things that make the opportunities happen. I feel real encouraged by thinking about this. If I—*MYSELF*—made that opportunity happen last summer, can I do it again? And I am really proud of what I learned by taking advantage of that opportunity. I remember that first night there. I slept in Dad's flannel pajamas, long Fruit-of-the-Loom underwear and lined ski socks. We had two beds, but the thermal coupling in the heater was broken, so my roommate and I slept in the same bed to keep warm. Also, I didn't want to sleep in my bed because there was a dead mouse in it. [Squiggles] I don't know what else to write. I'm tired of thinking about opportunities. I wish the timer would go off and I could stop this loop. Great, there it is.

Center of gravity sentence: *I made my own opportunity.*

When Debbi finished these three loops, she had a subject for her essay. She decided to write on the idea that occurred in her second loop, "My biggest opportunity is *MYSELF*, and I proved this by working in Colorado this summer." Now read the essay she wrote on this subject. You will easily see the connection between her creating activity and the content of the essay itself.

CONFIDENCE   STUDENT ESSAY

Last April my telephone rang early in the morning, and it took me a full thirty seconds to recognize Mrs. Holt's voice. She wanted me to come to Colorado that summer and clean the guest cabins at her ranch. I thought about it a while and decided to go. I told myself, "This is a great opportunity to make money." What I learned during the summer, however, was that there is a bigger opportunity than making money. That opportunity is having confidence in yourself.

I flew from my hometown on May 19. When we arrived in Colorado, the temperature was 38 degrees. I got off the plane and realized that I had to carry both my suitcases and my clothes bag myself. This was just one of the things I was to discover during the summer that I had to do for myself. All the way up the drive in the canyon to the ranch, I kept thinking, "Don't forget how much money you are going to make. It will be worth it all." I was really scared.

It is true that the summer was a great opportunity to make money. I saved $500. My salary was $250 a month plus room and board. With all the baked

Expanded Creating Techniques

potatoes and gravy and even some boiled cabbage that I finally learned to swallow, I felt I came out on the good end of the room and board part of the deal. I was able to save almost all my salary because there was nothing to spend it on except maybe an occasional tube of toothpaste at Sherm Cranor's Taylor Park Trading Post.

Sometime during the early summer, I quit thinking about the opportunity to make money. I began to experience the opportunity of proving myself and accomplishing hard and new things by myself. It was really rough running a guest ranch. There was always a pilot light that had gone out or a toilet that wouldn't flush. There was always a beaver to clog up the irrigation ditch or a guest who needed dry bath towels at the strangest moment. I learned all about leaky pipes and the parts of a toilet. I spent hours plunging with my plumber's friend. I even learned how to run a "snake" through sewer pipes. I made beds in three minutes flat, and I washed three million dirty bath and tea towels every day. I set thousands of mouse traps. I learned how to light the pilot on cooking and heating stoves. I helped flip refrigerators so their freon would circulate, and I exploded them when they wouldn't draw the air up. I painted signs and cleaned the fireplace and dusted furniture and even helped lay linoleum in the laundry room. (It got a big wrinkle down the middle. We nicknamed it the Continental Divide.)

So, what I had thought would be just an opportunity to make money turned out to be an opportunity to grow with myself. I found out so many things about me. I became very proud of myself and what I was able to learn and do. I found out I really liked people. It made me feel good to work hard and accomplish things. I even learned to like cabbage.

Someday, I'll go back. By then I am sure that I will have grabbed a lot more opportunities to make myself proud of me. And I will probably even make money on top of it.

APPLICATION

1. Pick *one* of the topics and do three ten-minute loops on it:

    FAMILIES   MUSIC   TRAVEL

    Be sure to include a center of gravity sentence at the end of each loop.

2. Read over everything you have written during this looping activity. If you were required to write an essay on some idea that occurred to you during this loop writing, what would you write on?

Be prepared to discuss this topic (the one you picked) with the class. Were you surprised when you hit on it? Was it something you hadn't thought about for a long time? What did you like about it? What makes it seem like a good subject for an essay? What is there about the essay that you think would interest other people?

CUBING

Cubing is a technique for swiftly considering a subject from 6 points of view. The emphasis is on *swiftly* and *6*.

Often writers can't get going on a subject because they are locked in on a single way of looking at the topic—and that's where **Cubing** works very well. **Cubing** lets you have a single point of view for only 3 to 5 minutes, then moves you on to the next point of view. When you've finished **cubing,** you've spent 18 to 30 minutes, and you've really loosened up the soil of your mind. This technique moves very swiftly and is quite structured.

RULES FOR CUBING

1. Use all six sides of the cube.
2. Move fast. Don't allow yourself more than 3 to 5 minutes on each side of the cube.

Use All 6 Sides of the Cube. Imagine a cube—think of it as a solid block. Now imagine that each side has something different written on it.

> One side of the cube says: **Describe it.**
> Another side says: **Compare it.**
> A third side says: **Associate it.**
> The fourth says: **Analyze it.**
> The fifth says: **Apply it.**
> The sixth side says: **Argue for or against it.**

For the cubing technique, you need to use *all six sides*. This is *not* an exercise in describing, analyzing, or arguing. It *is* a technique to help you learn to look at a subject from a variety of perspectives. Consequently, doing just one of the sides won't work. Doing just one side is like a mechanical assignment—"describe this picture." You may decide after doing all six sides that you *do* want to describe it; but by then your decision will be meaningful and intelligent, based on your having something to say in the form of a description. So remember: **cubing** takes all six sides.

Expanded Creating Techniques

Move Fast. Don't Allow Yourself More Than 3 to 5 Minutes on Each Side of the Cube. The energy in this creating technique comes from shifting your perspective on the subject often. By moving around the cube, one side after another, in rapid succession, you see that you can look at your subject from a lot of different angles and that you can talk about it in a lot of different ways. You are not hunting for something to say from each perspective; you are taking a *quick* run into your mind for whatever presents itself on that angle, and the quickness of the run is important. It is the quick switch that makes the **Cubing** work.

PRACTICING CUBING

To practice this creating technique, let's use the picture of a luscious chocolate-covered cherry. Remember the rules: *use all 6 sides of the cube and move fast, allowing no more than 3 to 5 minutes per side.* Look at the chocolate-covered cherry. Get your paper and pen ready.

TOPIC: Chocolate-covered cherry

Begin. Do each of the 6 steps in order, spending no more than 3 to 5 minutes on each.

1. **Describe it.** Look at the subject closely and describe what you see. Colors, shapes, sizes, and so forth.
2. **Compare it.** What is it similar to? What is it different from?
3. **Associate it.** What does it make you think of? What comes into your mind? It can be similar things, or you can think of different things, different times, places, people. Just let your mind go and see what associations you have for this subject.
4. **Analyze it.** Tell how it's made. (You don't have to *know*; you can make it up.)
5. **Apply it.** Tell what you can do with it, how it can be used.
6. **Argue for or against it.** Go ahead and take a stand. Use any kind of reasons you want to—rational, silly, or anywhere in between.

When you have finished all six, read over what you have written. If one angle or perspective strikes you as particularly promising, you probably have come up with a focus for an essay. There very likely was one thing you really enjoyed writing during the cubing activity, something that made you smile, something that caused your pen to move faster, something you felt some interest in and even some excitement about. What is amazing and encouraging is that you can find *something* to say on this frivolous subject, a chocolate-covered cherry! Get used to the pleasure and security of having such a full repertory of creating techniques that you will *never* be given a subject without knowing *at once* how to find something you really want to say about it.

Here is student David Hill cubing the topic *My Home State,* which in David's case was Texas. Read his **cubings**; then see how he used that material in the essay he wrote later.

STUDENT SAMPLE: CUBING

Texas—big, bold, BIG, GIANT. Everything is big, so big that there's too many different things in it to mention. Texas has girls—girls on the beaches, in the cities, at the parks, in the country. The girls in Texas are something else! The main thing about Texas is that there isn't ONE MAIN THING. DIVERSITY. One can drive all night and never make it out of the state. There are so many different kinds of land—if you get tired of the desert, go to the mountains—if you get tired of the mountains—go to the beach. If you get tired of Texas get the H . . . OUT of here. Economically, it's great.

DESCRIBE IT

Texas is similar to and different from *itself*. Strange—instead of comparing the whole Texas to another whole anything you have to compare a little part of Texas to a whole something else. The beaches—let's compare the beaches—well, now which part? Aren't they all the same? No. Well, now, the South Padre beaches are white—not quite as beautiful as the Bahamas but you can't drink Lone Star on the Bahama beaches. The mountains are another thing. SOME ARE BIG—like the ones in the dramatic exploration movies. The rivers are like the ones in wilderness movies—movies—maybe that's why the movies are moving headquarters to Texas.

COMPARE IT

THE SUN—THE HOT, BIG, LONGTIME-RUNNING SUN. Cowboy hats—to keep the sun from burning. The sun of west Texas can make a person crazy if under it for a while—you can't make sandwiches out doors because the sun will toast the bread. Colors—bright colors—paisley colors—psychedelic SUN —old cowboys with leather necks and lines around their eyes from squinting while out in the sun—the weather—where else can it rain for one short 20 minutes and shine brightly soon after, then the next day it'll be cold and the day after hot again, with of course some rain and always THE SUN.

ASSOCIATE IT

90,000,000 miles of sun, a million beautiful girls, natural flavor, natural psychedelic colors, no preservatives, nothing artificial added. Take above ingredients and mix in one large area—put a little jalepeño pepper in if Mexican flavor is your gig. The only thing left out are the cows—leave them out: they are messy. The Food and Drug administration said that Texas is good for indigestion. Texas is made of a little bit of everything.

ANALYZE IT

You could use it as a wall decoration but you would have to have a
BIG WALL!

APPLY IT

Expanded Creating Techniques

You could use it for a place to meet a friend. "Meet me in Texas at 3:00." No—someone might want to use it for a place to go on vacation, but they might not leave. Look at me—I'm here on a life-long vacation. The only obvious thing to use Texas for is a place to live and stretch out.

ARGUE FOR OR AGAINST IT

Oh, yeah! Well, I happen to live in Texas, and I know that I not only don't have to pay state income tax (do you?) but sales tax is only 5%. There is no tax on groceries and the beef is local and fresh—best in the world. Where else can you drive on such good highways and don't forget the rest stops. Yes.

This cubing of the state of Texas has allowed David to explore what he thinks about the state and to see what ideas might surface in his mind about the topic. He actually got very excited about what he discovered when he did these cubes, and he chose one of the ideas as the subject for his essay.

STUDENT ESSAY

THE LONE STAR?

Any veteran of fourth grade geography can tell you that Texas is the biggest state in the United States, next to Alaska. Many can also tell you that Texas is called the Lone Star State. But when one of these little scholars asked me *why* Texas is called the Lone Star State, I was stumped. I knew full well that the state flag has only one star on it, but I knew equally well that if I used that as the reason for Texas' nickname, the kid's next question would undoubtedly be, "Why does the flag have only one star?" I never did answer the question; I merely mumbled something about flags and retired to my library where I pondered the phrase "the Lone Star State."

The more I thought about it the more I convinced myself that Texas was anything except a lone star. As far as galactical comparisons go, Texas is more like the entire universe than a single star. Ask any cowboy if the ranches, pastures, and cattle-raising plains aren't the universe, and he will say if they aren't he isn't interested in knowing about it. Ask corporate leaders in oil and gas if there is a bigger place, and they are likely to answer no without even thinking. Stop in Houston and the citizens there will tell you how advanced science, technology, and medicine are in their city and that there is no other place like it. The people who live in Texas feel it is their universe. They can't imagine any need to live anywhere else.

This paradox is so typical of Texas. A symbol that is a lone star, which might suggest smallness, aloneness, tinyness; and a state that is so big, so varied, and so self-sufficient that its citizens think it is the universe. I turned off the light on my desk and headed for the door, mumbling aloud, "Nowhere except Texas—that's for sure." Just then I heard a small voice that sounded a lot like that fourth grader. Suddenly, I knew why a universe like Texas could be symbolized by a lone star. There absolutely is no other place like it!

Stage 1/Creating

CLASSICAL INVENTION

In ancient Athens there were people who gave speeches in public places as a way of life. These speeches were designed to persuade listeners on controversial subjects, and the arguments were often intense and always serious. One of the most distinguished of these ancient orators, Aristotle, decided to write a how-to manual for these speakers. In it, he covers subjects like how to make emotional yet ethical appeals to the listeners and how to deliver a speech most effectively; he also passes on valuable hints about how to find the "best" thing to say. Aristotle's advice summarized the best that was known in his time; it also added an extra dimension to the subject—his own particular clarity and insight. Not only has his work survived through the centuries, but it also continues to be very valuable today.

Although Aristotle's advice was aimed at speakers, not writers, his principles can easily be applied to writing. In fact, many of his original guidelines for organizing and presenting a speech still appear in current textbooks on writing, even though Aristotle himself may not be mentioned. Let's look at Aristotle's original advice on finding ideas, then see how we can use this for our modern-day purposes.

When you sit down to think of content for a speech, Aristotle suggested, picture your mind as a land with several kinds of places or regions or haunts in it. These places (called *topoi* in Greek; "topics" is a loose translation) stand for different *kinds* of ways to view or think of a subject. Just as each part of the country—desert or mountains—would have a climate of its own, so each area of the mind has its characteristic way of thinking.

Obviously, this is merely a figurative, picturesque way of describing different mental processes—and of course Aristotle lived many centuries before modern brain research. Nevertheless, thinking of these different "areas" of the

INVENT:
To conceive of or devise first; originate.
To fabricate; to make up.
(From Middle English *enventen*, to come upon, to find.)

Expanded Creating Techniques

mind can serve as a kind of **checklist,** a way of seeing what ideas might occur to you as you examined the subject from each different perspective, or place.

ARISTOTLE'S COMMON TOPICS

DEFINITION
   A. Genus
   B. Division
 	
COMPARISON
   A. Similarity
   B. Difference
   C. Degree
 	
RELATIONSHIP
   A. Cause and effect
   B. Antecedent and consequence
   C. Contraries
   D. Contradictions
 	
CIRCUMSTANCE
   A. Possible and impossible
   B. Past fact and future fact
 	
TESTIMONY
   A. Authority
   B. Testimonial
   C. Statistics
   D. Maxims
   E. Law
   F. Precedents

    With your subject in mind look at the *topoi*. The first one is *Definition,* so ask yourself questions like "Does this subject *need* to be defined?" "If I defined it, what would I do with the definition?" "What if I broke my subject down into parts; what parts would I have?" "Is there any problem about my subject that defining it would show up?"—and so on until you feel you have asked enough questions about defining your subject. Then go to the next topic on the list, *Comparison,* and ask the questions that the topic makes you think of. Somewhere along the line, this methodical, orderly, deliberate search for ideas will pay off; you will think of something you want to say on the subject.
    After a little practice with this creating technique, you'll find that as soon as you know your subject, you instinctively go directly to the *topoi* that will work best with that subject, the *topoi* most likely to give you ideas. Until then, however, you will need to go through all five *topoi,* checking each one to see if, using that perspective, you can think of something to say.

> **RULES FOR CLASSICAL INVENTION**
> 1. Take the questions one at a time, thoughtfully.
> 2. Write brief notes about the answers.
> 3. If you get stuck or have nothing to say, move on.
> 4. When you finish the questions, reread your answers and check those that are most useful in generating material, information, or energy.

Take the Questions One at a Time, Thoughtfully. Following this rule is the key to using **classical invention** successfully. The power of **classical invention** comes from its relationship to common, ordinary patterns of human thought. There are probably a number of times each day when you are discovering the meaning of a new term (definition), comparing one thing to another, considering relationships, deciding whether to accept or reject some advertiser's claim, or weighing whether some action will or won't be possible (circumstance). Taking the questions one at a time and allowing yourself to be thoughtful about answers (for example, giving more than a yes or no answer) will strengthen that particular way of thinking. When you work on questions in the *Definition* section, you strengthen that mental skill in exactly the same way a weightlifter or violinist will practice specific movements to develop one specific physical skill. You may find some of the *topoi* less comfortable than some of the others. Remember that few of us can juggle, water ski, or type without a lot of practice; also, you may be exercising a kind of thinking that is entirely new to you. So be kind to yourself, and allow this new mental skill to develop at its own rate, even if it means slowly, thoughtfully.

Write Brief Notes About the Answers. You will want some kind of notes so that you can re-create your thinking later. Also, because your mind will probably range widely—especially on a question that seems particularly stimulating and appropriate to your subject—you'll want to have some notes, *outline, key words* or *phrases* that will let you retrace your thoughts. But you'll want to **keep the notes brief**—otherwise, you'll be writing long, sometimes exhaustive (and exhausting!) answers.

If You Get Stuck or Have Nothing to Say, Move On. Although you'll want to give yourself a reasonable amount of time to come up with an answer for every question—and sometimes several answers—there are some questions that simply don't apply, or that you don't want to deal with. For example, Question 5 *Testimony* asks what sources you've looked into. That's a useful question if you need ideas on places to look for testimony, or if it jogs your memory about something you've recently read or heard. But unless you really intend to do research on a subject, it's best to use Question 5 as a memory aid and let it go at that. If you find other questions that clearly just don't apply, pass them by. Remember, though, that surprises *can* happen; sometimes a seemingly useless question can provide a subject that you had never dreamed you would be interested in writing about.

When You Finish the Questions, Reread Your Answers and Star Those That Are Most Useful in Generating Material, Information, or Energy. Your brief notes will have already established, for a while, thought patterns connected with each of the different *topoi* or questions. Later, when you reread your answers, you'll already know which areas look most promising. You've used the process to discover which questions seem to work best for your subject. You can follow up, perhaps by looping, to develop—in more detail and depth—those questions and answers that serve you best.

PRACTICING CLASSICAL INVENTION

Let's practice the creating technique of **classical invention** by using the subject *My Retirement Place*. Don't groan! We're deliberately choosing an unpromising subject to demonstrate that the creating technique of **classical invention** really helps you come up with something to say on any topic. According to the Roman orator Cicero, a speaker relies on three things to find appropriate subject matter: native genius, diligence, and method (or art). As for genius, you're already operating on whatever level of native genius you've got; and as for diligence, you owe it to yourself, right? And method, fortunately, is something you *can* learn. That's comforting. Given your level of native genius and your willingness to look for ideas diligently, you can learn methods that will *always* work to find content for your writing.

And we believe any method you learn has to work on unpromising subjects just as well as on promising ones. Usually a person doesn't get sparkling subjects to write on in real-life, everyday situations, so we want you to know several methods for finding something to say that will enable you to feel confident about any subject you may be required to write about.

Here are the questions we will use in practicing **classical invention.** Go through these questions, seeing what ideas emerge about my retirement place. Remember, too, that these same questions will work for any subject you might come across at a later time.

DEFINITION

1. How does the dictionary define _____?
2. What earlier words did _____ come from?
3. What do *I* mean by _____?
4. What group of things does _____ seem to belong to? How is _____ different from other things in this group?
5. What parts can _____ be divided into?
6. Does _____ mean something now that it didn't years ago? If so, what?
7. What other words mean approximately the same as _____?
8. What are some concrete examples of _____?
9. When is the meaning of _____ misunderstood?

COMPARISON

1. What is _____ similar to? In what ways?
2. What is _____ different from? In what ways?
3. _____ is superior to what? In what ways?
4. _____ is inferior to what? In what ways?
5. _____ is most unlike what? (What is it opposite to?) In what ways?
6. _____ is most like what? In what ways?

RELATIONSHIP

1. What causes _____?
2. What are the effects of _____?
3. What is the purpose of _____?
4. Why does _____ happen?
5. What is the consequence of _____?
6. What comes before _____?
7. What comes after _____?

TESTIMONY

1. What have I heard people say about _____?
2. Do I know any facts or statistics about _____? If so, what?
3. Have I talked with anyone about _____?
4. Do I know any famous or well-known saying (e.g. "A bird in hand is worth two in the bush") about _____?
5. Can I quote any proverbs or any poems about _____?
6. Are there any laws about _____?
7. Do I remember any songs about _____? Do I remember anything I've read about _____ in books or magazines? Anything I've seen in a movie or on television?
8. Do I want to do any research on _____?

CIRCUMSTANCE

1. Is _____ possible or impossible?
2. What qualities, conditions, or circumstances make _____ possible or impossible?
3. Supposing that _____ is possible, is it also feasible? Why?
4. When did _____ happen previously?
5. Who has done or experienced _____?
6. Who can do _____?
7. If _____ starts, what makes it end?
8. What would it take for _____ to happen now?
9. What would prevent _____ from happening?

Expanded Creating Techniques

Begin. Go through each of the questions in each of the *topoi* groups. Write your answers to the questions in brief notes. If other questions occur to you, make a note of them, too. If you get stuck or have nothing to say on any particular question, move on. When you've finished all the questions, reread your answers and star the ones that you think will be the most useful in giving you something to say on the subject.

At the end of this process, you will have used several ways of thinking to consider your subject. Having a method like **classical invention** lets you switch from one thought pattern to another deliberately and lets you do a systematic, *thorough* investigation of your subject and arrive at ideas that have depth and a lot of potential for your writing.

Let's look at what one student—Rachel Harper—discovered about her retirement place by using the **classical invention** creating technique.

STUDENT EXAMPLE:
CLASSICAL INVENTION

DEFINITION

* 1. How does the dictionary define _____?
  A private or secluded place.

2. What earlier words did _____ come from?
  From French word which meant to withdraw.

3. What do *I* mean by _____?
  A place that gives me pleasure and a sense of well-being.

4. What group of things does _____ seem to belong to?
  Places to live.
  How is _____ different from other things in this group?
  It's different because a retirement place has to be really satisfying since you're in it all the time. Other places you might live can be not so satisfying because you're gone a lot.

* 5. What parts can _____ be divided into?
  Different characteristics of the place, different ways to use it, reasons why it is nice.

6. Does _____ mean something now that it didn't years ago? If so, what?
  It does to me because I've just retired. I used to not think much about the place I lived. Now it means a lot to me.

7. What other words mean approximately the same as _____?
  resting place, vacationing place, easy place.

8. What are some concrete examples of _____?
  Trailer villages, rest homes, senior-citizen communities.

9. When is the meaning of _____ misunderstood?
  People think that a retirement place has to be where a lot of people have retired to.

COMPARISON

* 1. What is _____ similar to? Why?
   It's similar to a campground, a vacation spot, a state park.

2. What is _____ different from? In what ways?
   Different from most senior-citizen communities, most apartment complexes. It's different from what people usually picture for a retirement place.

* 3. _____ is superior to what? In what ways?
   Superior to any other retirement place I have ever visited because it doesn't feel or look like a retirement place. A lot of young people live here or they come for the weekend.

4. _____ is inferior to what? In what ways?
   Inferior to . . .

5. _____ is most unlike what? In what ways?
   Most unlike a jail, a hospital, room with no windows.

6. _____ is most like what? In what ways?
   Most like a beautiful park

RELATIONSHIP

1. What causes _____?
   The trees, lake, quietness.

* 2. What are the effects of _____?
   Peace, easygoing life, satisfaction, quietness, being with nature.

3. What is the purpose of _____?
   For people to get away from hustle and bustle of city life, be alone or with only a few people, be out of doors.

4. Why does _____ happen?
   It happened for me because I was lucky and found it.

5. What is the consequence of _____?
   I'm much happier and content.

6. What comes before _____?
   A lot of frantic, hurried life.

7. What comes after _____?
   Depends on how I live, I guess.

TESTIMONY

1. What have I heard people say about _____?
   That my retirement place is ideal.

* 2. Do I know any facts or statistics about _____? If so, what?
   Yes, I know that it was a fishing village first. I know it started around the turn of the century. There are about forty houses here and about twenty families live here year-round. I know that my

Expanded Creating Techniques

retirement place is well cared for and protected because we have a full-time caretaker. I know a lot more.

3. Have I talked with anyone about _____?
   Yes, a lot of people.

4. Do I know any famous or well-known sayings about _____?
   "Too much work makes Jack a dull boy." "Here today, gone tomorrow."

5. Can I quote any proverbs or poems about _____?
   A picture is worth a thousand words.
   "Gather Ye Roses While Ye May."

6. Are there any laws about _____?
   Yes, rules that keep the place nice.

* 7. Do I remember any songs about _____?
   "A Little Bit of Heaven."
   "By the Old Mill Stream."
   "My Blue Heaven."
   Any books or magazines I've read?
   I've read enough to know how good mine is.
   Anything I've seen in a movie or on television?
   I've seen TV programs on the aged and where many of them live.

8. Do I want to do any research on _____?
   No.

CIRCUMSTANCE

1. Is _____ possible or impossible?
   Possible.

2. What qualities, conditions, or circumstances make _____ possible or impossible?
   Having enough money to buy a place here; knowing about it in the first place.

3. Supposing that _____ is possible, is it also feasible? Why?
   Yes. It's not too expensive.

4. When did _____ happen previously?
   As early as 1900.

5. Who has done or experienced _____?
   A lot of people.

6. Who can do _____?
   Anybody who likes this kind of environment.

7. If _____ starts, what makes it end?
   Dying.

8. What would it take for _____ to happen now?
   People to be ready to retire and to know about this place.

9. What would prevent _____ from happening now?
   Not knowing about it; not liking the isolation or the quietness. Not having enough money.

Here is Rachel's essay for her *Association of Retired Persons' Newsletter*.

MY RETIREMENT PLACE   STUDENT ESSAY

There's an old saying that good luck comes when you least expect it. That was certainly true for me the day I discovered the clubgrounds which have now become my retirement place. I never dreamed that day about 15 years ago when some friends brought me to the Chickamauga Fly and Bait Casting Club for a picnic that I would come here to live when I quit work. I did, however, and I am extremely pleased. This club is a perfect place for a person who loves peace, quiet, and the out-of-doors.

The appearance of Chickamauga Fly and Bait Casting Club is one of its greatest assets. It certainly isn't grand, but it does look old in a comfortable sort of way. It started around the turn of the century as a fishing camp (in fact, that's how it got its name), and it looks settled and well developed. It's also very natural. Although the area is well taken care of, the trees and plants have been left to grow in their natural condition, so when you drive in you feel as if you are on a state campground. The club is also beautiful. The gravel road that you come in on ends at a large lake which has high mountains all around it. Many days I go down to the lake early just to see the mist rise off the water and into the trees of the mountains.

I think I would have chosen the club as my retirement place on its appearance alone, but it has even more good things about it. The management, for example. There is a full-time caretaker couple who keep the grounds in good shape and who protect the club. They lock the gate every night. If you are going away, they will check your mail or pick up your paper. There is also a pot-luck supper organized once a month by the club's officers. People who live at the club permanently and people who just belong get together for the meal and some kind of program. Every Wednesday the women who are on the grounds that day get together for some special activity. Once we painted the boatdock. Another time we went into town to a photography show. One day last winter we skated on the frozen lake. There's a governing board, also, that keeps very up-to-date on what the club needs and authorizes repairs and improvements. Right now they are getting a new water line so that people who have wells can hook up to county water, and they are inquiring about the cost of surfacing the road. I couldn't ask for more from a management standpoint.

The appearance and management of my retirement place are great, but there's something even more important to me. That's how I *feel* living at the Chickamauga Fly and Bait Casting Club. I feel content, happy, and alive. I walk by myself a lot on Daddy Jack Trail. I take my pole some mornings about 5:00 and catch a big brim for breakfast. I watch the leaves turn, the dogwoods bloom. This is the most important thing to me—the happiness I feel daily in my retirement place. I think the luck that was with me 15 years ago is still holding. Every day I wake up feeling that I've come home.

APPLICATION

1. Using the checklist for **classical invention,** explore one of these subjects to see what you have to say about it:

    INDEPENDENCE   LONELINESS   HUNGER

    Use the student sample as a guide for your work.

2. Be prepared to discuss with the class what occurred as you used the classical invention technique. Where did you first become interested in the subject? What part caused you to think of something that really surprised you? What parts turned up ideas that you think would really appeal to a reader? Which parts were helpful in clarifying your own thinking?

    Of all the ideas you generated during the activity, which seems the most promising to you if you were to write an essay on the subject?

SUMMARY

ALL MEN (AND WOMEN!) Are created equal—but not all creating techniques are equal! Each, in fact, is different.

You have now practiced several distinctly different creating techniques, and you may already have your favorite among them, the one that works best when you are searching for ideas. You will certainly have noticed the ways the techniques are different. Some work like a fishing expedition—you lower a net and catch whatever thoughts you have on the subject. Some work like a reminder or checklist to help you think up things you already knew but had forgotten. Some actually let you invent something new by rubbing together thoughts, ideas, and information you already had to come up with new combinations, insights, and relationships. Some work best when you don't have a single thing to say; others work best when you already have several ideas on a subject and need to decide which is the most promising. Some of the techniques are unstructured and loose; some are tightly controlled. No single one is inherently better than another. Each works for its own purpose.

Learning what each technique will do for you may be trial and error at the beginning, but as you become more and more familiar with the ways to create, you will develop a feel for which one to use when. There will always be a unique mix of subject, what you already know and/or think about the subject, your mindset on a particular day, and many other variables that will affect which creating technique works best for you when.

"Keep on going and the chances are you will stumble on something, perhaps when you are least expecting it. I have never heard of anyone stumbling on something sitting down."
—Charles Kettering

The important thing to remember is that there is a *creating stage* in the writing process—that you need to let yourself hunt for ideas before you begin writing a paper. Now you know how to get started, no matter what the writing task or assignment is. You know something you *can* do. You know how to get *some* words on the page! You will never again have to say, "But I can't think of anything to say. I don't know how to start." Because now you do know how to start. *You start by creating. You don't start by writing the piece of writing itself.* In fact, you don't worry at all in this stage about the essay or report or whatever you must write; you just set yourself to have ideas on the subject of that essay, report, or whatever by doing a creating technique.

SUMMARY

TECHNIQUE	CHARACTERISTIC	WORKS BEST FOR	STRENGTHS	WEAKNESSES
REPORTER'S FORMULA	familiar, a set pattern	viewing subject as "thing" or separate entity; giving clear, objective information	produces factual information, detail; can suggest actual order/organization of finished writing	can be routine, unimaginative; can be applied only to *some* subjects (not all); separates writer from subject
BRAINSTORMING	group activity	breaking mental blocks, getting fresh approaches	ranges widely; uncritical; works off other people's ideas	may seem merely silly, horseplay
LISTING	simple, direct	gathering facts, details, points which already exist	quick, easy	limited application; requires the previous information to be there and within reach
LOOPING	unstructured; a fishing expedition	exploring in a free, wide-ranging way	uses right lobe, brings surprises and pleasures; lets the strongest thing emerge	usually takes several loops to work; may not always give depth
CUBING	fast-moving, structured; combination of fishing expedition and planned search	considering subject from six points of view to set up a variety of perspectives	"loosens the soil" of your mind; corresponds to way people usually think about subjects; shows writer perspective most likely to yield ideas for the essay	doesn't work on all classroom assignments; may not give enough depth
CLASSICAL INVENTION	structured; a planned search; goes into depth	exploring regions of the mind; handling subjects that benefit from logical, planned investigation	well-developed, traditionally useful, corresponds to human thought processes	can result in mechanical writing or writing that is more interesting in form than in content; takes considerable time

And there is a bonus for you when you create—even if you never write the essay or the report, even if you never go a step further, the creating activity gives you clarity by letting you see a thing and know it. During the creating stage you find out what you actually think about this subject, what you believe, what you know. What is more, you not only come to *know* the subject by writing about it, but you also have *words on a page* to use as a starting point for sending your ideas to someone else. The *creating stage* serves both purposes. You find out what you know, and you get ideas that you can shape into a coherent message for another person.

APPLICATION
Double Technique

Taking the same subject through more than one *creating technique is an excellent way to see which techniques you find most beneficial for which kinds of subjects. To get practice in knowing the characteristics of various creating techniques, choose one of the topics below and* run it through two different creating techniques. *Be ready to discuss with the class what you discovered in this process, what one technique did that the other didn't, which you found most beneficial, what idea(s) you came up with that you could write on if you were required to do so, and the like.*

I.
  CHOOSE ONE   CHOOSE TWO
  Getting along with (parents, children).   Cubing
  Finding work.   Looping
  Problems of growing up.   Classical Invention

II.
  CHOOSE ONE   CHOOSE TWO
  Things wrong with holidays.   Cubing
  A skill you have and are proud of.   Looping
  A problem you had and how you   Classical Invention
     solved it.   Reporter's Formula
  Ways people act that you don't like.   Brainstorming
  A movie you just saw.   Writing a List
  A book you just read.
  Soap operas.

DISCUSSION

1. What is the direct connection between the writing you do during the *Creating Stage* and the completely finished final essay?
2. What are some possible disadvantages of doing creating techniques?
3. What arguments would you give to a friend who said he or she didn't have to do a *Creating Stage* for a piece of writing?
4. What is the best state of mind to be in when you approach the *Creating Stage*?
5. Which technique works best for a subject you already know something about? Which works best for a subject you are absolutely blank on?
6. When would a quick technique, such as a list, work best?

WRITING ASSIGNMENT: THE PERSONAL EXPERIENCE ESSAY

You are now ready to put *creating* to the test by writing a complete essay. With each additional section of this book you will, of course, learn more and more about the writing process. However, you are at a good spot, right now, for a practical application of what you've been learning. Here is an opportunity for you to discover (and demonstrate) what a truly successful *Creating Stage* can contribute to a finished essay. If your experience is like mine, you know that every time you write, you learn something new, and you extend your command of writing skills. So consider this assignment as a chance to grow, specifically to increase your mastery of *Creating* and to increase your ability to incorporate the *Creating Stage* into a piece of finished writing.

The first assignment is a personal experience essay. People write about what happens to them for a number of reasons:

- To tell something that happened to them which caused them to have an insight about life which they believe is universal enough or important enough for other people to take their time to read.
- To relate an experience that the writer thinks will be interesting simply because the facts, description, and the like will be new, unfamiliar, or even unknown to the readers.
- To use a personal experience to teach a lesson or warn the reader, sometimes explicitly or directly stated, sometimes not stated but understood.
- To entertain the reader.
- To write about something very emotional, disturbing, or upsetting that happened to the writer in order to get it off the writer's mind or to complete the experience.
- To give the reader facts about the writer which the reader will be interested in knowing simply because the writer is so well known or famous.

---

1. CONTEXTS

Look over the following writing contexts and decide on one that you would like to use as the basis for your own personal experience essay.

A. A close friend of yours has just really disappointed you. Because of this person's actions, you have discovered something about life that you hadn't realized before. You decide to write about this personal experience in order to share your insight with other people. Since your college newspaper solicits writing from the students, you decide to prepare your essay to submit to the editor, thinking that what you have learned will strike a responsive chord for a lot of your classmates because they have probably had similar experiences.

B. You have just had a run-in with the police, for what you thought was a minor offense. You (a) took a plastic cone from the street where a work crew was painting the center line; (b) were going _____ in a _____ mile zone and got stopped for speeding; (c) had a party which ended up moving out of doors at 2 A.M., and the neighbors complained to the authorities. You discover, however, much to your sorrow, that the police think the offense is much more serious than you do, and they take you down to the station. You have to appear before the judge to post bail. The judge says that the fine will be $200, but that $100 of it will be reduced if you write an account of this incident and get it published in your college newspaper as a warning to other students. You gladly agree to write the essay and get it published for your classmates to read. Perhaps, then, they won't make the same mistake.

C. You are taking an introductory geography course your freshman year in college, and the first assignment of the year is this: "Write an essay about the most unusual and interesting place you have ever been. Be sure that this place is likely to be a location your classmates will not have been." The instructor is planning to compile all the essays into a booklet; each member of the class will get a copy. The instructor believes this collection of essays will make the study of geography much more interesting and personal for everyone in the class. Write the essay you want printed.

D. A magazine like *Reader's Digest* is having an essay contest. Each contestant is asked to complete this sentence and write an essay about the experience: "The day I learned something I will never forget was when. . . ." The magazine announcement contains some sample essays: one about a birth, another about a death, a car wreck, a storm, an illness, a celebration. You want to enter the contest and win the $1000 first prize. Write the essay you will submit.

2. CREATING

After you have selected the writing context, you are ready to do the *Creating Stage* for the essay. Choose **looping, cubing,** or **classical invention** and do a complete *Creating Stage*. Don't worry at this point about the essay itself. Just follow the rules for the particular creating technique you choose and get your thoughts down on paper.

3. WRITING THE ESSAY

After you complete the creating activity, you are ready to write the essay. You will learn many pointers about writing good essays in the *shaping* and *completing* sections later in this book. For now, however, here are just a few general facts that you can use to make your essay more interesting and worthwhile to your readers.

Remember that writing for the creating stage and writing for the essay are different in these ways:

CREATING	ESSAY
Has to matter only to you; doesn't have to be important to anyone else.	Has to matter to someone else; must seem important or significant to him or her.

Can be messy.	Has to be readable.
Wanders around as your mind explores.	Has one main idea and sticks to it.
Is done to give you ideas on a subject.	Is done to share with someone else something you think is important.

What these differences highlight is that the creating stage is for *you* and the essay writing stage for another person, your *reader*. This means, then, that as you write the essay, you will want to keep your readers always in mind, thinking about *getting your message to them*.

Remember that your readers want to see *the point* or *significance* of your personal experience; they are almost always bored by just a recounting of facts. Tell a good story and use a lot of vivid description so that your reader can *see* the event. Successful personal experience essays are interesting because the writers put their stories in an order you can follow easily, make you feel you are living the story with them, and use detail after detail to bring the scene to life. You want to do the same in your writing.

4. FINAL CHECK

When you have finished writing the essay, be sure to put it in the best form possible for your reader. Make it neat and easy to read. After all, the essay will be the piece of "you" that the reader will have when the *real you* isn't there in person. Make it as impressive as you can.

STAGE 2 / SHAPING

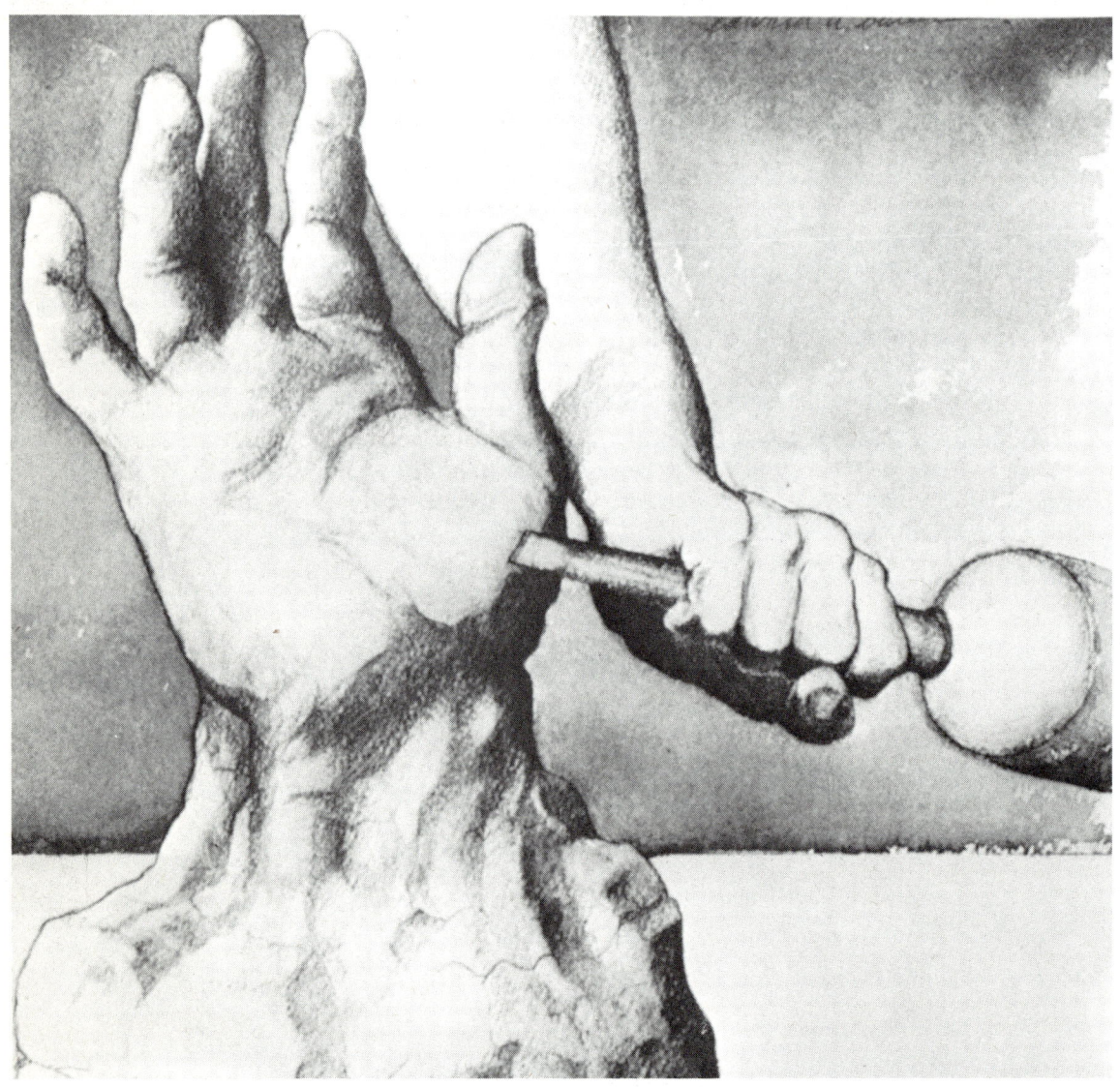

HOW TO PUT WRITING IN ORDER

OVERVIEW

Going Public: Writing for an Audience
How Communication Happens
Writing to Communicate
Early Shaping
Preliminary Agreements

**WRITING ASSIGNMENT:
THE HOW-TO ESSAY**

The Trial Draft
Between Early and Late Shaping
Reader
Thesis
Form

**WRITING ASSIGNMENT:
THE PROBLEM/SOLUTION ESSAY**

Late Shaping
Make the Most of Your Introduction
Stick to Your Thesis
Develop Your Thesis
Make the Most of Your Conclusion
The Promise and Delivery System

**WRITING ASSIGNMENT:
THE EXPLANATION ESSAY**

PURPOSE

Bridge the gap between private writing and public writing
Look at the act of communication
Develop preliminary agreements about audience, purpose, and message
Draft a rough version of the essay
Analyze and evaluate the trial draft
Create effective and well-developed beginnings, middles, and endings

GOING PUBLIC: WRITING FOR AN AUDIENCE

AUDIENCE:
The readers, hearers, or viewers reached by a book, broadcast, or performance; an opportunity to be heard or to express one's views.

PUBLIC:
Open to the knowledge or judgment of all; participated in by the people or community; connected with or acting on behalf of the people or community.

PRIVATE:
Of or confined to one person; not available for public use or participation.

During the *Creating Stage,* nothing outside yourself and your project matters much. It's a time for clearing your mind, learning what you think about a thing, having some ideas to write on, or just giving yourself pleasure. You explore *your* thoughts, images, associations, attitudes, ideas; you find what *you* want to say.

If you set out only to find out what *you* think on a subject, then you are finished when you have done the creating stage. If, however, you did the creating stage in order to have some ideas *to share with someone else,* you move into a second stage in the writing process—one determined by the demands of a *reader,* not one determined by you alone. You move from your private world to the public world, from writing for yourself to writing for someone else.

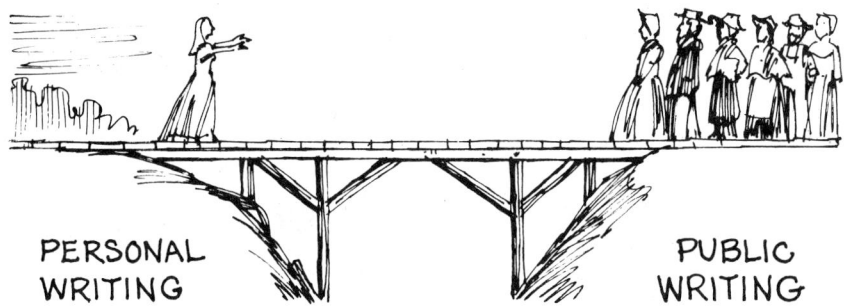

THE DIFFERENCE BETWEEN PUBLIC AND PRIVATE WRITING

Anyone who has ever peeked on the sly into another person's diary knows that private writing can be fun to read. People's journals—like Lewis and Clark's when they cut the Oregon Trail, or May Sarton's when she moved to an isolated spot to live alone by the sea—illustrate that private writing can make good public reading. With private writing, however, the reader is always a visitor, a viewer on the outside looking in. The reader may get value or enjoyment or pleasure from reading the writer's private jottings, but that is just a by-product of the writing, which was written for the writer alone.

In **private writing,** the writer doesn't have to do anything in the interests of any readers: *no explanations, no connections, no clarifications*. It's totally up to the readers (and perhaps an editor who prepares the private writing) to make sense of the writing on their own.

The situation changes immediately, however, when a person intends from the outset to write something for somebody else. In **public writing,** a writer must do everything possible to get the reader interested in what the writer has to say and to say it so clearly that the reader will experience no confusion. That is why a writer *shapes* the ideas that surface in the creating stage of the writing process. Readers want order, clarity, and stimulation. Therefore, the writer must be aware of what readers demand and what conditions are usually present when communication actually occurs between a writer and a reader. With this knowledge of the nature of readers and the nature of communication, a writer can plan and produce a piece of public writing that will do just exactly what he or she wants it to do: engage the reader in the act of understanding what the writer is saying.

HOW COMMUNICATION HAPPENS

Since the purpose of public writing is to communicate something, we should understand what happens when communication takes place. Let's take a look at what goes on when people talk (something you mastered so early and so thoroughly that you now take it pretty much for granted). Then we'll examine the differences between talking and writing, which you'll want to be aware of as you transform your own writing from private to public.

SPEAKING—"PERSON A"

When two people meet—say, Person *A* and Person *B*—they meet at some specific place (on a corner, at a laundromat, over a cup of coffee, at the office, in a hallway). Already Person *A* has some real advantages that she wouldn't have if she were writing:

- the audience is somebody specific;
- the place (location) is real;
- the person can be seen face to face.

If the meeting were arranged in advance, presumably that would help too. If it's a date, you say things appropriate about a date—maybe deciding about where to go. If it's a business appointment, you discuss the business at hand.

If it's a chance meeting, then you know that, too. Some more advantages:

- the circumstances are known;
- the situation is known;
- subjects will fit the person and the situation (so will the words);
- all these elements enter the speaker's mind fairly automatically.

If Person **A** decides to communicate with Person **B** (more than "Hi" or "Hello"), that communication involves three more things: (1) Person **A** has a lifetime of stored knowledge, past experiences, feelings, attitudes, emotions, images. That's where it starts. (2) Person **A** makes a lightning-quick sorting and selecting from among all that's in the mind, choosing exactly the ideas, experiences, knowledge, emotions, attitudes—whatever—to be communicated to Person **B**. (3) After deciding what to communicate (and this happens so fast that we often don't even know we've done it), Person **A** "encodes" the message—puts the selected experience, knowledge, emotion, etc., into words and speaks those words to Person **B**.

LISTENING—"PERSON B"

So far, that's what Person **A** has done. Has any communication happened yet? Not until Person **B** gets involved. And Person **B**, to have communication take place, must hear what's said (not be hindered by mumbling, impaired hearing, or loud noises outside), understand the words (presumably **A** and **B** are using a common language), understand **A**'s intention, find it appropriate to the situation and circumstances, and be willing/able to reconstruct the message according to his own experience/knowledge/attitudes/images. It is that **re-creation** that counts—without **B**'s re-creation, not much happens. And if **B** re-creates something far, far different from what Person **A** sent, then there has been little if any communication.

GET IT?

The chance of **B** re-creating **A**'s message *exactly* is pretty small. Given good will, few distractions, and an appropriate setting, Person **A** has a lot going for her to help get through to Person **B**: spoken words, tone, facial expression, gesture, volume, pitch, delivery, visual contact to see how it's going and change whatever is necessary right on the spot.

You can ask questions. Looks on faces can be noticed. The speaker can say, "I don't think you see what I mean; let me start over." Or the listener can say, "I understand the first point but I don't see where you are going on the second." If the speaker sees a quizzical look on the listener's face, it's possible to give some more examples or explanations. If the listener looks bored, the speaker can stop or do something to get the listener's attention again. If there is a bulldozer that suddenly starts up outside the window while the conversation is going on, the speaker can say, "Let's go into another room." If the speaker wants to emphasize a point it's possible to talk louder or make hand gestures.

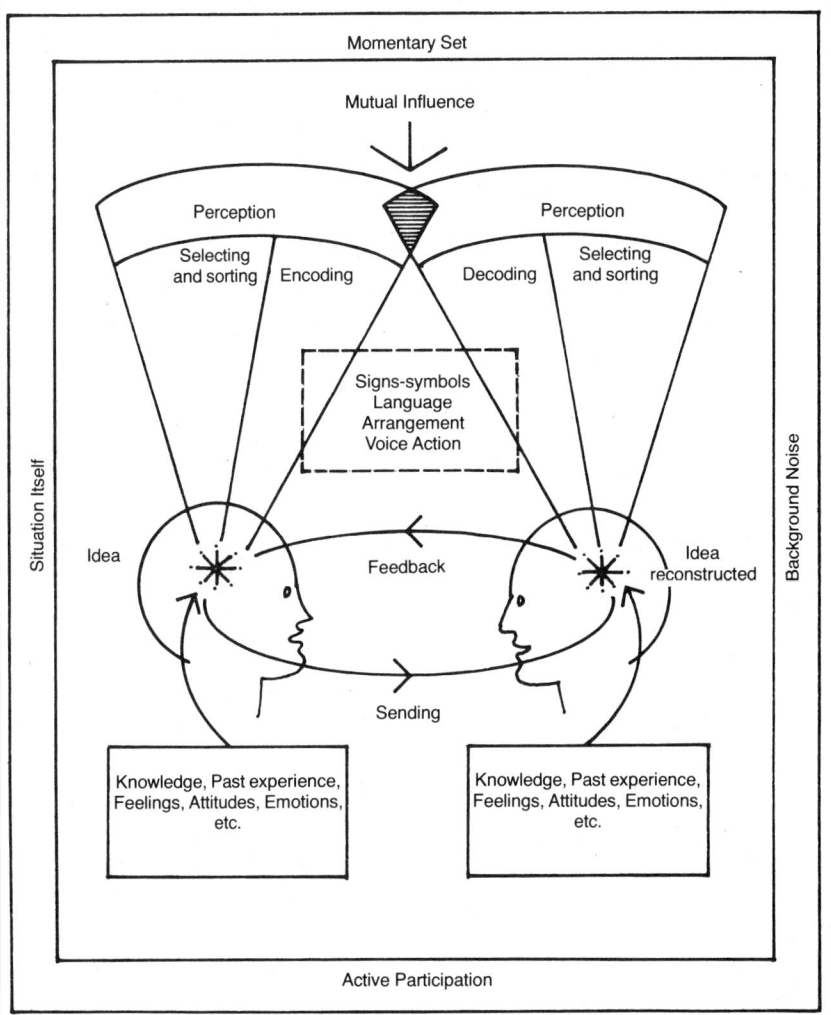

The Ross Model shows how little overlap—*Mutual Influence*—there is when people communicate. Even so, mutual influence is vastly greater in speaking than in writing, simply because the two of you are together and because of the whole support system that goes with speaking.

APPLICATION

1. Choose someone in your class to be your listener. Then tell him or her how to get from one specific place to another specific place. For instance, how to get from a building on one end of the campus to a fountain at the other end; or how to get from the campus to the bus station; or how to get from the dorm to the new pizza house.

How Communication Happens

Check how many things besides words that you use to communicate this information. Also check how many things the listener does to make the communication clear.

SPEAKER	LISTENER
___ used hands to gesture or point	___ used hands to indicate understanding or lack of understanding
___ started over again when listener was not understanding	___ showed by look on face that he/she did not understand
___ asked listener questions to determine what information to give	___ asked speaker questions when did not understand
___ others	___ others

2. Now, write out the directions telling someone how to get from one specific place to another. (Use the same two places that you used in 1 above.) Give these written directions to someone else in class, not the person you just talked to.

Next, make a list of all the ways writing the directions was harder for you than talking. Get as complete a list as you can. If it was easier in any ways, list those too.

Then, after your classmate has read the directions, talk with him or her about how well she or he understood them. What wasn't clear that you thought would be; what did you assume the reader would know that he/she didn't know?

3. Write a paragraph in which you summarize the differences you experienced between telling a message and writing it.

WRITING TO COMMUNICATE

So, what have you got going for yourself in writing? Nothing in sight except you, your pen, and some paper. *Blank* paper! And when you finally send your communication to someone else, what's in sight? Nothing but that same paper—this time with words on it.

Because there is a big difference between the liveliness of talking to someone who is right there and the act of writing on blank paper all by yourself, it's no surprise to learn that many people don't really think of writing as *communicating* at all. But if writing isn't communicating, it is merely an empty and unsatisfactory activity to the writer, not to mention the reader.

However, writing can be communication when you intend it to be. And since in writing you do not have the many advantages that you have when you speak, you'd better do what you can in advance to ensure that your reader will stick with you all the way.

It's because communicating in writing is such a different activity from communicating face to face that you even have to study writing at all. You especially have to study how to communicate in writing when that writing is **public**

IN WRITING,
If it doesn't happen *on paper*.
It doesn't happen *at all!*

because no explanation can accompany the writing—your writing must be its own explanation.

What *can* you do?

This section on *Shaping* shows you, exactly. Writing has its conventions that compensate for the absence of personal contact, voice, facial expressions, and the like. In fact, that's why people study writing—to learn how to compensate for not having the audience right there and not being able to change the message on the spot.

> Public ↔ Communication ↔ Audience Writing Theory

Just realizing the differences between talking and writing can be a real step ahead. You soon begin to see that writing has got to change from being a "guessing game" to becoming a "choosing game." You learn to control, as much as possible, the reader's reaction by making deliberate decisions about what will work.

Shaping is exactly what works in public writing, and it is a much more deliberate activity than creating. In shaping you consider all the raw material you have generated or brought to the surface in the *Creating Stage*. From that, you choose what to focus on, what to develop for another person. Then you decide *how* that material is going to be put together—what comes first, second, or third, and what gets top billing and what comes in as supporting roles. All of these conscious decisions are necessary because if you intend communication to happen, you need to do in advance everything possible to put the message into a form that will leave no room for misunderstanding or, worse yet, cause the reader to just stop reading in the middle of your paper.

Even though shaping is much more structured and deliberate than creating, you will soon discover that in the *Shaping Stage* you also create, just as at times in the *Creating Stage* you actually begin to shape your public writing without even knowing it. You will see, for instance, that although shaping is usually much more organized and planned than creating, shaping itself begins with some steps that are exploratory (much like *creating*) and moves finally to some firm and concrete choices (much like *completing*).

It would be much simpler if writing happened in three totally separate stages that didn't overlap or contain each other at times. What happens, however, is that right in the middle of shaping your essay you may discover something new you want to say. Actually, writing is a recursive process: the stages happen once (creating occurs in the *creating stage*) and then later appear again, in a modified form, in other stages (*creating* recurs, in a lesser degree, in *shaping* and *completing*). Inside each stage the other two stages are likely to pop up.

The three stages can be separated as you learn them because each one—creating, shaping, and completing—does have its own characteristic activities that set it apart from the other two. Each has a specific purpose that the others do not have. Just remember that while you definitely do move through three distinct stages, each of these will also contain elements of the other two. Because writing is recursive, you won't be able to finish the creating stage and say, "Well, that's that; I won't be creating any more in writing this essay!" What you *can* say is, "Well, I've finished the *Creating Stage* of the writing process, which allowed me to find something to say. I may actually do some more creating later in the other two stages, but not for the purpose of getting my initial ideas for the paper."

> RECURSIVE:
> Each step depends on the step before; movement tends to return to point of origin, or to redo, with slight modification, something already done.

EARLY SHAPING

PRELIMINARY AGREEMENTS

The *Shaping Stage* actually begins before you start organizing and arranging your material. Shaping begins by your making some "preliminary agreements" about why you are writing, to whom you are writing, and what is to be communicated. Let's compare this idea of preliminary agreements to the second stage of cabin building discussed at the beginning of the text. In that second stage, you stop dreaming and make a firm decision to build a cabin. First, you buy the land. Then you select the contractor (or people to help you if you are going to be the contractor). You decide on the floorplan, maybe hire someone to draw the blueprints. Only after you have done all these things—made these preliminary decisions—will you start laying the foundation and putting up the studs.

That's how it is as you start the shaping stage in the writing process. You will already have gathered your ideas. You will already have collected information. Now you have to begin to make some firm decisions. You decide to whom you are writing (or review to whom you are writing, if the audience is assigned), why you are writing, and what you want the writing to accomplish. In other words, in early shaping you handle all "contracts" and preliminary agreements. Then and only then are you ready to start the rough work of indicating what shape the whole essay will take.

Let's take a detailed look at the preliminary agreements you have to make early in the shaping stage.

WHY YOU ARE WRITING?

You write because some *situation* or *motivation* or *demand* brings you to put pen to paper. For some people the stimulation is the internal need or desire to say something that is burning inside them. For most writers, however, particularly beginning writers, there has to be some *external situation*—some encounter in the outside world—that requires that writing be done: an assignment, a business report or memo, a request that a certain thing happen, an explanation. This external situation itself begins the *Shaping stage* for you. It helps to review for yourself why you are writing so that your mind can begin to select and sort for a particular circumstance.

- I am writing to give information to . . .
- I am writing to persuade them to . . .
- I am writing to get someone to do . . .
- I am writing to get this off my chest . . .
- I am writing to share an insight I have had . . .

> MODES:
> To describe, narrate, classify and evaluate
> AIMS:
> Self-expression, literature, information, persuasion

Making the *situation* real for yourself before you begin writing provides a kind of general "guide to the mind" so that ideas (and probably even the form) appropriate to the *purpose* for which you are writing begins to emerge.

TO WHOM ARE YOU WRITING?

When you talk, you don't have to invent an audience because an audience is there. You may have to *analyze* your audience when you talk—for example, find out what age they are, what they already know about your subject, etc.—but you don't have to make up an audience. In writing, however, because the audience is not actually present in the room with you, you have to both make up your audience and analyze that audience. But what if I don't invent and know my audience before I start writing?

Well, if you write a paper to no one, then the only audience you are likely to attract are people who like papers written with no particular audience in mind. How many people like that can there be? If you choose to write an essay with no audience in mind, or "forget" about the audience, or write for "a general audience," it all comes to the same thing: you are actually deciding that your audience will be those few souls in the universe who like dull prose. If you invent and/or know your audience in advance, however, you can plan the whole essay around this person or group of people. You gain enormously by having your audience in mind from the very start.

Dear Nobody,
Nothing, nothing, nothing. Nothing at all. Nothing and nothing and blah blah blah.......

PICTURE A SPECIFIC AUDIENCE

The problem with writing to "a general audience" is that you tend to shotgun your message rather than rifle it—you scatter your efforts broadly rather than train them on real people awake and reading your paper. It's the difference between sunlight falling broadly on the earth and sunlight focused through a lens—one can light a fire, the other can't.

It is crucial to note who your specific audience is at the outset (or to invent an audience if the choice is yours) because your approach to the subject will be determined by who this audience is. Just suppose that you were writing an essay to inform your readers about the attractiveness of the town you live in as a vacation spot. Sure, why not? People always think they have to go *somewhere* to have a vacation. What might happen if they came to your town? Of course, the question has more obvious answers if you live in a place like San Francisco or Las Vegas, but even the most unpromising places can be appealing—if you bother to work out the appeal.

If you were to explain the attractions of your town to potential tourists, what would you say? What would the differences be in how you approached the subject if your audience were

people your own age   *out-of-state visitors*
people already living in your home town   *foreign travelers*
people with small children   *retired persons*

You can see right away how many decisions would turn out one way for one group of people, another way for other people. Almost everything would depend on which audience you wanted to attract.

CHECKLIST: INVENT AND KNOW YOUR AUDIENCE BEFORE YOU BEGIN TO WRITE TO THEM

1. Know the truth about *all* audiences.
   They do not like to be bored; they do like to be stimulated.
   They want a feeling of achievement or accomplishment.
   They want to get something out of what they read.
   They are busy and don't want their time wasted.
   They often have things to do besides reading.
   They need explanations and details.
   They like order and hate chaos.
2. Picture a *specific* audience.
   Who is the audience?
   What do you know about this audience?
   How old? What educational background? What kind of work?
   What will be the audience's attitude toward the subject?
   How much does the audience already know about the subject?
   Will they already be interested in the subject? Why?
3. Decide what your audience is like and what it is likely to understand, find stimulating, need to know, enjoy . . . and
4. Deliver that.

If you were writing for someone your own age, you would likely emphasize the things you like to do; you could probably count on your audience liking these things too. You could also be more informal; the words you used could sound like your normal conversation with friends, and you wouldn't have to worry much about the readers knowing the definitions or getting the drift of what you had to say. However, think of the difference in how you would write the essay if you were praising the town as a vacation spot for foreign travelers. Foreign visitors would have to be given more background, would need directions, and would need to be persuaded to choose this town over a hundred other places they could visit while in America. If you were writing for people who already lived in your town, however, you could skip much of the description, location, directions, and the like, and instead write about the places to go and things to do that even residents might have overlooked. For this audience, your purpose would be to write about the possibilities "right in their own backyards."

As you can see, not only the approach and purpose in writing are influenced by the audience, but also the very content of the writing itself—what points you make, what examples you use. Getting to know your audience before you write the paper is crucial."

WHAT DO YOU WANT TO COMMUNICATE IN THE WRITING?

You will know only vaguely what you want to communicate when you begin the *Shaping Stage* of writing—in fact, you will know mostly what you think you want to say at this point. Sometime in the *Creating Stage* the idea you want to communicate began to emerge. Now you have to communicate this idea to someone else to see what you do think and what you want that person to know. So, it is a case of both knowing and not knowing: you have an idea of what you want to communicate, and yet you won't really know what you want to communicate about that idea and just how you are going to present that idea until you put it down on paper intended for another person. The only thing for you to do at this point, when you know vaguely what you want to say, is to *get started*. And the way to do that is just to jump right in and begin writing your first trial draft.

There is, however, one crucial question you must ask yourself before you jump: "Am I an insider in this matter?" The answer is "maybe" if you know something about the subject that the reader doesn't know or have a special expertise in the matter. Figure out and establish your own special qualifications as an expert in this matter. Be certain that *you* are the appropriate person to write on this subject. If that sounds too hard, you may need to look for another subject, since you obviously don't want to waste your reader's time by writing simply to have something to turn in. And, in fact, it wouldn't be a very good preparation for life after school, where "turning in assignments" means more than merely going through the motions.

But don't be too hasty in deciding that you're *not* an expert. Just be sure that you're thinking about it, and thinking about the ways that you *are* an insider.

Who knows where the shadow lurks...

WRITE AS AN EXPERT, SPECIALIST, INSIDER

Preliminary Agreements

APPLICATION

1. Think of writing an essay that would describe your town as an attractive vacation spot. Make a list of things you would talk about for each of the following audiences:

    people already living in your home town   out-of-state visitors
    people with small children   a group you make up yourself
    retired people

    When you finish your five lists, look at the ways each list differs from the others because of what is needed for the specific readers. Which audience seems to you easiest to write for? Which is hardest? Why? Which would you most enjoy writing for? Why? (Do you see, now, how having a *specific* set of readers in mind at the outset of your writing process takes care of a lot of those initial decisions?)

2. Read and evaluate the four writing contexts below. Then apply the following questions to each context, discussing your answers with your class.
    a. If you had to write in this situation, what would your basic purpose be?
    b. Who is the audience? Does this audience have any special characteristics or needs that you would have to keep in mind?
    c. What do you think your message would be?
    d. Could you write as an insider on this subject?
    e. Do you notice any ways in which the audience might influence your message or purpose?

CONTEXTS

A. The local Chamber of Commerce has organized a travel tour to a country (or state) with which you are very familiar. Over one hundred Chamber members—both male and female business leaders—have signed up for the tour. The Chamber president asked you to write a short essay for the next edition of the *Chamber News,* which will go out to all who are going on the trip. He requested that your essay focus on something about the country (or state) that probably will not appear in an average tourist guidebook.

B. You are a person who really enjoys going to the movies, especially western films. It is the anniversary of the death of John Wayne, and you have been asked to write an essay on what John Wayne represented to you and how you feel about his place in movie history. There has never been a time when you didn't "know" John Wayne, and you are thrilled to have this opportunity to give your personal viewpoint. The essay will appear in the film column of your local paper.

C. You are a young woman with several small children to support. In an effort to better yourself, you want to enroll in the local university. However, the school does not provide day-care facilities, and you cannot afford the private ones. Write a letter to the chancellor, who has denied such petitions in the past, in which you attempt to get him to take the steps necessary to establish such facilities.

D. Your English instructor has assigned you a composition on this topic: "An Absurd Experience." The student writing the best essay will be exempted from the final examination in this course.

WRITING ASSIGNMENT
THE HOW-TO ESSAY

A how-to essay tells readers how to do a certain thing. A good how-to essay has these characteristics:

1. The content of the essay is directly related to the audience.

   Knowing who the readers will be, a writer makes decisions about just what kind of information to include and how much to include. Judging from how much the readers already know and how likely they are to be interested already, a writer can determine what kind of instructions or directions are needed and what details should be included.

2. The process being described in the essay is divided into clear, logical steps.

   The writer is careful to break the process down so that the readers can follow it easily, seeing exactly how one step leads to the next. The writer works to be certain there are no gaps in the directions, no faulty assumptions about what the readers will "automatically understand."

3. The essay is full of vivid, concrete details so that the reader can see exactly how to do the thing the writer is describing.

   The writer realizes that words have to do all the teaching in a how-to essay. These words must be as clear and sharp in detail as possible.

4. The information in the essay is presented in an interesting framework rather than just as cut and dried directions.

   The opening of a good how-to essay must get the reader's attention. It will have an interesting lead-in to or a frame around the information itself—something to move the reader into the subject. No writer expects anyone to be interested in just a set of dull instructions.

5. The essay sounds as though a human being, not a mechanical robot, wrote it.

   A good how-to essay is more than a list of directions; it is a *piece of communication* from one *person* to other *people*. The writer takes into account the fact that readers like to hear a "voice" behind the words, like to think someone alive and enthusiastic wrote the essay.

---

1. CONTEXTS

Choose one of the following contexts and write a how-to essay based upon the information. At the top of your essay state the purpose, audience, and message.

A. The local Y is having a special summer sports program. Free lessons are available for all teenagers who have never played tennis, racketball, handball, basketball, or volleyball. When someone joins the program and signs up for lessons in one of the available sports, he or she receives a booklet which explains how to play that particular game. Write the how-to essay that will appear in the booklet.

B. Imagine that you are out of school and have a good job or perhaps even own your own business. As part of the publicity and advertising campaign for your company or business, you plan to write a how-to essay telling your customers how to do something you think they will be interested in learning. You plan to have this how-to essay printed up with a colorful cover and attractive format and give it to everyone who comes to your place of business. Write the essay which you are going to give away.

C. You have been nominated by a local civic club as a candidate for Woman or Man of the Year. One of the things all candidates must do in the competition is write an essay in which they describe how to do something that most people don't know how to do. The information you have received from the club lists some possibilities:

If you collect stamps or records or books, tell how to make a really good collection.

If you can cook ethnic food, tell how to prepare a little-known dish.

If you know how to build things, tell how to do some particular building project.

The information for the competition also tells you that you are to write the how-to essay for an audience who has had no experience in what you are describing. Choose the thing you know how to do that most people might not and write the how-to essay that will win you the award.

2. CREATING

Several of the creating techniques you have learned will help you find ideas for your how-to essay. You may, in fact, want to do a two part creating activity for this essay. First, if you have no idea what you want to use for your subject, write "What do I know how to do well that might interest other people?" at the top of the page and then do three 5–10 minute loops. (See **Looping.**) By the end of the third loop an idea will very likely have occurred to you. Second, after you know what you are going to talk about in the essay, a creating technique like listing will help you get the steps clearly in order. You could also use looping again, this time writing the subject of your essay at the top of the page and then doing three 5–10 minute loops to get in your mind exactly what procedure you are going to use to tell your reader how to do whatever you're discussing.

3. SPECIFIC AUDIENCE

After you have finished this Creating Stage, you are ready to write the essay. Now your audience becomes crucial. You have to think first about whether the subject you have settled on is one *(a)* you really do know enough about to teach to someone else and *(b)* your readers will get value from reading.

The aim of a how-to essay is to give value to the reader. This means that the subject must be something potentially interesting to the readers, not something ordinary like how to tie your shoes—unless you are writing for a preschooler's magazine. Nothing cute like how not to bowl—unless you are writing specifically for a light publication that solicits humorous, tongue-in-cheek pieces.

Remember, you must be an insider. Pick a subject that you know extremely well. Don't try to tell someone how to change the points and plugs in a car if you don't really know how to do it yourself. Don't pick something that a reader is likely to know as much about as you do. If you really want to tell how to bake a cake, why not direct the essay to an audience of ten-year-olds who have never cooked or a bachelor afraid of the oven and sure his cake will fall. Or tell how to bake a cake so special that even veteran bakers will be interested. Aim always to give value to the readers so that they will not feel they have wasted their time when they finish reading the essay.

You must also think about your audience in order to decide just what kind of, and how much, information to put into the essay. Your decision will be based on how much your readers are already likely to know. For instance, if you are writing an essay on how to water-ski, it would be helpful to know if your readers have ever been in the water, have ever seen skis, or have any experience in other sports. Not only the amount of details and explanation but also the tone of the essay will be determined by who the audience is going to be.

In second-guessing your audience for a how-to essay, you have to think of even the simplest step in your process and include it in the discussion. You might know what a lug wrench is when you're telling about points and plugs, but your reader probably won't. If you are telling how to weatherproof a mobile home, you will just take it for granted that you pull the plastic tight over the windows before you staple it on, but your reader might never think of this and have plastic billowing out all winter sounding like clothes flapping on a line. Think through every step of your process and anticipate *anything* the reader might not understand or might overlook.

4. FINAL CHECK

When you have written your essay, read it to someone who does not know how to do what you have discussed. Find out if you have been thorough and clear enough for another person to understand the process. Ask the listener if the essay is *interesting* as well as informative. When you are satisfied that the essay can teach your reader how to do what you have discussed, put it in the best form you possibly can and turn it in.

RULES FOR A HOW-TO ESSAY

1. Be sure to choose a process that you know thoroughly.
2. Be certain that your essay will give value to your reader.
3. Know exactly what audience you are writing for and tailor your discussion of the process to that particular group of people.
4. Anticipate anything your specific audience might not know; make every step clear and in order and define all terms and procedures that might be unfamiliar.
5. Use vivid details that are relevant to the point you are making and that will give the reader a clear picture of what you are discussing.
6. Put the information into an interesting framework.

THE TRIAL DRAFT

You are now ready to do the first draft of your paper. You are clear who your audience is; you know why you are writing. You have decided on what you think you want to tell your readers. It is now time to see if your idea is going to fly. To check this out, you do a dry run of the paper, your trial draft.

HOW TO WRITE THE TRIAL DRAFT

1. Remind yourself about why, to whom and about what you are writing the essay.
2. Keep in mind the basic arrangement of all essays—beginning/middle/end.
3. Get started on the draft itself.
4. Aim to involve the reader from the start.
5. Write more instead of less.
6. Don't get bogged down.
7. Wrap up the essay.
8. Put the trial draft aside to cool.

> "How do I know what I think until I see what I say?"—E. M. Forster

TRIAL:
Act or process of testing, trying, or putting to the proof by actual or simulated use or experience.

DRAFT:
Preliminary version of a document.

ROUGH:
Having an uneven surface, full of bumps, ridges, or other irregularities; coarse, shaggy, uneven in texture; lacking polish or finesse; not perfected.

It is really important that you accept that this *is* a trial draft. *Trial* means to test out to see what the results will be, and that is exactly what you will be doing in this first draft of the paper. You are taking your idea and actually putting it into essay form to see if the idea is *(a)* what you really want to say and *(b)* something you can develop adequately.

There is no way for you to know this until you do it. That is why it is crucial for you to be willing to let this first trial draft be whatever it turns out to be. You may discover that you have to start over completely because you really don't know as much as you thought you did about your subject. You may find out that when you've stated your thesis you can't think of a single other thing to say. You may feel that you are sounding absolutely stupid. You may be certain by the second or third paragraph that no person in the universe will be interested in what you have to say. All of these feelings are legitimate. In fact, you will be lucky when you feel them—at least you won't be living in some blissful dream that's completely divorced from reality. Yet, you can handle the feelings, overcome them, merely by being willing to let your trial draft be just that—a *trial* effort. That way you'll at least be able to put some words on the paper. And, as an old French philosopher used to say, until you are willing to put black on white, you won't have anything to change, refine, improve, or fix. So just plow ahead and write the essay. Whatever you produce will bring you closer to that really fine essay you want eventually.

There is no question but that this trial draft can be rough, uneven, imperfect (unless you are writing that day under the luckiest stars in the heavens). In the first place, most of us have to do some writing to learn what we think; in the second place, most of us need to write some more to see how we want to say what we think. Writing is an act of discovery, whatever stage you are doing, and the trial draft is a perfect illustration of the back-and-forth motion that occurs between *creating, shaping,* and *completing,* the three stages of the writing process. Even though you may think you have in mind almost everything you are going to say before you begin the trial draft, you will often find that actually doing the draft itself will lead you to new and even better ideas on your subject.

There are some distinct differences, however, between writing this draft and *creating*.

1. You have a definite audience in mind rather than just yourself.
2. You are now writing to communicate something you really want to say.
3. Your writing now clusters around the idea or message or information that you think you want to deliver to someone else instead of roaming over anything that might come into your mind on the subject.
4. You are now writing toward form and shape, something that looks like an essay.

HOW TO WRITE THE TRIAL DRAFT

Remind Yourself of "Why," "What," and "to Whom". Begin your trial draft by putting three things at the top of the first page: your **purpose** for writing, a short **description** of your audience, and the general **idea** you want to communicate. These won't appear on the final paper itself, of course, but for now they will remind you of the *reason* you are writing, the person or persons *to whom* you are writing, and the *message* you intend to deliver. They will set your mind in the right channel as you begin. If worst comes to worst—you still aren't sure of exactly what you want to tell the readers and you have no time left for creating activities—just put down your best guess and start the trial draft anyway. The shaping process will probably chase some good ideas out of hiding, and you can rewrite more purposefully later.

Keep In Mind the Basic Arrangement of All Essays. The basic arrangement for all essays is beginning/middle/end. Sooner or later, the opening paragraph or paragraphs of your paper will have to:

- Get your readers' attention.
- Reveal or suggest the message you intend to send in the essay.
- Ease your readers into the very aspect/perspective of your subject that you want them to think about.

The middle paragraphs or body of the essay will have to:

- Stick to your thesis.
- Deliver the message promised.
- Get the idea that was in your head into your readers' heads.

THE BIG THREE:
Beginning
Middle
End

The ending of the paper will have to:

- Remind your readers of what you said.
- Give your readers at least one new thing or twist on the subject to think about.
- Provide a gentle completing of the paper so that your readers are not left hanging in mid-air.

It isn't likely that you will be able to accomplish all of these in the trial draft, but keeping in mind the purposes of each basic part of the essay will often feed your creativity and help you make spontaneous, even unconscious, decisions about what you want to say and how you want to say it.

Get Started on the Draft Itself. Actually start putting words on the page. Don't get caught in the cycle of writing and crossing out. And don't think of the hundred other things you could be doing—cleaning out your bureau drawers, washing the top of the refrigerator, calling your friend you haven't seen in four years. Handle this draft the way you handle swimming in cold water—just jump in! Start writing even if what you are putting down seems so obviously stupid that you are embarrassed to see it on the page. **Put it down.**

You already know that an essay always opens with some kind of introduction, so start there. Think of *anything* that can serve as an introduction. Tell a story; give a quote; ask some questions—anything that leads into what you want to discuss with the reader. Aim, if you can, for something interesting and catchy (since an introduction must finally be both). If you produce a workable introduction this time around, fine. If not, don't let that stop you. Keep moving; keep writing. The point is to start the trial draft, not to get stuck at the very beginning. If all else fails, just write *Introduction* across the page and go on.

Aim to Involve the Reader from the Start. Keep reminding yourself that you are writing to a person. You will be amazed at how many decisions you can make about what details to put into your paper and how to arrange them if you will only keep *this* reader and *this* situation in mind. On the other hand, remember that your reader won't be reading your trial draft, so don't worry too much about writing correctly. If the idea of an audience begins to hinder instead of help you, just concentrate on expressing your ideas. You can get back to audience later.

Write More Instead of Less. Write every idea you can think of to communicate what you want your reader to know. This is the main part of your trial draft. Your reader has very likely *not* been thinking about your subject and certainly hasn't done the creating activities you have done. And the reader probably has a different background and set of experiences from yours, too. So write plenty. Make all the points you can think of to convince or inform or explain. And when you suppose you have given enough information for your message to be very clear, add about 10 percent.

Don't Get Bogged Down! Don't worry at this point whether *this* example should come before *that* one. Don't worry if you can't spell some of the words, or if you can't recall a specific thing you are trying to think of. *You have to keep moving on.* You can worry about all the rest later—you can take out, put in, fix up, skin down. Right now, however, you have to get the material onto the paper. Until you do, there simply isn't anything to revise.

Wrap Up the Essay. Go on and finish it, even if you think it is the worst thing you ever wrote. What was the main idea you wanted to leave in your readers' heads—even if you are sure you didn't achieve your intention? Put that idea down again now. Having written the trial draft, you may have a better idea of what you actually do want to communicate than you did when you began writing. This restatement will help you later to revise. Some writers have to write the last paragraph of the trial draft before they really know what they want to say in the opening paragraph of the revised draft. (This often happens because the idea actually grows and perhaps even changes during the trial draft.) What value is your reader likely to find in what you have communicated? Write that down too. You may have insights now that you didn't have when you started. So don't lose them. They may be the inspirations that will encourage you to do the hard work of transforming this "diamond in the rough"—your first draft—into a polished gem.

When you think you have given the reader enough information so that he or she can understand exactly what you have been saying, it's time to bring the writing to a close. It would be easy if you could do what the writers suggest about bringing a hymn to a close—just write Amen, and let it go at that. Or THE END, and let the reader's feelings fall where they may.

Put your Trial Draft aside to Cool. When you have completed the trial draft, you will probably feel wonderful, and you're certainly entitled to. Whatever the faults of this draft, you have at least tested your idea and done a preliminary version of your writing. Sure, it looks rough. But you do have a complete paper, something you can work on later, and having *that* is exactly what you set out to achieve. Put the paper aside with a sigh of contentment—or at least of relief. Leave it for several hours or more. Set it on the windowsill to cool.

If you are working on a very tight schedule and don't have time to let the paper cool for a few hours, at least do this: find a friend and read the paper out loud to him or her. Ask what message the person hears in the paper. Watch your listener's face and see if he or she looks confused as you read the paper. Listen to yourself and notice if you stumble anywhere as you read it *(research shows that wherever you stumble there is usually something that can stand to be changed in the writing).* Ask your listener if the paper was boring. In general, get another person's response to what you have written.

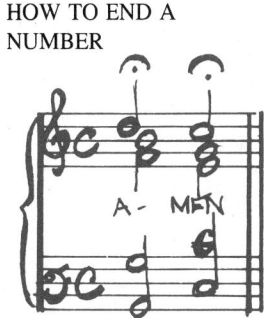

HOW TO END A NUMBER

BETWEEN EARLY AND LATE SHAPING

If you do have time to let the paper sit for a while, go about your daily rounds. Study for other subjects, attend classes, take a walk, eat some food. Do what you normally do, and let some psychic distance come between you and what you have written. This psychic distance is exactly what you need to be able to look at the essay with new eyes and a clear head when you return to it. If you have been able to put this psychic distance between you and the essay, you will see—even before reading the paper to someone else—a number of places you want to rewrite or gaps you want to fill in.

While your trial draft is cooling, you can occupy your time very profitably by thinking about your reader, your message, and the form of the writing itself. Now that you have words on paper, you have something to check.

READER: THE READER IS A PERSON, NOT A WALL

It's always tempting to assume that anything interesting to *you* will also be interesting to the reader—but that's not always the case. You're interested in something simply because you're interested. The reader, though, may or may not agree with what interests you.

Often, it is possible to tell from the first paragraph of an essay whether the reader is being treated as a wall or as a person. Compare the following two opening paragraphs, for example. The first strains to catch the effect of the sunrise in the mountains and concludes with an expression that is rather worn ("the first day of the rest of your life"). It's clear that the writer wants to describe the Great Outdoors. It is not clear that he cares at all whether the reader wants to read about the Great Outdoors. He seems to be assuming that the reader is going to enjoy hearing about this scenery just because he enjoyed seeing it and writing about it.

> There, on the horizon, are the majestic mountains, stretching their peaks so that they might be seen over the top of the towering bristlecone pines. You awaken in awe of this sight, and even more awed are you as you see the sky change from a shade of pink, to orange, to red, and finally, in a glorious burst of yellow light, the sun shoots up over the mountains, signaling the beginning of the first day of the rest of your life.
> —*Howard Marshburn*

Now look at the opening of the next essay. It is written on the same subject, the out-of-doors, but from the very start the writer was aware that he has to interest his audience, to write as though there were people out there, not walls, and that those people would put the writing down if it didn't provide them some sense of satisfaction. He begins by making the reader a partner, the person on the other end for whom he has done all this work.

> An inaudible yawn was the best answer I could give to Bobby at six in the morning. Besides, what kind of a question is "Are you awake yet?" at this early hour? Slowly, my sleepy mind began to focus. Today was the day of our hike into the hill country. I was certain this day would be the low point of my visit with Bobby. However, Bobby was my older brother, as well as my host, and I felt that I should struggle through this journey for his sake. I could think of nothing more boring and worthless than wandering through some barren hills all day long. Nevertheless, I decided to crawl out of bed and get dressed, straining to open each eyelid. Before this day was over, I would realize that my eyes had never really been open before. —*Tim Wold*

What did Tim do that Howard didn't do? He "talked" to the reader by using vivid details, "drawing" the picture so that the reader can see exactly where the writer was. He let the reader know what the reader can expect to read in this essay—about a day he hiked in the hill country. And even more important, he was courteous enough to let the reader know more exactly what will be important about that day—that it was the day his eyes really opened to the out of doors. *The reader has been considered and included.* Tim took very little for granted; he wanted to tell the reader this particular thing, and he knew that to do so he had to bring the reader into the transaction from the very start. He did not take it for granted that someone would read his paper just because he wrote it.

There's nothing at all wrong with writing just to have the pleasure of expressing your own private feelings or opinions, but it's absolutely essential to realize that this kind of writing may have very little in it for a *reader*. To illustrate this point, let's look at one more example of "Here's How I Feel" writing.

> The color of a day makes life worth living. There are many interesting aspects to the colors of a day. To sit and observe them it is evident that you could be sitting and observing for an eternity. The mysterious blue sky with its billowing white clouds is like seeing imaginary objects returning a look. Also, in the sky is the beaming yellow sun. It is a gorgeous object that should bring happiness to everyone. It can brighten up even the saddest of days. There is a secret spy in the sky too, but he only comes out of hiding at night. He is like a wise old owl, only revealing himself at the appropriate time. Coming down to earth we find many new colors. There is green which includes many things. Trees can be many various colors of green. Variety is. . . .

Want to read any further? *Not on your life!* You'd probably agree that the paragraph does, hit or miss, show *something* about how the writer feels, though most of us would be hard put to say *what* exactly. But what's a *reader* likely to think? It might be something like this:

ESSAY	READER'S REACTION
"The color of a day makes life worth living."	(Huh? What does "color of a day" mean? I haven't the foggiest idea! And how in the world can *it* make life worth living?)
"There are many interesting aspects to the colors of a day."	(I get sleepy reading glumpy stuff like "many interesting aspects." And I'm sure not interested in "aspects" of a thing I didn't understand in the first place.)
"To sit and observe them . . ."	(Observe *what?* Those silly aspects? Or colors? Or what?)
". . . it is evident . . ."	(*What* is evident? I don't even know what I am "observing.")
". . . that you could be sitting and observing for an eternity."	(Not me, baby! *You* sit there for an eternity if you want to, and observe away. As for me, forget it!)

If you really want to get a message across, you have to treat the reader as a separate person, not merely as a wall to bounce your feelings off of. Treating the reader as a separate human being, like yourself but also different from yourself, you want to consider what, exactly, you might have to do to move that reader, to get him or her to join up with you, subscribe, agree, feel strongly, be convinced, know in the same way you, the writer, do. To do that, you have to be sure that he or she will have the same images for your words that you do. If you are using terms like "colors of the day," you had better make sure that you show or explain what you mean by them. And if you want your reader to share your wonder about a thing, you had better do more than *say* that it is wonderful—or that *you* think or feel that it is wonderful. You have to *show* the reader exactly *what* is so wonderful about it.

What you have to do is make your reader feel like a partner in the communication exchange. You have to act as though it were a privilege for you to be able to tell your reader whatever it is you are telling; you do not act as though it were the reader's obligation to read what you write just because you write it.

You Can't Be Sure But . . . Finally, the truth is that you can't always know whether the reader will be interested. A lot of very expensive shows open every year on Broadway, with all the people from author to cast to stage crew doing their best to interest the audience—and most of the shows don't last a full season. Still, there are new shows that open the curtains to long and successful runs. So it stands to reason that the more attention you give toward taking an approach that gives value to the reader, the more likely you are to be rewarded by that reader's interest, though you can never be *absolutely* sure.

CHECKLIST: TREAT THE READER LIKE A PERSON, NOT LIKE A WALL

1. Have you considered and included the reader?
2. Does the writing let the reader participate, or does it merely fling feelings at him or her?
3. Have you used vivid details to "draw" a picture for the reader?

APPLICATION

Here are the complete essays by Howard Marshburn and Tim Wold. Compare them, and you'll get a good deal of insight into the differences between treating the reader as a wall and treating the reader as a person. Because both essays have the same theme—an appreciation of nature—they have elements in common that invite comparison. Answer these questions:

1. How does each author treat the encounter with a wild living thing—(the snake in Tim's essay, the trout in Howard's)?
2. What is the event that causes each author to "realize" the significance of his experience?
3. Which descriptions do you consider "seeable"? Which bring no picture at all to your mind?
4. Which conclusion relates back to the beginning of the essay, and how?
5. Which author uses more exaggerated emotion? Which uses more restraint? (Give examples from each essay to support your opinion.)
6. What do you suppose led Howard to write the way he did?

When you finish this comparison, you will have a lot of concrete knowledge about how to know your audience and how to take your readers into partnership when you write. Be able to discuss the comparisons of the two essays with your class.

Reader 63

LIFE IN THE WILD

There, on the horizon, are the majestic mountains, stretching their peaks so that they might be seen over the top of the towering bristlecone pines. You awaken in awe of this sight, and even more awed are you as you see the sky change from a shade of pink, to orange, to red, and finally, in a glorious burst of yellow light, the sun shoots up over the mountains, signaling the beginning of the first day of the rest of your life.

In this grandiose setting the human senses spark to life, as the air is filled with the pungent smells of cedar and pine, and tranquility is broken by the sounds of birds and animals frolicking in the sun of the newfound day. You realize then that you are either dreaming or you are truly experiencing some of the most beautiful sights in the world. You can imagine this scene, but I have and am experiencing it. After gazing at the beautiful scenario for a while, I reluctantly come back to reality.

I realize now that it is time to eat and all I have at my disposal is Mother Nature. I quickly set to work. My ears are way ahead of me as they have picked up the sound of running water over a nearby ridge. "Fish," I think out loud, "of course." I dart over the ridge and I come upon a babbling brook, and believe it or not, in the middle of this pool of Heaven's tears is the biggest rainbow trout ever beheld by human eyes. Can I catch it? The question becomes academic as I know I must if I wish to eat. So, I toss my baited hook into the stream and silently plead with the fish to take my morsel. Slowly he approaches the bait, and in an explosion of air and water that tears at the serenity of the surrounding area, the behemoth strikes and breakfast is mine.

After breakfast, one can do many things, including hiking through the wilderness and survey the splendor God hath wrought upon this land. As I top a ridge, overlooking the land our forefathers once fought for to make us free, I hear a sound that I think at first to be the whispering wind. I then recognize something that sounds like a storyteller, describing this land and how it got to be what it is today. Now I know what the sound is—it is the voice of the Spirit of the Pioneer. After hours of hearing the story of our land recreated, I grow proud to have the distinction of being able to say that by coexisting with nature I can contribute to our great land.

As I walk through this great land, I come upon an old tree and subconsciously wonder what stories it could tell me about this great land. Could it tell me how my forefathers treated this land as a frontier? I think of that and realize that, though my children will refer to this area as a landmark, I can call it home; for I know that I can appreciate the resources this land has to offer. Am I the last of a vanishing breed? I doubt it, for it is the instinct of Man to try to communicate with Nature and to be free. These feelings are the essence of life. This is the life, then, necessary for Man to truly live, and also the essence necessary for Man to break the bonds of humdrum routine of city life, for that can be called something less than living.   —*Howard Marshburn*

HILL COUNTRY HIKE

An inaudible yawn was the best answer I could give to Bobby at six in the morning. Besides, what kind of a question is 'Are you awake yet?' at this early hour? Slowly, my sleepy mind began to focus. Today was the day of our hike into the hill country. I was certain this day would be the low point of my visit with Bobby. However, Bobby was my older brother, as well as my host, and I felt that I should struggle through this journey for his sake. I could think of nothing more boring and worthless than wandering through some barren hills all day long. Nevertheless, I decided to crawl out of bed and get dressed, straining to open each eyelid. Before this day was over, I would realize that my eyes had never really been open before.

I could see a pale blue haze above the peaks of the hills as Bobby drove the Volkswagen farther away from the city. Soon the sun had risen completely, giving definition to the rocky hills on either side of the road. I was uncomfortable in hiking boots, and the drone of the car's engine made me sleepier. I felt miserable. Finally, Bobby led the VW off the road, parking on a flat, grassy plain at the crest of a steep incline. I got out of the car and followed Bobby, who waded through knee high grass, rather than walking down the worn trail many others had traveled before us. As Bobby and I labored up a rugged slope, I found myself wishing for the smooth trail we had passed by.

In any direction, as far as I could see, there was little else but rocks, grass, and an occasional mesquite. Yet there was a certain beauty about this place, a beauty I simply acknowledged rather than appreciated. Bobby spoke very little. He seemed to be interested in the smallest of details. After about thirty minutes of walking, I fell behind; Bobby and I were separated by a small ridge. I stopped in mid-stride, spotting a coral snake coiled beneath a rock in my intended path. I froze: not out of fear or even surprise. I simply stood still and watched. It seemed so odd to find life in such bare surroundings. I had never before encountered a snake and not felt the impulse to kill. Yet, all I wanted to do was watch. The snake jutted its tongue, sensing my presence, yet not the least bit anxious about it. It was so different from the snakes behind the window in a zoo. The colors were brilliant, and the symmetry was absolute perfection. Simply by taking the time to look, I noticed details no photograph could show or word could describe. The sun shifted, throwing light upon the snake and sending it racing for the shadows deep between two rocks. I walked on with a new impression of the land which surrounded me.

I ran over the ridge, catching up to Bobby, who had zig-zagged his way to the bottom of the ravine. We followed its sandy bottom for several hundred yards. I didn't mention the snake to Bobby, preferring to barrage him with questions about the kinds of plants and animals he had seen in the Hill Country. He answered my questions, half-smiling at the new interest I had taken in the surroundings. Before now, I had never understood why he was so observant of nature. Even now, I couldn't describe the feeling in words.

We followed the ravine between two hills where it led to a small pool of water, completely shaded from the afternoon sun. In the moist sand surrounding the water were the imprints of dozens of different animals. Perhaps this was the only source of water for miles. My thoughts flashed back to the snake—there was a drama of survival here. Some animals lived by killing others; some lived because others were killed. There were those who were victims, those who were predators, and those who were scavengers. This land has thousands of different cacti; its rocks contain fossils of animals that no longer exist! How could I ever have looked on this environment so superficially?

The day was such an awakening. Before it ended we were to spot several deer and actually watch a baby bird peck its way out of the shell. Exhausted, I settled into the seat of the VW with a strange feeling of contentment. Bobby returned my smile. I was proud of my older brother, for what he understood about life, and for teaching me the lesson I had only begun to learn.

—Tim Wold

THESIS: THE THESIS IS A MAGIC STRING

> All through *The Elements of Style* one finds evidences of the author's deep sympathy for the reader. Will felt that the reader was in serious trouble most of the time, a man floundering in a swamp, and that it was the duty of anyone attempting to write English to drain this swamp quickly and get his man up on dry ground, or at least throw him a rope
> —E. B. White

There is a beautiful children's book called *The Princess and the Goblin* in which the great grandmother provides the little princess Irene a magic string which she can follow to find her way out of wherever she is or to go wherever she needs to go. And in the quote in the margin of this page, E. B. White talks about throwing readers a rope to help them find their way. As you read your trial draft, you need to look for the thread or rope you have provided the readers so that they know which way to go.

This thread/rope will be the center of your writing; it will be the thing you are spending all this effort and energy to communicate to another person. In conventions of writing, this thread/rope is often called a *thesis*.

Many people make the mistake of thinking that having a "subject" is the same as having a "thesis" for a piece of writing. However, the thesis of your writing is something much more definite than the general subject. The thesis expresses the *subject* of the writing, but also says what the *central point* of your writing about that subject will be. The thesis expresses the topic (thing you'll write about) and your assertion about the topic (what you'll say about it).

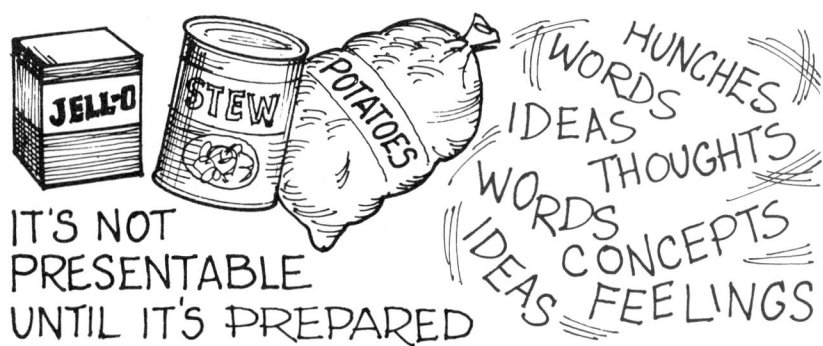

Narrowed Topic	1
+ Specific Meassage	+ 1
= Thesis	= 2

(and it's not true if any piece is missing)

When you look at your trial draft you may discover that you have said a lot *about* or *around* your main idea and that the main idea itself is not clearly visible to your readers. Unless you have a clear thesis that holds your writing together, it will be like inviting some friends over for a meal and when they arrive handing them an uncooked steak, a box of Jell-o, and a raw potato and saying, "Here is dinner." To move from all your private writings on a subject, you have to prepare the thesis, the specific subject, and a statement *about* the subject—just as you have to prepare the ingredients before you can serve dinner. From all the ideas you had in the Creating Stage and all the things you said in your trial draft, you must form a statement, stated or implied, that can hold all your thoughts together.

When you read your trial draft, you will see that you return at least once in a while to the same point or that you write *about* the same idea a lot or that one main thing stands out or seems the most interesting. It is your responsibility now, as you think about revising your writing, to make this thesis obvious and central in your paper. This thesis should be narrow enough for you to be able to discuss it completely in the time and space you are going to have to write the essay. The thesis should make an assertion about your subject. It should be specific enough to guide your readers and yet comprehensive enough to "hold" all the points you want to make. It should be a proposition you can discuss as an insider.

THESIS:
A setting down; something set down; a proposition stated or put forward for consideration, especially to be discussed or proved or maintained.

Your thesis may come to you in several ways. If some time elapses after the Creating Stage, this period of incubation may produce the thesis without your even being aware of it—there will just be a flash of the idea at the oddest moment. If there isn't incubation time, however, or if no promising central idea emerges in the trial draft, loop the idea that has the most energy in it as you read back over it, even if that energy is just a little spark. This looping specifically to define or refine the exact thing you want to communicate to the reader is an example of the recursive nature of the writing process. It lets you be exploratory even in the act of shaping your writing for other readers.

The question to ask is "What *exactly* do I want to say about it?"

On the other hand, sometimes a sentence can "look," like a thesis, yet because it is either too broad, or muddy, or both, it really doesn't serve either reader or writer very substantially. For example, you may remember Howard Marshburn's essay, earlier in the text, about "Life in the Wild," which had "majestic mountains stretching their peaks" and the sun "shooting up over the mountains, signaling the beginning of the first day of the rest of your life." Howard's "thesis" was: "The beauty and splendor of the Great Outdoors is exhibited throughout the heritage of our country, and it is the exploration of this heritage that remains as one of the last frontiers." It looks a little like a thesis, and he calls it a thesis; but *is* it?

For example, "the beauty and splendor of the Great Outdoors" *sounds* like a subject. What *about* the beauty and splendor? It is "exhibited throughout the heritage of our country." Well, that's a puzzler. What, in fact, does it mean? What *can* it mean? If beauty and splendor exist, how then can they be *exhibited?* And while it is possible to say that certain characteristics of the population are exhibited through certain *actions* and that the history of the country can therefore be partly accounted for by some of these traits, how does the character of the population relate to the Great Outdoors? The last part of the statement comes closer to making sense to the reader: "exploration of the beauty and splendor of the Great Outdoors remains as one of the last frontiers"—except that it's still too broad in the subject and a bit fuzzy, too, in the assertion (what makes the Great Outdoors like a "last frontier"?). So while this particular thesis fails to measure up to the criteria—and certainly there's no evidence of writing as an expert or insider—still it is extremely valuable in

BEWARE OF A VAGUE THESIS.

Thesis

showing the writer that *he hasn't yet got enough mastery of either the subject or the approach*. However, even a bad thesis at this stage can be valuable because it can reveal the need for clearer thinking before the actual rewrite.

SUMMARY OF THESIS

Asking yourself exactly what the paper is going to accomplish for your readers is absolutely necessary. To be sure that readers should take their valuable time to read your writing, to be sure they'll get something out of your writing, to be sure that they will be interested and that you'll tell them something they don't already know, you can ask these question:

- Am I writing on a *single aspect* of the subject?
- Am I writing as an *insider* in the matter?
- Have I stated (or suggested by implication) the thesis *early* and *clearly?*
- Is the reader likely to *care?*

When you can answer yes to these questions, you will know your specific purpose for writing and the specific message you want to send.

A CHECKLIST FOR THESIS

1. The message I am communicating in this paper is _____.
2. I am the appropriate person to write on this thesis because I am an insider on the subject. I know it from the point of view of _____.
3. I have clearly let my reader know what I am writing about by telling him or her on page _____ in paragraphs _____.
4. This thesis will probably matter to my readers because _____.

APPLICATIONS

1. Read the following paragraphs. Answer these questions about them.

- Does each paragraph have a **clear thesis statement?** If so, what is this statement?
- If a thesis statement is present, does the writer limit the subject to a **single aspect?**
- Has the **writer been clear** about what she or he is going to say about the thesis?
- Can the **reader** know what he or she is **going to get** from reading the paper?

Be able to discuss your answers for each paragraph in class.

A. "Gee, Mom, it smells good in here! What's cooking?" asks a boy as he walks through the kitchen. Slam! Mom watches her son come in and walk by without even noticing her presence. In tears she looks on as he hunts through the refrigerator for a mid-afternoon snack and thinks, "You call this a family."

B. I cannot believe that it is all over. When I was little, all I ever wanted to be was a teenager. I longed for the days when I would do nothing but chase boys, talk on the telephone and blast my stereo. I wonder now, if I had not talked quite so long on the phone and had not listened to my loud stereo quite so avidly, if my high school years would have gone by any slower. I never really took the time to stop and say, "Hey! I am now one normal, 100 percent, full-fledged teenager!" Instead, it seems as if I made a transition straight from babydoll little girl life into womanhood without even stopping to think twice.

C. The serene atmosphere surrounding the neighborhood was pierced by an echoing scream. A teenager turned and ran in the direction of the noise. Rounding a corner he was confronted by a mother and father standing over their son. The teenager took note of the situation and immediately began artificial respiration. Within a few minutes the child was conscious and active. Why was the teenager able to save the child while the mother and father stood helplessly by? Were they overcome by the shock of seeing their son in trouble, or did they not know how to administer first aid? In either case their son might have died if it had not been for a total stranger. The teenager was able to save the child's life because he had been taught first aid.

D. It took me twelve years of school to finally realize that I did not know how to study. When I was in high school, I did about twenty minutes of studying a night (excluding Fridays and Saturdays). Plus, for a test, I kicked in about thirty extra minutes. Despite the lack of study I still pulled out a 3.325. Then came the shock of my life, college.

2. Which of these paragraphs convince you the writer can give some unique value on the thesis? When you've made your decision, look closely at the convincing paragraphs and examine them for features that suggest the writer has the reader in mind. Explain what techniques a writer can use to convince the reader that there will be value in the writing.

A. Have you ever had the courage to work with little kids and not only try to teach them how to play soccer, but, at the same time, have them enjoy what you are teaching? Chances are your answer is no, but then again you probably never thought about it quite like that. This act of bravery is not a subject to be taken lightly, mainly because teaching is one of the hardest ways to relate to kids. While you are teaching them, you need to do it in such a manner that they can enjoy what they are learning. Some people just do not understand that kids can enjoy what they are being taught.

B. The American way has always been toward progress but not always toward every aspect of the future ahead. Americans in their race for progressive happiness have damaged one integral part of their future, their own lands. Now the people are beginning to see their wrongs and are correcting these problems. The only natural wild lands they have left to save are those in the national parks and forests and their time for repenting their ways grows short.

C. I have some grim facts concerning the automobile's future. According to the Ryman's study (Standard Oil Co. of New Jersey) in 1967, there are $30-50 \times 10^9$ tons of oil on the North Slope. There are just 200

× 10^9 tons of oil in reserves in the U.S., with the average automobile using 2 tons of oil a year in the U.S. (1 ton = 8 barrels). If the energy usage of the U.S. continues to go up at the present rate (1% and $3/10^9$ tons used per year), the U.S. will have to import as much oil from the Middle East in the 1980s as it produced in 1970. There is evidence that shows the automobile will have to use one-tenth less gasoline in the year 2000. According to most studies, the automobile is responsible for over half the energy consumption in the U.S. The excessive use (or waste) of gasoline will soon spell an end for the automobile.

3. Look at these opening paragraphs from student essays, and see if the writers seem to be *insiders* on the subject. What passages, words, sentences, establish them as *insiders* (or *outsiders,* as the case may be)? Be able to discuss these paragraphs in class.

   A. Dating is an important part of every young person's maturing process. One's social growth is very likely to be stunted by the limiting of himself or herself to a single steady date. Young adults are quick to believe they are in love and believe that marriage would be the only way to truly express it. True, some of these marriages work out fine but most result in divorces.

   B. Racquetball is the youngest of the racquet sports. And, in many ways, it is the best. The game can be enjoyed at any level of competition. Almost anyone can hit a rubber ball against the wall, but few can do it with the power, velocity, and finesse of a racquetball champion.

   C. "You know that class is awful. I never learn anything from it, but it seems to last for hours."

   "I know what you mean. The lectures are so disorganized. He doesn't even know what he's talking about."

   "Well, I won't be there next class. I have better ways to spend my time."

   This conversation is often heard after many college classes. However, this attitude can be reversed through the efforts of the professor. By inspiring confidence in the student and through an organized and knowledgeable presentation of the material, a professor can make any class interesting as well as instructive.

FORM: THE MESSAGE CONTAINS THE FORM

> The acorn contains a mighty oak

Much of what determines the shape and the movement of your writing is not *consciously* decided by you. Your writing generally results from the mix of purpose or aim, audience, content of the message itself, your own thought patterns, mental collection of images and memories, ways of seeing and stating connections—and probably a hundred more things personal to yourself. Therefore, there is little that you need to do deliberately about the overall form of your essay. Putting these principles about form into your mind, however, can make you a better reader of your writing when you return to work on the draft.

Nobody is sure exactly how writers decide the form that their writing will finally take. Usually a writer doesn't really *decide*. The essay, once the thesis is thought out, seems to take its form organically. Form is often a subconscious or automatic activity with experienced writers.

There is a clear application for your own writing. When you wonder what form to arrange your writing into, don't look for some rules from outside to help you, to make it absolutely clear for all time. What researchers currently know about form is that the message itself—the main idea, the thesis that you are going to expand and develop—will determine to a very great extent the form the essay will take. And though there are no hard and fast textbook rules, there is one truth you can hold onto:

The message will have *the* form, or at least *a* form, inherent in it.

> "But after he has at least analyzed the subject in his mind and decided what his purpose requires . . . the writer will usually find that a satisfactory pattern suggests itself."
> —Randall E. Decker

Yet, as we have seen before, beginning writers must often be more conscious and even maybe a little artificial when they are first learning to write, until they get the hang of it and can just "know" things automatically the way experienced writers often do.

What, then, can you learn specifically that will help you have form, arrangement, and organization in your essays as you develop that natural feel of writing? There are a few hints and suggestions that will probably help you in the beginning.

SPECIFIC PATTERNS OF ORGANIZATION

Time Order
Narration
Process
Cause Effect

Spatial Order
Description

General-Specific Order
Definition
Induction

Break-down Order
Analysis
Classification
Examples

Relationship Order
Comparison/Contrast
Analogy

The specific patterns of organization you are about to examine come naturally and organically out of an essay thesis. They are "natural" patterns of thought that all human beings use every day. In fact, even if you wanted to, you couldn't stop yourself from thinking in these patterns. So it follows that you will also write in these patterns; in fact, you will find they come to you easily. The purpose of studying these patterns, then, is to become *(a)* aware of the types of thought patterns that are natural, and *(b)* alert to the combinations—that is, what kinds of thinking patterns usually occur with what kinds of thesis statements and writing purposes. The more you write, the more proficient you will get in actually seeing the specific pattern of organization that will work best for your message—even before you start writing, or certainly by the end of your trial draft. And knowing the pattern that is natural for your thesis can help you improve the shape of your essay when you revise it.

> Be aware of the Patterns;
> Be alert to the Combinations

Form

TIME ORDER

NARRATION
Introduction
Body: (choice of pattern)
   Natural
     Past
       | Happening 1
       | Happening 2
       ↓ Happening . . .
     Present
or **Reverse**
     Present
       | Happening . . .
       | Happening 2
       ↓ Happening 1
     Past
or **Flashback**
     Recent
       ↓ Happening . . .
     Past
       ↓ Happening . . .
     Present
       Happening . . .
Conclusion

Your paper may fall into a *chronological* or *time order* if you have a thesis like this one:

THESIS: **The story of man's first landing on the moon excited the world.**

Here your purpose in writing the essay is to tell this story and to show why the story has excited the world. You naturally begin,

> First, the rocket was launched . . .
> Then, the team . . .
> After that, the module . . .
> Next this happened . . .
> Finally, . . .

and on to the end of the story. You close off the essay with some discussion of the significance of this story for the reader, and there is your specific pattern of organization—*time order*, which you have not imposed arbitrarily. *The pattern of organization has emerged from the thesis of your essay.*

The narrative pattern can easily be varied by reversing the time order or by using a flashback technique. For example, the following thesis:

THESIS: **The brief life and death of my brain-damaged son, Danny, was a painful blessing.**

The writer might begin with the tragic moment of the child's death, then go back to his birth and narrate the natural sequence of happenings in the bittersweet experience of having and then losing this son.

PROCESS
Introduction
Body: (choice of pattern)
   Enumeration
       1
       2
       3
       4
or **Steps**
     Step one
     Step two
     Step three
     Step . . .
or **Sequence**
     First
     Next
     Then
     After that
     Finally
Conclusion

Here is another thesis that leads naturally to *time order* as a pattern of organization in an essay:

THESIS: **Following these steps, a person can spend less for groceries, even in these days of high inflation.**

Do you see how the development that follows a process thesis will also just automatically take a chronological shape?

> First, you do this . . .
> Then, you do that . . .
> After that, you do . . .
> Another thing you can do is . . .

and so on to the end of the steps.

Stage 2/Shaping

A third kind of *time order* pattern appears in this thesis:

THESIS: **The 1954 Supreme Court decision on *Oliver Brown et al* v. *Board of Education of Topeka* caused American education to change.**

To develop this thesis, you would follow a *time order* again because you would say first there is this cause—a court decision—and after that there are these effects—a historic shift in a nation's attitude. If *x* hadn't happened before, *y* wouldn't have happened afterwards. It is an organic organization pattern for this thesis, then, when you discuss first the cause and then the effects.

Sometimes the pattern might be reversed; you might want to discuss the effects first and then the cause, as in a paper written on a thesis like this:

THESIS: **Although integrated education is common in America today, it began in 1954 with the famous Supreme Court "Brown" decision.**

Then your paper would fall into a discussion of the effect first and then a longer discussion of the causes of this effect. You would still be moving in *time order*, however, because the cause occurred first and the effects second.

CAUSE AND EFFECT
Introduction
Body: (choice of pattern)

Cause	or	Effect
1		1
2		2
3		3
4		4
. . .		. . .
Effect		Cause
1		1
2		2
3		3
4		4
. . .		. . .

Conclusion

SPATIAL ORDER

Here is another specific pattern of organization that occurs again and again in writing because all of us see the world this way too, just as we all think in *time order*. The following thesis would result in a paper organized on *spatial order* principles:

THESIS: **The newest aid for tennis players is a specially designed ball thrower.**

It isn't hard to see how this thesis would have as its organic development a description of the new machine. The writer might describe the ball thrower from *left to right, inside to outside, top to bottom*. The important thing is that the writer's pattern of organization should in some way be "built into" the thesis of the paper.

Here's another example:

THESIS: **The most unusual costume I have ever seen was worn by the bass player in a family rock band.**

In the body of an essay written on this thesis, you would naturally describe the costume (how it looked) from top to bottom. Your organizational principle would come directly from the message you were sending in the paper.

DESCRIPTION
Introduction
Body: (choice of pattern)

North
↓
South

Top
↓
Bottom

Near
↓
Far

Inside
↓
Outside

Left
↓
Right

Conclusion

Form

DEFINITION

Introduction
Body: (choice of pattern)

    Define by synonym

    Define by origin

    Define by class

    Define by details, description, etc.

Conclusion

GENERAL-SPECIFIC ORDER

A general statement is one that covers a lot, applies to many things, includes many cases or instances or examples. A specific statement gives one *particular* example, incident, etc. Thought patterns that move from the general to the specific help us to understand new terms or concepts. A thesis like this would lead to a *general-to-specific order:*

THESIS: **Szechwan is a kind of Chinese cooking closely tied to the region of the country where it first began.**

This thesis would lead to a definition of Szechwan cooking. It begins by a generalization: that Szechwan is a kind of Chinese cooking. But, of course, there are many kinds of Chinese cooking, just as there are many kinds of American, French, German, and Italian cooking. So to move from the general to the specific, it will be necessary to show how Szechwan cooking stands out from all other kinds of Chinese cooking—Cantonese, Peking, Mandarin. The movement is broad-to-narrow (all cooking in China to Szechwan cooking), with the main part of the essay devoted to the definition of the more narrow, Szechwan, cooking. Definition results in *general-to-specific order* because you are moving from a large group of things to show how one specific thing stands out from that larger group.

Here is another thesis that would result in a *general-specific order* for an essay:

THESIS: **Lawyers are expected to have offices that look conservative, but nowadays some are showing a real individual flair in how they decorate the place in which they work.**

An essay written on this thesis would begin with a discussion of the generalization contained in the first part of the thesis: that lawyers are expected to have conservative-looking offices. After this discussion the writer would move to something more specific: evidence that some are now decorating with an individual flair.

DEDUCTION
Introduction
Body:
    General
    Specific
Conclusion

The *general-specific order* can also be reversed. You might have a thesis like this:

THESIS: **Just because hunger and starvation have been on earth a long time is no reason to suppose that they will always be.**

You could develop that thesis nicely with a series of specific examples of things people used to believe but which are no longer true. You might use beliefs about the world being flat (which ended around 1492), that humans couldn't fly (which ended in 1903), that running a mile in under four minutes was physically impossible (which ended in 1954), that traveling to the moon was an unattainable dream (which ended in 1969). From those specifics you could move to a generalization: other "impossible" things have been achieved; we can also achieve the end of starvation. And the shape of the paper emerges effortlessly from the thesis.

INDUCTION
Introduction
Body:
    Specific 1
    Specific 2
    Specific 3
    Specific. . .
    Generalization
Conclusion

BREAK-DOWN ORDER

Another common thought pattern of organization is illustrated by this thesis:

THESIS: **All pieces of good writing have some characteristics in common.**

As you wrote the essay that developed this thesis, you would naturally discuss the *specific characteristics*—you would *analyze* good writing to see what its parts were.

Here is another thesis that would just automatically result in a *break-down* pattern of organization:

THESIS: **This magazine advertisement is extremely effective in getting people to buy Vim chewing gum.**

The rest of your paper would consist of your analysis of the ad; you would talk first about one characteristic and then another. You would be breaking the subject down into *component parts* and that would provide the order for your paper.

ANALYSIS
Introduction
Body: (choice of pattern)
    Part 1
    Part 2
    Part 3
    Part. . .
or
    Characteristic 1
    Characteristic 2
    Characteristic 3
    Characteristic. . .
Conclusion

Form

CLASSIFICATION
Introduction
Body:

    Group 1
    Group 2
    Group 3
    Group. . .

Conclusion

Here is another kind of thesis that results in a *break-down* pattern of organization:

THESIS: **Television shows can be divided into those that are produced to entertain and those that are produced to educate.**

As the writer who was going to develop this thesis, you would not even have to decide what organization pattern you were going to use. The parts of the essay would just naturally be (1) the shows that entertain, and discussion about these; (2) the shows that educate, and discussion about these.

EXAMPLES
Introduction
Body:

    Example 1
    Example 2
    Example 3
    Example. . .

Conclusion

A third kind of *break-down* shape appears in this thesis sentence:

THESIS: **The Smoky Mountains in east Tennessee are a great vacation spot.**

To develop this thesis, you would give examples. Your aim in this essay would be to convince your reader by citing specifics that you think prove that the Smokies are good vacation country. You wouldn't have to worry about the overall shape of the essay because it's inherent in your thesis. (This is also known as the *string-of-beads shape* because examples follow the thesis like beads on a string.)

COMPARISON/ CONTRAST
Introduction
Body (choice of pattern)

I	Or	II
Item A		Point 1
Point 1		Item A
2		B
. . .		. . .
Item B		Point 2
Point 1		Item A
2		B
Item. . .		Point. . .
Point 1		Item A
2		B

Conclusion

RELATIONSHIP ORDER

Imagine that the thesis of your essay was this:

THESIS: **City dwellers often dream of living in the country, but those dreams miss the reality by a country mile.**

You would be setting up your paper to discuss two things: dreams about life in the country, and the real life. This kind of *comparison/contrast* built into a thesis gives the writer his or her organizational pattern.

Here is another example:

THESIS: **The question of whether to rent or to buy your own home is becoming more complex every day.**

The organization pattern for this essay will be to discuss renting and to discuss owning. The only decision you will have to make is whether to say everything you want to say about renting before going on to owning, or whether to talk about a *particular aspect* of the thesis—say, tax relief—and, in the discussion of tax relief, talk about *both* renting and owning, and then go on to *another aspect* of the thesis—say, initial investment—and talk about both renting and owning under that. At any rate, no matter which variation you choose, the basic pattern of organization—*comparison/contrast*—is an organic part of the thesis itself.

Another relationship pattern is inherent in this thesis:

ANALOGY
Introduction
Body:

    Example 1:
    _____is like
    _____in this way

THESIS: **Partnership is a legal arrangement something like marriage.**

    Example 2:
    _____is like
    _____in this way

    Example . . .

The organization pattern comes directly out of the thesis: a discussion of something probably unfamiliar to the reader (partnership) by comparing it to something familiar (marriage). This is a form of comparison that carries *one point extended all the way through the essay* with examples or details to show how the comparison is accurate.

Conclusion

MIXED FORMS

You have perhaps noticed that a group of essays might appear together in a collection and be introduced as, say, Essays of Definition. Then, when you started reading the essays, you saw that a lot of other ways of writing besides *defining* appeared in the essays—for instance, *describing, comparing, narrating*. Don't let this confuse you. Remember that terms like *comparing, defining, analyzing, classifying,* and the like are actually names of ways in which all of us human beings think. Any of these can be the *general form* of an essay and/or one of the several *specific ways* that the essay is developed within the *general form*. Just remember that although the general overall *pattern* of your essay may be, say, comparison, you will use several other kinds of thinking to *develop* that essay.

Read the following student essay and notice (a) how the overall shape of the essay is determined by the writer's thesis and (b) how other forms of thinking also appear inside the overall shape or pattern.

OFTEN THE GENERAL FORM OF THE ESSAY IS DEVELOPED BY SEVERAL OTHER KINDS OF THINKING

COMPARISON / CONTRAST
CAUSE AND EFFECT
| DESCRIPTION | ANALYSIS |
| NARRATIVE | CHRONOLOGY |

Freshman to Freshman: Surprises in English

STUDENT ESSAY

Every time I go to get my hair cut, I ask the hairdresser if there isn't some way he could cut my hair so that I wouldn't have to wash it everyday, blow it dry, curl it, or roll it—and, of course, it would have to look perfect all the time. I would be willing to wash it occasionally and comb it once a day. Although I appear to be joking with the hairdresser, subconsciously I think that, if he really knew his job, he ought to be able to perform this impossible task.

That's the same attitude I had about freshman composition. I didn't want to put out much effort, but I thought I should get good grades. My prof, after all, was being paid to teach me to write well. And I was paying that salary. Therefore, by the end of the semester I should be able to write well.

Very early in the semester I learned how wrong I was. I had to wash my hair everyday and keep it fixed if I wanted to look nice (oh, sure, some people

Form

can jump out of the swimming pool and look like a million dollars, but they're the exceptions); and I had to work on my writing skills and put forth some effort on my own if I wanted my writing skills to improve.

I also discovered that writing was similar to hair styling in other ways. I never realized that, just as a beautician often looks at a picture of the finished hair style before he begins cutting my hair, I have to know what my finished theme should do before I ever begin writing. Hair has to be properly shaped to hold a certain style; themes, too, must be shaped to achieve their purposes. And, just like certain hair styles work on some people and don't on others, I had to decide how to write my theme to interest and convince the audience of readers.

Before I took freshman English, I had concentrated most of my efforts in writing on making sure that all words were spelled correctly and all commas were placed correctly. I soon discovered that that was like a hairdresser spending five minutes cutting, washing, drying and styling hair and thirty minutes applying hairspray. When writing, all the correctly spelled words in the world won't help if the message is not carefully planned to be clear to the audience. I started spending much more time coming up with an interesting way to present my ideas and making sure that my audience understands my message.

That brings up another important part of writing. I've spent months sometimes going through magazines to find the exact hair style that would look right on me; I knew where to go to look for ideas. When preparing a theme, I had no idea that there were ways to create a topic and make my message more interesting and more effective. Finding a topic was always the worst part of writing; creating techniques—discovering ways to find a topic—were a welcomed surprise in freshman English.

I also quickly learned that my comp texts weren't much help. It seemed like the authors assumed that we already could write C+ essays and just needed help correcting mechanics so that we could all make A's or B's. Most of my help in freshman English came from the prof, from reading and discussing examples of good and bad essays, and from endless hours of writing and thinking.

I never expected my freshman comp course to have so much writing and thinking. Don't ask me why. Maybe it's because we really never wrote much in high school and I was hoping to make it through college English without writing.

But, now that I think about it, that would be like going to the hairdresser to have my car fixed.

—*Karen Davis*

This essay is written in the **break-down** pattern with **examples.** The writer's thesis is that **there were many surprises for her in freshman English.** The shape of the essay is organically present in this thesis: she gives examples of how she was surprised. These surprises turn out to be:

- She had to work hard and put forth effort.
- She learned that writing had to be shaped.

- She learned there was more than editing to do when she wrote.
- She learned about creating techniques.
- She learned that her textbook wasn't much help.
- She learned she had to do a lot of writing.

Notice, however, that even though this essay has the *break-down* shaping pattern of examples as its overall form, the writer does many other things inside the essay besides give examples. She *narrates, describes, compares,* uses an *analogy,* and does other things, all in the overall *break-down* pattern of shaping called *examples*.

> *"Purpose* is the greatest influence on form."
> —Henry Boettinger

REVIEW OF PATTERNS OF ORGANIZATION

Here are the main points for you to remember about patterns of organization:

1. Be aware that a thesis does suggest its own pattern of organization.
2. Realize that although the overall pattern of organization may be defined as one word (*classification, definition,* etc.), many patterns of thinking will appear in the essay. The form of almost all essays is a *mixed form*.
3. Become familiar with and conscious of the basic patterns of organization, but don't make these patterns the reason you write.

Don't worry about memorizing such terms as *comparison, chronology, definition,* etc., because you will probably never have to stop and think that *analogy* produces *relationship order* while *definition* produces *general-specific* order, or the like. We are considering this matter simply to demonstrate how the thesis does result in its own appropriate form and to show that these forms can be discussed if need be. Knowing this form or that form, however, won't help you know how to write unless you really understand the central principle: your thesis will lead automatically, especially the more you write, to a particular form for your writing.

Writing in order to fit a pattern is writing backwards. Always begin with a *purpose,* an *audience,* and a *message*. Write because you have something to say to someone, and then be aware after that of the variety of methods of organization you might use for that message. Be confident, though, that if you have a *purpose* for writing, a particular *audience* in mind, and a *message* you really want to send, then an *organizing principle* will naturally and organically follow. Your essay will definitely have a shape.

APPLICATION

1. Read these thesis sentences and decide what organizational patterns are present in them:
   a. There are only three basic types of running shoes.
   b. Nancy Lopez's rise in golf is a Cinderella story.
   c. The new office building has a very unusual shape.
   d. The book *Being Seventy* is extremely well written.

e. *Self-actualization* is a word everybody ought to learn.
f. People are eating better all over the country; this is causing some significant changes in health, illness, and death.
g. *Moving Mountains* tells the reader how to give an effective speech.
h. Stories abound about the danger of microwave ovens.
i. Our new senator is a flamboyant person.
j. *Poetry* is a hard word to pin down.
k. Swimming doesn't use the same muscles that badminton does.
l. Subways are picturesque.

2. Here are two lists of thesis sentences. Choose *one* from each list. When you've chosen, begin at *once* to write an essay on each subject. The point is to notice how each thesis carries with it an organic shape. Therefore, deliberately avoid thinking about shape for the essay; bypass the creating stage too. Instead, move directly into the essay and watch the shape emerge.

You don't need to write two whole essays. Just write enough of each essay to experience how the shape is contained within the thesis.

GROUP 1	GROUP 2
1. Red is not a good color to wear on a hot day.	1. Red is a better color than blue for decorating a playroom.
2. Organizing recipes requires some kind of system.	2. Recipes for making pie dough are easy to follow.
3. Artificial respiration saved the life of a friend of mine.	3. Artificial respiration makes the lungs continue functioning.
4. The mountains were breathtaking	4. The mountains have interesting geological features.
5. You can recognize my neighborhood by its distinct boundaries.	5. My neighborhood has a feeling all its own.
6. My father's (mother's) face is a record of his (her) life.	6. There is more to fatherhood (or motherhood) than just producing offspring.
7. Although my mother and father are both parents, each has a different role.	7. Although my mother and father each have very different roles, they both are described by the word *parent*.

WRITING ASSIGNMENT
THE PROBLEM/SOLUTION ESSAY

All of us experience problems—plenty of them too. Certainly they help keep life challenging. Since dealing with problems and working on solutions can be an important part of our lives, it's no wonder that much of the writing required of us in life has to do with problems and/or solutions. The essay form you are about to practice will appear in your life probably in hundreds of guises—in reports you write, in speeches and talks you give, in letters you send, at meetings you attend. It is one of the most useful and common essay forms you can have. Fortunately, this form is also fairly simple and seems almost to write itself—provided you are discussing a problem you know something about.

A good problem/solution essay will have these characteristics:

1. The writer will thoroughly discuss (a) the problem, (b) the solution, or (c) both.

Problem/solution writing does not always cover both the problem and the solution with equal thoroughness. Sometimes a writer's purpose is to emphasize the problem so that people will think more about it. Perhaps the writer isn't even sure of the solution. Other times a writer's purpose will be to present the solution to a problem, and the problem itself will be mentioned only briefly. The writer will assume that the problem is evident to and agreed upon by the reader. At still other times the problem and the solution will be given equal space. The form that the problem/solution writing takes—emphasis on problem, emphasis on solution, or emphasis on both—depends on the purpose of the writer and the nature of the audience.

2. Examples and illustrations will be used in abundance.

The writer cannot expect the reader to understand the problem or to agree with the solution unless they are really discussed in the essay. The best way to help the reader see the situation as the writer sees it is to use many examples and illustrations. A problem/solution essay, then, will be filled with phrases like, "For instance . . .," "An example of what I mean is . . .," "To illustrate my point. . . ."

3. The writer will choose examples and illustrations that will have meaning for the particular audience to whom she or he is writing.

Just the presence of examples and illustrations won't get the problem and solution across. The examples must mean something to the people who will be reading the essay. They should, then, be about things, people, places familiar to the audience and preferably be examples that have a direct bearing on the readers' lives.

1. CONTEXTS   Choose one of the situations below as the basis of your problem/solution essay. At the top of the essay write the context.

   A. You are running for a student government or city government position. You, along with all the other candidates, have been asked to prepare a position paper in which you discuss some problem you would solve if you won the election. The paper will be published in a special section of the school or city paper. Naturally, the audience will be making up their minds whom to vote for as they read about the problems discussed and, more importantly, the solutions offered. You sit down to begin this position paper and realize that that you aren't going to have any trouble thinking of the problem because so many come to mind. It will just be a matter of choosing the one you think the audience feels is most pressing in their lives. If you're running for student government, you think of things like parking space, library hours, quality of the food, lack of equal sports facilities for women and men. If you're running for a city seat, you think of things like taxes, school improvement, city spending, garbage pickup, corruption. Choose the problem for which you have a really terrific solution, and write the essay that will win you the election.

   B. Your boss has just held a special meeting of the employees. You learn at the meeting that the company is going to adopt participatory management as its way of operating, and one of the first steps in this direction is to ask the employees to discuss the problems in the company and to present solutions to these problems. You now have the chance not only to get off your chest a complaint you've had about how things are done, but you also have an opportunity to make a contribution to the company. Write the paper that discusses these problems and solutions clearly and concisely, and watch changes that you have been longing for come to pass.

   C. You can't believe it! For years you have been plagued with (1) a problem around the house, (2) a problem with a friend or relative, or (3) a personal problem (overweight, smoking). Suddenly you come up with the perfect solution. It's so simple or obvious or workable that you can't imagine why it took you so long to think about it. And it's something you think other people could profit from by hearing of your experience. Write about this problem/solution, inventing an appropriate context and audience for the essay.

   D. You have just had an experience that *really* made you aware personally of a problem you'd heard a lot of people talk about but that you had never thought very much about until now. Perhaps it was having inflation really hit you in the face when you made a certain purchase. Or perhaps you realized how difficult life can be for someone trying to live on a fixed income like social security. You may have experienced the stereotyped attitudes toward people when they get old, the effect on a mother who does not work outside the home when the children are gone, etc. You are motivated to write about this problem, perhaps for a sound-off column in a local newspaper, church bulletin, club newsletter, etc. Prepare the essay you want published so that other people become aware of the problem.

2. CHOOSING A PROBLEM

One of the pitfalls for students when they start to write a problem/solution essay is the inclination to pick a problem that is too big or too complex. Perhaps the subject will be something so complex that people working on it for the past fifty years haven't made a dent in the problem—like balancing the federal budget. Or maybe the solution the student decides to give is such a cliché that people get bored just hearing it—like "Don't be a litterbug."

Somehow, when students think "problem," one of these all-time biggies like conservation is what comes to mind—together with war, energy crisis, environment, health care, and world peace. Resist such problems for all you are worth—unless you are truly an expert in the matter or have given a lot of thought to the problem and genuinely believe you have a solution to offer. If you don't know a good solution for the problem from your own first-hand experience, or your own reading, don't write about it. Remember that, as always, you write to give your reader value.

3. CREATING

Both **cubing** and **classical invention** are excellent creating techniques for a problem/solution essay. If you cannot think of a problem to discuss, try *looping* the words "Problem/Solution Essay," and see if an idea doesn't emerge. Then take this idea through **cubing** or **classical invention** because both of these will lead you to think about many aspects of the problem and solution. You will thus be able to go beyond a mere surface discussion—one that is not thought through but is merely an emotional or parroted reaction. Remember, too, that a problem/solution essay, to be effective for the most readers, must make its impact from its *evidence, examples, illustrations, facts, logic,* and *wisdom*. **Cubing** and **classical invention** will let you settle down and really look at what you know and think about the problem and its solution.

4. SHAPING

The purpose of the problem/solution essay will produce its form or shape. If your purpose is to discuss the problem, then the essay can be arranged in an order that answers these questions:

1. So, what's the problem?
2. Why should the reader care about this problem?
3. Here's a full description of the problem with several examples. Do you understand it?
4. So? What should the reader do or know as a result of reading this essay?

If your purpose in the essay is to discuss the solution to a problem, writing an essay that answers these questions in this order provides form for the essay.

1. So, what's the problem?
2. Why should you, the reader, care about this problem?
3. OK, here's the solution described fully with many examples. Do you understand it?
4. Why will this solution work?
5. So? What does the reader do or know as a result of this essay?

If your purpose is to discuss both the problems and the solutions, writing an essay that answers these questions in this order gives you shape for the essay.

1. So, what's the problem?
2. Why should you, the reader, care about this problem?
3. Here's a full description of the problem with many examples. Do you understand it?
4. OK, then what is the solution?
5. Here's a full description of the solution with many examples. Do you understand it?
6. So? And finally what?

If your essay answers these questions for the reader, you will have a clear and effective piece of writing. And, as always, you must make decisions about your audience in your *shaping stage*. There is no way to answer the questions above unless you can picture who will be reading them. Decide in advance whom you want to read this essay and plan everything you do in light of those particular people.

5. FINAL CHECK

After you have written your essay, read it to someone to see if the listener:

- stays interested
- understands the problem or finds the solution believable
- feels that you, as writer, were genuinely concerned
- feels that you, as writer, sounded like an insider on the subject.

When you are satisfied that the essay really communicates to another person, put it in the final form for turning in. Make it as correct and attractive as you possibly can. Don't let a hurriedly put together final draft steal all the effectiveness of the hard work you did in creating ideas and putting them into a shape that communicated to another person.

RULES FOR A PROBLEM/SOLUTION ESSAY

1. Select a problem and/or solution that you have experienced personally. Be positive that you have something to say on the subject.
2. Decide whether you want to discuss the problem, the solution, or both.
3. Know your audience and intend to give them value in the essay. Make certain that the subject is going to matter to them.
4. Use many examples and illustrations throughout the essay. Be sure these examples and illustrations will strike home to the audience.
5. Assist the readers in understanding any complex issues by breaking them down into their simpler parts.
6. End the essay by letting the readers know what to make of all you have said.

LATE SHAPING

Now that you have looked at your trial draft to see if you have treated your reader like a person and not a wall, to see if you have a thesis that holds everything together, and to notice what form seems to be emerging or could emerge from what you have written, you are ready to write a second draft. If you could find no thesis at all or just wrote with a total absence of audience or rambled so much that you know that this isn't the direction you want to go, you may want to write a second trial draft. If not, you are ready to move right on to *rewriting* the essay itself. You are ready for *Late Shaping*.

HOW TO REWRITE: PROMISE AND DELIVERY

1. Make the most of your introduction.
2. Stick to the thesis.
3. Develop the thesis.
4. Make the most of your conclusion.

What do you do after you have written your trial draft? By the very act of writing the essay in order to send a message to someone else, you have tacitly made an agreement with your readers. The agreement goes like this:

PROMISE:
A declaration that one will do or not do something; to afford a basis for expectation.

DELIVER:
To take to the intended recipient; to perform as desired or promised; to transfer to another.

You may notice that most of the responsibility for this agreement falls on *your* side. That's because it is the *writer's* job to get the message across, and it is the *writer* who is asking others to trust that if they take their valuable time to read what's been written, they will get some kind of benefit from it. The responsibility is *yours,* then, because *you* started the whole arrangement, and because *you* get results when you keep your promise.

Late Shaping

MAKE THE MOST OF YOUR INTRODUCTION: MAKE CLEAR WHAT YOU ARE PROMISING

You would be surprised how many writers don't take advantage of the chance to capitalize on a good opening. Ignoring this opportunity is risky business. If you don't get your readers hooked right away, they may not stay around long enough to see what you have to say. Unless you just got lucky when you were writing your trial draft, you will need to rewrite to make the most of your introduction.

The opening paragraphs of your paper must do three things:

1. Get your readers' attention.
2. Reveal the message you intend to send in the essay.
3. Ease your readers into the very. *aspect/perspective* of the subject that you want them to think about.

YOU'VE GOT 2 SENTENCES OR 20 SECONDS TO HOOK THE READER

Get Your Readers' Attention. This requirement of the introduction is easy enough to understand. Since you know that boredom is a writer's worst enemy and that there is enormous competition for your readers' attention, you have to begin with something that will make them listen to you instead of doing the thousand other things they could be doing. In real life, unfortunately, very few people will be paid to read your writing—as your English teacher is—so you must hook the reader immediately. You probably have about **two sentences,** or **20 seconds,** to do that. David Pichaske, in *How to Do Well in Freshman English,* thinks you should look at your essay and ask, "If this were a novel at the drug store, would I pay $2.50 for it?" Of course it's an exaggeration to compare an essay with a novel, yet the point is clear: the reader should be strongly drawn into the writing at once, or else he or she is likely to wander.

Reveal the Message You Intend to Send. You can almost always *get* anybody's attention for a second or two, but you won't *keep* it very long if there isn't something in what you say that seems clear and valuable. So after you have your readers' attention, you must let them know what your purpose is, what you are going to write about; you must point them in the direction in which you want them to begin thinking. They can't simply be left in mid-air, entertained with some snazzy opening; they have also got to see your *point* in the essay. But don't jar your reader with some klunky and obvious "I'm going to tell you about . . ." statement, either. Gaps and jars are hard on readers. Do remember though, that the introduction must contain, either explicitly or implicitly, the thesis of the writing.

Ease Your Readers Into the Very Aspect/Perspective of Your Subject That You Want Them to Think About. You could spend the entire introduction talking about your subject in general, but it is more efficient to go directly to the angle of your subject that you are going to be discussing. The following two examples will show you the difference. Both deal with the same message—telling the reader that canning one's own pickles gives two advantages: the fun of canning and the pleasure of having good healthy food. Here is the first version, which begins—as you can see—far, far too wide.

> Health foods. Do those words make you think of seaweed cookies and sawdust-tasting soup? More and more people are beginning to learn that health foods can look and even taste like ordinary food, yet they can really make a difference in length and quality of life. Health foods may be nothing more than ordinary foods grown or prepared in an organic and pure way such as apples grown with no insecticide or peaches canned without additives. Realizing this, many people are more receptive to health foods and are willing to give them a try. A lot of people are beginning to do home canning. Pickles are a favorite thing to put up.

Well, this introduction finally *does* get to talking about canning pickles, but the reader first had to wade through too much information about health food and the advantages of home canning in general. The writer is taking far too long to get to the subject and is not directing the reader's attention enough—or soon enough—to the very specific aspect that is the subject of the essay. She has to jump very awkwardly from people being willing to try health foods to home canning. The reader feels stretched and senses too big a gap there.

Let's look at the second version:

> Home canning used to be a drag. Women would slave over a hot stove, heaving large pots of boiling water and taking all day to put up perhaps just one batch of beans. Home canning now is a hobby for men and women alike, and a lot of the pleasure comes from the ease of modern canning processes and the satisfaction of knowing that you are putting up clean, healthy food with no additives or preservatives. The new inexpensive equipment available for canners and the new awareness of the dangers of many commercially canned products makes even a job like making pickles a real pleasure. . . .

The second version does a much better job of moving right into the subject of home canning. It gives the reader a clear focus on the area to be concentrated on; it lets the reader know right away why the essay was written and what the reader ought to be thinking about immediately.

APPLICATION

1. Read the following introductions to essays. Notice how they (a) get the readers' attention, (b) tell the readers what the thesis of the writing is going to be, either directly or indirectly, and (c) move quickly into the exact angle of the subject the writer wants the reader to think about. Be able to discuss the specifics of these introductions with your class.
   A. We live in a country with the highest per capita income ever known to mankind; yet of every 100 of our citizens who reach the age of 65, 95 are flat broke! Of every 100 who reach their "golden years," only 2 are financially independent, 23 must continue to work, and 75 are dependent on friends, relatives, or charity.

From Venita Van Caspel, *The New Money Dynamics,* 1978, p. xiii. Reprinted with permission of Reston Publishing Company, a Prentice-Hall Co., 11480 Sunset Hills Road, Reston, VA 22090.

They lost the money game. The money game is not like any other game. You cannot choose whether you'll play. You cannot choose to sit out a hand or move to another game. For this game—the money game—is the only game in town.

Since you have no choice but to play, then the only intelligent thing to do is to learn the rules and play to win! Losing means spending 20 to 30 years of your life in angry frustration in a state of financial insecurity. —Venita Van Caspel, *The New Money Dynamics*.

B. Teaching ten-year-olds how to play tennis is like teaching them how to play the piano. The only reason they are out on the court is because "Mommy" signed them up. And since learning tennis takes many hours of repetition and concentration, this causes a problem. The ten-year-old has an attention span only long enough to allow his or her little mind to come up with something mischievous. After the first ten minutes are up, well, Billy and Jim start to fight, Terry puts gum in Nancy's hair, Nancy starts to push him, and the tennis teacher is ready to call it a day.

The trick to solving this problem is keeping the kids from thinking they are being taught. They could be at home watching television or riding bicycles which would be fun. So, the teacher must make learning to play tennis look like fun. That is the key to effective teaching.

—*Rick Jones*

C. An eight-year-old boy at summer camp lies on his bed crying. He feels empty, and he wants to go home. Ten years later, he stares out the window of his apartment with the same desolate feeling. Now, he realizes that he cannot run home, so he searches for some cure for his homesickness.

Almost everyone has experienced this feeling at some point in his or her life. It is perfectly normal. It is the type of problem that must be confronted and then solved. As in all problems, there are ways to solve it. —*Mark Shelton*

2. Read these opening paragraphs from student essays and notice how you respond as a reader. Are you interested? Can you tell what the writer is going to write to you about? Does the writer give you an angle on the subject? Be ready to discuss your answer in class.

A. "Do you want to go to the show tonight?" "I don't know." "Aw, come on. I don't have anybody to go with." "Well, all right, I guess I will."

Oops, has another "yes" slipped out again when a "no" was intended? Don't worry. It's a common problem many people share. "No" seems to be a word that sticks to the tongue while "yes" blurts right on out and past it. How does a person learn to say "no"?

B. The small-block Chevrolet V8, without a doubt, has become the most popular engine in America. During the past 22 years, Chevrolet has produced more than 32,000,000 small-block V8's. Since its debut in 1955, enthusiasts quickly recognized the small-block's power-to-weight benefits. This started new development and almost total modification of the small-block. To improve perfomance, the factor increased the small-block's size from the original 265 inches to displacements as large as 400 cubic inches. They also tested and produced many off-road performance parts at unbelievably low prices.

But the development of the small-block by the factory was only the beginning. . . .

C. After waiting for what seemed like an eternity for my twenty-dollar steak, I noticed a wisp of smoke float over my shoulder. I glanced behind me to see if the kitchen was on fire and caught a blast of poisonous smoke in my face. The effects of this attack were immediate; my eyes became red and watery and my once-hungry stomach suddenly felt sick and queasy.

I am sure all of you nonsmokers can empathize with my feelings that night as I was attacked by a foe who was wielding that omnipotent weapon, the cigarette. The physical and mental strain that nonsmokers get from smokers is intolerable. My anticipated pleasant meal that evening was ruined by an inconsiderate smoker. How can we nonsmokers stop this assault on ourselves?

D. Wouldn't it be super if you could just swallow a pill about the size of a vitamin and in a few minutes know everything there is to know about a certain subject? Jump into a machine and have it pop you into the middle of an atom to watch the electrons whirl about you? How about slipping back into the 1800's and seeing Abraham Lincoln and the way he lived his life? Just imagine how much time we wouldn't have to spend in school and how much more interesting learning would be.

Well, getting back to reality, I think learning is a very difficult thing to get a hold of. It seems that a subject has to be interesting to enable it to sink into our head and stay there for a while. . . .

STICK TO YOUR THESIS

One of the first things to check is whether you veered off your subject when you wrote the trial draft. If you tell the readers in so many words, "You can count on me; I'm going to tell you this particular thing," and you get started on that but then think of something else and jump off in another direction, you are failing to keep your agreement; and the reader has every reason to just stop reading then and there. **You can't set up reader expectations and then ignore them.** Readers expect you to say exactly what you said you would say, period. They look for a discussion that stays on the subject throughout the essay; otherwise, they tend to feel frustrated, teased, or set up. They don't want to be told to expect one thing and then have the writer surprise them with something else.

Campfire Dance. You can almost imagine the thesis working like a cheerful campfire, a bright and inviting spot where people can gather and feel cozy and quietly sociable. It's a natural place for tall tales, yarns, ghost stories. Everybody gets nicely settled, and one person begins a story. Then, a couple

of sentences into a story about a shipwreck, he suddenly jumps into a story about graverobbers. Without finishing more than a sentence or two, suddenly he's telling about a magic beetle. In a few more sentences he's begun describing a cold-blooded murder and then starts a new tale about a broken-hearted lover. It's as though he's jumping, hopping, and whirling all around the topic rather than really delivering on any *one* thing. And the folks who have settled down to hear a good story are certainly going to be put off by this disjointed drifting, shuffling, pouncing from one thing to another. We call this the Campfire Dance. The writer is bounding all around the campfire (the special subject for his essay) while the readers are forced to change position constantly in order to try to follow what's going on.

What causes a paper to be like this Campfire Dance? Sometimes the writer comes to the topic without any clear idea what to say—so he or she circles round and round the topic saying anything and everything that pops into mind. That can happen, and often does, when the writer has a *topic* but no clear *thesis*. A disjointed paper can also happen when the writer has *too many aspects* of the topic to cover in a single essay. Eager to cover them all, the writer shifts from position to position, and the reader is dragged along behind. When that happens, the problem usually is that the writer has not *narrowed* the thesis enough.

Here is an example of a student paper that does the Campfire Dance. We've made notes in the margin to help you see how the author jumps from aspect to aspect of the general topic.

FAMILY CLOSENESS

Title says that general subject is family closeness.

Can you find a main statement that the essay will discuss, consider, prove, etc.?

Special occasions seem to bring families together. There is usually a party consisting of the whole family during Christmas. Relatives from far away always come together to eat and enjoy each other's company. I have a relatively small family; my father has only one brother and my mother has none. Small families seem to be closer knit. During Christmas, nobody at the dinner table is shy to talk to one another because everybody is so closely related. It is a wonderful time of year; presents are passed about. Imagine yourself as a little kid and think about how excited you were when you opened the beautiful presents.

    My father is a hard worker. He owns a restaurant, and my mother is a housewife. They are usually very busy, and it is a shame that they do not have time to enjoy themselves more. Another time that we are all together is the two weeks in June when my father takes off for a vacation. We usually go to a different part of the United States.

    My first time to New York was when I was a child of 6. Things seemed so big. That was my first impression of New York. I can remember the time when my grandfather took me shopping at toy stores. We walked on endless streets and we went into all the shops. To close off the day, we would go to a drugstore and have ice cream. I always got chocolate and my grandpa got strawberry. In the month of June in New York, things are bright and warm.

    I can still picture my grandparents' apartment. It consisted of four rooms, a kitchen, restroom, living room, and bedroom. It was an old beatup place. Walls were torn, and on one of the walls were two pictures, one of my grandmother and one of my grandfather. My grandfather is an outgoing person. He was the one who took my brother and me to see the streets of New York.

    Last year was the last time I went to New York. This time the city gave me a drab feeling. It was cold and there was snow at least two feet high. New York did not feel the same as the time before.

    The first thing you can notice about this essay is that the writer had no clear message that he was sending. Nowhere in the first paragraph or so of the essay can you find a statement/idea/subject that the writer is going to consider, discuss, prove, or maintain. This, then, is the writer's first serious mistake. It leads directly, of course, to his doing the Campfire Dance. He takes the subject "family closeness" and then mentally hops from one thing to another.

Special occasions, Christmas, relatives, small families, dinner, presents.

Parents' work, vacations, trips.

Trip to New York, grandfather, toy stores, streets, ice cream, June.

Grandparents' apartment, grandfather's character.

Most recent trip to New York.

Stick to Your Thesis

> It is an ancient Mariner,
> And he stoppeth one of three.
> "By thy long gray beard and glittering eye,
> Now wherefore stopp'st thou me?
>
> "The Bridegroom's doors are opened wide,
> And I am next of kin,
> The guests are met, the feast is set:
> May'st hear the merry din."
>
> He holds him with his skinny hand;
> "There was a ship," quoth he.
> "Hold off! unhand me, gray-beard loon!"
> Eftsoons his hand dropt he.
>
> He holds him with his glittering eye—
> The Wedding-Guest stood still,
> And listens like a three years' child.
> The Mariner hath his will.
>
> The Wedding-Guest sat on a stone:
> He cannot choose but hear;
> And thus spake on that ancient man.
> The bright-eyed Mariner.
> —Samuel Taylor Coleridge, *The Rime of the Ancient Mariner*

Dramatic beginning, to get readers' attention.

Transition to essay and main point.

Paragrah 1: He begins by talking about special occasions that bring families together. Then he gives some specific information about his family. Then he refers to Christmas and presents, with a strange reference to the reader that seems completely off the subject ("Imagine yourself as a little kid and think. . . .").

Paragraph 2: He talks about his father and mother, the work they do, and mentions that they go on vacation and take trips. But he doesn't relate this to family closeness.

Paragraph 3: Evidently when he mentioned vacations the writer next thought of a time when he went to New York—so, off we all go to New York. The Campfire Dance.

Paragraph 4: You can almost see the free association that is going on in the writer's mind. He thought of going to New York, then he thought of his grandparents' apartment. Free association is a valuable creating device, and it's even fun just to play with when you are doing private writing for yourself only. But for *readers* it doesn't work very satisfactorily because readers expect *messages* to be delivered and are, therefore, mostly unsatisfied to follow anything that just pops into the writer's mind.

Paragraph 5: Finally, the writer tells us about one more time when he went to New York, and there is no connection with the subject of family closeness. We hear of the trip, and that is it.

Possibly this student was beginning to get in touch with the special closeness he felt toward his grandfather. Maybe the contrast in the moods of New York in June and in winter had something to do with his grandfather. There's just no way for the reader to tell. Most likely this student skipped Early Shaping and thus stopped short of finding exactly what he wanted to discuss in this paper or how he meant to interest the reader. And that's enough to see how a paper looks and feels when it fails to stick to the subject and fails to develop one aspect of that subject.

Master Storyteller. The opposite of the Campfire Dance is the Master Storyteller, the one who settles down beside the fire with everyone else, and without stirring from that spot spins out a story so well developed, so tightly crafted that the listeners know exactly what it is about and are made to hang on every word and every detail.

Here's a student paper that clearly sets down the subject and sticks to it all the way through and develops that point and that point only.

AS THE SOAP TURNS

Soft, intriguing music plays in the background. Martha, a pretty brunette, walks into the living room. Her husband, Paul, is sitting anxiously on the couch. "Martha, where have you been?"; then, taking a closer look, he adds, "You haven't been down at Ted's Nightclub again, have you?" She remains silent for a moment and then speaks defensively, "What difference does it make to you? You spend every night at the clinic! What do you expect me to do, stay home and watch T.V. by myself?" And so another dramatic episode begins.

Each weekday, many stories similar to this one are broadcast on T.V. Soap operas are viewed by thousands of people across the country. Now soap operas are also shown at night. Men are enjoying what used to be considered a show for women. They have become an American pastime. Why do people watch soap operas? Why have they become so popular?

Many people watch soap operas because they can identify with the characters. They can relate their own problems to those of the characters in the show. Lana, on *One Life to Live,* is contemplating whether to have an abortion or to have Brad's child. Her situation often occurs in the lives of real women. Their decision, as well as Lana's, will affect them for the rest of their lives. While watching the show, these women can see how Lana reacts to her problem and possibly make their decision according to hers.

Divorce is another common situation in soap operas. Recently on *All My Children* Frank and Nancy got a divorce. Before they went to court, both of them wondered if divorce was what they really wanted. Men and women can see themselves in Frank and Nancy. The frustrations of indecision, the agonies encountered while carrying out a decision and the enjoyments of later realizing that the right decision was made are felt by the viewer in his or her own personal experiences. Seeing the same thing happening to someone else is comforting to the viewer.

Soap operas also provide a dream world in which an individual can fantasize. You can imagine what you might do if the same situation confronted you. If you were pregnant, or getting a divorce, or experiencing any one of the number of things that happen to the characters, would you make the same decision they did? Soap operas allow you to forget your own worries and momentarily focus on something else. Thinking about the character's problem creates a distraction from your own. This distraction sometimes makes your problems easier to take in stride.

Soap operas are also beneficial in helping viewers see that their own life isn't as bad as it may seem. After watching a soap opera, you might find that the character's life is more complicated than your own. Almost any soap opera character's life could be considered complicated when compared to real life. For example, on *All My Children,* Mrs. Tyler, a wealthy doctor's wife, is an alcoholic. Her husband filed for divorce. She has blackmailed him by getting her chauffeur to take some pictures and to record a telephone conversation. She has been sentenced to seven days in jail for driving without a license, her daughter is in a mental hospital, and her grandson has just disgraced the family by marrying a prostitute. Realizing that your life is not worse than theirs can encourage you. You have living evidence that things are much worse on the other side of the street.

Soap operas will remain part of American life. They are unending stories that are enjoyed by men and women alike. Martha and Paul may have reconciled their differences for today, but what will happen tomorrow? Will another argument arise? Why does Martha like to go to Ted's Nightclub? Does Paul really have to work nights at the clinic? The questions about the soap opera

---

Generalization from the specific example.

Questions: an indirect way of putting the thesis.

First reason: people identify with the characters.

Conclusion ties example back to main point: the watchers identify with characters

Second example: divorce.

Tying this example to the point.

Tying example to point again.

Third point: dream world fantasy.

Tying example to point.

Tying example to point.

Fourth point: related to paragraph above, but slightly different.

Specific example.

Tying example to point.

Return to examples used in introduction.

Again tying it to point.

Stick to Your Thesis

characters' lives never end. This is also true for people who watch the programs. Their lives are filled with questions needing to be answered.

Somehow it seems reassuring to think that all these questions and more might be answered in tomorrow's episode. —*Julie Meyer*

<small>Conclusion finishes essay, gives final reason why soap operas are popular.</small>

Julie's purpose in writing the essay is stated at the end of the second paragraph: she is going to concentrate on telling the reader why soap operas are so popular. She then gives three reasons that account for their popularity. Each reason is stated clearly and followed by enough explanation for the reader to be able to "see" what Julie means by the statement (paragraphs 3, 4, and 5). Then she closes the essay by giving the reader a final clue why soap operas are so popular. Nowhere does she get off on another topic. Readers always appreciate this kind of clarity. In fact, they don't just appreciate it: they demand it. If you are going to take up a reader's valuable time, you better say something and then stick to it. If you don't, you very likely will lose one more reader.

APPLICATION

Read the following student themes. In each, spot the thesis—the statement/position/subject to be discussed. Then decide whether the writer stays on this subject or does a Campfire Dance. If you spot a Campfire Dance, mark the places in the essay where the writer jumps from one aspect of the subject to another.

DISCO AND COUNTRY MUSIC

In this section of the country, two types of music are very popular: disco/rock and country/western. Disco is better for dancing; country is better for laid-back listening. Some students love disco, and some love country. Very rarely will you find someone who likes both.

Disco is fun and entertaining. It has a fast beat that makes you want to get on your feet and dance. There are many types of disco dances. One of the most popular is touch-disco. Touch-disco means that partners are actually in contact with each other throughout the entire dance. It consists of several loops, turns, and spins while holding hands. Some well-known types of these dances are the Hustle, Pretzel, and Latin-Hustle. Another type of disco dancing is freestyle. Freestyle is individual dancing with little or no partner contact. The Freak is a popular freestyle dance.

Country music can also be entertaining or at least funny. Most of the lyrics have to do with a man, his girlfriend; wife, lover, or mistress. (Sometimes his best dog or pick-up truck.) Almost all country music is very chauvinistic. Country is more to be listened to (if you like $99^{44}/_{100}$ percent pure love) than danced to. However, if you do want to dance to country, you will be dancing what is known as kikker. (I think this has something to do with the foreign matter found on most dancers' boots.) There are two popular kikker dances. One is known as the "Country Star" where everyone simply turns. The other is known as the "Cotton-eyed Joe." Now this is an interesting dance. People form lines and walk in a two-step circle. At the end of every 16 steps, a back step is taken, and everyone yells. It is quite amusing.

Dancing is a favorite pastime of many college students, and it's good exercise as well. No matter what type of dancing, it's fun. If you like fast dancing to good music, disco is the choice. If kikker is what you want, it's available. There are other types of music college students listen to, but disco and country seem to be the big rivals.

A FIVE-LETTER WORD

It is thin and crinkles when you handle it. It is just white paper with green printing on it. It is a small collection of silver and copper discs which jingle in your pocket when you walk. It is a commodity certain people say they cannot live without. How much of it one has determines a person's social status. "It" is a five-letter word—*money*.

According to certain theories, our present-day monetary system evolved from Primitive Man using seashells or coconuts or some other article in exchange for something that he wanted. Someone would trade a bunch of seashells for a piece of fruit someone else grew. This person would then give the seashells to someone else for a cutting utensil and so on. The amount of seashells one had determined one's wealth or social position. Over the years the seashells became gold and silver coins and finally evolved into the system we use today. As with the seashells, the amount of money one has determines one's social position.

There are three main social divisions in this country: the rich, who are few; the poor, who are many; and the middle class, who pay all the taxes and bear the brunt of every social crunch. The rich have more money than you can shake a stick at. They always have high-salaried lawyers who find every loophole they can to prevent their employer from paying "more than he or she truly owes" in taxes. The rich can also afford to hire people to lobby for those issues they feel will benefit themselves either immediately or in the long run. The rich also have benefits people do not usually think of, such as being well known if one is rich enough, and having the opportunity to rub elbows with other well-known individuals, like movie stars. But, then, what can you expect from someone whose main worry is how to spend $50,000 just to keep from paying that amount in taxes.

Then there are the poor. These are generally those people who live in what is referred to as the "inner city," "the ghetto," or the "poverty pocket." Whatever name you like, it all means the same. It means that these people have very little income and, subsequently, a lesser amount of money. These are the people who can really stretch a dollar, mainly because they usually have to. The poor also benefit in some ways from today's society, in a form of relief, i.e. welfare, medicare, and medicaid. Despite all the drawbacks, some of the happiest people in the world fall into this category of social status.

Last, but not least, there is the middle class. These people are the backbone and make up the fiber of today's society. These are the people that have to pay for the programs which give relief to the poor and the class that answers "How high'' when the rich yell "Jump." The middle class is more mobile, in that one can still improve one's stature in society. This can be done many ways, but the main way is hard work. Some advantages for the middle class are that big business is set up to satisfy the average middle-class person; one can set up a small business with relatively little capital and move up in position; and the government is starting to swing toward the side of the average citizen. All things considered, middle class is pretty well off.

In going from seashells to dollar bills, the economic setup has changed and stayed the same. The rich have certain advantages over the other classes. The rich and poor can be more easily defined and distinguished now. There are three main classes with several divisions in each class. This is the main difference between now and seashells. People are still judged by how much they have.

DEVELOP YOUR THESIS: DELIVER WHAT YOU PROMISE

After you have looked at your trial draft to see if you stuck to the same point all the way through, you are ready to check to see if you gave your reader enough information. You are ready to see how you need to expand what you wrote.

There is no doubt about it: knowing how much to expand is a very thin line. How much development will the reader *really* need?

DEVELOP:
To cause to grow or expand; to elaborate or expand in detail.

EXPAND:
To spread out or stretch out; to unfold; to express in fuller form or greater detail.

This is a big part of the "guessing game" we considered earlier. You, as the writer, have to anticipate what the reader is going to know and what the reader is *not* going to know. (All the more reason, of course, to know or invent your audience before you begin writing.) It's really a matter of second-guessing your readers. Will they be bored if you give them more examples on a particular point? Will they understand what you are saying if you don't give them a few more illustrations on another point?

Since you do have to guess about this, you may over- or underdevelop at times. Experience, however, teaches that beginning writers underdevelop much more often than they overdevelop. They assume readers will see and understand—but the readers often don't! They have different backgrounds, different frames of reference, different experiences. What *they* picture when a writer says a particular thing may not be at all what the *writer* is picturing. So until you have had a lot of practice at second-guessing readers and really have a feel for how much or how little to develop and expand, go for more instead of less.

Another way of thinking about it is this: before the human mind can take in a new thought, it must first find something already there that is compatible with the new thought. According to this model, the writer's job is to put a thought, approach, idea or insight into such a form (or in such a way) that it is compatible with the reader's previous collection of information, facts, opinions, insights, and experiences. You can appreciate how building that kind of compatibility takes a little time and a lot of awareness of the audience. You can also see how a point that is compatible with one reader might not match up in the mind of another reader—and so on. Of course the writer can never know for certain what is going to work for individual readers. The only thing to do is to give *enough* development or expansion of the idea so that there is a pretty good chance that *most* readers in the audience will be able to find a match and a synthesis between what you are telling them and what they already know.

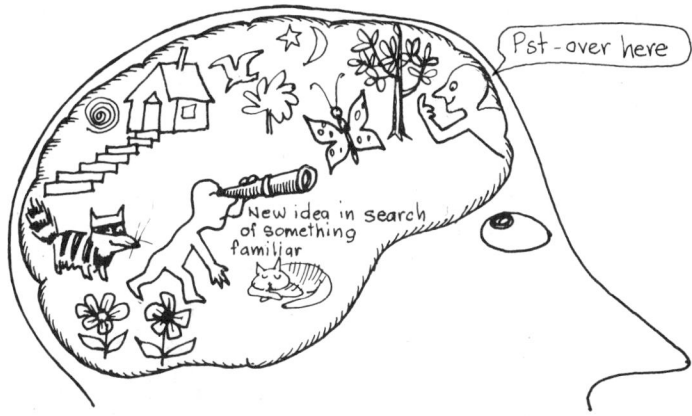

Now, how can you check to see how well you have developed matters in your trial draft so that you will know what you need to do when you rewrite? What follows is a sure-fire check that we call the Bare Bones Outline. If you will put your essay up against the Bare Bones Outline, you can see immediately where you need more development. Here's how it works.

THE BARE BONES OUTLINE

This Bare Bones Outline shows the structure of your essay in just the same way that an X-ray machine shows the skeleton of your body. By applying the Bare Bones Outline to your essay, you will be able to see exactly how many points you used to develop your thesis in your trial draft, how you developed each point, and whether there are gaps you need to fill in.

Here are the instructions for doing a Bare Bones Outline:

1. **Write your thesis at the top of the page.** (This may be actually stated in your essay or it may be implied. It is what you wrote the essay to say.)

    I wrote this essay to tell the reader. . . .

2. **State how you began your paper.**

    In my introduction, I. . . .

3. **Next, make a list of the points you made to develop and expand your thesis. Following each point, state *how* you developed that particular point.**

    I made these points to develop the thesis, and I explained each point like this:

OUTLINE:
To give the essential features or main aspects; to sketch the main points.

BARE BONES OUTLINE

THESIS: I wrote this essay to tell the reader. . . .
I began my essay by. . . .
I made these points to develop and expand my thesis; each point is developed this way:

POINT 1: Developed this way:

POINT 2: Developed this way:

POINT 3: Developed this way:

POINT 4: Developed this way:

POINT 5: Developed this way:

I closed the essay by saying. . . .

4. **Finally, state how you closed your paper.**

    I closed the essay by saying. . . .

What if you do the Bare Bones Outline and find out that you made only *one point* in the whole paper and maybe just said that single thing over and over again in different words? Well, there is no reason to despair. Finding out that you didn't make enough points is as valuable as finding out you made just the right number—it proves that your Bare Bones Outline is working for you, reporting what you have done. There is plenty of time (and a really enjoyable variety of ways) to put the development in. If you find out that you have enough development, fine and good; you can move on to the next stage. If you find out that you don't, no harm done. You will just get busy putting some in. You're still in good shape.

WHAT DOES DEVELOPMENT LOOK LIKE?

First of all, let's see what *no* development looks like. Here is a student's paper that has no development of the message.

A controversy over taking vitamins is going on across the country. Some people say that vitamins will keep you from getting sick. Other people say that vitamins are a waste of money. Research shows that the people favoring vitamins are right.

There are articles that show that some vitamins can help clear the bloodstream of cholesterol. Vitamins also can make burns heal faster. Large dosages of vitamins can help people get over emotional problems. Vitamins can keep you from getting a cold. The people who believe in vitamins are definitely right.

That's it—the whole works. What will a Bare Bones Outline reveal? Let's take a look.

BARE BONES OUTLINE: Vitamin essay

THESIS: I wrote this essay to tell the reader that taking vitamins is a good thing.
I began this essay by stating that there is a controversy about vitamins.

I made these points to develop and expand my thesis. Each point is developed this way:

POINT 1. Vitamins clear the bloodstream.
 Developed . . . (nothing to put here—nothing in essay about point)
POINT 2. Vitamins help heal burns.
 Developed . . . (nothing to say here)
POINT 3. Vitamins help people get over emotional problems.
 Developed . . . (nothing here)
POINT 4. Vitamins keep you from getting a cold.
 Developed . . . (nothing here)

I closed this essay with one sentence: The people who believe in vitamins are definitely right.

And that tells the tale. *The student developed none of the points.*

POINT:
A single, separate item in a large whole; a detail.

There *is* a framework—a skeleton—to support the thesis of the paper, but this skeleton doesn't have any meat on it. If a reader didn't agree with the writer, there is nothing in the essay to convince, illustrate, or explain. The writer seems to be assuming that the reader is automatically going to accept the statements made (vitamins help heal burns, for example) *just because the writer says so*. Well, that isn't how it works. A reader will hardly accept anything—unless it is something he or she already knows about and believes. This writer has got to back up what is being said with a *lot* of information, or else he has wasted his time in writing the essay.

If you look at your Bare Bones Outline and see that you need some development, what can you do? Well, here are some possibilities:

EXAMPLES AND ILLUSTRATIONS
How to Help the Reader See

1. An example or illustration is a specific instance that helps clarify a more general statement by allowing the reader to *see*. It is one single thing that shows the character of the whole.

2. Be as colorful, descriptive, detailed, and specific as you possibly can when you give examples and illustrations. Appeal to the readers' *senses*. Transport the readers to the spot and *show* what you mean.

3. Use *concrete* words. Abstract terms don't produce pictures in readers' minds. General words, too, can mean different things to different people. Concrete words appearing in examples and illustrations will let the readers know what *you* mean by the general terms. And if you've used any abstract terms, concrete words will help make them clear to the readers.

4. Choose examples and illustrations that will mean something to the particular audience for whom you are writing.

5. Be generous with examples and illustrations. A minimum ratio is one specific example or illustration to one general statement. Often, however, a higher ratio—say, two or three examples or illustrations to one general statement—will be necessary to let your reader *see* exactly what you mean. You will probably never err by having too many examples and illustrations.

DESCRIPTION
How to Present Sharp, Focused Pictures

1. When you *describe* to develop a point, you draw images or impressions in words that *reveal* the thing described.

2. Appeal to *all* the reader's senses: sight, smell, touch, hearing, taste. Be very specific.

3. *Select* the details you want to include in the description so that they give one main impression of the object, person, or scene. Don't try to describe everything at once. This means that you will choose details according to what your purpose is at the time.

NARRATION
How to Tell a Good Story

1. The word *narrate* comes from Latin words that mean "to acquaint with"—so you could use a story, or narration, to make your reader know your point a little better.
2. Be sure to give the reader a clear time order. Provide a clear sequence of events. Often this sequence will be *chronological*—first this happened, then this, then that. . . . You may, however, use a *flashback* technique in which you show an earlier scene and then relate that scene to the main story you are telling at the moment.
3. Let your readers feel the *action* of your story. Don't just tell them *about* what happened. Let them *live* through what happened. Make a movie of the sequence of actions. The more *immediate* the details and the more *descriptive* the scenes, the more your readers will feel a part of what is going on in the story.
4. Be very *selective* in the details you choose. Don't give the readers a lot of information they don't need to understand or see your story. Stick to details that are directly related to your purpose in telling the story.
5. Decide on a *point of view*. Point of view is how the story is told. Very likely the *first person point of view* (when the author is a character in the story) will be the easiest way to tell a story that has happened to you. Later, however, when you are using narration as part of other pieces of writing, you may want to adopt the *omniscient point of view*, in which the writer knows everything and gives an objective, outside account of the sequence of events.

DETAILS
How to be Specific

1. Details are individual or minute parts of a whole. When included in a piece of writing, details give the reader a much clearer picture of what is being discussed.
2. Select details that are relevant to the point you are making. Don't try to include everything.
3. Among those relevant details, select only the most important ones to include.
4. Make the details as specific and concise as possible.

COMPARISON AND CONTRAST
How to Show Similarities and Differences

1. *Compare* comes from a Latin word which means *equal* and means to examine in order to observe or discover similarities or differences.
2. *Contrast* comes from an Italian word that meant *to stand opposed to* and implies a comparing for the purpose of emphasizing differences.
3. When comparing or contrasting two things, you will probably use one of two common patterns: discussing A completely and then discussing B or discussing a particular characteristic of A and B, then another characteristic of A and B, then another . . . until you've completed the comparison.

Develop Your Thesis

4. You may discover that an item is similar to another thing in an exact way—that house has the same floor plan as the one I lived in as a child—or is similar in a nonliteral way—that house is like a tomb. Both kinds of comparison are valuable to a reader who is attempting to understand your subject just the way you do.

5. Differences you spot among things may be differences of characteristics—their car has bench seats; ours has bucket seats—or the differences may be differences of degree—the back seat of the Volkswagen Rabbit is bigger than the back seat of the Volkswagen Beetle. Both kinds of contrast help the reader see the subject the way you wish to communicate it.

CAUSE/EFFECT
How to Explain the Reasons and Consequences

1. *Explain* means to give complete particulars that tell something fully and distinctly.

2. Giving the cause and effect of a situation means that you (a) identify the thing/person/act that brings about a particular result and (b) show *how* it caused that result.

3. Be sure that the causes you give are sufficient to convince the reader. Even after you have isolated the cause of a situation in your mind, ask yourself, "Are there any other causes I should include?"

4. Be sure that there actually *is* a relationship between the cause and effect. If you can't prove this relationship exists in some logical, objective way, be sure that your reader understands that you are offering a personal view of the relationship between the cause and effect. Take the time in your essay to explain to the reader the connections you see.

5. Let the purpose of your writing determine the form your essay takes.

ANALYSIS
How to Help the Reader Understand

1. The word *analyze* means to divide anything complex into its simple parts or pieces by separating a whole into its parts. It also means to show the relationship among the single parts of a larger, more complex subject.

2. A good analysis actually shows the reader how to *think* about the subject.

3. To use analysis in your writing, decide what parts you can break the larger subject down into. Then take these parts one at a time. Discuss or describe them, either on an individual basis or as a group, showing how to relate to each other. Finally, put the parts back together in a whole. The reader will then have been able to *understand* what may have otherwise been baffling or confusing.

ANALYSIS BY DIVISION
How to Explain a Process

1. Divide the process into distinct steps.
2. Discuss these steps in the *exact order* in which they occur when the process is done.
3. If there are a large number of steps in the process, group the steps into categories and then discuss them.

Stage 2/Shaping

4. Define all terms and procedures that might be unfamiliar.
5. Do not omit *any* step in the procedure.

CLASSIFICATION
How to Show Common Characteristics

1. *To classify* means *to organize into groups according to common characteristics, qualities, traits,* etc., *to put into basic categories,* or *to break down into component parts.*
2. When you set up a classification system, be certain that the categories don't overlap. Also make very clear to the reader what the groups are and how you decided what went into each group.
3. Don't oversimplify when you classify. Sometimes in an attempt to make everything orderly, a person will push a subject, person, item, etc., into a category where it doesn't really belong just to make the classification systematic. Don't undercut your credibility with your audience by forcing an item into a group where it doesn't clearly belong.
4. Use a classification system when it will help your reader follow your thoughts or explanation point by point. Classification helps the reader know how to think about the subject: how to group it with things that are like it or unlike it, how to see it in relation to some bigger thing the subject belongs to.

DEFINITION
How to Tell What Something Means

1. *To define* means *to explain the nature or essential qualities of a word, function,* etc. A definition determines or fixes the boundaries of the thing being discussed. The origin of the word *definition* was *to set boundaries,* and that is what a good definition does for the reader: it helps him or her stake out, limit, see the boundaries of a term.
2. A formal definition includes the term being defined, the class to which it belongs, and what differentiates it from other things in that class.
3. An informal definition takes several forms: defining by using a word that means approximately the same thing (*to gloat* means *to act superior and proud*); by using an opposite (*love* is *not using someone*); by showing the term's origin (*defining* originally meant *to set boundaries*); by using personal experience (*summer* means *time off, rest, and fun*); by giving examples (*eating well* is *having fresh vegetables and fruit, avoiding sugar, and staying off fried foods*).
4. Use definitions in your writing when there is any chance that your readers will not know the formal meaning of a word or the informal way you are using it. Being clear on the terms in a piece of writing is absolutely necessary for both the reader and the writer if communication is to occur.

You can see that you really have a rich variety of ways to deliver what you promise your reader. The important thing is that you do give the reader enough information for him or her to *see* what you are saying. Did you notice how many of the words in the explanations above have to do with *seeing* or with getting the reader *closer* to the subject: *reveal, makes a point clear, something specific which gives clarity, to acquaint, to match, to convey an image.* That's really all development is about: getting your reader up close to the subject in order to see clearly what you are trying to say. Let's look at this brief essay by Shana Alexander to see how she developed her message:

MOTHERLINESS

THESIS — "Motherly," to most of us, means gentle, open, warm, uncritical, and adoring. By these lights, some of the most motherly people I know are fathers.

EXAMPLE — Take a look at any beach in summertime. Here the motherly fathers are out in force. They help build the sand castles, they rub on the sun creme, go for the ice cream, and carry the toddlers into the surf. For this is the height of America's custody season and these are the weekend fathers. The bright summer sunshine reveals all the new patterns in part-time parenthood which our soaring divorce rate has forced us to devise.

FACTS — About a third of all American marriages now end in divorce. In some communities, like Southern California, the divorce rate has passed 120 per cent, which means that the mythical "average citizen" has been divorced one and one-fifth times. Divorce, here, is considered a normal part of marriage, much the same as death is accepted as a part of life.

DISCUSSION — But what of the children? What does a man do with a four-, or a six-, or an eight-year-old child, or perhaps all three of them, when "Daddy's Day" rolls around? Visits with the new wife or girl friend are difficult; Disneyland is expensive. Every spare cent Daddy has already goes for alimony and child-support. So it comes down to a choice of the beach—or visiting your children in your ex-wife's living room.

ILLUSTRATION — One stretch of California coastline has become so chockablock with weekend fathers and their offspring, it is known as Alimony Beach. The regulars here do not greet each other by name, but by number—"two-two-five," or "three-five-o," according to the amount the divorce is costing them per month, in cash. One day across the sand lurched a lone man festooned with beach towels, umbrella, hamper, and thermos jug, and followed by five small children. "That's seven-five-o!" someone whispered.

EXAMPLE WITH DESCRIPTION — I watched seven-five-o all the long day—finding lost sneakers, settling fights, and brushing sand out of the peanut butter—and I have never seen a more gentle, more patient, and—well—more motherly parent.

CONCLUSION — That qualities like "motherliness" or "fatherliness" are not inborn, nor God-given, but are really states of mind, is something men and women both must remember as drastic changes in patterns of marriage and family life tug at the fabric of our society. —CBS "Spectrum," August 3, 1971

MAKE THE MOST OF YOUR CONCLUSION

Like the introduction, the conclusion must be "concocted." It is not organically contained in the thesis as the middle of an essay is, so it has to come entirely out of your head.

As with introductions, many writers fail to make the most of conclusions. Yet if your paper fizzles out at the end, the reader may forget what you said the minute he finishes reading it. Having come this far, you should want to make sure your reader doesn't end with a "Ho hum! So what?" So make the most of your conclusion.

ESSAY CONCLUSIONS

The ending of your paper ought to do three things:

1. Remind your readers of what you have said.
2. Give your readers at least one new thing to think about.
3. Provide a gentle completing of the paper so that your readers are not left hanging in the air.

Remind the Readers of What You Have Said. Since the whole purpose of your essay was to get a point across to your readers—some information that you wanted them to have, some opinions or experience of yours that you wanted to share—reminding them of what you have said and how this is significant (or what it means) is a very smart thing to do at the end of the writing. You don't want to insult the reader by simply saying over again what you have already said, using the same words, because the reader is likely to think, "How stupid does this writer think I am?" What you *do* want to do, however, is **assist the reader by summing up for him or her your main points, pulling together what you have said into one tight statement or group of statements, and in some way helping the reader know exactly what you said in the paper.** You want to bring back into the reader's attention the gist of what you have taken the whole paper to tell. Remember that readers have very short memory spans (in fact, research shows that readers remember the linguistic form of a piece of writing about 20 seconds), and your ending must, in a very brief space, help the readers reconstruct what you said. Yet, you need only a few sentences because you have already explained it fully for the reader in the body of the essay. All you need at this point is to pull it together, say it one more time for the reader's benefit, and bring the writing to a close.

Give the Reader at Least One New Thing to Think About. How can this be sound advice? Isn't the writer supposed to work hard to keep a reader's mind on the message being written? Why should the reader be told something *new* to think about at the end of the essay? Well, for this reason: **the something new will be some spin-off from the thesis of the essay, some sharp,** *extra* **point you can make about the thesis that you didn't make in the paper, some new way of saying something you have already said that will** *cause the reader to continue to think* **about your writing after the reading is over.** You want to make a difference to your reader, not have an essay that can be forgotten the minute the reading is finished. You want the reader to be affected by the writing, stimulated by it, intrigued by it, aggravated by it, entertained by it, to the extent that the writing will have a ripple effect. Telling one new thing in the conclusion can be the pebble you drop into the well of his or her consciousness to produce those ripples.

Provide a Gentle Completing of the Paper So That the Reader is Not Left Hanging in the Air. Be sure your reader knows when you are finished. Although we all like to be left hanging for a short period of time (during a murder mystery, a western, or a ferris wheel ride), we don't like to hang indefinitely. Your reader is willing to move with you through the essay while you prove your point or develop your message, but then she or he wants to be let down back to earth easily and told, "This is the end."

Concluding your paper merely carries out the principle of closure which is absolutely central to human beings: you have opened a discussion and brought the reader into this discussion with you; not closing the discussion deliberately and clearly would leave your reader feeling unfinished, tricked, and waiting. So, let your conclusion bring to a gentle and clear ending the exchange you began when you sat down to write.

In Closing* . . .   The important thing to remember for both the introduction and the conclusion is that they are not just there as window dressing. Having a clear opening and a clear closing will not make a bad essay good; in

---

*Q.: Does *this* paragraph satisfy any of the three criteria of a good conclusion?

fact, they will only make a bad essay look even more mechanical and fake! Introductions and conclusions, however, can assist you in getting the message to your reader. They can be a valuable part of your strategy, not mere parts that are "supposed" to be there for custom or fashion.

---

1. Read these conclusions from student essays. Decide if each conclusion meets the three requirements for a good ending: **APPLICATION**
   Does the ending remind the readers of what has been said?
   Does the ending give the readers one new thing to think about?
   Does the ending provide a gentle completing of the paper so that the readers are not left hanging in the air?

   A. To sum up, here are the steps you should follow if you are interested in installing solar heating in your home. First, see your banker and see what kind of loan you can get. Next, talk to your local power company; some companies help citizens install the system. Some even put in the system free of charge as long as the owner lets them collect data from it. If your power company will not help you with your system, then see if you can find a nearby installer of solar equipment, or do it yourself. Design a system and its installation around your loan. Get your loan for as long a period as possible; the longer the loan the more likely it is that a solar system will pay for itself. And, finally, start installing the system knowing that you are one of a growing number of people who are tired of paying high utility bills and tired of worrying if they are going to be warm this winter and who have turned to the sun for their energy needs.
   B. Campus life is not, then, an individual effort. It is learning, studying, and making conversation and friends. Look around, smile, and be friendly, because friends are one of the greatest assets a college student has.
   C. Time management includes more than just studying and having fun. Good time management should tell you when to get up, when to go to class, what to do in between classes, and everything else almost. Good time management is the efficient use of the time you have. Therefore, good time management is very important to college students, especially freshmen.
   D. With the use of these new parts and the parts perfected in the past, it is now possible to reach over 2 horsepower per cubic inch in the small-block. Each year the power-to-weight ratio has increased, but can this go on forever? Can the Chevy small-block engine continue to improve and stay the favorite of most Americans for the years to come? Even if it can't, the Chevy small-block has already achieved more success than any other American-made engine, and it will not soon be surpassed.

THE PROMISE AND DELIVERY SYSTEM—WHAT SHAPING IS ALL ABOUT

WRITING IS A CHAIN OF AGREEMENTS

Do you see how an essay is just a chain of making an agreement with the readers to tell them a particular thing and then keeping that agreement by actually telling them? And that the whole agreement set-up begins with the thesis that you promise to deliver? Then the agreements turn on smaller units—the individual points that you use to deliver your thesis. You have a secondary set of agreements with which to set up each point and then deliver it by developing the idea with examples, details, specifics of some sort or other. All along the way you are telling the readers that if they stick with you, they will find out x, y, or z. Keeping those agreements means the readers' expectations are fulfilled and your message gets delivered.

The system of agreements-plus-delivery also gives you a great way to check on the shaping of your paper. You have something to look for as you check to verify whether you have really communicated your message. Filling out a Bare Bones Outline after your trial draft and then again after the first revision will show you exactly where you have holes in your essay. You can plug them up *before* the reader ever sees the essay. Now that you know how to check your shaping carefully, you need never again miss the whole purpose by giving the reader so little information that he or she can't get your message.

APPLICATION

1. Read the following student essays. Answer these questions for each essay:
    a. Does the writer have a clear thesis?
    b. Is the writer an insider on this subject in a valuable way?
    c. Does the entire paper stay on the thesis?
    d. Has the writer developed the thesis enough? Explain.
    e. What methods of development has the writer used? Be specific. Be able to point to sections in the essay to support your answer.
    f. Does the introduction attract you immediately? Does it start "close" enough to the exact subject of the paper?
    g. Does the conclusion remind the reader of what was said, provide one new thing to think about, and let you feel closure and completeness at the end of the essay?

    Be ready to discuss these essays in class.

GARDENING FOR PROFIT

CONTEXT *Written for a community senior citizens' newsletter*
AUDIENCE *Retired people, many of whom are on social security*

Mrs. Sanford pointed to her garden and explained her admiration for it. As the chitchat continued, I got my turn and I explained how gardens were economical. Gardens on a small scale are similar to commercial farms that show a healthy net profit every year. Hence, if large gardens are profitable, it follows that small gardens are profitable, also.

Gardens have only one major expense. That is a soil tiller which can run from $200 to $1,000 at any Montgomery Ward's. The size and type are dependent on the area of the garden. Gardens also have yearly costs. Water, for example, varies in cost from $10 to $100 per year. Fertilizer such as 10–15–10 will cost around $10 per year, while manure, mulch, seed, poison, and plants will run from $5 to $100 per year, depending on size, geographic location, and thriftiness of the person running the operation.

You really can't measure the money made in a garden, because who can put a price on the taste of homegrown fresh vegetables? There is nothing like them. But, even putting the taste aside, if you go just on money spent and produce received, your final accounting will go something like this. If you have a garden 75 feet by 50 feet, filled with ¼ corn, ¼ beans, ⅛ okra, ⅛ sweet peppers, and the remainder in tomatoes, onions, cabbage, and lettuce, you can produce enough vegetables to amount to about $1,000 if bought in the store. Your cost, after the purchase of the tiller, is about $150 per year for the above-mentioned things. This is a very good yearly profit margin.

THE EGGHEAD IS NOT DEAD

CONTEXT *Written as an editorial for college newspaper*

AUDIENCE *College students and faculty*

Do you know those smart people in your classes, the ones who sit in the front of the room right in front of the teacher's desk? The ones who rarely speak and when they do, it is to ask an impressive question or to remind the teacher to give the homework? Now you know who I am talking about, the so-called "brain" or "egghead." They usually wear glasses and clothes which are out of style. They do not participate in extracurricular activities. All they do is sit at home and study. Most likely, these people are not really this way. They want to participate in other activities, but they are shy and do not know how to make friends, and they have been labeled "egghead." This word itself can ruin a person's entire social life.

Most of these "eggheads" have been pushed into their way of life by their parents. When they were young, their parents insisted on good grades, so all they have been striving for is academic awards. They finally reach high school and realize that they have been missing so much, such as doing things with their friends and just being a teenager. Since most of them do not know how to make friends, because up until now the only thing that was important was good grades, what can they do? How can they come out of their shell? Somehow their intelligence has outshined their other qualities.

If you have been labeled an "egghead," fear being labeled one, or even know someone who is a "brain," I have some good news! Here are a few tips on how to come out that "egghead" shell. Try to be more outgoing; get involved in clubs or organizations. Remember, academics are not everything. One B on your report card is not so much to pay for meeting new friends and having fun. Is it now? Help the people in your classes, but do not act like a "know-it-all." This will only confirm your peers' assumptions. Also, be more independent of your parents. I am not saying to disown them; just think more for yourself. Do things for yourself, too.

This advice may help people you know. Help them out; give them a few tips, and, remember, the "egghead" is not dead—yet.

WRITING ASSIGNMENT
THE EXPLANATION ESSAY

One of the most frequent reasons that you will write after you get out of school is to explain something to somebody. An explanation always operates out of these conditions:

- there must be someone who doesn't know or understand something
- there must be someone else who does know and understand the thing
- the person who knows must be able to discuss the matter so clearly that the one who doesn't know at the beginning will understand fully when the explanation is completed.

These conditions put a serious constraint on a writer who must be the one who understands and the one who can discuss the matter so clearly that someone else will also understand. The writer must attempt to explain, then, only those things she or he knows thoroughly. And the writer must find a way to explain so effectively that the person who doesn't know will be absolutely clear on the subject by the end of the explanation.

A good explanation essay, therefore, will have these characteristics:

1. Early in the essay the writer will identify what is going to be explained.

2. The essay will then center totally on this thesis.

3. The writer will take into account the particular audience who will be reading the explanation and will make decisions about how much and what kind of explanation is needed, based on the specific requirements of these readers.

4. The writer will give a *full* explanation so that the reader feels satisfied and complete at the end. This means that the writer must give enough information to resolve all tension in the reader's mind.

TO EXPLAIN:
To make plain or clear; render intelligible; to make known in detail; to assign a meaning to; to interpret; account for; to make clear the cause or reason for; to make understandable something not known or understood.

1. CONTEXTS

Choose one of the following contexts as the basis for your essay. Be sure to indicate your context and audience on the top of the first page.

A. A greeting card company that prints those little books on subjects like Happiness is . . ., A Friend is . . ., etc., is soliciting copy for additional books. If it buys the copy you send in, you will receive a $500 fee. The company will mail you $10, however, for every essay you send in, whether or not it is selected for publication. You are tempted. All the advertisement states is that persons interested should write an essay in which they define one of these terms:

> Family togetherness is . . .
> Bossiness is . . .
> A vacation is . . .
> Unhappiness is . . .
> Success is . . .
> An enemy is . . .
> The good life is . . .

If the company feels your essay could be turned into copy for one of its books and would lend itself to great illustrations, you'll be $500 richer. Write the essay. After all, you can't lose. At least you'll get the $10 for trying.

B. Your manager or supervisor often has to hire people on a part-time basis during heavy workload periods to do the same job that you do on a regular basis. Every time someone new gets hired, your boss must take time out to explain to the temporary employee how the company operates, what to do on the job, etc. Realizing that much of this is a duplication of effort and a waste of time, the manager has asked you to write a pamphlet in which you explain everything the temporary help will need to know. The boss specifically asked you to include the rules of the company, the way to do the particular job (it's the same one you do), and how people get asked to stay on in a permanent position. You eagerly write the essay that the graphics department at the printing company will turn into a colorful pamphlet. After all, you're going to be saving yourself a lot of time, too, because you have to give out the same information time after time when the new employee has forgotten what the boss had to say.

C. The teacher of a sixth grade class in a local school wants your help in preparing a learning package on hobbies to be used to get the students interested in taking up some hobby for themselves. He has asked you to write an essay for the package which will inform the students about your own hobby. He wants you to give the pupils enough information to let them know what the hobby requires, why it is fun, and what benefits can be gained from it. You know this is a tough assignment because you have to put your information on a level that sixth graders can understand, but give it a try. Write the essay for the learning package and enjoy making a contribution to the sixth graders. And they just might take up the hobby that you love best.

D. You have just had your first class in an introductory course in world religions. Your instructor has assigned an essay on this topic: "Religious Types I Have Observed." The instructor plans to have students read their essays aloud in class to provide a basis for discussing the rich variety of ways people reflect their beliefs in their lives. Your instructor has planned these activities to get students ready to learn about world religions.

E. You have just missed the final exam in one of your most important courses. Although you have a legitimate, but complicated, excuse, the professor has not agreed to let you make up the test. She says that under school policy she is not allowed to do so. She has suggested, however, that you write a statement to the Dean of Student Affairs, explaining the situation and asking special permission to make up the exam. Write the essay that you are going to send to the Dean. Be sure that your explanation includes the fact about missing the test, the cause for your absence, the effect a decision not to let you take the test would have, and what you want the Dean to do.

F. Last night you received a telephone call from a regional marketing company that wanted to hire you to give them some information about the people in your school. This marketing firm wants to know specifically how the people in your school dress. They represent several shoe and clothing companies that want to increase their sales in the area. The marketing firm offered you $250 to write an essay in which you describe the three basic ways people dress in your school. What they are actually asking you to do is to divide your classmates into three groups, based on how they dress. You realize that you will have to generalize to make this division, but you do think you could come up with three basic ways the people dress. The woman from the marketing firm said your report would have to be very descriptive, with a lot of specific details, because the firm would have to be able to make definite recommendations based upon what you have to say. You decide to write the report, using the general explanation essay format you have learned in school. It seems like something you might even enjoy doing.

2. CREATING

The first thing you may want to do in the *Creating Stage* is to **loop** the contexts to see which one you want to choose as the basis for your essay. (You may also discover in the looping another context that you would rather write on. If so, discuss this new context with your instructor.) If you know immediately which context you want to use and don't need the looping activity to help you decide, you can move right into a creating technique that will produce ideas for the content of the essay itself. The best creating technique will depend upon the context you have chosen and upon your own preference. By this time you probably prefer one creating technique over the others and may also already be experiencing how different techniques work best for different purposes in writing and even how they lead to different ways of thinking. Whatever creating technique you choose, give yourself thirty to forty-five minutes or longer to come up with ideas for your essay.

3. SHAPING

1. Make your preliminary agreements. Know or invent the exact audience for whom you are writing. Make a list of the characteristics describing these readers if it will help you stay clear on what they are likely to respond to. Write *to* (not *at*) your readers; remember they are people, not walls.
2. Check your thesis. Do you have one specific thing you are writing the essay to explain? Is this point very clearly stated early in the essay so that the reader knows from the beginning just where the writing is headed? Did you stay on this point all the way through the essay? Did you adequately explain it? Do you show that you are an insider on the matter and do actually have something to contribute to the reader? Does the essay sound like something you are *communicating* rather than something you are doing because you have a class assignment?
3. Do a Bare Bones Outline after you write the trial draft. This outline will show you any gaps or underdeveloped areas in the essay.

4. FINAL CHECK

Write a second draft of the essay and read this to another person. Find out (a) if the person stayed interested all the way through (b) understood exactly what you were explaining (c) got value from the essay. After you have read the piece of writing to someone else and made any changes necessary after this reading, put the paper in its final form. Use a format that is as correct and attractive as you possibly can. Remember that the *appearance* of the essay can often make or break it as a piece of communication. How the essay looks is the first thing that strikes a reader. So don't undercut all the fine work you have done by letting the essay look incorrect and sloppy. Good luck!

STAGE 3/COMPLETING

HOW TO TURN GOOD WRITING INTO EXCELLENT WRITING

OVERVIEW

Why Complete?

Revising for Flow: Paragraphs

The Topic Sentence Paragraph

The Function Paragraph

Transitions and Reminder Signs

**WRITING ASSIGNMENT:
THE EVALUATION ESSAY**

Revising for Energy: Sentences

Making Variety Happen in Your Sentences

Sentence Combining

Combining for Emphasis

Getting Energy Through Style

Revising for Punch: Words

Exactness, Specifics, Pictures, and Images

Dissecting Your Paper

Final Considerations

**WRITING ASSIGNMENT:
THE ASSERTION-WITH-PROOF ESSAY**

PURPOSE   Make life easier for yourself
Make the reader more receptive to your message
Remove the last sources of confusion in the writing
Perfect what you say so that you can be proud of your writing
Release your paper and yourself

WHY COMPLETE?

You have now finished the first two stages of the writing process. In Stage 1 you **created** something you wanted to say. In Stage 2 you **shaped** your writing by inventing your audience, turning your unruly thoughts into a single message that you could send to another person, and then doing everything you possibly could—organizing *beginning/middle/end,* fully developing your points—to get that message delivered to the reader.

After all this, you may be asking, *"What else is there to do?"*

Actually, all that *is* left to do is some check-up reviewing of the paper and some fine-tuning revisions. That's the third and final stage in the writing process—**completing**—and you're ready for it. In the *Completing Stage* you turn a really critical eye on your writing to see what you have actually done and to detect any remaining weaknesses that might interfere with your message. You dissect your essay, examining its parts—paragraphs, sentences, and words—as carefully as you examined its basic promise and delivery system in the *Late Shaping Stage*. The critical eye can help you make your writing the very best it can be.

THE CONSTRUCTIVE CRITICAL EYE

When you turn a *critical eye* on your work, you are doing something you actually do in life many times a day. Have you ever hung posters or pictures on a wall and then stepped back to see how they looked? "That one is too high . . . no, a little too low, put it back up just an inch or so . . . that's just right; hold it while I get the hammer." That is turning a critical eye on your work.

Or you've looked at yourself in the mirror as you put the finishing touches on your hair, your outfit, your make-up. You think, "Should this shirt collar be on the outside of the sweater or on the inside?" Or you wonder, "Do I have that part in my hair straight; is it too far down on the left side?" Or you ask yourself whether your shoes can get by one more time without being polished. That's turning a *critical eye* on your appearance before you go out to meet the world.

Well, what you have done with pictures on a wall or your image in a mirror is exactly what you do to your writing when you move to the *Completing Stage* of the process. You examine it critically, but constructively. Your purpose isn't to find fault or to blame, but merely to see how it might look to someone else.

Then see what you can do to make it better. *Have I made everything perfectly clear to my reader? Can the reader always see where I am going? Have I made any silly errors that will keep the reader from getting the message? What improvements and polish can I give this so that it is the very best writing I can possibly do?*

One big difference between putting the finishing touches on yourself before you go out and putting the finishing touches on your writing before you give it to someone else is that you *know* what to look for as you check yourself over in the mirror. It's not so easy with an essay. You're much more likely to read it over and think, "Well, that looks all right to me," because it takes a specially trained eye to know what to look for and to spot the ways the writing might be improved. This section will enable you to develop that "trained eye," and practice will perfect your use of it.

Although you might suppose that nobody would send out a paper without polishing, editing, and correcting it, experience shows that almost all beginning writers tend to skip this stage. Perhaps they lack the special skills required to do the job, or maybe they feel so burdened throughout the creating and shaping stages they figure that *any* kind of first draft is victory enough. Whatever the cause, many people omit this final stage. They shouldn't, however, and neither should you. To help you see the value of doing the *Completing Stage* on your own writing, and of doing it well, let's look at five substantial reasons.

WHAT COMPLETING WILL DO

Make Life Easier for Yourself. There are certain rules of correctness and propriety associated with writing. If you violate these established principles—say, have no margins or write in choppy, incomplete thoughts—then you are asking for the same kind of rebuff a barefoot person gets who tries to go into a roadside restaurant with a sign on the door saying, "No shoes, No shirt, No service." There may be something to be proved by going against the rules, but

NO SHIRT
NO SHOES
NO SERVICE

NOT CORRECT
NOT POLISHED
NOT READ

in the case of writing, it's just plain smart to know the rules and to go by them. *"It's easier to ride the horse in the direction it's going."*

Make the Reader More Receptive to Your Message. The *Completing Stage* is certainly a way of making life easier for your *message*. People do have certain expectations of a paper—they want it to be neat, to make sense, to be readable, to be correctly spelled and punctuated, and to have an order that they can follow. Because that's so, many people see only the error or weakness—the smudge, the misspelled word, the awkward sentence—and fail to see anything else in the paper, no matter how important that "anything else" might be. You may not think it is fair to equate mistakes in papers with sloppy thinking, but many people do just that. They pay so much attention to one or two faults that they miss the whole message. To give your message the best chance possible, you have to make it free of blemishes.

Remove the Last Sources of Confusion. Things written in haste sometimes confuse a reader because the message is actually blocked by gaps in the organization, too little development of the main points, or a lack of coherence. The *Completing Stage* gives you a final chance to make the message totally clear. Perhaps the reader will be tolerant. Maybe he or she doesn't mind a smudge or is "understanding" about a misspelled word (although it's dangerous to count on that). But even if the errors or weaknesses don't upset the reader, they may still steal the punch or cloud the clarity of the message you are trying to get across. It is a shame to spend hours on a piece of writing, only to have it less effective than it could be simply because you didn't do a thorough *Completing Stage* and remove the last sources of confusion.

Perfect What You Say So That You Can Be Proud of Your Writing. There is nothing like the good feeling that is yours when you say something important in *just* the way you want it said. But it's impossible to check on the *way* it is said while the thoughts are still hot and rolling in. It's only after the words are "cold" that you can do the fine tuning that turns work from "OK" into "Good" or "Good" into "Best." Going back over your work gives you a chance to (a) say what you mean, (b) put on any finishing touches that you want to make, (c) rearrange for better effect, and (d) put your absolutely best foot forward. It's your final chance to make the writing something you are very proud of—both for what you say and how you say it.

Release Your Paper and Yourself. Of the three stages of writing, the third one is very valuable to you symbolically because doing the third stage says, *"I'm finished!* It is the final act of this project in my life. I started it; I worked on it; I've finished it. I'm now ready to move on to something else." There is liberation and freedom in this act. You've in effect said, "This is the best I can do on this at the moment. I've finished it. I'm ready for a new thing." Skipping the third stage will always leave you with an incomplete feeling and a knowledge that you did not give the writing your best.

REVISING FOR FLOW: PARAGRAPHS

In the *Completing Stage,* the first thing you want to check with a critical eye is *how your writing flows. Flow* is a great concept: it means to proceed continuously and smoothly, and that is exactly what you want your writing to do. If your writing *flows,* not only will your thoughts proceed continuously and smoothly, but your reader, too, will be able to proceed continuously and smoothly along the course you have set.

However, there are several things that might keep the reader from proceeding continuously and smoothly. One is the overall *organization* and *development* of the essay. Of course, you have already done the Bare Bones Outline in the *Shaping Stage,* and you have become conscious of what your thesis is, how many points you used to develop that thesis, and how you supported each of these points. So the basic organization and development are probably handled. Now, in the *Completing Stage,* you can do a much more detailed internal analysis of your writing and develop more sophisticated and subtle means of having everything flow smoothly.

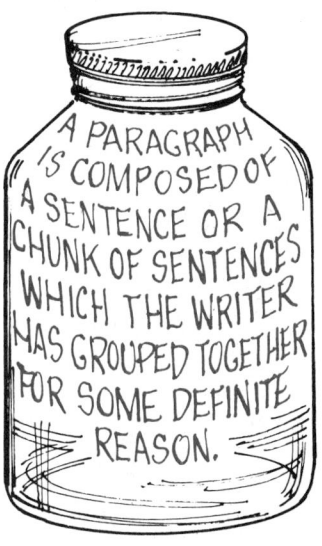

To learn how to look critically at the flow of your writing, begin with the concept of **paragraphing.** Once you understand precisely *what a paragraph does* and *how it* does it, you will be able to check your writing for smoothness. You will be able to revise it so that it really *flows.*

Think of a paragraph as a container that holds words and sentences that you want to keep together for some reason or other, and you will have a good starting point for thinking about the concept of paragraphing. Like a container, a paragraph can be used for different purposes. It's like having a jar that can contain berries or cherries or marbles or milk, or having a jar that you could use to prop up a window at your beach cabin, throw at a cat, or use as a magnifying glass. Paragraphs are similar. To see how this works, let's examine the two basic kinds of paragraphs.

The Topic Sentence Paragraph has a clear logic; there is a main idea, either stated or implied, and a group of sentences that develop that idea. Thus, the Topic Sentence Paragraph is a miniature promise and delivery system. The *topic sentence* itself (sometimes stated, sometimes implied) tells the readers what you are about to discuss and focuses the readers' minds on that particular thing. The additional sentences provide enough information to prove or explain or illustrate or otherwise develop that main idea. It is the Topic Sentence Paragraph that carries the information or content of the writing and is essential in getting the message across to the reader.

The Function Paragraph is a different matter entirely. In it, you won't find one main idea set forth and developed. In fact, at times a Function Paragraph may be only one sentence; it's a ''paragraph'' only because it is indented. **Function Paragraphs usually have no logic except the author's own.** They aren't caused by a new thought. They don't have main idea sentences. They don't develop a topic. They do, however, keep the reader moving, provide continuity in the essay, give a sense of drama, and reflect the individual personality of the writer.

Without Topic Sentence Paragraphs there can be no developed message. Without Function Paragraphs, however, the reader would probably be bored by the sameness of the writing (a characteristic of a lot of classroom essays) and a lack of consideration for the reader's attention span.

Of course the descriptions of the two paragraph types are not exclusive. That is, it's possible to have a Topic Sentence Paragraph that is also dramatic, and it's possible to have a Function Paragraph that adds details. A close look at both types will help you use them to your best advantage.

THE TOPIC SENTENCE PARAGRAPH

THE TOPIC SENTENCE PARAGRAPH presents and develops a point or thought within the paragraph, defines or limits the reader's thoughts, and provides the reader with a feeling of completeness.

> "I knew a woman,
>   lovely in her bones,
> When small birds sighed,
>   she would sigh back at
>   them;
> Ah, when she moved,
>   she moved more ways
>   than one:
> The shapes a bright con-
>   tainer can contain!"
> —Theodore Roethke

All essays must have several good Topic Sentence Paragraphs; it is these paragraphs that let you focus and limit the reader's attention to the particular thing you want the reader to think about. A good Topic Sentence Paragraph will never leave your reader guessing. It will also never let the reader's mind wander from your subject.

That tends to sound a bit marvelous, a bit miraculous. Imagine having the reader think what *you* want her to think about, rather than what *she* wants to think about! Well, in a way it *is* kind of wonderful, but it is also quite *systematic* and a "miracle" that anyone can *repeat* again and again, once the principles are understood.

Watch how a Topic Sentence Paragraph operates:
Here's a word:

Sea

I write it down, and you read it.

Then you "see" in your mind's eye whatever the word makes you think of. Perhaps a vacation you took at the beach, a program you saw on TV, the time you were in the Navy, jogging on sand, a storm, whales, or drowning. You think of whatever *you* think of; all I've done by writing down the word is to stimulate you to remember.

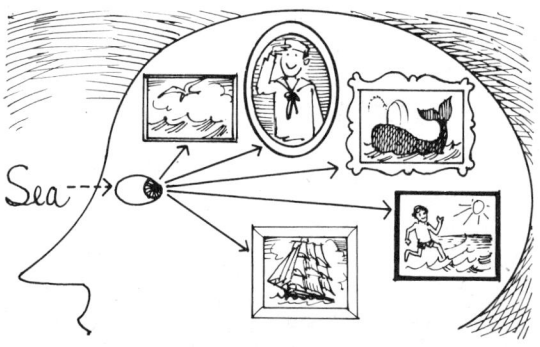

I add a few more words, giving you a phrase:

The Dead Sea

Now what has happened?

I've *limited* your thinking, directed it to what *I* am thinking about the word *sea*. Instead of entertaining any personal memory that you might remember connected with the word *sea*, now you are limiting your thinking (momentarily at least) to *The Dead Sea*. Maybe you think of Dead Sea Scrolls. Or you might think, "Isn't that where you can float more easily than on the ocean?" or "I don't know anything about the Dead Sea." Whatever happens, you concentrate on *The Dead Sea* instead of just *sea*, simply because I have given you more information. I'm narrowing your attention.

Now, watch this. I give you a whole sentence:

The Dead Sea is not a sea at all.

What will probably happen when I write this sentence is that you will stop looking into your own memory for something you know about the Dead Sea and will instead pay attention to me because I've caused you to be interested in what I have to say. If you aren't actually interested, at least **I've limited the things that at the moment you are thinking about *seas* in general and have directed you to the thing about *seas* that I want to say to you.** So, the Topic Sentence Paragraph allows you to direct and control the reader's attention to what you want to communicate.

But is this one sentence enough?

What if I don't go on? How long would I keep your attention? If I added nothing to that sentence, you would be perfectly within your rights to say, "Well, what about it?" or "So what?"

Thus, if I want to *keep* your attention and get a message across to you that is *complete*, I have to add some more sentences to this one. So that's what I do:

    Despite its name, the Dead Sea is not a sea at all. It is actually a lake. The lake ranges in depth from 33 meters in the north basin to 2 meters in the south basin. The lake is 45 miles long by 9 miles wide. The two basins which make up the lake were joined in Biblical times by a neck of land which could be crossed on foot; today that neck of land is submerged and the lake looks like one continuous body of water.*

—*Harvey Arden*

You can see now how a paragraph works. I can't deliver my complete message unless I give you enough additional information. Maybe the single sentence *Despite its name, the Dead Sea is not a sea at all* would be enough for me, the writer, if I know all the facts about it already. But if I want another person to believe or pay attention to what I say, I have to provide enough information—enough sentences—so that the reader will feel *complete* and *convinced* when the paragraph is finished.

It is ironic that the more information you give, the tighter you pull the circle of your reader's attention. The single sentence alone won't say enough. It's only when you put sentence to sentence that you can tell the reader any *meaning* about the subject. With each additional sentence, you're drawing your reader more and more into your circle of information. And you're directing—in fact to a certain extent controlling—what he or she thinks about your subject. A Topic Sentence Paragraph can really put you in command and let you give the reader exactly the information you've chosen.

TOPIC SENTENCE PARAGRAPH:
A group of sentences that are connected one to the other to cause the reader to know some particular point the writer is making; the smallest unit of writing that a writer can use to get a *Developed message* over to the reader.

APPLICATION

1. Practice limiting your reader's thoughts by adding more information. You can do this by pretending to be both the writer and the reader. Start with a single word. Write down what you think of when you see the word:

   Street: _____

   Now, add some words to the single word *(street)* and make a phrase that limits the reader's thinking:

   Phrase about *street:* _____

   Now, turn the group of words into a sentence:

   Sentence about *street:* _____

   Do you see how with each step you are drawing a tighter circle around what your reader will think? You are directing the reader to what *you* want to say instead of letting the reader think whatever random thoughts might come up.

2. Take each of the following words through the same three steps. Notice every time how the writer can direct and control the reader's attention by giving additional information.

         mountain   pizza   work   dancing   children

3. Here are some sentences that could be good topic sentences for a Topic

---

*This paragraph is excerpted from "The Living Dead Sea" (see page 144).

Sentence Paragraph. Write the *additional* sentences that will develop, or relate to, the topic sentence.
- A. Paying bills has its humorous side.
- B. Apartment living is for the birds.
- C. Going to college as an adult requires special skills.
- D. Working and going to school at the same time can be frustrating.

4. Now, let's apply this information about Topic Sentence Paragraphs to one of your essays. First of all, go through the paper and label each paragraph that carried a message *TSP* for *Topic Sentence Paragraph*. Next, look at the paragraphs that you have labeled *TSP* and check them by answering the following questions:
   - A. Have you told the reader clearly the main idea that the paragraph is built around, or have you made that idea so clear by implication that the reader can't miss it?
   - B. Have you made sure that every sentence in the Topic Sentence Paragraph is related to the main idea?
   - C. Have you given the reader enough information so that the main idea gets across?

CHECKING YOUR WRITING FOR FLOW: Looking at the Topic Sentence Paragraphs

---

The three questions you've just answered in checking your own paragraphs can be restated as principles. If there is anything that needs improvement in your Topic Sentence Paragraphs, it will probably be something in one of these three areas. Let's look at them one at a time.

PRINCIPLE 1: TELL THE READER CLEARLY WHAT THE PARAGRAPH IS ABOUT

It is absolutely in your own best interest to have topic sentences in your Topic Sentence Paragraphs. Since your whole purpose is to get a message across to another person, you need to do everything possible to make it *easy*. Remember that the reader gets impatient. The reader wants to *know* what you are going to talk about, and wants to know *quickly*.

The first thing you should check each Topic Sentence Paragraph for is the topic sentence itself. Is a main idea clearly stated in black and white, or is it still in your head? Is it anywhere? Although it is sometimes best to imply rather than state the topic sentence, the explicitly stated topic sentence has two enormous advantages: it helps you check the order of your own thoughts, and it helps you direct your readers' thoughts.

The topic sentence helps your writing flow by giving readers expectations that the rest of the paragraph fulfills. Readers proceed smoothly because the topic sentence lets them know where you are going and why the sentences in the paragraph are grouped together. They don't get stuck because they don't have to stop to second guess what your main point is.

Without a topic sentence, there's nothing to direct the readers to the particular aspect of the subject you want them to think about, and there's nothing to hold the sentences together as a group. A paragraph without a topic sentence looks like this:

> Jogging is a fast-growing sport. Sports really contribute to good health. There is a new sports magazine on the market this month. Playing ball was a sport done thousands of years ago in primitive societies. People get injured in sports every year. Tennis players do not have a wide variety of shoes available to them. Sports can be expensive.

Reading that jumble of sentences, you feel as though you were being pushed from this to that, never knowing what was coming up. There was not a single "leader" sentence in the bunch that directed your thoughts and served to hold all the other sentences together.

How *could* this paragraph become a good Topic Sentence Paragraph? In fact, it's impossible to use all these sentences in one coherent paragraph; the best you could do is choose *one* of them, make it the topic sentence, and add the necessary sentences to develop the point.

Where does the topic sentence go in the paragraph? Usually in one of three places: 1) at the beginning, 2) at the end, 3) nowhere—it's just "understood."

Placing the Topic Sentence at the Beginning. By far the most common location for the topic sentence is at the beginning of a Topic Sentence Paragraph. It is easy to see the advantage of putting it there. The reader knows immediately what you are going to talk about. And *you* have a constant reminder too—from the very start—of what you are concentrating on in this paragraph. The topic sentence will help you stay on the subject.

Here is a paragraph written by a college student. The writer took pains to let the reader know *immediately* what she was going to talk about. See how her topic sentence signals the reader about what is going to be discussed.

> *What happens when ducks swallow lead?* The pellets pass through the digestive tract to the gizzard where they are converted to a soluble form and absorbed by the bloodstream. Lead causes a reduction in oxygen supplies to all tissues. It interferes with the body's ability to break down glucose, leading to weight loss. Lead also disrupts the production of hemoglobin and anemia is the likely result. This imbalance in blood chemistry impairs the functioning of the liver and heart and causes severe damage to these organs. The external symptoms are an extreme loss of weight, wing droop, refusal to eat, a tendency to seek isolation and cover, and loss of the ability to walk or fly.

Placing the Topic Sentence at the End. One good reason for putting the topic sentence at the end of the paragraph is to keep the reader in suspense and, therefore, interested. The reader reads on to see what you are going to say when you get through, but only if what comes first is really compelling. Imagine a bicycle rider picking up a book that started, "You should study the interior and function of the muscle cell." Do you think she would be interested in reading on? But imagine the same cyclist with a different beginning for the paragraph:

> Each of us is composed of a hundred trillion cells or more. With each movement the body requires the collaboration of thousands of nerve and muscle cells. The muscle cell in particular shows a remarkable ability for obtaining and using energy. *Exploring the interior and function of the muscle cell is an exciting beginning to the appreciation, knowledge, and understanding of the cycling body.* —Irvin Faria and Peter Cavanagh

The reader is much more likely to be willing to read on because the writers built up to their point.

Another reason for putting the topic sentence at the end of a paragraph is to build point by point toward the conclusion so that the reader will be prepared to agree by the time he or she arrives. This type of paragraph is sometimes called *inductive,* since it induces the reader through a series of specific details toward a conclusion that draws those details all together. Here is an example:

> Now that they've taught pigeons to play table tennis and chimpanzees to play word games and computers to play chess, it's becoming quite difficult to distinguish humans from the rest of the landscape. So, if you set out to ask what makes people people rather than animals or machines, by and by you have to look into the subject of music. *It appears that the ability to make music is a characteristic of human nature only.*
> —Ward Cannel and Fred Marx

Placing the Topic Sentence Nowhere—Having It "Understood."

Sometimes you may feel that the reader will know the main idea in the paragraph without being told. In fact, sometimes formally stating the main idea is somewhat artificial and stiff, so you put in only the specific details. In the following example, Lawrence Durrell is describing the Greek island of Mykonos. There is no one sentence that says so; the main idea of the paragraph is, therefore, just understood.

> Everywhere the white arcades and chapels repeat themselves in an obsessive rhythm of originality and congruence; and what is marvelous is that in Mykonos there are no foreign echoes from Venice, Genoa and the rest. Everything is as newly minted as a new-laid Easter egg, and just as beautiful. You can walk for hours in what is an imitation *souk* hung with carpets, brocades, island blankets, donkey bags, shawls in all their bewildering variety. Relentless perspectives of light and shade marry the voluptuous shapes of breasts translated into cupolas and apses, into squinches and dovecots. Take Picasso, Brancusi and Gaudi, knock their heads together, and you might get something like Mykonos by evening light, foundering into violet whiteness against a blue-black sea. At the end of every gyre or whorl (you are inside a seashell), you suddenly plunge out upon the harbor with its welcoming lines of cafés and chophouses, set out under brilliant awnings or in some places shaded by tall

mulberries. Nightfall is the time, ouzo time, after an exhausting day of doing nothing purposefully (the opposite of killing time), when you feel the need of these cafés. The violets, pinks, rose and gray of the sinking sun on the walls—just before the wink of the green ray which says goodnight—are all the more haunting for being reproduced in the cloudy glass of ouzo before you on the table. It is like inhabiting a rainbow.

—Lawrence Durrell

And Please Note: It's very important to recognize the difference between a paragraph with an implied or understood topic sentence, such as the one above, and a paragraph that is just a collection of unconnected sentences. **If you are in the slightest doubt, put in the topic sentence.** That way you are *certain* not to go wrong.

APPLICATION
Finding the Topic Sentence

1. Pick out the topic sentence in the following paragraphs. If the topic sentence is implied, compose an appropriate sentence that describes the paragraph. Be prepared to evaluate the writer's placement of the topic sentence.

   A. The alcohol-drunk driver usually finds it hard to hide his condition, if stopped by the police. But the pot-high driver often believes he can "come down" and carry on a seemingly normal conversation with a police officer. This apparent ability to "hide their high" gives many pot smokers confidence that they can drive stoned.   —Peggy Mann

   B. We get home from church around 12:30. After a late lunch, the afternoon seems to stretch before us unendingly. We leisurely read the Sunday paper—there's always more to it than there is to the weekly papers. Usually, there's homework to do, but no one feels like doing it, so we postpone it, choosing to nap or to go for a ride instead. Occasionally, there's an old movie worth watching on television. And, of course, it's always nice just to sit in the shade sipping a Coke or lemonade while the afternoon wears on.

   C. When we first saw the barracks apartments, I told myself I would never live there. Five minutes later, we were turning the key to an apartment in one of those horrible buildings. (None of the nicer apartments were vacant, and we needed a place that day.) The first thing I didn't like was the stove that faced the door as you entered the apartment. Walking right into the kitchen as you came in reminded me of the crowded ghetto apartments I've seen on television. Then the couch looked like something you'd find in a cheaply furnished, rundown bus station. It was a gaudy orange vinyl and had no arms, and only two people could sit on it at a time because it was so small. There was no backboard on the bed, and the dresser drawer was made of brown, ugly metal. In the bathroom sink, there were separate hot and cold water faucets. I hated everything about that apartment—but we lived there three years!

D. I think the stature of humor must vary some with the times. The court fool in Shakespeare's day had no social standing and was no better than a lackey, but he did have some artistic standing and was listened to with considerable attention, there being a well-founded belief that he had the truth hidden somewhere about his person. Artistically he stood probably higher than the humorist of today, who has gained social position but not the ear of the mighty. (Think of the trouble the world would save itself if it would pay some attention to nonsense!) A narrative poet at court, singing of great deeds, enjoyed a higher standing than the fool and was allowed to wear fine clothes; yet I suspect that the ballad singer was more often than not a second-rate stooge, flattering his monarch lyrically, while the fool must often have been a first-rate character, giving his monarch good advice in bad puns. —E. B. White

2. Here are some "additional" sentences that might be added to a topic sentence. Write the topic sentence that will tie each unit together.

Writing the Topic Sentence

A. Red makes you feel aggressive and alive. Blue, on the other hand, can be calming or it can be depressing. If you wear yellow, you will probably feel cheerful, if for no other reason than because people say, "You look cheerful today dressed in yellow." Black can look smashing and chic, or it can look drab, depending on how you accent it. Probably the worst color to wear at all is gray. You just fade into the crowd.

   Topic Sentence: _____

B. When the day is cloudy and gloomy, I get depressed. Even if I have a busy day planned, the gloominess of a day without sunshine makes it difficult for me to function effectively. But rainy days don't depress me at all. Sometimes, though, they make me angry—especially when I have to do a lot of walking that day. I hate to arrive at work soaking wet. Other times, rainy days cheer me up. There is nothing as refreshing as a rain shower after several days of hot, muggy weather. My best moods, however, occur on warm, sunny days. The brightness of the sun lifts my spirits; I feel energetic and ready to work. The only problem then is that I'd rather be outdoors than indoors.

   Topic Sentence: _____

C. Some advertisers suggest that their cigarette will make you masculine or feminine. Marlboro and Virginia Slims ads are good examples of this. Others would like us to believe that their cigarettes will bring romance into our lives. Their ads feature happy couples usually strolling hand-in-hand; no doubt, we are to assume that the cigarette was instrumental in forming the romance. Still others claim that their cigarette is refreshing, that its taste will make you feel springtime fresh. Now that we know cigarette smoking may cause lung cancer, some advertisers try a logical appeal by comparing tar and nicotine levels:

the smart smoker buys the cigarette with the least tar and nicotine and the best flavor. Actually, the smart person enjoys the ads and buys no cigarettes!

Topic Sentence: _____

CHECKING FOR TOPIC SENTENCES: APPLYING PRINCIPLE 1

3. You have already marked the Topic Sentence Paragraphs in your trial draft. Now, for each paragraph that you marked *TSP* in your essay, find the topic sentence. *Underline it so that it really stands out.* If you don't have a topic sentence, either stated or implied, *now* is the time to find that out. It means that your reader will probably have no idea why you have grouped the sentences together that you did. As a result, you will lose the reader's attention while she or he tries to figure out the organizing idea of the paragraph. Mark any paragraph that does not have a topic sentence so that you can rewrite it when you get ready to make your next revision.

PRINCIPLE 2: MAKE SURE THAT EVERY SENTENCE IN THE TOPIC SENTENCE PARAGRAPH IS RELATED TO THE TOPIC SENTENCE

In the process of writing, ideas can pop up anywhere, sometimes even surprising you, the writer. Often these surprising ideas are so original or intriguing that you veer off in happy pursuit of them. This is fine in the early stages of writing—in fact, it can even be desirable because you may discover some really good point that hadn't been thought of before. But when the writing process gets down to thinking about the reader and to making everything as easy as possible for the reader, a Topic Sentence Paragraph must be examined carefully to be sure that the reader doesn't get surprised. Sudden veering off can be fun for the writer but confusing for the reader.

Because thoughts are at least as involuntary as they are deliberate, it's extremely useful to have a means of testing whether they are behaving or dashing off in all directions. For example, this paragraph from a student paper shows how the writer's thoughts veered while the paragraph was in progress.

> The sand dunes on the Oregon coast are as much fun as a carnival ride. You get into a modified pick-up truck, and the driver, who is probably 35, acts 14. He races up the dunes, stops suddenly, then takes off so fast that the truck—and you—leap several feet into the air. One man in our truck lost his glasses and his cigarette lighter on one of those leaps. His wife got very angry because the man could not find his belongings. The sand was so white and the truck had gone so far before the driver could hear us yelling "Stop!" that the glasses and lighter were nowhere to be seen. The wife wouldn't talk to the man all the way back to the ticket office. The spirit in the back of the truck just wasn't the same after that accident. The man was mad at the truck driver, and his wife was mad at him.

What has happened here? The writer began with a good topic sentence: *The sand dunes on the Oregon coast are as much fun as a carnival ride*. The next couple of sentences give additional information about *why* the dunes are fun and like a carnival ride. But then the writer veers off course: after telling about the man who lost his glasses and lighter, the writer gets onto a different topic—anger and resentful feelings associated with loss of the articles. Suddenly we've been shunted from *fun* to *anger*. And although there is some connection here—the articles got lost and the anger came up during the dune buggy ride—the writer has not stayed on the topic as announced in the topic sentence.

The paragraph could be easily fixed, and attention to the topic sentence makes the remedy obvious. Here's the revised version, with all the sentences related to the topic sentence.

> The sand dunes on the Oregon coast are as much fun as a carnival ride. You get into a modified pick-up truck with a driver who is probably 35 but acts 14. He races up the dunes, stops suddenly, then takes off so fast that the truck—and you—leap several feet into the air. One man in our truck lost his glasses and his cigarette lighter on one of those leaps. The driver will also spot another truck in the distance. The two will run right toward each other, swerving only at the last minute to avoid a head-on collision. Once our truck ran to the top of a dune, and suddenly there was nowhere to go. The dune went straight down so suddenly that you couldn't see the bottom at all. We all thought we were sailing off into the far-blue yonder and said our last goodbyes. When the ride was over, we all jumped off the truck saying, "I'll never do that again," but in fact we could hardly wait to get back in line to take the ride again.

Here the writer sticks to telling *why the truck ride on the dunes is so much fun*. The writer doesn't get sidetracked onto the story about the man's glasses or his wife's anger. Everything in the paragraph connects to the topic sentence.

APPLICATION
PARAGRAPHS THAT DO OR DO NOT STAY ON TOPIC

1. Determine which of the paragraphs below stay on the topic and which stray off. Rewrite the ones that go off the topic.

    A. Successful cooking can't be done quickly. The good cook reads recipes carefully *before* using them, and he rereads them as he goes along. He must assemble needed ingredients—or go out and buy them if they aren't available in his kitchen. He must gather utensils, and when the specified utensil isn't available, he must try to come up with a suitable substitute. As he begins the recipe, he measures patiently and exactly and adds things in the order specified. He follows instructions exactly, beating, cooking, and mixing for specified periods of time; he knows that failing to do this may result in a less than perfect product. Then, he cooks the whole thing for as long as the recipe says—not five or ten minutes more or less. After everything is mixed and cooking, he takes time to clean up right away. Bowls, measuring spoons, beaters, and measuring cups must be washed. Unused ingredients must be returned to their proper places. Sometimes the kitchen floor must be mopped to clean up spilled flour or broken egg shells. But for the person who enjoys cooking, all this is time well spent.

B. These days, deciding how to spend your leisure time requires wisdom. If you watch television, you must determine which programs are worth watching and which should be turned off. Sometimes I think the people who produce TV programs aim to insult the public. There's nothing on but silly, unrealistic "sitcoms," violent, unrealistic adventure series, or ridiculous game shows. Do the producers think we have no taste when it comes to TV viewing? Do they think we don't use our minds when we watch television? The least they could do is offer something realistic. Sometimes I get so mad, I seriously consider getting rid of my set.

C. What I like most about going to college is the chance to meet new and exciting people. My roommate is one of the nicest persons I've ever met. He is good-natured, understanding, and generally easy to get along with. There's only one thing I don't like about him—he studies too much. He gets up early to study and stays up late. I can't sleep when his study lamp is on. And I don't appreciate being awakened at 6 A.M. by his alarm clock. I sure wish he'd ease up on his studying. He'll end up going through college without having any fun—and I'll go through college without enough sleep!

CHECKING FOR RELATEDNESS: APPLYING PRINCIPLE 2

2. It is time now to do another check on the Topic Sentence Paragraphs in your essay. *Does each sentence in the paragraph clearly relate to the topic sentence?* A good way to check this is to ask yourself about *every sentence* in the paragraph: how does this sentence relate to my main idea? If you can't see that it does, mark the paragraph to be revised. If all the sentences do relate, you know you are in good shape in the "related" department.

PRINCIPLE 3: ALWAYS GIVE THE READER ENOUGH INFORMATION

The old truth that *a confused or unsatisfied reader is a lost reader* holds here as much as anywhere else. If a writer raises the expectations of the reader and then doesn't fulfill them with enough information, the reader is likely to resent what feels like a set-up. It's like a hotel that advertises deluxe accommodations when it has only canvas cots. Of course you wouldn't deliberately mislead your reader; using the topic sentence check-up, you can always be certain of having provided plenty of information.

Here are two versions of a paragraph that illustrate this principle. The first version clearly does *not* give enough information:

Stage 3/Completing

> Cooking southern food is something anybody can learn to do. The most important thing the cook has to learn is to be patient. The cook must also learn to think imaginatively. Finally, someone cooking southern food must think big instead of small.

This paragraph is almost provoking in its skimpiness of detail! Why is *patience* important? What makes *imagination* necessary? And what on earth does the writer mean by "think big instead of small"? This is a beautiful example of a paragraph in which the writer knows more than the reader *and* isn't telling enough. Perhaps if the reader already knew about southern cooking, the writer would not be in trouble. But if the reader didn't, the paragraph wouldn't tell very much.

Now see what happens when the writer rewrites the paragraph, this time *making sure* that the reader knows what the topic sentence means:

> Cooking southern food is something anybody can learn to do. The most important thing the cook has to know how to do is to be patient. Almost all southern dishes cook for an enormously long time. Black-eyed peas simmer for half a day. Chicken and dumplings take hours. Green beans are cooked until they are pearl gray. The cook must also know how to use meat for seasoning, because almost all southern vegetable dishes are seasoned with meat. Green beans and black-eyed peas are cooked with fat-back or salted pork. Bacon grease is put into corn bread. Biscuits are made with lard. Finally, someone cooking southern food must think big instead of small. A southern meal is likely to have at least two meats, four or five vegetables, three pies, and several cakes. And the portions are large, too. So the cook has to make plenty and think in large menus. With these characteristics, however—patience, imagination, and willingness to think big—anybody can cook southern food.

These details added to the revision bring life to the paragraph and let the reader *know* what the message means.

What makes this principle—give the reader enough information—so important? There are two reasons:

1. **Readers do not remember *general statements* very long at all.** What they do remember are images, specifics, "pictures" that the writer gives them. This is why the topic sentence is not enough within itself. There must be concrete details, examples that the reader can hold on to. It's the same principle at work when a set of instructions contains both written information *and* a picture or chart: you have a much better chance of understanding how to put an appliance or component together. And this is what you are doing in paragraphs when you give specifics to back up the topic sentence. You are giving the reader a double opportunity of getting the message: one way with the general topic sentence and another way with the specifics you give that paint pictures for the reader.

2. **Readers are more likely to get the message if you give it to them several times.** Not only are you sending it in two different ways—through a

topic sentence and through back-up details—but you are also just plain sending it *x* amount of times. And you can hope that at least *one* of those times the reader will get it. This isn't because readers aren't smart. It's just because the communication process has to operate across space, time, and distance, and without the communicator even being present. That makes for certain difficulties. The reader's phone might ring; the reader might not have a particular interest in what you are communicating; a bird might fly by the reader's window—a lot of things might happen, including any or all of the things that distract *you* when you try to write. So you can see that if you are sending your message in just one sentence, just one time, just one way, the odds are stacked against you.

How Much is Enough? How can you know what is *enough* information? There is no sure formula that answers this question. *Who your readers are* is part of the answer, because how much they already know or don't know will determine how much or how little you, the writer, have to explain. So, the first thing you can do as you look at your Topic Sentence Paragraphs to see if you have given enough information is to make as good a guess as you can about what your readers will need to be told. This will be an estimate on your part; and if you are undecided about whether they will or won't know something, go with the *won't* because it is better to give too much information than too little.

The second thing you can do when trying to decide how much information is enough is to recognize some givens that are almost always true for all readers:

- Readers do not remember general statements very long at all.
- Readers are skeptical; they often have a "show me" attitude, and you have to accept the responsibility for doing just that.
- Readers always want to be filled in. "Fill me in, won't you?" says your friend who wants to get the whole picture, avoid confusion, and be in the know. So even readers who may know a lot about what you are writing on still want to be filled in on what *you* mean, on what *you* are attempting to say. You still have to give them enough information about your thinking, even if they know quite a bit about the subject.

How Do You Give Enough? The methods for adding information to Topic Sentence Paragraphs are the same as those used to develop your main points in previous drafts of your essay. In the Completing Stage, you simply check out the promise and delivery system of each Topic Sentence Paragraph as carefully as you checked out the promise and delivery system of your trial draft in Late Shaping. Any paragraph that still does not give enough information can be filled out in one or more of the following ways:

1. **Illustrations, Examples, and Details.** Will your readers be likely to *see* more clearly what you mean if you *show* them by adding one or more examples? Remember that it can sometimes take two or three examples or

illustrations to clarify one general statement. Details give the reader a clearer picture of what is being discussed.

2. **Description.** Is there any point made in the paragraph that you can *reveal* more clearly if you draw a picture of it with words? Description answers such questions for the reader as "What does it look like?" or "What does it feel like?"

3. **Definition.** Is there any chance that your readers will not understand a term you have used, especially a word that the message of your paragraph depends on? Words that are unfamiliar, words that mean different things in different contexts, words that can mean different things to different people—these will cloud your message if they are not defined. If you find any words like this, tell your reader exactly what they mean or what *you* mean by them.

4. **Explanation and Analysis.** Will your readers be likely to understand you better if you add more particulars? Are there any reasons or consequences that need to be explained? Any characteristics or parts of the subject of the paragraph that need to be identified or discussed in more detail?

5. **Facts and Figures.** Are there any statistics or facts you can add to help your readers believe what you say, agree with what you say, listen to what you say, notice what you say?

6. **Comparison and Contrast.** Can you help your readers *see* what you mean by comparing it to something else, showing how the two things are alike; or by contrasting it with something else, showing how your idea is different from something else? Putting two things up together can throw light on the point that you, the writer, really want to get across.

7. **Narration.** Is there a story you can tell to explain or illustrate the point you are making? "Once upon a time . . .": you can never fail to get a reader's attention with this strategy.

APPLICATION
Method of Paragraph Development

1. Read the paragraphs below and identify as closely as possible the method of development which has been used.

   A. Shaking off from my spirit what *must* have been a dream, I scanned more narrowly the real aspect of the building. Its principal feature seemed to be that of an excessive antiquity. The discoloration of ages had been great. Minute fungi overspread the whole exterior, hanging in a fine tangled webwork from the eaves. Yet all this was apart from any extraordinary dilapidation. No portion of the masonry had fallen; and there appeared to be a wild inconsistency between its still perfect adaptation of parts and the crumbling condition of the individual stones. In this there was much that reminded me of the specious totality of old woodwork which had rotted for long years in some neglected vault, with no disturbance from the breath of the external air. Beyond this indication of excessive decay, however, the fabric gave little token of instability. Perhaps the eye of a scrutinizing observer might have discovered a barely perceptible fissure, which, extending from the roof of the building in front, made its way down the wall in a zigzag direction, until it became lost in the sullen waters of the tarn. —Edgar Allen Poe

B. Have you ever noticed the kinds of shoppers you see in a grocery store? Some women dress up to go out and buy their groceries. Their hair and nails immaculately done and their outfits elegantly in style, they breeze from aisle to aisle leaving a whiff of expensive perfume lingering in the air. Other women don't seem to bother to change the sloppy clothes they were wearing at home. They dart from aisle to aisle in hair rollers, baggy, dirty shirts, and house shoes. Many times, they are trailed by a small army of equally sloppy, dirty children. Other shoppers are more noticeable for their approach to shopping rather than for their appearance. Some carry lists and carefully cross off each item as they put it in their baskets. Some spend minutes frugally comparing the "national" brand to the store brand. Others compare prices per pound for packages of different sizes. Others just take items off the shelves impulsively without regard for cost.

C. According to the story pieced together by astronomers, a star's life begins in swirling mists of hydrogen that surge and eddy through space. The Universe is filled with tenuous clouds of this abundant gas, which makes up 90 per cent of all the matter in the Cosmos. In the random motions of such clouds, atoms sometimes come together by accident to form small, condensed pockets of gas. Stars are born in these accidents. —Robert Jastrow

D. I think this is the fourth spring the coon has occupied the big tree in front of the house, but I have lost count, so smoothly do the years run together. She is like a member of our family. She has her kittens in a hole in the tree about thirty-five feet above the ground, which places her bedchamber a few feet from my bedchamber but at a slightly greater elevation. It strikes me as odd (and quite satisfactory) that I should go to sleep every night so close to a litter of raccoons. The mother's comings and goings are as much a part of my life at this season of the year as my morning shave and my evening drink.
—E. B. White

E. Americans tend to think of Islam as just another religion, which explains in part why the Islamic revival has been so little understood in Washington. Actually, Islam is much more than a theology; it is also an idea of how society should be organized. The Koran and subsequent interpretations of Mohammad's thinking spell out rules for individual behavior from cradle to grave, and detailed precepts of how governments should conduct their affairs. The concept of separating church and state is meaningless to orthodox Muslims. Mohammad and his successors were not only the supreme religious leaders, but heads of government and commanders of its armies as well. Perhaps

most important of all, Islam demands—and receives—an unquestioned faith from its believers. Western church-goers will listen politely while preachers thunder against immodest dress or sex in movies, but they hardly ever do anything about it. By contrast, the cry of a *mullah,* warning that Islam is in danger, is often enough in itself to send tens of thousands of Muslims surging through the streets.
—William E. Griffith

F. The past is completely eliminated in Orwell's *1984*. History is revised. Books are destroyed. Without print media, there is no evidence that anything has been different. Even keeping diaries is forbidden. People are expected to absorb and accept the new information delivered by the television sets even if it directly contradicts the news of a month ago. Since it is impossible to prove the contradiction, it is useless to try to resist. Without points of comparison, all information is equally real. The Underground, for example, or a distant war between Oceania and Eastasia, might have existed or they might not have; there is no way of knowing. —Jerry Mander

G. The skin is the body's largest and one of its most complex organs. Spread flat, it would cover approximately 18 square feet, every square inch of which includes about a yard of blood vessels, four yards of nerves, a hundred sweat glands and more than three million cells. Without this natural spacesuit we would be prey to all sorts of deadly bacteria and, in any case, would quickly perish from loss of body heat. —*Reader's Digest*

H. A basic understanding of euthanasia is needed before the controversy over it can be discussed. Euthanasia is the painless putting to death of a person terminally ill. In most cases these people are in pain and only kept alive by machines. In some cases, there is the question of whether the patient is human or vegetable. The term "vegetable" refers to the idea that because of no brain activity the "person" is dead. This mercy killing is usually accomplished by disconnecting the life-supporting machines. The controversy springs from the question of whether it is morally or legally right to take another person's life even though he would die without modern technology.

2. The paragraphs in the passage below are undeveloped. Using any of the methods discussed above, rewrite each paragraph so that the topic is developed fully for the reader.

Undeveloped Paragraphs

   Although a college degree is a form of success in itself, only the individual can determine if that degree is the beginning or the end of the road. A person must want success in order to attain it.
   In today's highly specialized and technical society, a university education is practically the only way to open doors of opportunity. Most good jobs require college degrees. But once on the job, a person must be willing to work hard and be the best that he can be.

The Topic Sentence Paragraph

Although a university education is not the only requirement for success, it is a necessary part of the make-up of a successful individual.

CHECKING FOR PARAGRAPH DEVELOPMENT: APPLYING PRINCIPLE 3

3. We want to emphasize the basic concept of giving enough information. The *method* you use is not the most important thing; that you give enough information to the reader is. Now make a final check on the Topic Sentence Paragraphs in your essay. Read them with a critical eye to see if they are fully developed. Have you given the reader enough information? Have you given some *specific* statements for each *general* statement that you made? The principle of general "progressing to" specific is at the heart of all good writing. The general statement lets the reader know what you are going to communicate, and the specifics make sure that the communication happens.

In your final check to see whether you have developed each of your Topic Sentence Paragraphs, fill out a chart like this one:

CHART FOR CHECKING DEVELOPMENT IN TOPIC SENTENCE PARAGRAPHS

Here is my topic sentence: _____

_____

Here are the specifics I used to develop this topic sentence:

1. _____

2. _____

3. _____

4. _____

(for however many points you have)

For some of my specifics I gave *additional* information about something in that specific point, in order to further explain it:

To explain specific _____, I gave this information: _____

_____

To explain specific _____, I gave this information: _____

_____

(for however much additional information you gave on specific points)

Actually, you can analyze any topic sentence paragraph in the world by using this chart. And if you apply the chart to your own topic sentence paragraphs, you'll see immediately whether you have developed your point fully. The chart works by making you look at *every sentence* to be sure you know *why* you put it there. And if you can see what the function of each sentence is, you can be pretty sure that each sentence is contributing to the flow of the paper.

Stage 3/Completing

APPLICATION
Topic Sentence Paragraphs

1. The following paragraphs do *not* follow the three principles of writing good topic sentence paragraphs.
   (a) What principle is missing in each paragraph?
   (b) Revise each paragraph so that the message has a better chance of getting across.

   Three Principles for Topic Sentence Paragraphs:
   1. Tell the reader clearly what the paragraph is about.
   2. Make sure every sentence relates to the topic sentence.
   3. Give the reader enough information.

   A. "No" is just a simple, one-syllable word used to express a negative answer. Agreed, the word "no" is easy to say, but to answer someone directly with it changes the entire situation.

   B. Education concerning the harmful effects of smoking should be increased. This can be done through the schools, starting with health programs for children at an early age. Some schools have initiated such programs, but a more widespread and intensive approach must be employed.

   C. Gardening of vegetables is one hobby that is money saving; not many hobbies can claim this. It is also fruitful, literally. Gardening of vegetables is relatively easy if you approach it in the right manner. First, you must have the proper location and tools. Pick a site that gets plenty of sunshine, is wind free, and preferably enclosed. You then must have some tool that breaks up the soil. I would recommend investing in a small tiller. You will also need an efficient watering system and common tools such as a hoe and garden rake.

PARAGRAPHS REPRESENTING THREE TYPES OF ERRORS

2. Explain how the following paragraphs violate all three principles of paragraph writing. Then explain how each might be corrected through rewriting.

   A. We are going to have to face the situation. We all have been brainwashed into the society we are by a variety of sources. Television is the main contributor of propaganda, followed by the government, other mass media, public education, the term "the American Dream," your neighbors, big business and labor, and, maybe even your own mother.

   B. Although it was hard for the man working long hours and not getting paid a high salary, the woman's day was not easy. The average wife in the fifties stayed at home and cooked, cleaned and waited for her husband to come home. There is nothing wrong with this except for the fact that there was no diversion except for the radio. The television did not yet exist. The average couple had only one car which the husband would take to work. This meant the wife was stuck at home all day. To buy groceries, the wife would walk and either carry the bags home or pull them in a small cart. Although a couple starting out in the 1950s had a hard financial struggle, they appreciated all they had worked for.

   C. To me the university is a place where I can go to fulfill my dream in

The Topic Sentence Paragraph

life. Granted, the university is not for everyone—just those who want it. A carpenter, construction worker, a farmer have no reason to attend universities, but a doctor, scientist, businessman, or teacher all have to continue their education in universities, which sometimes can be expensive.

THE FUNCTION PARAGRAPH

The **Function Paragraph** guides the reader through the piece of writing, keeps the reader's interest whetted, and expresses the writer's personality, whims, style, and purposes.

List 20 things you can't do with a hammer:
1. Play the violin.
2. Comb your hair.
3.
4.

Someone has said that if the only tool you have is a hammer, you tend to treat everything as if it were a nail. The same thing is true in writing an essay. If the only kind of paragraph you know about is the Topic Sentence Paragraph, you have to treat all your thoughts as if they were points to be developed.

Fortunately, this isn't the case.

As wonderful, useful, and necessary as the Topic Sentence Paragraph is, it isn't the only kind, even though it is the most commonly known. To get any *developed* message across, of course, Topic Sentence Paragraphs are necessary. But there are other uses of paragraphs—and you see lots of them in magazine articles and in books—that are *not* topic sentence + development. Rather, they are **Function Paragraphs,** paragraphs that do things other than give the reader information about a topic sentence.

Function Paragraphs are amusing, quirky, and fascinating to learn about, but the main thing about them is that they are *useful*. Knowing about Function Paragraphs, you aren't confused when you look at writing in books and magazines and find paragraphs that don't always begin with a new thought and give a developed message. More importantly, however, when you know about Function Paragraphs you are aware of the many more choices available to you when you write. You can discover new ways of controlling your writing and your reader, and you will find new possibilities for putting energy, personality, and variety into your writing.

Function Paragraphs help you get attention, show what things you consider important to notice, and, in general, work like the time signatures and notations on a piece of music. They assist you in orchestrating the essay and in telling the reader how to read it.

Following are some uses of Function Paragraphs.

ADD DRAMA AND GET THE READER'S ATTENTION

Often when people are talking and really want to get someone's attention, they will shout or say emphatically, "Listen to me!" Or they will use their hands in a dramatic gesture to keep the listener's eye right on them. When you are writing, of course, you can do none of these things, so you have to depend on other means to get the reader's attention or to be dramatic. Function Paragraphs will do this for you. See how Isabella Bird uses a one-sentence Function Paragraph to set up the reader in anticipation for what is coming next.

I shall not soon forget my first night here.

Somewhat dazed by the rarefied air, entranced by the glorious beauty, slightly puzzled by the motley company, whose faces loomed not always quite distinctly through the cloud of smoke produced by eleven pipes, I went to my solitary cabin at nine, attended by Evans. It was very dark, and it seemed a long way off. Something howled—Evans said it was a wolf—and owls apparently innumerable hooted incessantly. The polestar, exactly opposite my cabin door, burned like a lamp. The frost was sharp. Evans opened the door, lighted a candle, and left me, and I was soon in my hay bed. I was frightened—that is, afraid of being frightened, it was so eerie—but sleep soon got the better of my fears. I was awoke by a heavy breathing, a noise something like sawing under the floor, and a pushing and upheaving, all very loud. My candle was all burned, and, in truth, I dared not stir. The noise went on for an hour fully, when, just as I thought the floor had been made sufficiently thin for all purposes of ingress, the sounds abruptly ceased, and I fell asleep again. My hair was not, as it ought to have been, white in the morning!

FUNCTION PARAGRAPH
Paragraph to keep the reader alert and interested, to dramatize or quicken the pace.

MAKE A TRANSITION FROM ONE PART OF THE WRITING TO ANOTHER

In a fascinating essay, "Toward a Theory of Creativity," Carl Rogers discusses what creativity is, what kind of people are most likely to be creative, what conditions must be present before creativity can emerge, and what some after-effects of creativity are. Then he prepares to discuss a new topic in the essay—how constructive creativity can be encouraged. To connect the parts of the essay, he had to write a paragraph that could work like a bridge that the reader could take to get from one part of the writing to the next. Here is that paragraph and the first paragraph on the new topic.

Thus far I have tried to describe the nature of creativity, to indicate that quality of individual experience which increases the likelihood that creativity will be constructive, to set forth the necessary conditions for the creative act and to state some of its concomitants. But if we are to make progress in meeting the social need which was presented initially, we must know whether constructive creativity can be fostered, and if so, how.

From the very nature of the inner conditions of creativity it is clear that they cannot be forced, but must be permitted to emerge. The farmer cannot make the germ develop and sprout from the seed; he can only supply the nurturing conditions which will permit the seed to develop its own potentialities. So it is with creativity. How can we establish the external conditions which will foster and nourish the internal conditions described above? My experience in psychotherapy leads me to believe that by setting up conditions of psychological safety and freedom, we maximize the likelihood of an emergence of constructive creativity. Let me spell out these conditions in some detail, labeling them as x and y.

The Function Paragraph

SET OFF CONVERSATIONAL DIALOGUE

At times writers will use conversational dialogue in order to get the reader's attention and make a point by *showing* instead of *telling*. When such dialogue is used, each conversational response is put in a new paragraph. So you may see multiple paragraph indentations simply because a conversation between two people is being recorded.

Here is a student essay that uses conversational dialogue and that emerges with Function Paragraphs as a result.

"You know, this class is awful. I never learn anything from it, but it seems to go on for hours."

"I know what you mean. The lectures are so disorganized. The professor doesn't ever act as though any time has been spent in preparing for class."

"Well, I won't be here for the next class. I have better ways to spend my time."

This conversation is often heard after many college classes. These attitudes, however, could be reversed by a concerned professor. By inspiring confidence in the students and by organizing a knowledgeable presentation, a professor could make any class interesting as well as instructive.

BREAK UP LONG PARAGRAPHS OR MAKE PARAGRAPHS OF ABOUT EQUAL LENGTH

Sometimes authors make new paragraphs simply because they think the reader's eyes will get tired if a paragraph is too long. Readers do need a break periodically—a *psychological* break if nothing else—and a paragraph indention can be just the break they need when the writing is long. In the following example Martin Luther King is writing what has now become a very famous document, "Letter from Birmingham Jail." When you look at these two paragraphs, you can sense that Dr. King divided them to avoid having one really long paragraph. Of course, we can't know his motive for sure, but there doesn't seem to be any other recognizable reason for the division of the two paragraphs except to break the length.

You speak of our activity in Birmingham as extreme. At first I was rather disappointed that fellow clergymen would see my nonviolent efforts as those of an extremist. I began thinking about the fact that I stand in the middle of two opposing forces in the Negro community. One is a force of complacency, made up in part of Negroes who, as a result of long years of oppression, are so drained of self-respect and a sense of "somebodiness" that they have adjusted to segregation; and in part of a few middle-class Negroes who, because of a degree of academic and economic security and because in some ways they profit by segregation, have become insensitive to the problems of the masses. The other force is one of bitterness and hatred, and it comes perilously close to advocating violence. It is expressed in the various black nationalist groups that are springing up across the nation, the largest and best-known being Elijah Muhammad's Muslim movement. Nourished by the Negro's frustration over the continued existence of racial discrimination, this movement is made up of people who have lost faith in America, who have absolutely repudiated Christianity, and who have concluded that the white man is an incorrigible "devil."

I have tried to stand between these two forces, saying that we need emulate neither the "do-nothingism" of the complacent nor the hatred and despair of the black nationalist. For there is the more excellent way of love and nonviolent protest. I am grateful to God that, through the influence of the Negro church, the way of nonviolence became an integral part of our struggle.

ACCOMMODATE THE AUTHOR'S PERSONAL WRITING STYLE

After you have read enough of a particular writer's work, you can often recognize his or her style without even seeing the author's name. Many things make up a writer's personal style, but how he or she paragraphs is definitely part of it. Here is an example from *Everything You've Always Wanted to Know about Energy but Were Too Weak to Ask.* You can probably tell from the title that the writing is going to be flippant, maybe a little breathless; and you are right. Naura Hayden, the author, writes in an excited, personal style. She paragraphs when she wants to, and you see the same style all the way through her book.

> If you were to ask people what they would like if they could have anything in the whole world they wanted, most would say energy. Energy is everything. Energy is good health. Energy, rightly channeled, will get you anything you want—love, friendship, money, power, success, fun—*everything*!
>
> Loaded with energy, you'll feel like a million bucks—you'll feel as though there's nothing you can't do. And you know something? There *will* be nothing you can't do. Anxiety and depression will disappear. Your whole life will change drastically for the better when your body is surging with energy. Believe me, a whole new world of adventure and accomplishment will open up for you.
>
> Now what most people don't know is that energy is not that hard to get once you know the secret.
>
> Before I learned this secret, I smoked a lot and drank cups and cups of coffee to stimulate myself. These were the "uppers" I needed to get through the day. I've since found that most people need these things plus lots of sugar. Sugar is mistakenly thought of as an energy booster; all it does is give you a short spurt up, then you plummet down and get depressed until you eat more sugar—a vicious circle. It's *Bad* for you—and it's found not only in the sugar bowl, but in cakes, pies, cookies, soft drinks, and in donuts, bread, spaghetti, macaroni and other starchy things.
>
> Before I discovered my great energy secret, I was tired a lot and falling apart physically at a very young age. . . .

EMPHASIZE A POINT, DEVELOP AN EXAMPLE, OR ADD DETAIL

In this use of the Function Paragraph the writer will begin a new paragraph to emphasize a point, to develop an example, or to add detail. Of course, without the preceding paragraph, the reader wouldn't have a context for the Function Paragraph used for this purpose. So, the Function Paragraph with the details, examples, etc., is definitely connected to the Topic Sentence Paragraph preceding it and must rely on it for meaning. The writer has made the example details a separate paragraph perhaps for emphasis or perhaps because developing the example in the same paragraph would make the paragraph too long. Here is an example from Henry Boettinger.

> The key to getting and holding attention lies in having something *new* happen continually. This calls for a sense of *movement* forward or backward, development, or the feeling of "something going on." Development suggests that what we are seeing *now* grew out of something before, and is going to turn into something else. Consider the difference between the attention a child gives to a basket of eggs on the kitchen table and his [her] concentration on an egg that is being cracked from the inside by a chick straining to emerge.
>
> Another illustration, probably old when the pyramids were under construction, is the attention given to workers and their machinery on a large building project by sidewalk superintendents. The same project on a Sunday morning will hold no interest from passing crowds, because "there is nothing going on." Yet the structure's design is clear, and all the machinery stands ready, but silent. Clearly, the sense of development is dead, and with it dies attention. The fundamental aspect of development derives from its continuity with the past and the future. This unfolding of your presentation must parallel nature. Even the most spectacular and dramatic event in the story must be related to what has gone before . . . . Clear problem-statement is important because it allows a development related constantly to both aspects of any problem: that which exists and that which is desired.

In the *Completing Stage* watch for the **flow** of the message. Sometimes a Topic Sentence Paragraph will be most appropriate; other times a Functional Paragraph will work just right. Just keep your eye out for ways of moving the essay along smoothly and continuously; that's the point of it all.

This doesn't mean, however, that you can be oblivious to rules for paragraphing. You can't just paragraph anywhere and everywhere—with no rhyme or reason and no thought on your part—and have your writing really work. If you are conscious about *why* you are paragraphing—what purpose each paragraph serves—then you *do* get to make the paragraphs wherever you want to. But if you don't have some explanation and are unconscious in making your paragraphs, the result will inevitably be a disjointed, undeveloped, incommunicative piece of writing.

What you want to do is make your decisions according to what you believe is best for the reader and for your own presentation of the material. But remember: almost no writing in the real world is ever one Topic Sentence Paragraph after another. Real messages usually don't fall into these neat packages. Function paragraphs add interest and assure flow. You will want some if for no other reason than to sound like *yourself* when you write instead of like some dull "voice of the past."

APPLICATION
Function Paragraphs

1. Explain which of the paragraphs in the following passages are Function Paragraphs. Describe what their function is in each passage.

    A. Try to remember a time when you *first* read a book or heard a radio show and then *later* saw a film or a television program on the same work.

    If you read, say, *Gone With the Wind, Roots, Marjorie Morningstar* or *From Here to Eternity,* or heard any radio show such as "The Lone Ranger" first, you created your own internal image of the events described while you read or listened. You imagined the characters, the events and the ambience. You made pictures in your mind. These pictures were yours. Of course, they were influenced by the author—what he or she told you—but the creation of the actual image was up to you.

    Marjorie Morningstar was an image in your mind *before* you saw the film. Then you saw the film with Natalie Wood playing Marjorie. Once you had seen Natalie Wood in the role, could you recover the image you had made up?   —Jerry Mander

    B. Style is organic to the person doing the writing, as much a part of him as his hair, or, if he is bald, his lack of it. Trying to add style is like adding a toupée. At first glance the formerly bald man looks young and even handsome. But at second glance—and with a toupée there is always a second glance—he doesn't look quite right. The problem is not that he doesn't look well groomed; he does, and we can only admire the wigmaker's almost perfect skill. The point is that he doesn't look like himself.

    This is the problem of the writer who sets out deliberately to garnish his prose. You lose whatever it is that makes you unique. The reader will usually notice if you are putting on airs. He wants the person who is talking to him to sound genuine. Therefore a fundamental rule is: be yourself.   —William Zinsser

    C. Come on, admit it.

    You've been living with someone for a while now and you sometimes think you've made a mistake, a big mistake. There are things you want to do that you can't because the person you are living with gets in the way.

    You feel cheated. You're missing a lot. You can't stand thinking

---

The Function Paragraph

about it because it hurts so much. Sometimes you just want to be alone, free to be and do whatever you want.   —David Viscott

Checking Your Writing for Flow: Considering Function Paragraphs

2. As you do the *Completing Stage* of your essay you have the time to see what you can do to make it move faster, interest the reader more, be better connected, or emphasize just what you want emphasized. You've checked all the Topic Sentence Paragraphs, and they are in good order. Now you can look to see if you want to add any Function Paragraphs. You may need some *transition paragraphs* to get the reader from one point to another. You may see some places you could use a little drama—maybe wake up the readers and keep them interested. Perhaps one of your thoughts could use another example, and you'll put in a Function Paragraph to highlight that extra information.

3. Here is a portion of the essay on the Dead Sea by Harvey Arden of the staff of *National Geographic,* which we have been quoting in this section. The beginning of the essay has been annotated so that you can see exactly how professional writers combine Topic Sentence Paragraphs and Functional Paragraphs in their writing. Beginning with paragraph (5), you should attempt to supply your own annotation or notes—your own analysis, in other words—similar to those provided for paragraphs (1) to (4).

You will observe how much (or how little) rhyme and reason there is to how professional writers use paragraphs. When you finish, you'll know and understand that there is no firm rule about paragraphing. Yet at the same time, you'll have a broader concept of how paragraphs can be effectively used in your own writing. This understanding should allow you more control and more energy in the essays that you write.

THE LIVING DEAD SEA

(1) FUNCTION PARAGRAPH: TO GET THE READER'S ATTENTION. The two-sentence introduction sets the scene and gets the essay moving swiftly. Writer gets reader's attention by being a little mysterious as he begins.

(1) Getting to the bottom of it all is not so difficult. If you happen to be in Jerusalem, as I was one rainy November, you need only hail a taxi and ask to be taken to the Dead Sea—the lowest spot on the surface of the earth.

(2) TOPIC SENTENCE PARAGRAPH: MAIN IDEA IS DEAD SEA; REST OF SENTENCES DEVELOP THIS MAIN IDEA.

(2) It's only a half-hour drive from Jerusalem's 760-meter spiritual height to the Dead Sea's netherworldish shore—399 meters (1,309 feet) *below sea level*. Snaking through sere Judaean hills where Abraham and Jesus once walked, you pass a sign that says "SEA LEVEL" in Hebrew, Arabic, and English. It may vaguely occur to you that there aren't too many places in the world where you can dip below sea level in a taxicab and keep going, but such thoughts are now shunted out of mind by the fact that your ears have begun to pop, your head is ringing slightly, and the wool sweater you'd snuggled into back in Jerusalem's 10°C (50°F) chill has become uncomfortably warm.

(3) FUNCTION PARAGRAPH: TO BREAK UP A LONG PARAGRAPH.

(3) Your Israeli driver, Shlomo, informs you that this new-looking road was modernized by Jordan's King Hussein just before the six-day war of 1967 brought the West Bank under Israeli military control.

(4) "Nice of the king," Shlomo remarks wryly, and you slouch back in your seat just a bit uncomfortably at the thought that this is occupied territory. Before 1967 only the southwest quadrant of the Dead Sea belonged to Israel. An Israeli in West Jerusalem, unable to cross into Jordanian territory, had to take an hours-long roundabout drive through Beersheba to get to the Dead Sea. Nowadays, using "King Hussein's road" across the West Bank, it's just a short trip . . . .

(5) Off to the left a splash of green brightens the ocher landscape. "That's Jericho," Shlomo says. "Oldest known town in the world. Been there 10,000 years. And that's the River Jordan just beyond, where Jesus was baptized by John. Over there"—he points to some caveriddled cliffs to the right—"is Qumran, where most of the Dead Sea Scrolls were found. And see those mountains? One of them is Mount Nebo, where Moses died. Joshua then led the Israelites into the Promised Land right down there, across the Jordan above the Dead Sea."

(6) He smiles. "It's easy to believe in the Bible when you come to a place like this."

(7) Ten minutes later you reach the Dead Sea shore at a former Jordanian spa called the Lido. Like most first-time visitors, you cross the salt-encrusted beach to the water's edge, crouch down, poke one finger through the oily-looking surface, then gingerly put it to your tongue.

(8) *Arghhh-h*! The taste is as strong and stinging as lye. "Worst-tasting stuff in the world!" Shlomo laughs, and you don't argue . . . .

(9) Despite its name, the Dead Sea is not a sea at all. It's actually a lake with a deep northern basin 331 meters (1,086 feet) deep, and a smaller southern basin averaging only about two meters deep. The two, totaling 75 kilometers (45 miles) long by 15 kilometers (9 miles) wide, are joined across a now submerged neck of land that could be crossed on foot in Biblical times, when the water was lower . . . .

(10) Nor is the Dead Sea "dead." While it's true that fish can't live in it, scientists have discovered in its waters a number of halophilic—salt-loving—microorganisms. One of them, *Halobacterium halobium,* has recently been found by U.S. scientist Dr. Walther Stoeckenius to yield a purple pigment that is the only known biological substance other than chlorophyll capable of photosynthesis—the conversion of sunlight directly into energy.

(4) FUNCTION PARAGRAPH: TO MAKE TRANSITION.
This paragraph hooks a new train of thought onto previous remark. The paragraph also allows writer to give additional detail about the road.

TRANSITIONS AND REMINDER SIGNS

There is one final thing you need to check before you can be sure your writing is moving smoothly and continuously for the reader. You need to see if you have all along given the reader **signals** that indicate your direction *(transitions)* and **reminder signs** that help the reader remember what you are writing about. Turning a critical eye on these two areas will be the final part of revising for flow and will complete this part of the *Completing Stage* of the writing process.

TRANSITIONS

Once you know the *concept* of "transitioning," you'll master the *forms* almost without effort.

The word *transition* comes from the Latin word *transire* which means "to pass from one place to another." As you learned in studying Function Paragraphs, transitions help the reader to pass from one place (or point) in your writing to the next. And while, as you have seen, transitions may indeed be whole paragraphs in length, they may also be only a sentence or even a few words—anything that indicates for the reader that you are changing from one point to another. Although the *forms* vary, it is the *concept* of "transitioning" you want to learn, because once you understand the concept you will be able to insert transitions into your work in *any* form—paragraphs, sentences, or even single words—and you will be able to judge for yourself *which* form will do the best job for any given situation.

Let's begin by examining the work of other writers to see how they indicate transitions, how they show the movement from thought to thought. Once you can spot the transitions in someone else's writing, and understand how they function (regardless of form), you'll be in good shape to look at your own writing to see whether there are enough (and adequate) transitions. In the essay by John Stewart and Gary d'Angelo that follows, the transition signals are marked.

GIVING WHAT YOU SAY A SENSE OF WHOLENESS

Signals condition.

(1) If your experience is anything like ours, people have been telling you to "get organized" ever since you were in diapers. Your toy box was to help you learn to organize your room. School and work taught you to organize your time. And invariably, one goal of English, speech, philosophy, and science classes is to teach you to organize your thinking and the ways to express yourself. Sometimes, I wonder whether we tend to go a little overboard. Gary's got a cartoon on his office door that shows a high-school-age girl deep in thought, and the caption is: "Sometimes they teach things out of me. And I feel like saying, 'I wanted to keep that.'" We sometimes wonder whether spontaneous chaos is one of those things that schools "Teach out of us" that we might enjoy—and profit from—keeping.

Signals addition.

Signals addition.

Signals contrast.

(2) On the other hand, most psychologists believe that we *naturally* structure our world, i.e., that order is more characteristically human than is disorder. But whether structure is natural or is an artifact of Western culture, it's here. We *do* tend to see things and people in wholes made up of parts that are somehow related to one another. Therefore, communication that has a sense of wholeness is usually easier for us to comprehend clearly than is communication that doesn't.

Signals contrast.

Signals conclusion.

Shift from conclusion to how people act.

Signals example.

(3) When people perceive something that's "incomplete" or "disordered," they sometimes fill in or add details so that it makes more sense to them. For example, as you watch a television program you may see an actor put a coffee cup to his lips and make drinking movements. Even though you don't actually see the coffee itself, you mentally "put" coffee

146   Stage 3/Completing

in the cup—you fill in the detail. <u>This same kind of process</u> can occur when you're talking with another person. If you don't provide a "whole" message, the other person may fill in missing details or examples and in so doing may make your message into something you didn't intend. To the extent that you don't come across as a "whole" person, the other person may fill in or infer things about you that don't adequately characterize you as an individual. <u>In short, giving a sense of wholeness and some structure to your communication gives you some control over how you</u> and your <u>ideas</u> are perceived by others. *Signals similarity.*

Signals summary.

(4) <u>The more formal the communication context, the more obvious that sense of wholeness can be.</u> Persons listening to a public speech usually expect the talk to be clearly structured. A public speech doesn't have to sound as if it's coming from a robot; the speaker can still promote some person-to-person contact. <u>But</u> the speech should usually be pretty clearly organized. Your <u>contribution</u> to a group discussion should also have fairly clear structure, <u>although</u> it can be less formal than the organization of a speech. *Shift to general principle about formal/informal contexts.*

Signals contrast.

Signals contrast.

(5) <u>An informal conversation, however, is obviously different from both a speech and a group discussion.</u> You don't sit down beforehand to <u>organize a conversation</u>—not usually, anyway. (Your <u>first date</u> might have been an exception to that rule. I remember frantically trying to plan topics of conversation for my first major boy-girl social engagements. You know how well that worked.)

(6) <u>Yet structure is important,</u> even in conversational communication. <u>For example,</u> have you ever had a conversation like this? *Signals reassertion.*
Signals example.

Fred: How many Christmas presents do we have left to get?
Wilma: Just a couple. You have any ideas for your brother? I don't remember what we got him last year.
Fred: That reminds me, I forgot to call that woman.
Wilma: Hunh? Should we call Ann and ask her? I always feel like . . . .
Fred: Damn, that makes me mad! Oh, well, he still does a lot of hunting.
Wilma: She remembers *Halloween* even.
Fred: Who?
Wilma: Was it you who told me about that guy who killed one of the six remaining animals of that one species?
Fred: Yeah, but how does *that* relate to Sam's present?

(7) In a conversation like that, the problem is *not* that there's a total lack of structure. Fred's contributions make all kinds of sense to him, and so do Wilma's—to Wilma. *The problem is that the implicit structure is not made explicit.* Fred knows the connections among his own statements, but he doesn't bother to show Wilma those relationships, and Wilma doesn't bother to explain anything to Fred.

(8) For example, when Wilma mentions Fred's brother (Sam), Fred pictures Sam on the job—Sam counsels handicapped children—which reminds Fred that he forgot to call a psychologist he works with—"that *Signals example.*

woman." Wilma hears "that woman" and assumes that Fred is talking about Sam's wife, Ann. Wilma feels uncomfortable around Ann and so begins to say to Fred, "I always feel like . . . " Fred doesn't even hear her. He's thinking that they might get Sam something he can use while hunting; when Wilma hears the word "hunting," she remembers a story Fred told her that she's been wanting to share with a friend, but forgot about until now, and so on.

Signals point.

Signals summary.

(9) The point we're trying to make is that there's structure even in an informal conversation, in the sense that each person's contributions "fit in" or "follow logically" or "make sense"—in short, connect—*for that person*. Problems arise when two (or more) persons' structures don't merge or fit together. Then you get the kind of confusing exchange Fred and Wilma had. You can avoid such confusion by thinking of the other person as unique, as someone who doesn't structure the world or the conversation as you do. Your thought patterns, the connections you see between ideas, are different from his or hers. So if you reveal your thought patterns, if you make them explicit by bringing them to the surface with verbal cues, then the structure of each person's contributions to the conversation becomes apparent to the other, and there will be less room for misinterpretation.

Signals conclusion.
Signals condition.

Signals rephrasing.

(10) In other words, there are ways to structure even informal conversation so that it makes sense. You don't necessarily have to give your conversation a beginning (introduction), middle (body), an end (conclusion). It would sound a little phony if you said to someone in an informal conversation: "Hi, I'm really glad to be talking with you today. As our conversation progresses I'd like to talk about three things: (1) the weather, (2) the movie I saw last night, and (3) our relationship." That kind of organization or structure fits many public speeches, but most people prefer spontaneity in informal conversation.

Signals contrast.

Signals qualification.
Signals rephrasing.
Contrasts conditions.

Signals rephrasing.

(11) Even in an informal conversation, however, you can verbalize the implicit structure, that is, talk about the links you're seeing between ideas. When you don't, you leave open the possibility for all kinds of misinterpretation. When you do, you significantly improve your chances of adequately limiting the range of interpretations, i.e., you improve your chances of "being clear."

This selection is rich with connectors that act as a map to guide the reader from major point to major point, and also as a blueprint of structure even within the sentences themselves. The reader appreciates this wealth of clues, too, even though some of them may not register on the conscious level. In fact, sometimes clues work best when they are so smooth and subtle that the reader doesn't even notice them, but rather takes them for granted. However, by means of such clues the writer's ideas are made to flow smoothly and steadily for the reader. Without the clues, the reader's head bobs from point to point in a hopelessly wobbling fashion.

This essay, with its signals marked in the margins, makes clear exactly how

Stage 3/Completing

these signals work. They *do* help the reader see where the writer is going at all times. And you will probably find that *you* usually put transitions into your own writing quite naturally and automatically, without thinking much about it. Yet sometimes as you're writing, your mind twists, turns, and shifts so fast that you forget to tell the reader where you have gone—or where your're headed. So it is always worthwhile to look over your paper to check if the transition signals are there. If they are, you are in good shape (and probably haven't lost much time in checking). If they are not, you can provide a thoughtful service—a courtesy—for your reader by inserting enough transition signal words so that the reader will always know exactly where you are going.

TRANSITION SIGNAL WORDS

Here is a short list of words and phrases mainly used to indicate relationships between one piece of writing and another. (Although there are many such words and phrases, this is a fairly illustrative list.)

TRANSITION SIGNAL WORDS	MEANING
for example, for instance, e.g.	"Here's an example of that principle or generalization."
because, consequently, since, therefore	"This caused that, or is a reason for that."
in other words, that is, so, i.e.	"Here is a restatement or a clarification."
but, however, on the other hand, yet, nevertheless, on the contrary	"This is different from that."
similarly, likewise, in the same manner, in the same way	"This is similar to that."
also, too, in addition, and, furthermore, moreover	"Here comes another one, just like the other one."
first, next, then, last, before, prior, subsequently, earlier, later	"These exist in time relationship."
aboard, above, beyond, on top of, under, alongside, upon, beneath, to the left	"These are related in space."
finally, at last, after all, in conclusion, to conclude, to sum up	"This wraps it up. The end is in sight."

Transitions and Reminder Signs

REMINDER SIGNS

> "The labor of writing and rewriting, correcting and re-correcting, is the due exacted by every good book from its author. . . . The easily flowing connection of sentence with sentence and paragraph with paragraph has always been won by the sweat of the brow."
> —G. M. Trevelyan

> "One should not aim at being possible to understand, but at being impossible to misunderstand."—Quintilian

People generally have a short memory of what they read. Since we have considered this aspect of the message in the *Creating* and *Shaping* stages, what bearing has this for us in the *Completing Stage?* Just this: **since a reader will tend to forget the order of the words themselves so easily, you must use reminder signs all along the way in your writing to refresh the reader's memory and to keep your subject clearly visible.**

What are reminder signs in writing? They are simply *key words or phrases repeated throughout the writing.* Sometimes it is the *same* word repeated exactly; other times it is a *variation* of that word, a *synonym* for the word, or a *pronoun* that stands for the word. Here is a paragraph illustrating the principle.

> Leaves fall in an annual cycle, and there is a natural cyclical pattern of normal hair loss on the human head, too. The greatest amount of hair loss occurs in November; the least amount in May. A single hair grows on your head for a little less than three years. Then it rests. After about three months of rest, it falls out and a new hair grows in its place in the same hair follicle, and the cycle begins again. This is the end of that resting period for old hair, so you can expect heavier accumulations than usual in your brush and comb. Up to one hundred hairs a day may fall out in the normal course of things, but healthy new hairs are growing as you read this. If you suspect that your hair loss is greater than normal, count the hairs that come out in your comb. If the total is higher than one hundred, take measures. See the hairologist at a good salon for treatments.
> —Vidal and Beverly Sassoon

Examining this paragraph, you can see that the key words are *cycle, normal hair loss, rest,* and *one hundred.* These key words are repeated all the way through the paragraph, and the reader is never allowed to forget what the subject is, never is obliged to double back to pick up the thought. In your own writing, you naturally have to beware of sounding monotonous, and so you will want to vary the wording, using pronouns or synonyms. However, you *will* need to do a certain amount of repeating of the main word or words in your message if you are going to keep the idea directly before your reader. This may finally—with the transitions—be the most important thing in your writing that causes it to really *flow.* A reader can't move in a straight line toward the goal—your total message—unless all along the way you give reminder signs to help overcome that twenty-second memory risk and to remember exactly what you are talking about at all times.

WHY TO USE TRANSITIONS AND REMINDER SIGNS

1. Your readers forget easily, within twenty seconds.
2. You have a lot of competition for your readers' attention.
3. The best way to keep your readers with you is to keep them moving in a straight line, never causing them to double back to see what you are talking about.

APPLICATION
Transitions and Reminder Signs

1. In the two samples below, find all the *transitions* and *reminder signs*. Underline them and be prepared to explain how they keep the reader moving smoothly through the paragraph and how they keep the subject at the front of the reader's attention.

   A. Shopping around for a car loan is not as much fun as shopping for the car. But just as the savvy shopper checks out several car dealers before that final handshake, he should also check out competing lenders. To help him, the Federal Trade Commission has prepared a handy pocket *Credit Shopping Guide*. It includes tips on borrowing and a series of tables so you can compare the cost of car loans, home improvement loans and mortgages at various interest rates and over different time periods.

   The total finance charge on a loan can depend on where you borrow. Let's say you need $3,000 for three years to buy a new car. If you finance it through the car dealer, where the average annual percentage rate—the true rate of interest—is 13½%, that $3,000 loan is likely to cost you $665. But if you go to a bank, where the average rate is 11%, the loan may cost $536; and if you can borrow against your life insurance, the rate will average 6%—for a cost of $286. . . .

   To get a copy of the free credit guide, write the Public Reference Branch, Federal Trade Commission, Washington, D.C. 20580.
   —from "A Pocket Borrowing Guide," *Money Magazine*, May, 1979.

   B. Samuel Johnson has fascinated more people than any other writer except Shakespeare. Statesmen, lawyers, and physicians quote him, as do writers and scientists, philosophers and farmers, manufacturers and leaders of labor unions. For generations people have been discovering new details about him and reexamining and correcting old ones. Interest in Johnson is by no means confined to the English-speaking world, though naturally it is strongest there. In Asia, Africa, and South America, groups of Johnsonians meet every year to talk about every aspect of him. The reason why Johnson has always fascinated so many people of different kinds is not simply that Johnson is so vividly picturesque and quotable, though these are the qualities that first catch our attention. The deeper secret of his hypnotic attraction, especially during our own generation, lies in the immense reassurance he gives to human nature, which needs—and quickly begins to value—every friend it can get.
   —Walter Jackson Bate, *Samuel Johnson,* 1979, p. 3.

2. Look over your essay now to see if you have given the reader enough transitions and reminder signs. If not, reword some of the sentences to allow you to repeat the key words from a previous sentence early in the next sentences to be sure that you take the reader along with you.

Checking Your Writing for Flow: Transitions and Reminder Signs

WRITING ASSIGNMENT: THE EVALUATION ESSAY

"This car isn't running as fast as it did before the tune up."
"That was really a good concert."
"The price of real estate in this town is too high."
"That book isn't worth reading."
"She may be the best president we have ever had."

TO EVALUATE:
To determine or set the value of; to estimate the nature, quality, or importance of; to determine the worth of.

A hundred times a day we evaluate things around us, determining their value, quality, importance, or worth. The presence of some kind of standard against which the thing being measured is judged is what distinguishes evaluative writing. Sometimes these standards are *external:* this blender is better than those because *(a)* it has a stronger motor, *(b)* it is easier to wash, and *(c)* it has an unbreakable glass bowl. These features can be observed by everyone who wants to check on them and are external to the person writing the evaluation. The only thing the evaluator is taking for granted is that the reader agrees that stronger motors, easy washability, and unbreakable glass bowls are more desirable.

In other kinds of evaluative writing, the standards the writer uses for judging are *internal:* this book isn't worth reading because *(a)* there is too much description, *(b)* the main character is unattractive, and *(c)* the plot has too many angles. In a case like this, the writer cannot assume that the reader will necessarily agree that a lot of description is bad, that a particular kind of person is unattractive, or that a complicated plot is not desirable. The evaluation is based on the internal standards of the writer, standards which may or may not be the same as the readers'. (Usually, we like an evaluation more quickly if the writer has the same standards we do. One of the finest ways to broaden oneself, however, is to read evaluative writing done by people who think very differently.) The use of internal criteria for judging assumes that the writer has some special expertise, knowledge, experience, or the like to merit being listened to. One of the first things readers want to know when they read an evaluation is, "What are the writer's qualifications?" Any person using internal criteria, then, runs a greater risk of disagreement and can only counteract this by making very clear and convincing to the reader why her or his personal standards should prevail.

A good evaluation will always make very clear *(a)* what the criteria for the evaluation are and *(b)* whether these standards against which the thing is being judged are *external* (capable of being checked on or proved) or are *internal* (based on the writer's personal experience, knowledge, view, or the like and not capable of being proved). Whether the criteria are external and objective or internal and subjective, the value in an evaluation essay finally lies in the relationship between the person doing the evaluation and the thing being evaluated. It is this interface or friction between the one doing the judging and the thing being judged that the reader is finally left with, rather than some kind of absolute proof or truth. Even when a writer has used *external* criteria, for example, the human nature of the evaluator still intrudes on the evaluation—how many blenders were tested the day this one was proved best, does the evaluator work for the company whose blender won, do other blenders have outstanding features that are more important than motor strength, washability, or the kind of glass?

There is little use, of course, even to attempt to separate an evaluation from the person doing the evaluation, and it's not even desirable. To do so would be to lose the quality—the variable—that makes evaluations interesting, real, and valuable or not valuable. Instead, when we write (and read) evaluations, we should realize that we are having the opportunity to observe both the person doing the evaluating and the thing being evaluated. We can't avoid learning about both.

A good evaluation essay will have these characteristics:

1. The criteria used will be clear to the reader.
2. The writer will explain how these criteria are appropriate to be used in the evaluation unless she or he can assume that the reader will automatically know.
3. The nature of the criteria—whether they are internal or external—will be established early in the essay.
4. The writer's qualifications for doing the evaluation will be apparent to the reader.
5. The writer will give ample facts, specific details, or examples to support the final judgment made in the evaluation.

1. CONTEXTS

Choose one of the following contexts for the basis of your essay, or make up a context for yourself.

A. You have been invited to be the guest reviewer (book, music, dance, food, or film) for the local newspaper while the regular reviewer goes on vacation. This delights you because you have been wanting to see a variety of types of _____ reviewed, and you welcome the chance to see your own standards and preferences reflected on the review page. The editor has just called to say the first review is due Tuesday. Write the essay that will put *you* in the public eye!

B. You have just heard from your brother, who lives in another state. He is shopping for a new car and wants your advice: what kind of car should he buy? You have a very decided opinion that a _____ is the best car on the market for his purposes and you sit down to write him an evaluation of this car.

C. You are president of an organization and in this capacity must serve on a national committee which selects the next site of the annual convention of the club. You and the group have now visited over a half dozen possible sites for the convention, and each of you has been asked to narrow your choices down to two. You must write an evaluation of these two cities to give to the chair of the committee who will do a composite report that the whole membership will vote on. Write the evaluation of the two cities that you liked best as possible places for the organization to meet, emphasizing the advantages and disadvantages of each.

D. A very good music group is coming to your college. Unfortunately, many of the students do not know much about them. You have been asked to write an evaluation of the group, highlighting their history, accomplishments, strong points, etc., for the school paper. You want to inform people about the group so that more will come to see them.

E. You belong to a lively young adults group that even has its own monthly newsletter. One of the columns in the newsletter is called "Personal Finance," and the editor has asked you to write a piece for the next issue to be used in the column. You have been asked to evaluate the good and bad aspects of renting an apartment and buying a house. Since you have done both—in fact, had pleasant experiences both renting and owning—you are a good choice to give a balanced evaluation. You look forward to writing the essay.

2. CREATING

Once you have decided upon the context for your evaluation essay, the creating stage will follow very naturally. A creating technique many writers find especially useful when they evaluate is the simple *list*. For instance, one person writing on Context C made a list early in her creating stage that looked like this:

POSSIBLE CONVENTION SITES

NEW ORLEANS	SANTA FE
great food	Old-World atmosphere
distinct Cajun culture	few hotels
many hotels	wonderful distinctive New Mexico food
high prices	
Mississippi River	great opera
Dixieland jazz	Chimayo weaving nearby
French Market	much fascinating history
great shopping	breathtaking scenery
Bourbon Street	unbelievable light
hard to get around in car because of traffic	not easily accessible by air
	pueblos nearby
easy to get to by air	very high quality arts and crafts available
plantations nearby	

The writer then decided to *loop* the two cities, too, just to be sure she had thought of every advantage and disadvantage that she wanted to include in the evaluation.

As you certainly know by this time, there is no right or wrong way to get ideas on your subject. The important thing is that you set aside time to do the *Creating Stage,* a time when you feel absolutely free to go wherever your mind takes you as you write.

---

3. SHAPING

A. As you move in doing the evaluation essay from private writing in the *Creating Stage* to public writing in the *Shaping Stage,* you need to be very conscious of some specific requirements of evaluative writing:

1. Be sure to let the reader know immediately what criteria you are using in making the evaluation.
2. Be sure that your criteria are fair, logical, and consistent.
3. If you have many criteria that you could choose among, pick those most likely to convince the specific readers for whom you are writing.
4. Let the reader know your qualifications for making the evaluation.
5. Use *many* details, facts, and examples to support your evaluation.

B. By now you are familiar with the various requirements of the *Shaping Stage:*

1. Write to a specific audience and treat them like people, not a wall.
2. Write a trial draft.
3. Have a thesis that is (a) clear to the reader, (b) something you are an insider on, (c) a promise that the rest of the essay delivers, (d) something you can be reasonably sure the reader will find valuable.
4. Do a Bare Bones Outline that checks for promise and delivery and for full development.
5. Rewrite the trial draft.

If you follow this progression in your writing and keep these courtesies to the reader always in mind, you will find that at the end of the *Shaping Stage* you will have an essay that actually does communicate exactly what you want to say to another person when you aren't present—the miracle of the pen! And you are the one doing it!

---

4. COMPLETING

A. In this evaluation essay you will have a chance to refine your work in the *Completing Stage* by checking to see if all your Topic Sentence Paragraphs are fully developed, if you have used Function Paragraphs for drama, emphasis, transition, and so forth and if you have clearly tied the paragraphs together with transition and signal words so that the writing flows for the reader smoothly and effortlessly.

B. When you have revised the essay for flow, put it in the best possible form—check the spelling, punctuation, any typos, correctness—and present it to your readers with a feeling of pride.

REVISING FOR ENERGY: SENTENCES

If you have ever heard the old saying "Where there's life, there's hope," it may just occur to you that the converse of that statement is usually true, too—and particularly when it comes to writing. If the writing has no life, there's little hope for it. A reader will react to dead writing the same way a bird will react to a bug that's playing dead—nose it around a bit, this way and that, then get bored, discouraged, and finally go off and leave it. But if there is some *life* in what you write, then there is real hope that the reader will stick with you long enough to get the message.

What makes writing have *life*? What can you do to be sure there is a lot of *energy* in what you put on the page?

When you are reading really *energetic* writing, you don't think, "Oh, look! There is energy here because the writer has done such-and-such!" You simply respond to the energy without even thinking. What is true, however, is that the writer did several things in the *Completing Stage* to make sure that you, the reader, felt the energy. Of course, sometimes the writing may have energy from the very beginning because the writer was *excited* about the subject; more often than not, though, the writer *revises* to put *energy* into the paper. It's like adding a few ounces of kerosene to a fire you have laid in the fireplace. You wad up the paper, then arrange the kindling, then the logs. When it's all tidy and ready to go, *then* you put on the kerosene, and light it. There's plenty of energy in the paper, kindling, and wood—but that extra little bit of kerosene makes it all take off.

Now—how can you put energy into your writing?

Here are two suggestions:

1. Give the reader a *variety* of kinds of sentences.
2. Combine sentences to make your main points shout out loud and your supporting points hum in the background.

   In other words, develop a little style.

MAKING VARIETY HAPPEN IN YOUR SENTENCES

Variety is the key to good writing. An essay chock full of similarly long sentences isn't any more interesting than an essay full of short, choppy ones. *Chu-whuffety, chu-whuffety, chu-whuffety* is about as monotonous as *thump, thump, thump.* Variation, the feel for change of movement and pace, a sense of when to spin it out and when to make it short and punchy—these are what make up *variety* and *style*.

Let's now take a closer look at the patterns you can experiment with as you revise for energy. You will want to get the hang of them, the knack of knowing when and how to couple or uncouple them, to develop a feel for the impact and effect of this kind over that kind. In short, you want to learn the techniques for producing *energy* in your writing.

Linguists tell us that basic English sentence patterns are few and simple, like these:

    Cows eat.
    Cows eat grass.
    Grass is green.

We rarely use such simple patterns in regular conversation or writing. Our "real" sentences are longer—they carry more information. We vary the basic patterns and add information to them through a process called *expansion*, adding single words or groups of words here and there.

This is an example of such an expansion:

 John has a job.

 Finally, John has a job.

 After three months of hunting, John has a job.

 John has a job after three months of hunting.

 Although he spent three months looking, John finally has a job.

When you are revising for energy in your writing, check to see if you use the simple patterns over and over again. If you do, you can probably count on your readers getting bored. *Give them some variety.* Begin sometimes with the end of the sentence first. At other times, start with a single phrase or a word and then put the main subject and verb of the sentence. You don't actually have to know a lot of terminology to do this (though knowing the names of the grammatical parts of the sentence will help you master sentence-combining for variety, and these are discussed in the Handbook). For now, however, during this *Completing Stage* of the writing process, you can vary your sentences by modeling the variations after some of the ones that follow even if you don't know the formal names for the parts of the sentence you are moving about. Take a simple, basic sentence like:

    Green peppers are good in spaghetti sauce.

Now look at the variations you can make of this basic pattern:

 To make really good spaghetti sauce, you should add green peppers.

 With green peppers added, spaghetti sauce is much better.

 By adding green peppers, you can really make good spaghetti sauce.

 Spaghetti is better with green peppers in the sauce.

 Those green peppers which have been added make this spaghetti sauce
  better.

The spaghetti sauce, with green peppers added, is better.

The spaghetti sauce, which has had green peppers added to it, is better.

Just for practice, see how many variations you can make of this sentence:

A grocery list aids shopping.

You can even make a kind of game out of seeing how many ways you can write a sentence—sometimes just by moving one word.

ONLY I saw Howard Smith in the morning.

I ONLY saw Howard Smith in the morning.

I saw ONLY Howard Smith in the morning.

I saw Howard Smith ONLY in the morning.

I saw Howard Smith in the morning ONLY.

Each shift produces a slight variation. By making a game of it and keeping alert for the various implications of each combination, you can enjoy revising your sentences for energy, and maybe even have fun. The bonus for you, besides an increased mastery of sentence varieties, is that you'll have gained a technique for helping the reader stay interested and stick with you all the way to the end of the paper.

APPLICATION
VARIETY

Rewrite the sentences in the following paragraph with the aim of improving variety in sentence patterns.

It was the last track meet of the season. The state championship. I was going to long jump and run the mile relay. Now the long jump is the first event at any track meet, so I got there early. The long jump started at 10:00 and went on until 12:30. Then the mile relay was at 5:00. I got to the field at about 8:30. I ran around the track four times to loosen up and stretch out. All this took about an hour. By 9:30 the stands were packed, and that's when this terrible nervousness hit me. I realized that over 2,000 people would be watching me as I would run down the runway and take my jump. I got a cold sweat; my entire body was shaking worse than jello in an earthquake. Then everyone started giving orders at once. My two other teammates were telling me what to do and what not to do. The official was telling me to get ready to jump. My coach was yelling at me to get a good jump the first time, and the crowd in the stands was going crazy because we were about to start. As I stepped out onto the runway, my entire mind and body went blank. I couldn't see anything or anybody except the long jump pit 104′ 6″ down the runway. My head was pounding, and all I could hear was the blood rushing through my body. I waited a second, said a little prayer and took off. It felt like I was moving in slow motion. My legs felt like lead weights. My arms didn't want to move the right way, and I thought I'd never get to the end of the runway to the take-off board. Finally, I saw it closing in on me.

SENTENCE COMBINING

One principle that will handle both suggestions for giving your writing more life is **Sentence Combining.** When you have caught on to the trick of this technique, you will be able to handle (1) giving the reader a variety of kinds of sentences and (2) giving the reader a way to distinguish more important from less important information.

One of the reasons you need variety in the kinds of sentences you write is to keep from sounding simple and monotonous. Here is a passage from a third-grade reader that really shows how sentences that are too short and choppy give the reader an impression that most adults wouldn't want to create:

> Most of the ways to turn salt water into fresh water cost a lot of money. The Symi factory on an island in Greece uses a way that costs very little.
>
> Right in the middle of the town are some long ponds. They are only a few inches deep. The men of Symi dug out earth to make the ponds.
>
> Over each pond is a low tent. It is made of plastic that you can see through.
>
> At night, sea water is pumped into the ponds. The next day, the hot sun shines through the tents. The sun's heat turns the water into vapor that rises from the ponds. The salt is left behind.

Of course, the very short paragraphs and the very simple vocabulary also contribute to the too-simple effect. But it is the repetition of sentence after sentence, each in the same pattern, each containing only a single unit of information, which makes that passage sound so childlike, immature, and undeveloped. The deadness, for adult readers, comes from dragging on and on through sentence after sentence, picking up only one lifeless bit of message per sentence. Combining those informational bits into longer, more varied sentences, would make them much more attractive and effective.

Now look at this passage from a college-level government book:

> John F. Kennedy's assassination on November 21, 1963, probably evoked—in the period that followed his death—greater feeling on the part of more people than the death of any other American. His assassination was as close to formal tragedy as is conceivable in a democracy. Kennedy had all the attributes of a hero: power, prestige, presence, the heroism of the warrior, affability, social standing, youth, physical attraction, religious belief, and wealth. He embodied all of these qualities with a special grace, and his death seemed associated with the death of youth in America. —Theodore Gross

By comparing this passage with the earlier one, you can see immediately the effect of short, simple sentences and the effect of longer, more varied sentences. The short little sentences are perfect for the third graders in elementary school, but unless that is your audience, you may insult your readers with sentences that sound as though they were written for eight-year-olds. The more you combine short, simple sentences together, the more sophisticated your

---

SENTENCE COMBINING:
(1) Handling variety;
(2) Highlighting importance

ENERGY
Vigor or power in action; vitality and intensity of expression; the capacity for action or accomplishment; power exercised with vigor and determination.

Sentence Combining

Oh, oh, Dick!
Oh, oh, Jane!
Oh, oh, *Phooey*!

writing seems to the reader—and the more information units the reader gets per sentence, too—which really facilitates communication by making it seem effortless. For example, take these two sentences:

Over each pond is a low tent.

It is made of plastic that you can see through.

Each one offers a niggling bit of information, yet the reader has to come to a complete stop at the end of each, and do all the work a reader does in beginning and ending sentences. However, *combining* them allows the information to come together in a neat and orderly way, and the reader is spared much unnecessary effort:

Over each pond is a low plastic tent that you can see through.

What's happened? You've produced some variation on that same dreary repeated sentence pattern, *and* you've shown what really *is* important—*that there is a tent over each pond*. The information about what material the tent is made of is clearly less important, and the combined sentence helps the reader to keep clear what's important and what isn't.

APPLICATION
CHOPPY SENTENCES

1. Rewrite the following paragraphs combining short, simple sentences to make the writing sound more mature.

    I was fortunate enough to be able to travel to Europe during my senior year in high school. We went during our spring break, March 17–26. The travelers consisted of eighteen students and two teachers. We traveled in a group known as the American Leadership Study Group.

    There was question of whether or not I would be able to go. During the Christmas holidays we had a family reunion. My parents asked me if I wanted to go on the European trip. I said no immediately because I thought it was out of the question. The trip was too expensive. I began thinking about the trip more and more, and I finally decided I wanted to go. I had done quite a bit of baby-sitting and saved the money.

    We proceeded to find out more information about the trip. My mother and I thought the only obstacle would be getting the passport in time. However, my teacher told me there was a waiting list for the trip. He told me he was an area representative for ALSG and that a friend of his owed him a favor. That information lifted our spirits. I would probably be first on the waiting list.

    My mother and I went to the post office to apply for a passport. We learned that we could receive a passport very quickly if we paid an extra fee. We paid the fee and received the passport in a week.

For your own writing

2. The first application of the sentence-combining principle, then, is to examine your paper to see if you have so many short, simple sentences that it sounds as though you were writing for children. If that's what you find, put some of those little dinky ones into longer, more sophisticated forms.

COMBINING FOR EMPHASIS

After you have revised and combined your sentences for variety to get more energy into your writing, you need to look at them to see if you have put, right up front, the information that you think is most important. One of the most valuable uses of sentence-combining is to let you show the reader what you want him or her to see, without seeming obvious about this at all. That is a better way than just saying, "What's important to me is . . ." As we saw, two sentences can be combined into one:

Over each pond is a low tent.

It is made of plastic that you can see through.

can become

Over each pond is a low, clear plastic tent.

And the result of the combining is not only sleeker and more adult-sounding, but it also combines the elements in a way that shows **what's important** (there's a tent over each pond) **and what's not so important** (the tent is made of clear plastic). This technique, *combining to show emphasis,* lets you control what the reader notices *and* lets you highlight the important thoughts efficiently and energetically. To see clearly how to combine sentences for the best emphasis, you'll need to consult two words:

COORDINATE and SUBORDINATE

These Latinate words may not immediately ring a bell, but understanding *coordinate* and *subordinate* will help you considerably in getting energy in your writing. Once you have the idea each term represents, you will extend your mastery as a writer to a considerable degree.

Coordinate you can associate with co-partner or co-worker, someone you are on an equal basis with, someone in the same position as you. *Subordinate* you can associate with subfloor or a substitute player in a ballgame—not the main one; somewhat less important than the main players. It may also help to know that the roots are from the Latin *sub-,* "below," *co-,* "equal," and *ordinare,* "to arrange in order." Thus *subordinate* is in the "lower order" and *coordinate* is of an "equal order."

When two sentences in your writing are of equal importance, they are *coordinate*. When the thought in one sentence is more important than the thought in the other, the less important one is *subordinate* to the more important one.

Why do you need to know this?

Because when you are revising for energy and are combining sentences to emphasize what you really want the reader to notice, you will have to think about coordination and subordination, even if you don't use those words.

COORDINATE: EQUAL
copartner
coworker
co-owner

SUBORDINATE: SECONDARY
subfloor
substitute
subcommittee

Coordination

Coordination—*linking together words, groups of words, or sentences of equal type and importance*—puts energy into your writing. Look at how this works:

Two subjects are supposed to be the hardest for freshmen.

One is math.

The other is English.

Linking the two **words** *math* and *English* makes perfect sense—they have equal value in the sentence: they are "of equal hardness for freshmen." That can be crisply expressed in this combination:

Math and English are supposed to be the hardest subjects for freshmen.

And that handles it. Here is the way sentence combining works with **phrases:**

He spent the evening typing his essay.

He also spent the evening studying for his chemistry test.

Linking the two phrases, *typing his essay* and *studying for his chemistry test,* cuts out a lot of extra words and suggests that his evening was spent fairly evenly divided between the typing and the studying.

He spent the evening *typing his essay* and *studying for his chemistry test.*

The same principle works for **clauses,** too.

John went to the concert for two reasons.

One reason was that he had nothing else to do.

Another reason was that he had sort of promised his sister he would go.

Look at the streamlining sentence combining gives to this example:

Since he had nothing else to do and *since he had sort of promised his sister that he would go,* John went to the concert.

You can also combine whole **sentences.**

I had planned to spend the afternoon in the library.

I took a nap instead.

I had planned to spend the afternoon in the library, but *I took a nap instead.*

COORDINATING CONJUNCTIONS
and   for   so
or   but   yet
nor

Adding the word *but* allows the reader to move more quickly through the information and makes the two sentences one thought. Coordination in your writing does two things:

1. By combining words and groups of words, you avoid the monotonous repetition that steals energy from what you say;
2. By combining whole sentences you reveal the relationship between the thoughts.

When sentences are joined together by a conjunction that shows that the sentences are equal, the reader knows that one sentence is as important as the other. This example will make it perfectly clear.

Stage 3/Completing

Here are two sentences:

John doesn't plan to go to college.

He believes that experience in the working world is more valuable than an academic degree.

Looking at them, we can infer that the second sentence is somehow related to the first, but we have to produce the inference in our own imaginations—the writer gives no clues, merely sets forth two sentences, period. But look what happens when the sentences are linked in a way that shows, explicitly, exactly how the two items relate to each other:

John doesn't plan to go to college, *for* he believes that experience in the working world is more valuable than an academic degree.

In the combined form, you know that the second sentence explains the first, *and* that the two ideas are of equal importance to understanding the writer's message.

APPLICATION
COORDINATION

Rewrite the following groups of sentences using coordination to link clauses, phrases, and words.

1. Many times cooking for a crowd can be fun.
   It can be expensive.
   It can be time-consuming.
   It can be frustrating.
2. Americans constantly criticize their leaders.
   They don't make an effort to vote in national elections.
   They forget to vote in local elections.
3. The energy crisis has made many people seriously consider their driving habits.
   Many people have bought smaller cars that use less gas.
   Many people are doing more walking and bicycling.
4. John had to make a decision about the summer.
   He could go to the local junior college and gain some extra hours toward his degree.
   He could work full-time for his uncle's construction firm.
5. Wearing clothes that are in style is very important to some people.
   Others don't seem at all concerned about their appearance.
   They wear jeans and T-shirts everywhere.
6. Everywhere you look you see people jogging.
   You see people walking.
   You see people climbing stairs instead of riding the elevator.
   More and more people are growing conscious of the importance of good health.

Combining for Emphasis

Subordination

COORDINATION:
All parts are created equal.

SUBORDINATION:
Some parts are more equal than others.

Using *coordination* is like setting up a democracy, with everybody having an equal vote in the matter. *Subordination,* though, is more like a monarchy, and royalty matter more than commoners in that system. Subordination puts energy in your writing by clearly emphasizing what is important and by displaying that importance in a way that the reader picks up clearly, promptly, without any doubt or wondering.

How, exactly, can subordination work for you? It's not at all complicated, actually, and in fact you already use it quite naturally. The point here is just to become aware of it, so that you can use it intentionally during Stage 3 to improve what may have been a less conscious version of your writing in Stage 1 or Stage 2. Here's an example:

We were unable to go to the show last night.

The car wouldn't start.

Both are equal, and they don't seem related (although a kind-hearted, imaginative, generous reader might be willing to invent or create an inference that the second sentence caused the first). Subordination sets matters straight:

We were unable to go to the show *because* the car wouldn't start.

Superficially, it seems that little has happened; *because* was added—not a big deal. But you can see that coupling the two sentences and using *because* shows that the second sentence wouldn't be very important if it weren't for the first one. *The car wouldn't start.* Well, what of it? *Because the car wouldn't start, we were unable to go to the show.* So there was a *consequence!* By linking the two sentences and showing how they relate to each other—how one part *causes* the other part—the writer saves the reader from having to process the relationship. And it provides energy in the writing because the *writer* has handled it already for the reader. The reader is spared the necessity for wondering and puzzling and imagining and creating the relationship—there's nothing at all to do but to *get the message*. And the message is *already* in motion.

SAVE ENERGY: Subordinate

SUBORDINATE CONJUNCTIONS
TIME: when, after, whenever, while, before
PLACE: where, wherever
CAUSE: because, since, in order that, so that
CONTRAST: although, though, while
CONDITION: if, unless, since, as long as

Admittedly, this discussion is like watching a movie in slow motion. Actually, the reader skims from word to word and sentence to sentence quite swiftly, and the mind either makes connections or it doesn't, and that happens in fractions of a second. Yet sometimes slow-motion films let us study what passes in a flash, so that we can become very clear about exactly what did happen, and therefore do something differently or more efficiently, as football players do in studying game films to see why the left side of the line didn't give the quarterback any protection on screen pass plays. Incredibly enough, saving the reader those tiny bits of energy and those millisecond decisions can amount to the difference between a reader who is cheerful and enthusiastic about your writing and one who is worn out and half-hearted about it. Give the reader that sense of complete clarity and certainty, instant-to-instant-to-instant. A word as simple as *because* could do the trick alone.

Rewrite the following groups of sentences using subordination wherever possible.

APPLICATION
SUBORDINATION

1. Mary hates housecleaning.
   She claims she's basically a neat person.

2. You can chop the vegetables for the stew.
   I can brown the meat and prepare the gravy.

3. The rain may stop soon.
   We may have to cancel the picnic scheduled for tomorrow.

4. Most people seem willing to cut down on their use of electricity, gas, and heating fuels.
   They don't want energy conservation to interfere with their established lifestyles.

5. We spent the afternoon in the library working on our history project.
   We all went out for pizza.

6. Old movies seem to get more popular every year.
   They offer plot and drama that modern movies often lack.

GETTING ENERGY THROUGH STYLE

Anybody who has ever heard Aretha Franklin or Janice Joplin sing knows that rhythm produces energy. The same thing is true of writing. One kind of rhythm, in speech and writing, is *Parallelism*. You've heard it much of your life and probably already use it in your writing, but you may not be consciously aware of it. It is almost fascinating to see how it works, psychologically: setting up a reader's or a listener's expectations, then satisfying those expectations—a kind of suspense and conclusion, tension and release. Becoming aware of this kind of rhythm and learning how to put it into your own writing, you will master a good bit of style and will control a source of energy and vigor of the sort that has even moved nations!

PARALLELISM:
a kind of rhythm

PARALLELISM

Using parallelism as a rhythm-making, energy-producing technique in your writing works because of ever-present factors: *the reader's sense of order* and *the reader's demand for fulfillment of expectations* (balance and delivery).

Let's examine some parallel sentences written by Mary McCarthy to see what we can discover about *order* and *expectation/fulfillment:*

> Sheridan was then about six years old, and this [tin] butterfly immediately became his most cherished possession—indeed, one of the few he had. He carried it about the house with him all the next week clutched in his hand or pinned to his shirt, and my other two brothers followed him, begging him to be allowed to play with it, which slightly disgusted me, at the age of ten, for I knew that I was too sophisticated to care for tin butterflies and I felt in this whole affair the instigation of my uncle.

In the second sentence, the parallelism is in the arranging of the sentence to have neatly recurring patterns or parts:

> He carried it about the house with him all the next week
> > *clutched in his hand*
> > or
> > *pinned to his shirt,*
>
> and my other two brothers followed him, begging him to be allowed to play with it, which slightly disgusted me, at the age of ten,
> > for
> > > *I knew* that I was too sophisticated to care for tin butterflies
> > and
> > > *I felt* in this whole affair the instigation of my uncle.

The effect of parallelism can be *swift* and *punchy,* as in this sentence by Malcolm X:

> In those days only three things in the world scared me: *jail, a job, and the army.*

John F. Kennedy used parallelism frequently, too, as in this speech delivered at the University of North Carolina in 1961:

> Our policy must blend whatever degree of firmness and flexibility is necessary to protect our vital interests, <u>by peaceful means if possible, by resolute action if necessary</u>. . . . While <u>we do not intend</u> to see the free world give up, <u>we shall make every effort to prevent</u> the world from being blown up.

And Lincoln, in the Gettysburg Address, managed in few words to produce writing so resonant and enduring that readers are shocked again and again to discover that the entire address is only 266 words long. In fact, the main speaker of the occasion was Edward Everett, who later wrote to Lincoln, "I should be glad if I could flatter myself that I came as near to the central idea of the occasion in two hours as you did in two minutes." The whole piece contains only three paragraphs. It is the last that is so full of parallelisms and so richly enduring:

> But, in a larger sense, we cannot dedicate—we cannot consecrate—we cannot hallow—this ground. The brave men, living and dead, who struggled here, have consecrated it far above our poor power to add or detract. The world will little note nor long remember what we say here, but it can never forget what they did here. It is for us, the living, rather, to be dedicated here to the unfinished work which they who fought here have thus far so nobly advanced. It is rather for us to be here dedicated to the great task remaining before us—that from these honored dead we take increased devotion to that cause for which they gave the last full measure of devotion; that we here highly resolve that these dead shall not have died in vain; that this nation, under God, shall have a new birth of freedom; and that government of the people, by the people, for the people, shall not perish from the earth.

Whether in the speech of presidents or prime ministers, or in the musings about a child's toy, parallelism moves with a kind of stately force. For one thing, since the human mind responds to rhythm and order, the reader automatically responds to the rhythmic repetition of the parallel parts of sentences. Readers get started with the particular structured order you set up in the first piece, then just move on with you quickly and satisfactorily through the second, and even third, parallel constructions. You have also set up an expectation for the reader, at least by the second parallel item, and by continuing with that particular pattern you are fulfilling the reader's subconscious expectations and giving pleasure, even though the reader may not actually know why.

Parallelism can certainly supply your reader with a sense of order. If you start off a list of things, and move from one kind of construction to another, you'll surely interrupt the expected pattern, the flow, and the energy. So check to see whether your own writing is structured with sequences, and if it is, **be sure they're developed in the same kinds of grammatical patterns.** Keeping a series of things in the same kind of construction will contribute immeasurably to the clarity and energy that the reader gets from you.

Next, check to see whether you may have used *too much* parallelism. Because parallelism tends to be elegant and formal, a little will contribute some class and style to your writing, but too much of it makes everything you say sound like a proclamation, whether you are commemorating the birth of a nation or simply calling the kids in to dinner. As you revise your writing for energy, insert parallelisms where they will really work for you, but *don't overformalize everything.* Used appropriately, parallel constructions work beautifully to add style, rhythm, and clarity to your writing—and that results in energy for your reader.

PARALLEL: having comparable parts, readily recognized similarities; having the same tendency or direction; moving consistently by the same intervals; near similarity or exact agreement in particulars.

APPLICATION
PARALLELISM

1. Transform each group of sentences below into a sentence that contains parallel elements.

    A. My grandmother bakes cookies and cakes for all of our birthdays.
       She rides horses.
       She gardens.
       She models.
       My grandmother is a remarkable woman.

    B. Studying requires determination.
       It frequently means sacrificing fun times.
       To study effectively, you must have a serious attitude toward your education.

    C. A good teacher is someone who thinks of each student as a person.
       He is willing to spend additional hours at school to counsel troubled students.
       He doesn't care if class discussions veer toward a relevant topic not scheduled for discussion.

    D. Walking whenever possible shows that a person is concerned with good health.
       Exercising regularly shows a concern with good health.
       Watching the kinds of foods you eat is important if you want to be healthy.

    E. I expected to feel independent when I moved away from home to go to college.
       I knew I would enjoy making my own rules.
       I expected to feel grown-up about paying my own bills.

2. Identify all the instances of parallelism in this passage by Norman Mailer.

    But what will America look like? How will its architecture appear? Will it be the architecture of a Great Society, or continue to be the architecture of an empty promiscuous panorama where no one can distinguish between hospitals and housing projects, factories and colleges, concert halls, civic centers, and airport terminals? The mind recoils from the thought of an America rebuilt completely in the shape of those blank skyscrapers forty stories high, their walls dead as an empty television screen, their form as interesting as a box of cleansing tissue propped on end. They are buildings which reveal nothing so much as the deterioration in real value of the dollar bill. They are denuded of ornament (which costs money); their windows are not subtly recessed into the wall but are laid flush with the surface like a patch of collodion on the skin; there is no instant where a roof with a tower, a gable, a spire, a mansard, a ridge or even a mooring mast for a dirigible intrudes itself into the sky, reminding us that every previous culture of man attempted to engage the heavens.

> No, our modern buildings go flat, flat at the top, flat as eternal monotony, flat as the last penny in a dollar. There is so much corruption in the building codes, overinflation in the value of land, featherbedding built into union rules, so much graft, so much waste, so much public relations, and so much emptiness inflated upon so much emptiness that no one tries to do more with the roof than leave it flat.

BALANCE AND REPETITION

Another way to revise for energy through stylistic changes is to use *balance* and *repetition* in some of your sentences. Here is a good example of balance from Bennett Cerf:

> He [Faulkner] saw all of the tragedy of the Old South, but he also saw the humor.

The symmetry isn't quite perfect, but the repetition of "he saw the . . ." gives this short sentence a certain gravity, a touch of sobriety that is appropriate to the message—visions of tragedy and of humor.

Here is another balanced sentence, this time from Abraham Maslow:

> A husband's conviction that his wife is beautiful, or a wife's firm belief that her husband is courageous, to some extent creates the beauty or the courage.

Chances are that if you were simply reading along, you'd go right past it; most people would. Yet closely examined, it's a wonderful sentence. Look how the parts match:

A husband's conviction	that his wife is beautiful,
or a wife's firm belief	that her husband is courageous,
to some extent creates	the beauty or the courage.

Not only do the parts match; the last part also manages to echo the main pieces of the first part: *beauty* and *courage*.

Now that your eyes are sharpened and you know what to look for, examine this longer sentence from Tillie Olsen's *Silences*. Notice particularly how she uses "fortunate are those" to introduce each particular assertion about the kind of environment that encourages rather than stifles talent.

> Fortunate are those of us who are daughters born into knowledgeable, ambitious families where no sons were born; fortunate are those in economic circumstance beyond the basic imperatives, thus affording some choice; fortunate are those in whose lives is another human being "protecting and stimulating the health of highest productivity"; fortunate are those of us to whom encouragement, approval, grants, publication, come at the foundering time before it is too late; fortunate as has been indicated here are those born into the better climates, when a movement has created a special interest in one's sex, or in one's special subject; fortunate are

those who live where relationships, opportunities, not everywhere available are.

You may be saying to yourself "That's all well and good, but I never write sentences like those." Indeed, most people don't write sentences like those—but that doesn't mean that we can't imitate those patterns if we choose to do so. Why not try your hand at imitating Cerf, Maslow, and Olsen? Simply follow their *patterns* and put in your own content. For example, here's a spin-off from Cerf's sentence:

> Grandmother knew all of the work of raising five children, but she also knew the satisfaction.

Simply replace the nouns and verbs with new ones, and keep the structure the same. To get the full benefit from this activity, you should probably do at least five each of the Cerf and Maslow patterns. The Olsen one is so long that you may want to do only two or three of them.

APPLICATION
BALANCE

1. Rewrite each group of sentences below into a single sentence that uses balance.

   A. I don't avoid jogging because I don't like running.
      I refuse to jog because everyone keeps telling me how great it is and that I should do it.

   B. Television can be used wisely as a means of dispersing important information.
      Television can be abused grossly as a source of pointless, unimaginative "entertainment."

   C. A good student knows that diligent studying yields the satisfaction of good grades.
      A poor student can only hope that her half-hearted efforts will get her a passing grade.

   D. To work without praise can be disheartening.
      To strive without results can be discouraging.
      To set a goal and reach it is always revitalizing.

   E. Friendship can be one of the greatest pleasures in life.
      Friendship can be the source of some of life's greatest pains.

2. Pick out the balanced structures in the passage below by Charles Dickens.

   It was the best of times, it was the worst of times, it was the age of wisdom, it was the age of foolishness, it was the epoch of belief, it was the epoch of incredulity, it was the season of Light, it was the season of Darkness, it was the spring of hope, it was the winter of despair, we had everything before us, we had nothing before us, we were all going direct to Heaven, we were all going direct the other way—in short, the period was so far like the present period, that some of its noisiest authorities insisted on its being received, for good or for evil, in the superlative degree of comparison only.

There were a king with a large jaw and a queen with a plain face, on the throne of England; there were a king with a large jaw and a queen with a fair face, on the throne of France. In both countries it was clearer than crystal to the lords of the State preserves of loaves and fishes, that things in general were settled for ever.

REVIEW EXERCISES
IMITATING PATTERNS

Rewrite each group of sentences below as a single sentence that follows Cerf's, Maslow's, or Olsen's patterns.

A. He acknowledged the importance of a college education.
   He recognized his immediate need for a job.

B. A student's response to class discussion contributes to the tone of the class.
   A teacher's encouragement of comments improves the quality of the comments.

C. I knew that planning the party would be a lot of work.
   I knew that everyone was eager to get together.

D. Women born into open-minded families where no stereotypes exist can be considered liberated.
   Those women who are not forced into roles they don't want, who feel free to change and choose their lifestyles, are also liberated.
   Liberated women are encouraged by equally liberated husbands, children, parents, and friends.
   Liberated women have been lucky enough to have been born in this generation, when the world is beginning to recognize the human, intellectual, and economic worth of women.
   Liberated women live in a country which offers them the educational and business opportunities other countries would deny.

E. I enjoyed the weekly paycheck from my first job.
   I enjoyed the responsibility my first job gave me.

REVISING FOR PUNCH: WORDS

Confucius is reported to have stated that if he were made emperor of China, his first official act would be to establish a precise meaning for every word.

You are very near the end of the *Completing Stage* of the writing process. We are now ready for the smallest units in your writing—the *words* themselves. Again, as in all other revising, the process *could* go on and on indefinitely and you could be exchanging this word for that until doomsday. This section will instead suggest just a few main ways you can be sure that your writing will have punch, will hit the reader squarely with its exactness and directness.

EXACTNESS, SPECIFICS, PICTURES, AND IMAGES

There is no doubt that you are writing for a television generation. This means that your readers are visually oriented; they are accustomed to *seeing* a thing instead of *reading* about it. To hold their attention—perhaps even to catch them enough to begin to get your message across—you are going to have to draw pictures for them, pictures in words.

Very likely, these *specific pictures* will be the thing your reader most remembers, so you should in the *Completing Stage* of the writing process make sure that you have many of these *specific pictures, exact references, images* that the reader can remember. Giving your writing power and punch through choice of words can mean the difference between being read and remembered and being read and dismissed.

A favorite for exact words, color, pictures, and images is Woody Guthrie's last book, *Seeds of Man*. You are challenged to read these two passages, the first about cornbread and the second about supper fixings, and then *try* to forget the pictures they'll put into your mind! Here's the first:

"I'll always remember Grandmaw Tanner's good cornbread. Wonder what th' secret was about it."

"Well, Mammy Ollie could dish it up just as good as your grandma Tanner could, any old time. Main secret was that she didn't put any sugar in her batter. Maybe an egg or so, which sometimes she did have and sometimes she didn't have, but anyway, she put in lots of salt and left out the sugar. Said that the sugar made cornbread taste too much like oatmeal cookies. She greased her pan with good hot lard, bacon grease, hog lard, whatever kind of grease she had, and she heated her pan in the oven, or up on the stove before she would pour her doughbatter into the pan. She used a good bit of buttermilk."

"Likkum my slikkum. Starvin' me t' death. Keep on."

Mainest secret, . . .

"Mainest secret, I suppose, was lots of hot lard. And she shoved it into the oven when the oven was scorching hot. And she threw the wood to the fire till she nearly burnt the whole place up, summer, winter, all of the time. She always did say that she had to chase her whole family out from the house before she could bake up good cornbread. But they always came a-running back after a bit when they got the <u>smells of it cooking up their nose holes</u>."

"I 'mem'er. Yeahhhm."

"Always did bake it a long time. Most of us liked it good and <u>curly brown all around the edges</u>. Most of us would fight to get the corner piece, or at least an outside chunk."

"I remember. Me, too."

"I guess this was where I learned how to be such a good fighting hand in the first place. Fighting to get the best piece of Mammy Ollie's cornbread. <u>Browny. Crispish. Real hot</u>."

"Big glass o' buttermilk. Yeahhhmmmannn."

"Big slice of green onion—I mean, dry onion. No wonder that Pawpaw Jerry swung onto Mammy Ollie the way that he did. He always did say that is was her cracklin' bread that brought them together and it was this same bread that kept them together. This same cornbread that kept the whole family fighting and growing all of the time. I can just feel it <u>sticking out of my belly button</u>, here, right this minute. Mmmmm. Mmmm. Mmmm." Papa's face lit up with thoughts he was seeing <u>walk acrost the places of his memory</u>.

"Ymmm."

. . . *smells of it cooking up their nose holes* . . .

. . . *curly brown* . . .

Browny. Crispish. Real hot.

. . . *sticking out of my belly button* . . .

. . . *walk acrost the places of his memory.*

"Ymmm."

If you haven't put this book down yet to go fix yourself a snack, then you might as well read the second of Woody's passages; but you'll *surely* want to eat after this one:

Skinny Mammy beat the bottom of a skillet with her wooden stirring spoon. "Break it up, you harvest hands!" she yelled. "Chow is now on! Red bean a green bean a white bean a flitter, corn bread dry bread a wheat bread fritter! Come get it before I throw it to th' hogs in th' pen! Got ham hock. Got beef steak. Come on! Come on! Slop it up and slip it down. Gotta kiss th' cook or you can't ride to town! Eats! Eats. C'mon git 'em!"

"I'll sign up!" I yelled.

"If you would be kind enough, Skinny, or Hell Cat," Papa said as we staggered up off the floor, "to twist my arm and to force me to eat just a few mouthfuls . . ."

Reenie and Helen filled all of our eating plates high and dry and soupy and droopy and all down dripping and saggling and smoking and moving and running all down over the sides; both of them forked and ladled and spooned and poured the <u>soupy thick cementy concretey stewbrowny hamhockery stuff</u> steamyhot from our cooking pot, and next dropped a big oversized chunk of Skinny's rusty brownish redderish goldedged yellerneck yallerback cornponey rough salty greasy cornmeal bread off down around our plates in the general direction of Skinny's black-eye peas. Both girls filled their own plates as they stood by the table's edge dumping ours full; then, whenever all of ours were ready to be claimstaked and blasted and forked and shoveled and dynamited into, they both grabbed their own burnyhot plates to forkle and gobble them down like hungry hogs.

. . . *the soupy thick cementy concretey stewbrowny hamhockery stuff* . . .

Exactness, Specifics, Pictures, and Images 173

Isn't that fantastic? Can't you just *see* those plates "high and dry and soupy and droopy and . . ." And will you forget the description of that wonderful cornbread? Those onions? Those black-eyed peas? No, the question is not whether you will memorize the words in this passage and be able to recite them. Not at all. The question, is, *did you get a powerful picture, or not?* The answer is most probably, *Yes*. And obviously the words contribute to that magic: "they both grabbed their own burnyhot plates to forkle and gobble them down like hungry hogs."

Here is a short excerpt from George Orwell's "Shooting an Elephant." Even though the passage is brief, it clearly shows the kind of mastery Orwell had in fashioning comparisons that make the picture not only vivid but also unforgettable. The point of the essay is that, for fear of appearing foolish or being laughed at, we often go to extreme lengths and sometimes even allow ourselves to be forced into quite hideous acts. The vivid details in this description assist the reader in *feeling* the message as well as understanding it.

. . . bang . . . kick . . .
. . . devilish roar of glee . . .
. . . mysterious, terrible change . . .
. . . altered . . .

When I pulled the trigger I did not hear the bang or feel the kick—one never does when a shot goes home—but I heard the devilish roar of glee that went up from the crowd. In that instant, in too short a time, one would have thought, even for the bullet to get there, a mysterious, terrible change had come over the elephant. He neither stirred nor fell, but every line of his body had altered. He looked suddenly stricken, shrunken, immensely old, as though the frightful impact of the bullet had paralysed him without knocking him down. At last, after what seemed a

. . . sagged flabbily . . . slobbered . . .
. . . thousands of years old . . .

long time—it might have been five seconds, I dare say—he sagged flabbily to his knees. His mouth slobbered. An enormous senility seemed to have settled upon him. One could have imagined him thousands of years old. I fired again into the same spot. At the second shot he did not collapse but climbed with desperate slowness to his feet and stood weakly upright, with legs sagging and head drooping. I fired a third time. That

. . . agony . . . jolt . . . remnant . . .

was the shot that did for him. You could see the agony of it jolt his whole body and knock the last remnant of strength from his legs. But in falling he seemed for a moment to rise, for as his hind legs collapsed beneath him he seemed to tower upwards like a huge rock toppling, his trunk reaching skywards like a tree. He trumpeted, for the first and only time. And then down he came, his belly towards me, with a crash that seemed to shake the ground even where I lay.

. . . not dead . . . rattling gasps . . .
. . . caverns of pale pink . . .
. . . red velvet . . .

I got up. The Burmans were already racing past me across the mud. It was obvious that the elephant would never rise again, but he was not dead. He was breathing very rhythmically with long rattling gasps, his great mound of a side painfully rising and falling. His mouth was wide open—I could see far down into caverns of pale pink throat. I waited a long time for him to die, but his breathing did not weaken. Finally I fired my two remaining shots into the spot where I thought his heart must be. The thick blood welled out of him like red velvet, but still he did not die. His body did not even jerk when the shots hit him, the tortured breathing continued without a pause. He was dying, very slowly and in great agony, but in some world remote from me where not even a bullet could damage him further. I felt that I had got to put an end to that dreadful noise. It seemed dreadful to see the great beast lying there, powerless to move and yet powerless to die, and not even to be able to finish him. I sent back for my small rifle and poured shot after shot into his heart and down his throat. They seemed to make no impression. The tortured gasps continued as steadily as the ticking of a clock.

. . . *remote* . . .

. . . *no impression* . . .
. . . *ticking of a clock* . . .

Here's a final excerpt, taken from "Who Killed King Kong?" by X. J. Kennedy:

> Intentionally or not, the producers of *King Kong* encourage this identification by etching the character of Kong with keen sympathy. For the ape is a figure in a tradition familiar to moviegoers: the tradition of the pitiable monster. We think of Lon Chaney in the role of Quasimodo, of Karloff in the original *Frankenstein*. As we watch the Frankenstein monster's fumbling and disastrous attempts to befriend a flower-picking child, our sympathies are enlisted with the monster in his impenetrable loneliness. And so with Kong. As he roars in his chains, while barkers sell tickets to boobs who gape at him, we perhaps feel something more deep than pathos. We begin to sense something of the problem that engaged Eugene O'Neill in *The Hairy Ape:* the dilemma of a displaced animal spirit forced to live in a jungle built by machines.

. . . *etching* . . .

. . . *pitiable monster* . . .
. . . *fumbling and disastrous* . . .
. . . *impenetrable loneliness* . . .
. . . *boobs* . . . *gape* . . .
. . . *pathos* . . .

All these samples show writers who are superb at drawing pictures for the reader. Whether it is a rather intellectual essay, like Kennedy's on King Kong, or a rough-and-tumble lark like Guthrie's, or a multilevel description like Orwell's, the principle remains the same. **They all use specific, concrete words, and they use them vigorously to draw pictures for the reader.**

Getting *punch* in your writing probably comes down to three simple things:

1. Replace vague, general words with specific, exact words;
2. Cut out every word you don't absolutely need;
3. Use action verbs.

These three will just about do it. If you revise your words with these principles in mind, you will have *power* and *punch* in your writing. Here are some specific examples that illustrate the three principles:

REPLACE VAGUE WORDS WITH SPECIFIC, CONCRETE WORDS

Look at the differences in these pairs of sentences:

VAGUE: The landscape is very varied.
SPECIFIC: The landscape changes from high, old mountains in the east to flat, horse-raising country in the middle to river-bottom delta land in the west.

Exactness, Specifics, Pictures, and Images

VAGUE: The people living in the housing project are diverse.
SPECIFIC: The people living in the housing project come from ten different countries on four different continents.

VAGUE: The pizza was great.
SPECIFIC: The pizza started with a crust made of fresh-baked dough on which was piled a layer of cheddar cheese, ground beef, mushrooms, anchovies, sliced meatballs, sausage, baloney, pepper, onions, green peppers, and finally another layer of cheese: mozzarella.

Whenever you supply a specific for a general word, you will add power and punch to what your write.

CUT OUT EVERY WORD YOU DON'T ABSOLUTELY NEED

Save your reader time and energy; cut out the flab. Make your writing lean. There is nothing that will steal your power sooner than a lot of extra, flabby words that the reader has to wade through and climb around and over to get to your message. See the difference for yourself:

FAT: There are many people alive in the world today who are living strange and unusual lives.
LEAN: Many people live strange lives.

FAT: Modern men and women of today are both alike in similar ways; they repeat again and again their messages after they have already said them once.
LEAN: Both men and women tend to repeat their messages.

FAT: Because of the fact that I don't have any money and am therefore flat and broke, I don't go inside a restaurant.
LEAN: Because I don't have any money, I don't go inside a restaurant.

USE ACTION VERBS

Students often use the passive voice to avoid taking a stand about anything. Occasionally, the passive is useful to the writer—as when a cause or agent is unknown. However, for now it will probably do more good to avoid passive verbs—and then later allow them into writing in only the places where they actually are appropriate.

Let your reader *see* what is happening. Here are some examples of action verbs that let the reader see exactly what is happening.

GENERAL: He *moved* toward us.

SPECIFIC:
leaped	loped	crept
slouched	trotted	crawled
jumped	paced	scooted
stumbled	staggered	barged
ambled	lurched	exploded
sauntered	fell	shot

"Dancing in all its forms cannot be excluded from the curriculum of all noble education: dancing with the feet, with ideas, with words, and need I add that one must also be able to dance with the pen?"—Nietzsche

jogged	strolled	whizzed
dashed	jigged	oozed
reeled	moseyed	marched

In contrast, passive verb forms kill writing, and nobody knows "who dunnit." It's a classic way of concealing the evidence or hiding the responsibility, but it usually makes for downright dull reading.

PASSIVE: The music was heard late at night. (Who heard it?)
ACTIVE: The landlord heard the music late at night. (Oh!)

PASSIVE: The missing funds were looked for. (Who did the looking?)
ACTIVE: The bank janitor looked for the missing funds. (Ah ha!)

As you revise for *specifics, lean sentences,* and *active verb forms,* you will put *punch* in your writing that will very likely cause your readers to remember for a long time what you had to say. *Give it to them!*

APPLICATION

1. Pick out the words that contribute to the vividness of the passage below.

> Little Stevie Cauthen sat down in the jockey quarters and peeled off his hot pink riding silks.
>
> "Where's my roses?" Cauthen asked.
>
> A moment later, the 18-year-old jockey, with the angelic face of a choirboy, clutched a giant bouquet of longstem roses to his thin, bare chest and ceremoniously began handing out the flowers, one by one, to other jockeys in the room.
>
> "Here you go," Cauthen said, in his soft, girlish voice. He reached out and offered a rose to 57-year-old Bobby Baird, Cauthen's chronological counterpoint in the Kentucky Derby. Baird was touched by the gesture. His eyes began to mist.

"Little Stevie Cauthen sat down. . ." is excerpted from a David Casstevens column from the May 7, 1978 issue of *The Houston Post.* Copyright © 1978 by The Houston Post. Reprinted by permission.

It was a private, poignant postscript to the drama that had just unfolded moments earlier at fabled old Churchill Downs, where for the last 104 years men have chased after stardust, riches and a measure of immortality.

Cauthen realized that dream Saturday in his very first Derby run, riding Affirmed to a 1⅓-length win over late-charging Alydar.

Baird, in contrast, has devoted 40 years of his life as a jockey but never even come close to winning America's most celebrated thoroughbred horse race known romantically as the Run for the Roses. And with his career in the home stretch, he probably won't get another chance, either.

But Steve Cauthen, still too young to buy a mint julep, has everything ahead of him, for years to come.

Cauthen clearly demonstrated a poise and savvy beyond his teenage years as he avoided being squeezed out on the first turn and then held off late charges by Believe It and Affirmed's chief rival, Alydar.

Bobbing like a pink blossom aboard his big chestnut steed, Cauthen held Affirmed in reserve for six furlongs as Sensitive Prince broke fast and angled sharply in front of the field from his far outside position.

Affirmed then moved up boldly on the second turn, relinquished the lead briefly a quarter mile out and then ran away from Believe It, keeping onrushing Alydar at bay.

Cauthen was well in command of the situation long before he ever reached the gate for this prestigious horse race that puts a premium on speed and courage and heart. —David Casstevens

2. Each of the following sentences contains problems in word use. Identify the problem and revise the sentence to correct it.

   A. The air smelled good, the trees looked nice, the breeze was just right, and we felt great.

   B. Exercise is something that should be tried by everyone.

   C. In my estimation, the requirement of additional classrooms is an unwise move undertaken by the school board.

   D. It is expected by most of the members of the community that the abandonment of the drive to retain the trees will be detrimental to the city.

   E. The old house on the corner was in sad need of repair: the porch was falling, most of windows were broken, the paint was peeling all over, the roof looked terrible.

   F. The Congress's insistence on backing up the unfair demands by the President only resulted in the creation of an atmosphere of resentment and mistrust among the voters.

   G. It was agreed by everyone that a good time was enjoyed at the great movie last night.

DISSECTING YOUR PAPER

In order to drive home the necessity for looking at your paper *after* you have finished examining it for surface errors, structural weaknesses, and lack of polish, we present a checklist that we call a Dissecting Sheet. It has been used with students for several years now, and many of them have said this was one of the most useful things ever taught to them.

The Dissecting Sheet works this way:

You examine your paper just as you would a cat in biology. Where are the bones? How are the parts of the skeleton connected? What has happened here? What occurs when you do this, that? **You will be taking your paper apart and putting it back together again.** And the questions all cover the major areas for improvement encountered in years of teaching. You will want to fill out a Dissecting Sheet for everything you write, and as you become more familiar with it, you will learn how to adapt it for any kind of writing—a business letter, a scientific report, etc. It is your author's gift to you. Use it any way you can. Change it as you like. If it helps you learn to complete a writing project, I am happy.

DISSECTING SHEET

Take a *good* look at the essay you have written. Look at its anatomy. Find its parts. See if there are any broken bones—or any bones at all. You know the constraints present when anyone tries to communicate by writing, so now is the time to check to see if you have done everything possible to get your message to the reader. By filling in the questions below, you will see if your writing "works."

1. Recall the communication chart in the Shaping section (or look at it again). Remember, there is the idea in the person's head on the left that has to travel across all those spaces and get into the other person's head on the right.

WHAT IS THE IDEA IN YOUR PAPER
·THAT WAS IN YOUR HEAD
THAT YOU NOW WANT TO GET INTO YOUR READER'S HEAD?

2. Read your first two sentences. (Remember, you have about that much space to get and keep your reader's attention.) Would *you* read past these two sentences? Mark the appropriate line below:

_____ first two sentences extremely interesting; I can hardly wait to read on.

_____ first two sentences OK, and I'm mainly counting on my reader's good will.

_____ first two sentences crummy. I wouldn't read another word.

3. Look at your opening paragraph. Do you have any pronouns in it? (Not that there's anything especially wrong with pronouns, but they often signal that generalizations have been made, and generalizations *unless specifically planned by a writer* are often death to your message.) If you have any pronouns, write them here. If not, write *none*.

4. Do you use any words like *people, everyone, society,* etc.? If so, what specific purpose do these words serve? (These words often signal nonperson writing, no personal interest in the subject.) If you used none of these words, write *none* here.

5. Have you been *very* clear in your opening paragraph to state exactly the message you are taking the trouble to write to another person? Write the sentence here that comes directly from your paper showing your purpose in writing the paper. (If this isn't in the first paragraph, tell where it is and how it happened to be in that place. If the purpose of your paper is found in more than one sentence, write as many of the sentences from the paper as are necessary to show what the purpose is.)

6. What is the connection between your first and second paragraphs?

7. Read over the rest of your paper. How many separate points do you make in order to get your message across? List them here:

(1.)

(2.)

(3.)

(4.)

(5.)

(If you made more than five, you probably tried to cover too much territory in a single writing; people usually do not remember over five pieces of information at one time.)

8. For each point you made, there should be several sentences following that point explaining it, illustrating it, describing it, analyzing it, defining it, developing it in some way. Take each point you made and answer the following questions about it:

FIRST POINT: (write it again here).

How many sentences are connected with this point to develop it?

Is this point alone in a paragraph, or is it among other points in the same paragraph?

If it is with other points, why is it? Because the points all go together in one paragraph? Because there weren't enough sentences about the point?

What method of development did you use to explain the point to your reader?

When you left this point and went to the next, did you connect the two in any way? Explain in detail:

SECOND POINT (Write it here).

How many sentences did you use to develop it?

How is this point connected to the one above it and the one below it?

Look at all the other points in your paper and answer these same questions about them.

9. It's hard to make a point to a reader if you don't use concrete examples. Read your paper and find 8 examples of very graphic, concrete word pictures. (If you can't find that many, pick out the ones you can find. If you don't have eight, put some more in before you turn the paper in.)

(1.)

(2.)

(3.)

(4.)

(5.)

(6.)

(7.)

(8.)

10. Pick out two things you *really* like in your paper and write them here:

11. How did you end the paper?

12. Would a reader feel *psychological closure* at the end of the paper? How did you provide this?

13. On a scale of 1 to 10, with 10 being the highest, how successful do you guess you were in getting your idea into another person's head?

14. Check appropriate boxes below (as many as apply):

_____ I spent the equivalent amount of time on this paper that I usually spend studying for a major exam.

_____ I wrote this paper at the last minute.

_____ I revised this paper.

_____ I liked what I wrote about.

_____ I took this assignment seriously.

_____ I wish I were a thousand miles from here.

Dissecting Sheet

FINAL CONSIDERATIONS

You have now done your final revising. *You have revised for flow*—to see that the thought runs smoothly and continuously throughout the essay. *You have revised for energy*—putting sentences in the best order possible, changing phrases to get the emphasis on just the right thing, cutting words to have the writing lean and to the point. *You have revised for punch*—using words that produce pictures for the reader and giving the exact word to capture an elusive thought. Though you could probably tinker with the essay indefinitely, improving the style or being just a centimeter more exact (writers almost never feel that they are really through), you know that at this point the writing contains a message that is stated clearly and directed specifically toward your reader. You are now ready to **edit** the paper and make the final copy to send to the reader.

EDITING

It is at this point that you start looking for errors and mistakes, for it is absolutely in your own best interest to make the paper perfect. Wouldn't it be terrible to have done all this work—made all these revisions and rough drafts—and then leave careless errors in the writing that will cause your reader to think you are a sloppy writer? Very likely the mistakes and errors in your writing will fall into one of a very few categories. And although it's true that there are really hundreds of possibilities, you've eliminated most of them by the careful three-stage process you've gone through. This means that, thanks to your good and careful work, most likely the errors will be one of these:

1. **Misspelled words** (or typing errors or handwriting errors).

2. **Apostrophes left out or put in the wrong place.**

3. **Punctuation errors and omissions**—particularly commas left out or in the wrong place.

4. **Sentence fragments.**

5. **Run-together sentences.**

6. **Verb errors.**

SUGGESTIONS:
1. Learn the rules *you* need to know.
2. Read your paper *out loud* to somebody else.

When you think about it, that isn't a very long list to have to check on. Of course, you may have a long history with any of those errors—perhaps extending back to elementary school days. So we suggest two things: First, study the information in the Handbook section that applies to your particular errors and learn the principles once and for all. Chances are almost nil that these principles will change in your lifetime, so once you learn them, that's it. *Learn the rules and you'll never have to learn them again*. The second recommendation is to *read the paper out loud to someone else*. This small thing—reading the

Stage 3/Completing

paper out loud—could actually be the secret to finding errors and mistakes in your work before you turn it in for final evaluation. You can be certain that if you stumble over something when you are reading it, there *is* something there to fix. Countless times students, when they are reading their papers out loud to other members of the class, are overheard to say something like "Oh, I left part of that sentence out" or "I didn't say what I thought I did or what I meant to say there; I'll fix it before I turn it in." Reading out loud will catch a lot of your mistakes.

The third thing you can do is *have someone else proofread your paper for you*. It is very difficult for the person who has written a paper to see mistakes in it. For one thing, the eye compensates for letters left out or words missing, and your brain will just fill in the blanks. Since you, the writer, *know* what you are saying, the words don't actually have to be there on the page for you to *think* them as you read. Also, you may not know certain principles of correctness (like commas or apostrophes) and it may take you a few weeks to learn these rules. In the meantime, your papers have to be evaluated. So get someone who is good at catching errors to go over your paper with you before you turn it in.

Finally, the most important thing we can say about mistakes and errors in your writing is **Be Aware.** Experience repeatedly shows that the problem isn't that students *can't learn* these things—it is just that they are not *conscious* of them. They don't realize how important the Completing Stage is in the writing process. They don't know that they create their own failure by being inconsiderate and passing on mistakes and errors that the reader has to cope with—something that the reader isn't willing to do. (The reader's word to you, the writer, is "That falls into *your* territory. *You* get it cleaned up and right if you want *me* to take *my* time to read it.") Many writers are just plain unaware, and that is their downfall. If you will just be *aware*—awake and conscious—of the lurking problems you *might* have with grammar mistakes, spelling errors, etc., you will be ahead of about half of all the people who are studying how to write.

MANUSCRIPT FORM

When you have checked your paper for errors and oversights, you are ready to write or type the very final copy for presentation to the reader. Now you want to think about the way the writing is going to look on the page. Be alert to this! As in editing, don't let carelessness or laziness cause you to do a halfway job. Nobody would spend hours building a beautiful walnut bookcase and then display it at a craft fair with sawdust and garbage all over it. The way your paper *looks* will have a considerable psychological effect on the reader. And while a good-looking paper with no content won't get you anywhere, a paper with excellent content but a sloppy appearance usually won't either. You can't win *either* way on this one. It has to be *both*. Good content + good appearance = success with reader.

The total is equal to the *sum* of its parts. Period! Parts alone don't make it.

Final Considerations

Whether your paper is handwritten or typewritten, there are some conventions that you should always observe.

1. **Make your paper as neat as possible.** Erase carefully, and whenever possible, use correction fluid instead of an eraser. Correction fluid is especially good for long corrections.
2. **Use one side of the paper only.**
3. **Use standard size (8″ × 10½″ or 8½″ × 11″) ruled paper if you are handwriting, or 8½″ × 11″ unruled paper if you are typing.** Do not use legal size, colored, or spiral-notebook paper or cheap typing paper.
4. **Always number your pages.**

Make a handwritten paper as attractive as possible.

1. **Always use a black or blue ball-point pen.** Do not use felt-tip markers; they tend to make your writing too bold and unattractive. Never use pencil for the final copy. It suggests that the paper is not yet in final form.

2. **Write neatly and legibly.** Remember that if your reader doesn't understand your writing, he or she is not likely to pay attention to your message. If double spacing makes your handwriting easier to read, then double space—but make sure your teacher doesn't object to this.
3. **If you have a title for the writing, put it on the top line of the first page.** Skip at least one line, preferably two or three, before beginning the text of your paper. If you don't have a title, begin on the second or third line of the page.
4. **Follow the margin on the left side of the paper and leave at least a half-inch margin on the right. Don't write on the last line of the page.** Your words should neither bleed off the right nor fall off the bottom edge of the page.

Make a typewritten paper look professional.

1. **Always double space when you type.** Single spacing is difficult to read.
2. **Use good quality paper.** It is difficult to read material typed on cheap typing paper or onionskin paper. Do not use erasable bond. Its finish, which makes erasures easy, also makes smudging more likely. Besides, unless you erase very carefully and professionally, erasures will still be noticeable and will often be messy. If you plan to type most of your papers, invest in several hundred sheets of good-quality typing paper bought at a book or office supply store, not at the local grocery store.
3. **Use a good black or blue ribbon.** Change your ribbon when it begins to look faint. A paper typed using a worn-out ribbon is difficult to read. Do not use italics or script characters except for special effects. See that the type in your typewriter is clean.
4. **Leave at least one-inch margins all around.** If you will bind your paper in a folder, the left margin should be slightly wider to avoid making that side of the page look cramped once it is in the folder. The top margin on the first page should always be about two inches. Type the title; then triple space before beginning the body of the paper.

How foolish it is to court disaster by not taking into account every *psychological* as well as rhetorical aspect of how a written message gets from the writer to the reader. Errors and sloppy appearance are so easy to fix that they should *never* be the cause of a person's failing to get your message. *Don't let it happen.* Value your message and your time too much! Play by every "rule" in the book that contributes to your writing being a success.

The important thing once again—in editing as well as in anything else—is **Think of Your Reader.** Let everything about your writing—appearance, correctness, message, form—contribute to the message getting across.

Final Considerations

WRITING ASSIGNMENT:
THE ASSERTION-WITH-PROOF ESSAY

ASSERT:
To state positively with great confidence.

PROOF:
Facts, examples, information so certain or convincing as to demonstrate the validity of a conclusion beyond reasonable doubt.

We all know somebody whom we can always count on to be making loud assertions, but who usually is just blowing off steam: there's no proof behind the declarations. Of course, there are occasions when a writer is expected to give her or his opinion and is not expected to substantiate that opinion in any way at all. No proof is required because the writer has clearly been given the opportunity to just sound off. Unless you are writing for one of these distinct occasions, however, you need to back up all your assertions with proof that will convince your readers that you are right. Sometimes that proof will be documentation from research; sometimes it will be carefully developed and logical discussion; sometimes it will be examples that the readers can check if they so desire. The stronger the proof, the quicker your assertion will be accepted by the reader.

The most convincing and well-written assertion-with-proof essays have these characteristics:

1. The assertion is clearly stated early in the essay.
2. The proof follows quickly and is obviously in support of the assertion.
3. The proof consists of facts, examples, information that the readers can check or of discussion so logical and convincing that the readers accept it without argument.
4. There is *sufficient* proof cited to convince the reader.

CONTEXTS

A. You are the parent of a small child; the two of you have just returned from the grocery store where he did nothing but whine and cry for the latest junk food cereal that was advertised on the Saturday morning cartoons. You know this cereal is coated with sugar and is not good for children, and, finally, you have had enough. You sit down and write an assertion-with-proof essay that you plan to mail to the network president. This essay will center on what you believe television commercials are doing to children. You plan also to send a copy of the essay to your local newspaper.

B. You are a senator who recently voted for an arms treaty that will result in the closing of a factory and the loss of hundreds of jobs in your district. Your constituents are furious with you for your vote, which they see as having cost them money and jobs. However, you feel morally justified for your vote and are firm in your conviction. Write an open letter asserting your convictions and reasons for voting as you did. This letter will appear in the monthly newsletter to your constituents who live in a middle-class urban area. These constituents depend either directly or indirectly on defense contracts for local factories for their livelihood.

Stage 3/Completing

C. You are a newly appointed football coach at a local high school. You are surprised to learn that the previous coach used pain-killing drugs to enable the better players to play even when injured. You know this is illegal and dangerous to the young men on your team. You make the decision that under no circumstances will you administer pain killers to a player. You must prepare an essay that will appear in the newspaper, be read in the locker room, and be posted on the school bulletin board. You want no doubt as to your position and the reasons for it. Your football team is composed of teenage boys from a rural community whose major interest is "winning" football.

D. You and your friend have always done things together, even crazy things like cutting classes and pulling pranks. Now your friend has started smoking and wants you to try it. You have strong feelings against smoking and vow that you will never join your friend. In fact, you are so upset about your friend's new habit that you decide to write an assertion-with-proof essay for your school newspaper in which you give your reasons for thinking that young people should not smoke.

E. Martin Luther turned history around the day he wrote down a list of statements telling exactly where he stood on matters of religion and nailed it to the front of the church door. Imagine that you have just had a blowout with your parents (or children). You are really steamed. You decide to write your own assertion of your rights in the family. You know, however, that you must use proof, also, to back up your assertion, else your parents (or children) won't read past the first line. You plan to leave the essay on the kitchen table so that it absolutely cannot be ignored.

F. You are an avid television watcher. In fact, you absolutely love television. Everywhere you go these days it seems as though someone is talking about how bad television watching is for you and how people ought to stop watching it. Finally, you decide to speak your piece. Your friend edits the little magazine that is put in all the stores, motels, etc., in town to be taken free of charge by anyone who wants a copy. She often runs a short essay by some local person; last week's topic was "How to Build a Tree House," which a friend of yours wrote. You call the editor and ask her if she will take your essay on the value of television. She says she'll be happy to—that it ought to make lively reading. So, you sit down and write the assertion-with-proof essay in which you declare that television watching is a good thing to do.

G. Go to the library and get evidence, facts about, information on some subject you are interested in learning about. Then, with your instructor, plan a context for an assertion-with-proof essay that will be based on your work in the library.

H. Write an assertion-with-proof essay on some book, poem, play, or movie you have recently read or seen. Work with your instructor on the context and audience for the essay.

PRACTICAL APPLICATIONS

HOW TO APPLY CREATING, SHAPING, AND COMPLETING

OVERVIEW

Writing the Research Paper

Watching a Research Paper Being Written

Questions to Ask About Your Research Paper

Something Extra

Writing Essay Tests

The Creating Stage

The Shaping Stage

The Completing Stage

Writing for Business

Features of Business Writing

Business Letters

Job Applications

Résumés

PURPOSE
: Learn to adapt the stages to different types of writing

Practice various kinds of writing that you will likely do after you are out of school

Experience the relationship between writing and research

Discover the secret to doing well on essay examinations

Practice writing skills that you can use to get a job and to do well on that job after you are hired

WRITING THE RESEARCH PAPER

You've just heard that one of the major requirements of a course you are taking is a research paper, and you groan. You *know* what hard work that kind of writing is. Probably the first thing you think of is how difficult the footnotes are to type and how many hours it takes to find the material in the library. Well, cheer up: much of the misery can be taken out of the activity for you. What you will need, and what you are about to be shown, is a *system*—a system that moves step by step, making the paper a manageable task. This chapter will teach you a system that should work for all the research projects you will ever need to do.

But: *Why does doing a research paper seem like such a job?*

Several things account for it, which, summed up, come to this: while you exercise all the ordinary and regular skills involved in the writing process—getting ideas, deciding about audience, shaping, revising, completing—you also exercise several *new* nonwriting skills simultaneously. And it is this load-on-load that makes it seem like so much work.

SOMETHING OLD, SOMETHING NEW . . .

What are the nonwriting skills that you have to master in order to do a good research paper?

First of all, the *Creating Stage* for a research paper is different from the *Creating Stage* in other kinds of writing. The creating techniques that you have learned to use—**cubing, looping, classical invention,** and others—all call for information and knowledge that you already possess. When you did the creating technique, you pulled out this old information—or discovered new thoughts that emerged from the interaction of facts, experiences, and information that you already possessed.

With the research paper, however, it's different. To do your initial creating for this kind of writing, you do not begin with what you already know. You actually begin by putting information *into* your head, not taking it out. This new information is then used some days or weeks later when you are planning and writing the paper itself. The assumption is that you don't already possess a lot of knowledge or information on the subject of your paper. (If you did, there wouldn't be much need to research the topic; it would be mostly a waste of time.) The idea in *research* paper writing is that you must gather new infor-

Practical Applications

mation from outside sources *before* you can have anything to say on the subject. Going to the library is actually *the creating technique* for this kind of writing. You may, of course, loop or cube some part of the new information later in a secondary creating activity, but the first step to finding an idea in this case is to go find out what other people have said on the subject.

And here's the rub.

This new creating technique requires a skill that you haven't had to use in other essays—**how to find material in the library.** Learning how to use the library is an extra thing to master (very valuable, of course, but still *extra*), so it is no wonder that you feel from the very start that doing a research paper is more work.

Another "extra" in research paper writing is learning **how to take notes, how to incorporate these notes into the body of an essay,** and **how to give credit for the information.** Again, this is a skill you haven't had to exercise in most of your other writing. And without question, it is tedious. Deciding when to give credit to an author and when not to requires a lot of thought. Getting the paragraphs based on your notes to sound like coherent, flowing sentences instead of separate items from your notecards requires a lot of rewriting. But these skills of notetaking, incorporating notes into your own writing, and documenting notes correctly are essential to an acceptable research paper. So, that's another skill to learn—on top of all the skills necessary in the writing process itself.

Finally, there's the *form* of the paper itself. **All the outside sources must be documented in footnotes and collected in a bibliography,** and knowing how to cite and to type footnotes and bibliography is a big job. Anyone who has ever typed too far down on the page and run out of space for the footnotes or who has forgotten to indent the second line of the bibliography when about one-third way down the page knows the frustration that the *form* of a research paper can bring. This, then, is a third nonwriting skill that you have to know how to do.

To do a good research paper, therefore, you have to have a large number of skills—some writing skills, some nonwriting.

WRITING SKILLS	NONWRITING SKILLS
Finding an angle or thesis	Learning how to use the library
Writing to a particular audience	Learning how to take notes
Fully developing the points	Learning how to incorporate notes into an essay
Shaping the essay for the reader	
Revising	Learning how to document
Editing and correcting	Learning research paper forms

Is it any wonder, then, that the project looks big?

But, you may say, if it's all this much work why do it? Is *anything* worth that much time and effort? Here are some reasons that may help you answer *yes* to your own question.

1. Learning to use the library is a skill which will stay with you for life. And it is a skill transferable to any kind of research you will ever want to do.

2. Once you learn the system for notetaking, citing information, and documenting sources, you'll know it for good. And the same system that you learn now will work when you do research projects for your company, when you look up legal briefs for an appearance in court, or when you search for the latest information on the income tax laws in order to beat an IRS audit.

3. Learning correct documentation form really means simply learning where to look something up. (It's *never* anything you have to memorize.) Getting practice in how to do it right is really nothing more than a matter of following the accepted practices in order to make reading your research paper as easy as possible. Good documentation also serves the readers by letting them know what books, articles, and other matter they could read if they wanted to know more about your subject.

4. Finally, what makes the research paper really worth doing is the sheer power it gives to you: *personal power.*

Here you are: Here's a subject:

You know something about *U, Y, Z* and *T,* but you don't know anything about *X*. With research paper know-how, however, you can go into the library and learn about *X*. You come out smarter.

You now *contain X* and, above all, you can *communicate X* to someone else! This means that if you know how to use the library, how to take notes, how to document, you can find out anything you want to know—*anything!* There is *no* worldly knowledge that can be kept from you. And that is power—the power to be knowledgeable, to find out anything you want to know on your own, and to be able to communicate this to other human beings—for the rest of your life. You may never have to do a formal research paper again (although you also may, depending on how you decide to make your living and fortune), but you *will* have opportunity after opportunity to use the skills you learn in this process *to your advantage.*

WATCHING A RESEARCH PAPER BEING WRITTEN

Recalling those public television specials where families were filmed as they went about their day-to-day lives, we are going to do something quite similar in this chapter. We shall be following a student as she writes her research paper for her freshman English class. Without having her before us on television, we shall nevertheless have her diary, notecards, bibliography, and several pieces of the information she used for the final paper. By following her progress, you can learn how to write a research paper yourself. All we need to know to follow Karen's work is that her teacher assigned the topics in the English class, and Karen's was this: *Do research on the book* Tom Jones *and the movie* Tom Jones. *Write a research paper based on a topic which surfaces when you do your reading in the library.* Of course, the instructor gave more information in class when the assignment was made, but this is basically what Karen had to go on as she began the work. As we follow her progress, Karen's diary appears in italics and our remarks on the progress she is making appear in regular type.

February 1. I just can't believe it. This is the absolute pits. A research paper on Tom Jones. *Who cares about* Tom Jones? *English teachers, I guess. That's why he gave us such a useless assignment. I've never even seen the movie so how can I compare it to the book? Come to think of it, I've never even read all the book. We were supposed to read it last year in senior English, but I never finished. 400 pages is just too long. I read* Cliff Notes *instead.*

I don't know where in the world I'll find time to do research. Teachers seem to think that their class is the only one. Well, I happen to be taking 12 hours besides English, and it's time everybody realized that.

The only research paper I've ever written was in high school, and that was on golf. I chose that topic because Dad had a million Golf *magazines on the floor behind his chair. So I just used a couple of those, one encyclopedia, and a dictionary as my sources.*

I'll never find anything in this school's library. I think they organized it for the graduate students. I do well to find the copy machine.

What does Karen's first diary entry tell us?

- She is very confused about the topic assigned to her by the teacher; it is about something she knows nothing about. She just hasn't realized yet that *she's not expected to know anything about it.* Right now all she feels is confused.
- She feels she has no time. This is a normal reaction to a project she doesn't think she can do anyway.
- She has no skills in research paper writing. She knows that the one term paper she did in high school was just a get-by situation. And she's very worried because she has no real experience or know-how.
- Finally, she feels lost in the library. Even if it does have everything she needs, she doesn't know how to find it.

What would be the best advice for Karen? It would go something like this:

1. **Don't worry at this point about the topic.** Your first visits to the library are *exploratory* anyway, and as you read and take notes you will see what possibilities there are in your topic. Just hold on to the comforting fact that you aren't *supposed* to know anything about it at this point.

2. **Begin early.** So many of the problems in doing a research paper come about because much or everything is left to the last minute. You may discover that the library has to borrow books for you from another library or that a book you need is already checked out, so leave time for things like this. Also, remember the rule of thumb that *an activity probably takes three times the amount of time you think it will.* Plan for this. So don't underestimate the amount of time it will take to write the paper itself and type it. *Begin early!*

3. **Begin the project in a treasure-hunt frame of mind.** Approach the library as though it were a field where some fantastic treasure is buried that you are going to discover and get to keep. Be willing to be surprised. And realize that everything is there that you are going to need to know. It may not look at first as though anything is there on your subject. (When did you ever find treasure placed right out in the open?) The topic may be listed under something you hadn't thought of; the library may have separate collections or divisions you don't know about; the topic may be included in a bigger subject. Ask the librarian before you waste much time at all. There is no chance that there is *nothing* on your subject. It will be there, and with time you will find it.

    You may, on the other hand, be overwhelmed by how much material you *do* find. There may seem to be two hundred times more material and information than you could ever use. In that case, ask a librarian where it would be best to start. If you approach the project with the frame of mind of "There's no telling what I might find!" or "Wonder what I will learn about this that I never knew existed before?" you will get pleasure out of the act of finding information even in the midst of all the seeming pain.

4. **You need to realize that librarians are professionals.** They know everything there is to know about the library, and *they expect to be asked for help*. People doing research almost never use these professionals enough. Don't wait until you have a question. Go to the librarian just as soon as you are ready to begin the research paper. Tell him or her what you are working on and that you will be asking for assistance when you need it. Establish contact by this courtesy visit and become known to the people who can help you the most in your work.

February 4. Tom Jones is worse than my little brother. At least brothers go to sleep sometimes. Tom Jones just haunts me and follows me day and night. I'm honestly afraid to go to the library. I don't even know where to start. I don't even have a topic yet, except the general idea of the assignment.

I finally confessed to the prof that I'd never seen the movie, and he wasn't even surprised. He said that didn't matter because he wanted me to research what other people thought about it. I've got to get to the library.

I didn't even know when the thing came out. He said in the early '60s. I guess that is someplace to start.

February 5. I feel relieved. I just found out that we don't need a topic until after we go to the library and read a bunch of stuff.
   I've got to get to the library.
   Heaven help me!

Karen is stalling for time. She's worrying and not working. The only thing to do is to plunge in—to get over to that library and start looking. If she doesn't do that soon, she won't have enough time when she does start, and she will see all her nervous fears realized. She'll actually create her failure! Here is good advice for her:

1. Go to the bookstore and load up on supplies.
2. Get 3 × 5 notecards for the bibliography sources (why not some color—they come in blue and pink and green and yellow—something that will cheer you up as you work).
3. Get 4 × 6 or 5 × 7 notecards for the notes themselves. (Again, go for color!)
4. Stock up on a handful of strong rubber bands to hold the cards together. If you really have the money, buy one of those bright plastic boxes to hold your cards. Again, the more ample and cheerful your work tools, the better you will feel.
5. Get several ballpoint pens and reserve them just for your research project.

The mere buying of these supplies will move Karen one step closer to the library. She will feel that she has *done something* about the assignment, and that's a great first step. She will also be prepared when she does go to the library.

February 7. I finally did it. I took my new supplies and went to the library. The most familiar thing I saw when I got in there was the card catalog, so I decided to start there. And I actually found something!
   First I looked for the subject Tom Jones *and couldn't find it. Then I looked under Henry Fielding, the author, and found a heading, "The History of Tom Jones." (I didn't even know that was the name of the book.) I was really excited to see 4 books that I thought I could use even though I wasn't familiar with the titles.*
   Next, I thought I'd see what the encyclopedia had to say. The librarian showed me a weird one that was divided into two parts—the Encyclopaedia Britannica. *She said look at the Macropedia for details, so that's where I looked. It said Fielding was pretty controversial. I xeroxed that page just in case of an emergency.*
   After that I asked the librarian where I could find out exactly when the movie came out, since I am supposed to do something about the movie and the book. She showed me a book called Film Facts, *and it has all the scoop on films. It said—under* Tom Jones, *of course—that the movie was produced in 1962. Progress! So I took my 4 books on the novel and wrote down the name of* Film

Facts *and the page the information was on, and decided to call it a night. I figured I had found enough for one evening.*

Going to the card catalog first was a smart thing for Karen to do; she did find four books listed there. What she missed, however, was something very important on the card—a notice that one of the books had a *bibliography* included.

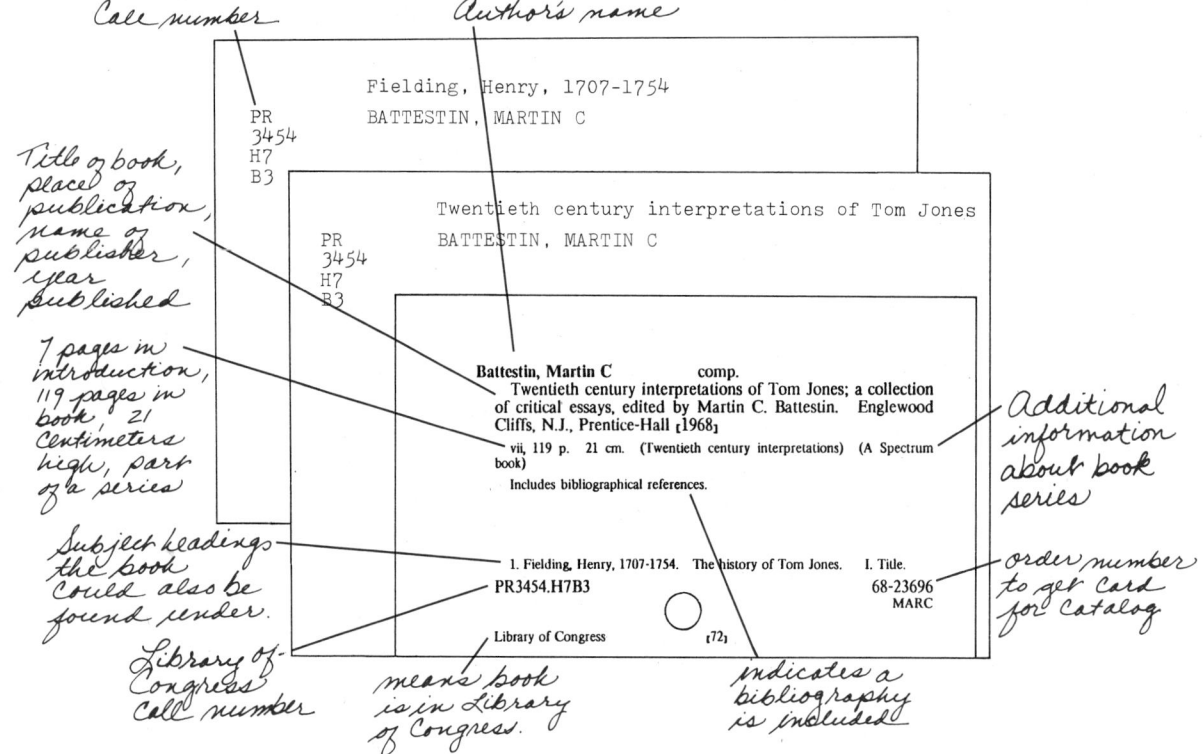

She didn't see that this particular book included a list of other books on the same subject. If she had noticed this, she could have turned to that list at once and had a large number of additional sources for her research without looking a bit further. It would have been a real short-cut. So our advice to her would be to **read the card carefully to see if the book cited can lead you to other books.**

Karen also has a lead on this card that she may not have noticed. **Near the bottom are *subject headings* that tell where to look in the Subject Catalog** (she's looking now in the Author Catalog). If she will go to the Subject Catalog and look under Henry Fielding or *The History of Tom Jones,* she will probably find several more sources very quickly. The subject card would look like the author card except that it would have a designation at the top of it saying what the book is about. (And a third way she might find the book listed is under its title, as on the title card.) *The clues are all there;* Karen just must be able to read them. If she can, she'll be able to find everything she needs and fast.

Another thing Karen needed to start doing immediately was to make her bibliography cards. Every time she finds a source, she should write down every piece of information she would need to find that book again or to cite it in her paper when it gets written. **Making bibliography cards (using 3 × 5 cards) *fully* and *correctly* will be one of the biggest time savers of the whole project.** If everything doesn't get written down, Karen will have to go back to the library later for the date of publication or the publisher or some other piece of information that she needs but neglected to write down. Here is how a bibliography card for a book should look:

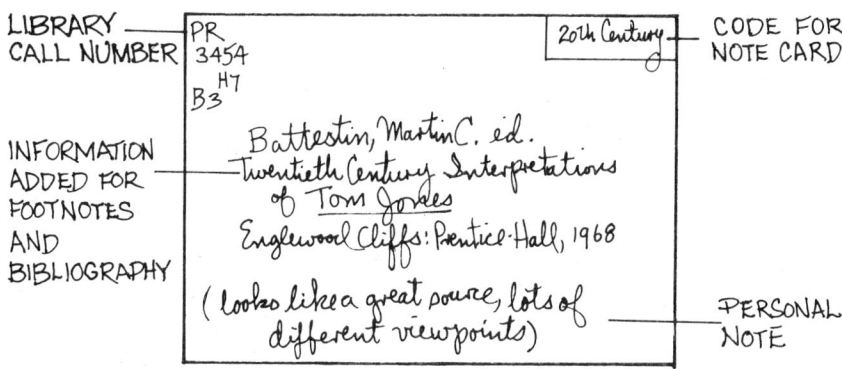

The bibliography card for Karen's encyclopedia article should look like this:

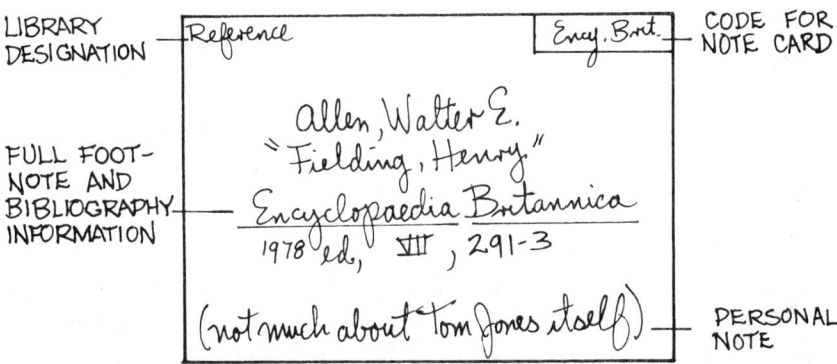

If she makes a bibliography card for every source *as she goes along*, Karen will make her job of looking for material and documenting the paper much easier and hassle-free. Even though it takes a little time, it will save *enormous* time in the long run.

> A stitch in time saves nine.

February 9. I looked through those 4 books, and they look as though they are written for graduate school research. Am I supposed to be a genius when I'm a freshman? There's only one of the 4 that I can even begin to read. And boring! Ugh!

  Back to the library. Why don't people write stuff that we can read?

Watching a Research Paper Being Written

February 10. This is really discouraging. I went to the Reader's Guide *to find magazine articles about the movie—that's where the librarian said to look. I looked under "Tom Jones," "Film," "Henry Fielding," and didn't find a single thing. "Tom Jones" wasn't even listed, and "Film" and "Fielding" didn't have anything about* Tom Jones. *I absolutely hate this.*

I guess I'll go back to the librarian and ask more questions.

February 11. The librarian suggested I go to the Reader's Guide, *which lists magazine articles, for the years around the time the movie came out. I had been looking in this year's* Reader's Guide. *When I went to 1961–63, I did find some entries, although I don't know yet how much they will help me.*

Subject headings

FILM adaptations
Bookmakers. il Newsweek 61:73 Ja 14 '63
Not by the book; film treatment of Advise and consent. H. Koningsberger. il Horizon 4:116-18 My '62
Rights and permissions. P. Nathan. See issues of Publishers weekly
Swifty the great. il Time 79:54-5 F 2 '62
When a book becomes a movie. J. M. Culkin. il Sr Schol 81:24T-26T O 10 '62

FILM censorship. See Moving picture censorship
FILM critics. See Critics
FILM dryers. See Photography—Apparatus and supplies
FILM festival, Cannes. See Cannes international film festival
FILM festivals. See Moving picture exhibits
FILM racks. See Photography—Apparatus and supplies
FILM speeds. See Photography—Exposure

Title of article, author, has pictures, found in Senior Scholastic magazine, Vol. 81 pages 24-26, October 10, 1962

FIELD trips. Nature study. See Nature study
FIELDING, Gabriel
To be continued. M. Cosman. Commonweal 75:78-9 O 13 '61
Uses of fear. Harper 224:92-5 F '62
FIELDING, Henry
Henry Fielding's pieceable animal. H. K. Miller. Sat R 44:36-7 Ag 5 '61
FIELDING, Marian
Bite back at insect bites. McCalls 88:154B Ag '61
FIELDING, Waldo L. and Benjamin, Lois
Medical case against natural childbirth. McCalls 89:106-7+ Je '62
FIELDS, Ann
Pueblo sketches; poem. Poetry 99:158-9 D '61

About author

Appears in Saturday Review Vol. 44, pages 36-7 August 5, 1961

February 14. I've finally had a real breakthrough. The listings in the Reader's Guide *helped some. The real progress came, though, when the librarian suggested I look in the* New York Times Index *to get newspaper reviews of the film. I didn't even know we had old newspapers in the library! They are all on microfilm, something else I had never used before. I am learning a lot!*

When I looked in the New York Times Index *under* Tom Jones, *there was nothing. Fielding, Henry—nothing. Motion Pictures—Hallelujah! I found it. Right there under motion picture reviews,* Tom Jones*—4 articles. I got the microfilm (sounds like real detective work) from the librarian and found out the library could make copies for me from the microfilm. I got copies of all 4 articles. I feel so much better. People in the 60s loved the movie, and I'm even starting to like it better myself. With these 4 articles from the newspaper and the magazine articles I found under* Tom Jones, *I ought to have something to work with!*

There are a couple of things we'd say to Karen here. First of all, she's doing great in her detective work. We applaud her for not being afraid to go back to the librarian when she needs assistance, and she deserves praise for not giving up when she gets discouraged.

However, **she should begin *now* to take notes** instead of paying so much money to have things copied. She's probably doing this for a feeling of security, but it isn't necessary and it isn't an efficient use of her time. She could glance at the articles in the *New York Times* and jot down anything she thought she might be able to use later. Of course, she doesn't know her exact topic yet, and that may be why she is collecting everything rather than making notes. If she began making notes, however, she would get into the subject matter of her topic much sooner (instead of merely having a pile of books and xeroxed copies stacked up). She would be clearer about exactly what she wanted to write about. Also, Karen may not always find herself in a library that has the expensive machines for copying microfilm. She needs to begin making notes *now*, particularly with short pieces like newspaper and magazine articles.

Here is the best advice about taking notes:

1. Use 4 × 6 notecards.
2. In the upper right-hand corner write the code words—last name of author, name of encyclopedia, etc.—from the bibliography card so that you will know what the source was for the information.
3. At the beginning of the note, write the page number of the source. (This is *critical* because you have to be able to footnote the exact page. Don't get caught in the library at midnight the day before the paper is due looking for page numbers!) As soon as the page in your source changes, write the new number immediately on the notecard, even if you are in the middle of a line.
4. Write the information in your own words. If you feel something *must* be stated just as the writer put it, copy it word for word and put quotation marks around it.
5. Number the notecard at the bottom for your own purposes. You'll probably drop the notecards a hundred times while you are doing the paper, and it takes hours to get them back in order if they aren't numbered.

BIBLIOGRAPHY CARD

ATKINSON

ATKINSON, BROOKS
"Critic at Large: Tom Jones film version is a reminder to reread Fielding masterpiece."
New York Times, November 8, 1963.
section 6, page 28, columns 4-5
(looks like great source)

NOTE CARD

> COMPARING BOOK AND MOVIE   ATKINSON
>
> PAGE 28 " To 18th century readers the Fielding novel must have been as refreshing as the film is to us."
>
> 1

NOTE CARD

> REAL LIFE IN BOOK AND MOVIE   ATKINSON
>
> P.28 Both the book and the movie catch the fun of life. They both show that vice can be fun too, even though it is usually virtue that people praise. People like the story because it shows real human nature.
>
> 2

6. When you have finished with one notecard, write a word or two at the top of the left-hand side which can be your index for the card—some words that tell you what the subject of that notecard is. This will help you when you start to sort the cards later.

February 21. I've read most of the material now that I got from the library, but I still don't have any idea what I am going to write on. I definitely don't want to write the usual boring paper that puts everybody to sleep. There must be something *interesting about* Tom Jones *to make so many people want to read and see him.*

That quote from Atkinson about people in the 18th century being as refreshed by the book as people in 1960 were by the film is the only thing that has seemed to have any promise at all *for a topic. I thought about writing a paper that compared the reactions of the 18th-century general public to the book with the reactions of the 20th-century general public to the movie. I don't really think I've got the material to do that, though. The only 18th-century reactions that I have found are mostly literary and don't mention much about the general public at all. Maybe the general public didn't read. They must have read the book, though, or at least have known a lot about it because the big scholars didn't care much for it, and I figure* somebody *had to like it to make it popular.*

February 22. I've decided that 3/4 of the work in doing research is thinking. *My brain has never worked this hard in my life. It's such a relief to come up with ideas and to find material, but it* hurts. *I don't think there's been one hour since I got this assignment that I haven't thought about Tom. I will be so glad when it's over, and I can think about something else for a while. I have a feeling that after I get my paper all thought out and come up with a definite idea most of the work will be over.*

Karen is absolutely right about the importance of *thinking* in the research paper process. Right now—after finding and reading as much material as she can and taking preliminary notes—she is at that point where writers usually sit down to begin their essay. She has completed that first nonwriting task of locating material in the library, and now she is ready to do the first stage of the actual writing process—creating or finding an idea.

The best advice for Karen at this point would be to do some of the creating techniques she learned earlier—*looping, cubing, classical invention*. She has put new information into her head, and now she can see what her own mind will do with this new knowledge. (That alone will be a pleasant thing for Karen to observe.) She could probably save herself a lot of worry and fretting if she did a few creating exercises at this point. Very likely some good ideas would emerge as possibilities for a focus for the paper. And doing creating activities would be a welcome break from the close reading she has been doing. They would also be a way to collect her thoughts and see just where things stand at this point.

February 23. I'm still toying with that idea of people being refreshed in the 18th century just as they were in the 20th. What is there about Tom Jones *that would make it fun for people living so many years apart? I went back to the encyclopedia to see if I could find anything on 18th-century England. I looked in* Britannica *and could find only very factual information—nothing I could compare to the 1960s. So I looked in the card catalog under the subject heading of Great Britain "Social Conditions and Customs—18th Century." The number of books was overwhelming, but I copied down several call numbers. By the time I finished I didn't feel like climbing all those stairs, so I just checked out one book that was on the first floor. I glanced at the introduction and read ". . . the conflicts and tensions of 1760 are identical with those of 1960." Maybe* this *is it! I think I'll read the whole book.*

There are a couple of things to notice here. One is that Karen is still playing with the idea that came after she read one sentence in the film review in the *New York Times,* an idea that fascinates her and yet that came from a very small piece of information. The point to notice is that you will never know when an idea will strike you—or from what source. It doesn't take a long piece of material to give you a thought, and you cannot set up "getting the thought." It just happens when it does. The thing you have to do is *keep moving.* If you stay in motion, something will finally turn up.

The second thing to notice is that luck was at play again in the one book Karen checked out the day she was tired. She had found so many, a lot were on other floors of the library, and she went for the one closest at hand—one that she wouldn't have to climb stairs to get. And *that* book turned out to have some information on just the thing she had been thinking about. There is no need to pretend that this kind of luck doesn't come to the aid of your research paper project. Sometimes just good fortune will cause you to put your hands on exactly the right thing. (Other times the greatest good will and effort in the world doesn't seem to turn up anything.) Serendipity plays a part, too: you will be looking for one thing and find another; it all falls within the territory of your research. And be certain of this: in the end, if you look enough and stick with your research, any "bad luck" you might be having will do a fade-out.

February 24. The name of that book I found on the first floor was The Augustan Vision. *I couldn't figure out why it was listed in the card catalog under 18th century. But then I looked in the introduction to the book and it said that this book is about the entire 18th century. The librarian suggested that I look up "Augustan Age" in the* Glossary of Literary Terms, *and I learned that it was an ancient period but that the same name was used for the first 45 years of the 18th century or the entire century. Why can't everybody just decide on a term for this period and make everybody use it? I'm really tired of coming across twelve different terms every time I open a book, just to discover that all the terms stand for the same thing. This is getting* very *exhausting. Already I've had to look up a million things in source books. I think I might qualify as a literary scholar if I live through this.*

No wonder people who do this for a living seem so strange. . . .

Frustrated again—and we can see why. But information is almost never in a concise package; it comes in bits and pieces, chaotic and squirmy. It's understandable why Karen is tired.

February 26. I can't believe I hadn't thought of this before! In the middle of the night last night, I realized that maybe I ought to check out the book Tom Jones *since I was doing research on it. What a stupid thing to miss. Well, I got a copy, and that was the smartest thing I've done yet. Not only did I get a copy of the book, but I got one that has all sorts of good stuff in the back. It has parts of papers and letters that people in Fielding's day wrote right after they had read the book, regular and normal people. That's just what I needed. And, as I suspected, they loved the book.*

This is definitely a breakthrough. I feel encouraged.

You have to ask, "Why in the world didn't she think of that sooner?" Well, just because she didn't! Your own mind isn't always orderly and smooth during the thinking process, and often it will be working for you when you are unaware that anything is going on. It's been said that the best thing to do with a question on a test that you can't answer is to "put the question on the back burner," meaning to put it out of your conscious mind and let the subconscious work on it for a while. Evidently, Karen's subconscious mind was working for her and threw in a very important suggestion when she was least expecting it. That's why it is very smart to *trust yourself* (provided, of course, that you are doing the necessary leg-work) and not get frantic. Good ideas will come.

February 27. Good luck strikes again! When I was looking over my notes, I realized that I had never looked under "Motion Pictures" in the Reader's Guide. *I went back and looked in the 1963 book and, sure enough, I found 7* articles listed in Life, Time, Newsweek, Saturday Review, *and other magazines. This is a* major *breakthrough!*

I had to look in this machine in the library to find out where the magazines were (I think it's called the microfish—*more detective work). I copied the call numbers and found the magazines. It was so neat to look through those old magazines and find the articles. I noticed that JFK was killed and that Viet Nam was going full force; this made me start thinking about what might have been going on in England when* Tom Jones *came out. I don't know much history, but I do know that in the 1770s England had a skirmish going on—in America. I wonder if I could find out something about conditions, events, concerns in England in the 18th century and in America in the 1960s. That might give me a clue to why people liked the book then and people like the movie now. That might make an interesting paper. I can find stuff on the 1960s—that's no problem. But I wonder where I can find stuff on the 18th century. I guess I'll go back to the encyclopedia, card catalog, and librarian.*

I'm so glad to have those articles.

Cross index

```
MOTION
    Bowling in the classroom. C. Randall. il Sci
        Digest 56:24-5 S '64
MOTION in art. See Action in art
MOTION picture production code. See Moving
        picture censorship
MOTION pictures. See Moving pictures
MOTION sculpture. See Mobiles
MOTION sickness
    Deaf personnel used in artificial-G test. R. D.
        Hibben. Aviation W 81:117+ S 14 '64
    Malady that motion can cause. A. Balk. il
        Todays Health 41:28-30 Jl '63
    Navy gains in effort to control canal sick-
        ness. H. M. David. il Miss & Roc 15:26
        Ag 31 '64
    Some comforting facts about motion sick-
        ness. G. G. Greer. Bet Hom & Gard 42:34
        Je '64
            See also
    Seasickness
```

finally! entries on Tom Jones itself!

```
To kill a mockingbird
    America 108:273+ F 23 '63
    Commonweal 77:572 F 22 '63
    Look il 27:84+ F 26 '63
    New Repub 148:30-1 F 2 '63
    New Yorker 39:125-6 F 23 '63
    Newsweek il 61:93 F 18 '63
    Time il 81:93 F 22 '63
To love
    Commonweal 81:390 D 11 '64
    New Repub 152:21 Ja 2 '65
    New Yorker 40:204 N 28 '64
    Time il 84:111+ D 4 '64
Tom Jones
    America 109:532 N 2 '63
    Cath World il 199:71-2 Ap '64
    Commonweal 79:141+ O 25 '63
    Esquire 61:32+ F '64
    Life il 55:120-3 O 11 '63
    Nat R 16:165 F 25 '64
    Nation 197:374 N 30 '63
    New Repub 149:27-8 O 19 '63
    N Y Times Mag il p 104-5 S 29 '63
    New Yorker 39:98+ S 7 '63
    New Yorker 39:169-70 O 12 '63
    Newsweek il 62:116-17 O 14 '63
    Reporter 29:54 N 21 '63
    Sat R il 46:52 O 5 '63
    Time il 82:117+ O 18 '63
Tomorrow is my turn
    Newsweek 62:78 Ag 19 '63
Topkapi
    America 111:391 O 3 '64
    Commonweal 81:168 O 30 '64
    Life il 57:55-6+ O 9 '64
    New Yorker 40:194 S 26 '64
    Newsweek 64:107A S 21 '64
    Sat R 47:27 S 12 '64
    Time 84:111 S 18 '64
```

Voilà!

It's good to watch Karen actually get excited over her ideas. She is now thinking about something she probably has never thought about before and is actually cooking up a "problem" that could become the focus for her paper: *what is there about the book and the movie that gives people of both centuries so much pleasure?* She's definitely making progress.

February 28. I have been reading a little in that book The Augustan Vision, *and I'm discovering some interesting things. The author tells how few people were financially supporting the entire population in England, how the sexes were trying to get their roles defined, how there was a growing movement toward humanitarianism. Well, if that doesn't describe movements going on today that began or got stronger in the 1960s, I don't know what does. There are obvious differences, of course, between the two centuries (like not so much mechanization, knowledge, etc., in 1700s), but the* conflicts *and* tensions *seem to be based on similar feelings. Maybe these conflicts and tensions made people need to lose themselves in a hilariously funny novel or movie.*

I can see the paper developing!

March 1. I am so relieved to have a topic. I just decided for certain that I would write about the reasons the book and movie were both popular, and when I decided on that for sure, I ran out of my room, down the hall, down the stairs, and out the door. I thought I deserved some fresh air, and I felt so light and happy. I feel like most of my work is over, although I haven't written one word of the paper yet.

Karen has finished a big chunk of the work—using the libarary to best advantage for finding material she needs and deciding on a *more specific* topic to base her paper on. She is ready now to begin the *Shaping Stage* of the writing process.

March 3. I just went out and bought a new pen. I've discovered that I have to take more notes. I don't have enough on the exact thing I am going to write about. I do have the sources, though, so it's just a matter of doing some more reading and notetaking. I am hoping the new pen will inspire me. I'm just not inspired to finish up. Everybody else is gone. The TV's off, and I'm sitting here having to take more notes.

March 4. I've just looked over all my notes to get ready to do the first draft of my paper. I turned out to have plenty of material, although I was afraid for a while that I would not find enough to say. I've got more cards than I can probably use. When I look at the cards, I can definitely see a concrete pattern emerging from my notes. Tom *the book and* Tom *the movie both laugh at and, in a sense, attack social institutions—like the Church and philosophers, the family and marriage, the military, social rank and class, and roles of sexes. It seems that in the 18th century, like in the 1960s, there was a general current of questioning these institutions and re-evaluating and changing some of them. These tensions, which sometimes came out in politics, made both cultures ready to read or view a story of an ordinary person who didn't blindly uphold all these institutions as sacred and absolutely perfect. This is what I am going to try to show in my paper.*

When I first got this research paper assignment, I never dreamed that I'd learn this much or be able to make such comparisons. I really feel smart. I really am learning, although I wouldn't admit it to my English prof!

The thoughts are jelling. Karen is beginning to make some sense out of all she has read. She now knows what the thesis for her research paper will be, and she can now write the first draft to see just how she can state and prove that thesis. As it turns out, Karen is writing the kind of research paper that *makes a statement and then proves it,* like the *assertion* essay you wrote earlier. Other people in her class are probably writing other types of research papers. Some may be doing a *problem and solution* research project, in which they state clearly some major problem and then use outside sources to find the solutions to this problem. Others may be doing a *report* type of research paper, where they merely set out to give the facts about some topic. Actually, a *research paper* could serve most of the purposes of the *essays* you have written earlier in this text; the difference is that outside information would be used instead of what you already knew.

March 5. I think I'm really beginning to see what research is all about. I didn't really do any research on that golf paper last year. It's one thing to talk *about some topic and another to* read *about a topic, come up with an idea based on the reading, and support that idea with details from the outside sources. The process of reading and gathering and organizing information to help an audience understand my ideas is really getting clear.*

I still think it is a dumb topic; I'd much rather be learning about something more useful. I was hoping to write a paper that I would use later on in other classes.

I really had a scare in class today. The teacher said something about "credibility of sources." Good Lord, what next? I don't even know what that means, much less whether or not I did it. This is just all one big pain. Anyway, I talked to him afterwards and found out that he meant that our sources had to be by reputable people. I don't even know these 18th-century people! He glanced over my bibliography cards and said my sources were credible. What a relief! What in the world would I have done if they weren't?

March 6. I just started trying to write my second draft. I did one, just going through my notecards very fast and trying to prove my thesis. Now I need to see what needs to be done to make the paper really stand up. Before I did my first draft, I divided my notecards into piles and then went from one pile to another as I wrote the paper. Now I see, though, that some things should come before others, etc. I was getting very confused, and then I came up with a brilliant plan. I wrote a real sketchy outline for my paper that looks like this:

1. *Establish mutual praise.*
   A. *Movie.*
   B. *Book.*

2. *Why?*
   Book and movie did same thing—dealt with institutions in satirical form.

    3.   *Briefly, why 2 centuries' audiences enjoyed these attacks?*
        18th.
        20th.

    4.   *Conclude that producer saw similarities between societies' attitudes and capitalized on this to produce an important movie of this century.*

This might even be the germ of my final outline that I include with the research paper itself. At any rate, it can serve as a guide for me as I do the second draft.

    March 7. When I read over my second draft today, I saw that I needed to give a slightly different slant to my groups. I think now they will look like this when I do the final version of the paper.
    1. Movie and book both well received by audiences.
    2. Both dealt with life.
    3. Both examine society and deal with issues of the day (reflect attitudes).
    4. That's what makes Fielding last two centuries.
I AM AN ABSOLUTE GENIUS!!!

    March 10. I'm in a state of shock. Writing the final version of my paper wasn't nearly as hard as I thought it would be. The biggest trouble I had was working in my quotes and outside information into my own sentences. The first version sounded just like my notecards strung along together. I even laughed to myself and thought, "I might as well just give the notecards to the teacher." But this last time I reworded things, added a lot of transition sentences to get from one point to another, and tried to paraphrase most everything. I got a little mixed up about whether to put a footnote in or not, and I'm still not sure about all that. But I think I've got it in pretty good shape.

    Unbelievable—the end is in sight. All I've got to do now is type the paper in its final form, do the footnotes and the bibliography, type the outline, and get it ready to hand in! I really feel good.

Tom Jones Lives a Long Life

by

Karen Brinkley

English 103
Professor Cowan
March 15, 1979

Tom Jones Lives a Long Life *— Title of research paper*

OUTLINE *— Optional heading*

Thesis: There are several reasons why *Tom Jones* was interesting to audiences who lived 200 years apart. *— Point the paper explains*

— Topic Outline

I. Introduction: *Tom Jones*'s Success in Two Centuries
  A. Twentieth-Century Movie
  B. Eighteenth-Century Novel
II. Explanation: Life as a Subject
  A. Eighteenth-Century Concern
  B. Twentieth-Century Concern
III. Reason: Society as an Issue
  A. Eighteenth-Century Hypocrisies and Issues
  B. Twentieth-Century Hypocrisies and Issues
IV. Conclusion: Lasting Success as a Masterpiece

1

Tom Jones Lives a Long Life

"Most of the critical excitement last week centered on 'Tom Jones,'" one American movie critic wrote in October 1963, "the brilliant and bawdy film of the Henry Fielding novel. . . . And it well should have been, for this rare rendering of the classic of 18th-century English literature . . . is a wonderfully energetic and entertaining film, one of the most completely antic that has ever been brought to the screen."[1] Another 20th-century critic agrees: "We are, in fact, still very much in the midst of the 'Fielding revival' . . . , one sign of which has been the brilliant success of the recent film Tom Jones."[2] Readers in 18th-century England were as excited about the book Tom Jones as moviegoers in 20th-century America were about the film. Brooks Atkinson, a critic for the New York Times, guessed that "to 18th-century readers the Fielding novel must have been as refreshing as the film is to us."[3] According to popular opinion in 18th-century England, Atkinson's guess was correct.

A 1751 anonymous reader called Tom Jones "on the whole . . . the most lively book ever published."[4] Two thousand copies were printed in its first edition and were sold before the announced date of publication (February 10, 1749). This was "perhaps an unheard of case."[5] By the end of February the second issue of 1,500 copies came out, and by the end of the year 6,500 copies had been printed. The book was "in every Hand, from the beardless Youth, up to the hoary Hairs of Age."[6] James Boswell, a famous writer in the 18th century, quoted Dr. Johnson as saying, "'Tom Jones' has stood the test of publick opinion with such success, as to have established its great merit. . . ."[7] Captain Lewis Thomas, a soldier in Fielding's day, agreed: "I am just got up from a very Amazing entertainment; to use a Metaphor in the Foundling, I have been these four or five days last past a fellow traveller of Harry Fieldings, and a very agreeable Journey I have had."[8]

[*Transition paragraph*] Obviously, then, the readers in 18th-century England enjoyed Henry Fielding's book Tom Jones as much as 20th-century Americans enjoyed the film version. [*Thesis of essay*] When I discovered this idea while doing research on the novel and the film, I began to wonder what a work could have that would make its topic so interesting to audiences two centuries apart in time.

[*These next 3 ¶'s establish that Tom Jones is about life*] Very simply stated, "Life is the subject matter of the writer of fiction . . . ,"[9] and this concern for life is one of the main reasons for Tom Jones's continued success. [*Corresponds to outline I A & B*] George Saintsbury called Tom Jones "an epic of life--not indeed of the highest, the rarest, the most impassioned of life's scenes and phases, but of the healthy average life of the average natural man. . . ."[10] The character Tom Jones was described in Life magazine as "one of the most engaging unheroic heroes in all English literature,"[11] and another source said "Tom Jones appears . . . as a kind of Everyman striving toward maturity against his own weaknesses and the pressures of a hostile world."[12] Since Tom Jones the novel and Tom Jones the movie are both concerned with ordinary people and everyday life, both have managed to captivate their audiences.

Some 18th-century critics disliked Tom Jones because it dealt with ordinary life; they thought "the 'lowness' of his themes--his preoccupation with the adventures . . . of footmen and foundlings, of country wenches and Mayfair demi-reps" was damaging.[13] A 20th-century critic, however, thinks these qualities are exactly what appeals to 20th-century Americans--"Fielding's wit and hearty good humor and, above all, his tolerant humanity . . . seem . . . congenial to us," he says.[14]

In addition, the Encyclopaedia Britannica states that Fielding is remembered today because of his concern for human weaknesses and morality.[15] Another source praises Fielding because he "described for the first time in English fiction a real man."[16] And this idea of a real man in a "country viewed through the wryly critical eyes of a man who knew too well the hypocrisies of his people and his age" is exactly what appealed to 20th-century viewers.[17] The movie presents a view of 18th-century England that most 20th-century viewers were not used to seeing; one critical review described it as "a great, sprawling boisterous film that is out to unbutton the elegant embroidered waistcoat . . . and show it dirty, cruel, yahooish, leching, and guzzling, as well as stylish."[18]

Because Fielding not only dealt with life but also with the hypocrisies of society, his subject matter appealed to people in the 18th-centuries. Pat Rogers, in his book The Augustan Vision, states that whenever a society becomes confident and politically stable, it will begin thinking about inward problems--"questions of personal identity and private relationships."[19] This is what

4

people in Fielding's time and the 1960s did. A census taken in the 1700s showed that a large portion of England was living in poverty; yet, generally speaking, it was described as "a period of prosperity with relatively few bad years" (Rogers, p. 11). England's economy was boosted and the population somewhat redistributed. People started to read at an earlier age because of the charity school movements; an increase in manufactured goods left housewives with more time to read; and more people on the lower social scale--footmen, apprentices, waiting-maids--were learning to read (Rogers, p. 85). Overall, England was advancing intellectually and scientifically (Rogers, p. 8).

The people of Fielding's day found a new liberalism because of the increase in education. Rogers said "whatever is, is right" became the "watchword of a whole optimistic philosophy" (Rogers, p. 9). As I have already stated, the public was very interested in humanity. Five new public hospitals were built in one decade, and the very rigid social classes were beginning to break down. Sons of the aristocracy were going into business; men with land married girls with money, and business became the fashionable thing among nobility (Rogers, p. 11). Many social institutions that were once sacred were being re-evaluated.

Marriage was one such institution. As seen in Tom Jones, fewer and fewer couples were quietly accepting the marriage arranged for them by their parents. On the other hand, although Tom loves Sophia, he felt free to indulge "in the pleasures of the flesh with any woman who was good-looking and facile."[20] There was also a growing interest in determining and rearranging roles for men and women. Women had freedom with leisure time and property that previous generations did not have. Although women did not have careers, the ones with property had a secure status without having to marry. Advances were being made.[21]

To people in the 18th century, possessions meant security, and the loss of possessions greatly threatened "social identity."[22] After glancing through several magazines printed at the time the movie Tom Jones was released, I discovered that the society of the 1960s was not too different.

Americans in the 1960s were concerned with improving the lot of humanity. In November of 1963 Life magazine ran a series of articles on the plight of the American Negro, and Congress was passing laws and making rulings to help them. Just as social classes were breaking down in the 18th century, minorities were gaining more fair treatment in the 1960s.

The women's liberation movement also grew and gained recognition in the 1960s. Betty Friedan gained popularity as she battled for her sex against the "feminine mystique."[23] Women were advancing in the 18th and 20th centuries.

Scientists made life a bit easier for people in the 1960s, too. The new interest in space brought many advancements to households, and great strides were made in medicine. One article of October 1963 in Life reported that scientists were closing in on the secret of life with the new research in DNA.

Perhaps the two biggest issues in the 1960s compare to major events in 18th-century England. In the 1960s, America was involved in the Viet Nam war, a war that proved to be as humiliating for Americans as was England's war of the 18th century. In 1776, England lost thirteen colonies and marked the war off as a minor skirmish, but the country felt humiliated to be defeated by such a small, powerless group of people. Americans' dissatisfaction in the 1960s over the Viet Nam conflict was evident in all magazines and newspapers of the decade. Some aspect of the Viet Nam war was the lead article for *Life* magazine almost every other week in early 1963.

The only event that affected America more than Viet Nam in 1963 was the assassination of President Kennedy. Eighteenth-century England was still concerned with the execution of Charles I. A sermon delivered in that century said that the execution of Charles I was worse than Christ's crucifixion since Charles (unlike Christ) was an anointed king.[24] When I read the pages and pages of articles written about President Kennedy after his death, I got the feeling that Americans felt the same way about his assassination.[25]

Since Americans in the 1960s were concerned about humanity and trying to question and improve their social institutions, they, like the people of 18th-century England, were ready to laugh at a book and movie that satirized these institutions. The film was called "a social satire written in blood with a broadaxe" since the producer "sharpens the author's satire to a cruel point.[26] In the movie, scenes of the slums were brief but vivid and vicious. This sort of scene, mixed in with hilarious scenes in the countryside, gave the audience an opportunity to laugh at the hypocrisies of people and society, yet they could not forget that something had to be done to end such hypocrisy.

"Certainly Henry Fielding's novel contains all the elements necessary for a good movie," one critic said. "It has lovers' misunderstandings, it deals with the very rich, it has comedy, chases, action, sex."27 But it has much more that has made the tale able to endure two centuries.

In the novel, Fielding wrote: "I have endeavoured to laugh Mankind out of their favourite Follies and Vices."28 This statement is the worth of the tale. "Two centuries have passed," Time magazine states; "Mankind still has its favourite Vices; and novelist Henry Fielding's sprawling, brawling masterpiece still stands as the greatest comic novel in the language."29 Because mankind has its vices and people in 18th-century England as well as 20th-century America were concerned with correcting those vices, Tom Jones appealed to audiences separated by centuries in time.

Frederick Hilles, a Fielding critic, quotes a character from a play who is standing in front of Fielding's tomb. He says to himself:

> Perhaps it was worth dying in your forties if two hundred years later you were the only non-contemporary novelist

who could be read with unaffected interest, the only one who never had to be apologised for or excused on the grounds of changing taste.[30]

That must be the mark of a true masterpiece--one that stands the test of time.

Notes

[1] Bosley Crowther, "Cinematic 'Tom Jones': Fielding's Classic Novel Made into Great Film," <u>New York Times</u>, 13 Oct. 1963, Sec. 8, p. 1, col. 6.

[2] <u>Twentieth-Century Interpretations of Tom Jones: A Collection of Critical Essays</u>, ed. Martin C. Battestin (Englewood Cliffs, N.J.: Prentice-Hall, 1968), p. 2.

[3] Brooks Atkinson, "Critic at Large: 'Tom Jones' Film Version Is a Reminder to Reread Fielding Masterpiece," <u>New York Times</u>, 8 Nov. 1963, Sec. 6, p. 28, cols. 4-5.

[4] Ian Watt, "Fielding as Novelist: Tom Jones," in <u>Twentieth-Century Interpretations of Tom Jones: A Collection of Critical Essays</u>, pp. 19-32.

[5] <u>Twentieth-Century</u>, p. 8.

[6] <u>Twentieth-Century</u>, p. 8.

[7] Samuel Johnson, "Samuel Johnson on Fielding," in <u>Tom Jones: An Authoritative Text</u>, ed. Sheridan Baker (New York: Norton, 1973), p. 787.

[8] Lewis Thomas, "A Very Amazing Entertainment," in <u>Tom Jones: An Authoritative Text</u>, p. 773.

[9] W. Somerset Maugham, ed., <u>The History of Tom Jones, A Foundling</u>, by Henry Fielding (Philadelphia: John C. Winston, 1948), p. xv.

[10] Maugham, p. xxvi.

[11] "Tom Jones Wins in a Romp," <u>Life</u>, 11 Oct. 1963, p. 120.

[12] <u>Twentieth-Century</u>, p. 15.

[13] *Twentieth-Century*, p. 1.

[14] *Twentieth-Century*, p. 2.

[15] Walter E. Allen, "Fielding, Henry," *Encyclopaedia Britannica*, 1978 ed., VII, p. 292.

[16] Maugham, p. xxii.

[17] Arthur Knight, "*SR* Goes to the Movies: Richardson's England," *Saturday Review*, 5 Oct. 1963, p. 52.

[18] "The Current Cinema," *New Yorker*, 7 Sept. 1963, p. 98.

[19] Pat Rogers, *The Augustan Vision* (New York: Barnes & Noble, 1974), p. 87.

[20] Maugham, p. xxiii.

[21] Rogers, pp. 87-90.

[22] Rogers, pp. 99-100.

[23] In November 1963, *Life* began a series of articles on Betty Friedan's attack on what she called the *feminine mystique*.

[24] Rogers, p. 9.

[25] Early December 1963 issues of *Life*, *Time*, *Newsweek*, etc., were devoted almost entirely to JFK.

[26] "Cinema: John Bull in His Barnyard," *Time*, 18 Oct. 1963, p. 117.

[27] Knight, p. 52.

[28] Henry Fielding, *The History of Tom Jones, A Foundling* (Mason Publishing, 1931), p. viii.

[29] "Cinema: John Bull," p. 117.

[30] Frederick W. Hilles, "Art and Artifice in *Tom Jones*," in *Tom Jones: An Authoritative Text*, p. 916.

Bibliography

Allen, Walter E. "Fielding, Henry." Encyclopaedia Britannica. 1978 ed., VII, pp. 291-3.

Atkinson, Brooks. "Critic at Large: 'Tom Jones' Film Version Is a Reminder to Reread Fielding Masterpiece." New York Times, 8 Nov. 1963, Sec. 6, p. 28, cols. 4-6.

"Cinema: John Bull in His Barnyard." Time, 18 Oct. 1963, p. 117.

Crowther, Bosley. "Cinematic 'Tom Jones': Fielding's Classic Novel Made into Great Film." New York Times, 13 Oct. 1963, Sec 8, p. 1, col. 6.

"The Current Cinema." New Yorker, 7 Sept. 1963, p. 98.

Fielding, Henry. The History of Tom Jones, A Foundling. Mason Publishing, 1931, pp. v-viii.

Hilles, Frederick W. "Art and Artifice in Tom Jones." In Tom Jones: An Authoritative Text. Ed. Sheridan Baker. New York: Norton, 1973, pp. 916-32.

Johnson, Samuel. "Samuel Johnson on Fielding." In Tom Jones: An Authoritative Text. Ed. Sheridan Baker. New York: Norton, 1973, pp. 784-8.

Knight, Arthur. "SR Goes to the Movies: Richardson's England." Saturday Review, 5 Oct. 1963, p. 52.

Maugham, Somerset, ed. The History of Tom Jones, A Foundling. By Henry Fielding. Philadelphia: John C. Winston, 1948, pp. xv-xxvi.

12

Rogers, Pat. <u>The Augustan Vision</u>. New York: Barnes & Noble, 1974.

Thomas, Lewis. "A Very Amazing Entertainment." In <u>Tom Jones: An Authoritative Text</u>. Ed. Sheridan Baker. New York: Norton, 1973, pp. 773-4.

"Tom Jones Wins in a Romp." <u>Life</u>, 11 Oct. 1963, pp. 120-5.

<u>Twentieth-Century Interpretations of Tom Jones: A Collection of Critical Essays</u>. Ed. Martin C. Battestin. Englewood Cliffs, N.J.: Prentice-Hall, 1968, pp. 19-32.

Watt, Ian. "Fielding as Novelist: Tom Jones." In <u>Twentieth-Century Interpretations of Tom Jones: A Collection of Critical Essays</u>. Ed. Martin C. Battestin. Englewood Cliffs, N.J.: Prentice-Hall, 1968, pp. 19-32.

QUESTIONS TO ASK ABOUT YOUR RESEARCH PAPER

1. Is the paper interesting and easy to read even if the subject is unfamiliar? **GENERAL**
2. Have I given some of my own thoughts, ideas, or opinions in addition to the information I got from my sources?

3. Does the title arouse curiosity and accurately reflect the content of the paper? **TITLE**

4. Is the outline in proper form? **OUTLINE**
5. Does the outline reflect the actual organization of the paper?

6. Is the thesis of the paper clear to the reader at the very start? **THESIS STATEMENT**
7. Does the thesis statement limit and focus the paper as well as illustrate the purpose of the paper?
8. Does the thesis statement do one of the following: *(a)* clearly state the assertion to be proven in the paper, *(b)* present the problem that the paper is going to concentrate on and suggest the solutions to be given, *(c)* set a context for the report of current conditions on the subject, *(d)* pose the question that the essay sets out to answer?

9. Does everything in the paper relate to the thesis? **DEVELOPMENT AND ORGANIZATION**
10. Is there a logical order in the development of the paper?
11. Are all the main points adequately supported with quotes and references? Are they fully developed?

12. Does the final paragraph or two pull the paper together by giving the reader a sense of completeness and closure? Is the thesis reviewed, summarized, or referred back to? **CONCLUSION**

13. Do transitions connect the sections of the essay? **MECHANICS**
14. Are there any spelling errors?
15. Did I punctuate correctly?
16. Did I use accepted grammatical forms?

17. Is there any plagiarism? **DOCUMENTATION**
18. Have I integrated my research material into the essay so that it doesn't sound like a paste-up job of my notecards? Did I use enough sources?
19. Are the footnotes in proper form? Is there a bibliography entry for each source cited in a footnote?
20. Is the bibliography in correct form?

SOMETHING EXTRA: A LAGNIAPPE

There is a lovely custom in the Cajun country of Louisiana: a merchant, fisherman, or even just a friend will give you, free of charge, a little something extra on top of what you just bought or received. This "something extra" is called a *lagniappe*.

That's what we are giving you here—some additional information about doing a research paper that we think you'll find helpful. Look at it whenever you need to.

DOCUMENTATION: MLA STYLE

Typing notes and bibliographical entires can be frustrating and time-consuming. The rules that govern mechanics and punctuation in these seem arbitrary and illogical. The fact that there is no definitive way to do this makes the whole process of documentation seem ridiculously detailed. Different areas of study (e.g. psychology) have their own style for documentation, so what you learn in your English class may be entirely wrong for a paper for chemistry, math, or history. To a certain extent, then, mechanics and punctuation in documentation *are* arbitrary—but they are never illogical. Each discipline can defend the logic behind its documentation system: one may strive for simplicity, another for brevity, another for completeness. Your instructor will tell you what system you should use in your English class. The system we use here is that given by the Modern Language Association in its *MLA Handbook*.

Because documentation is so detailed and meticulous, you may be tempted to think of the Notes and Bibliography pages as insignificant parts of your paper. Actually, these pages are very important. They provide a reader with all the information needed in order to consult—if he or she wants to—the sources you have used in your paper. This is why punctuation and mechanics are so important in documentation. A reader must be able to determine from your documentation whether the source is a book, an article in a book or journal, a newspaper, and so on. The conventions of punctuation and mechanics that you observe in documentation tell your reader these things.

The notes, which should appear at the end of the paper on a sheet titled *Notes,* document your use of borrowed material. **They include the author's name, the title of the work you are referring to, publication information, and the page number for the specific reference.** All this information must conform to standard conventions if it is to be useful to your reader. Study this sample note, paying close attention to the *mechanics* that govern its form:

Superscript number matches note number in the text
First line indented
Author's name in regular order
Publication information enclosed in parentheses
Name of State abbreviated
Comma after author's name

   [1] Leon V. Sigal, <u>Reporters and Officials</u> (Lexington, Mass.: Heath, 1973), p. 11.

Colon follows place of publication
Comma separates publisher and copyright date
Comma follows publication information
Entry ends with a period

The bibliography, which is usually the last page of your paper, lists in alphabetical order all the sources you directly cite in your paper. Each bibliographical entry presents the same information as a corresponding note, but in a slightly different form.

First line not indented
Last name first
Period after author's name even when there is no initial
Period after title

Sigal, Leon V. <u>Reporters and Officials.</u> Lexington, Mass.: Heath, 1973.

Punctuation, form, and information change slightly for other kinds of materials—articles, newspaper stories, essays, government documents—but the basic conventions remain the same.

The following examples illustrate the proper form for the most common notes and bibliographical entries. The note form *(N)* and the bibliographical form *(B)* are given together to help you compare the differences between the two.

Something Extra 225

Books with one author

N   ¹ Lewis Thomas, <u>The Lives of a Cell: Notes of a Biology Watcher</u> (New York: Bantam, 1974), p. 4.

B   Thomas, Lewis. <u>The Lives of a Cell: Notes of a Biology Watcher</u>. New York: Bantam, 1974.

Two or three authors

N   ² Arthur Shulman and Roger Youman, <u>The Television Years</u> (New York: Popular Library, 1973), p. 90.

B   Shulman, Arthur, and Roger Youman. <u>The Television Years</u>. New York: Popular Library, 1973.

Four or more authors

N   ³ Robert E. Burns et al., <u>Episodes in American History</u> (Lexington, Mass.: Ginn, 1973), pp. 103–105.

B   Burns, Robert E., et al. <u>Episodes in American History</u>. Lexington, Mass.: Ginn, 1973.

No author cited

N   ⁴ <u>Protect Your Pet Against Heartworm Disease</u> (Princeton, N.J.: American Cyanamid Co., 1975), p. 78.

B   <u>Protect Your Pet Against Heartworm Disease</u>. Princeton, N.J.: American Cyanamid Co., 1975.

Editors

N   ⁵ <u>Leukemia</u>, ed. Frederick Gunz and Albert G. Baikie (New York: Grune & Stratton, 1974), p. 137.

B   <u>Leukemia</u>. Ed. Gunz, Frederick, and Albert G. Baikie. New York: Grune & Stratton, 1974.

Editions

N   ⁶ Harold L. Nelson and Dwight L. Teeter, Jr., <u>Law of Mass Communications: Freedom and Control of Print and Broadcast Media</u>, 2nd ed. (Mineola, N.Y.: Foundation Press, 1973), p. 92.

B   Nelson, Harold L., and Dwight L. Teeter, Jr. <u>Law of Mass Communications: Freedom and Control of Print and Broadcast Media</u>. 2nd ed. Mineola, N.Y.: Foundation Press, 1973.

More than one volume

N   [7] Jay B. Hubbell, <u>American Life in Literature</u> (New York: Harper & Brothers, 1949), II, 53.

B   Hubbell, Jay B. <u>American Life in Literature</u>. 2 vols. New York: Harper & Brothers, 1949.

Essay or chapter from book

N   [8] Nancy McLaurin, ''Pfeiffer College Undergraduate Curriculum,'' in <u>Options for the Teaching of English: The Undergraduate Curriculum</u>, ed. Elizabeth Wooten Cowan (New York: MLA, 1975), pp. 70–76.

B   McLaurin, Nancy. ''Pfeiffer College Undergraduate Curriculum.'' In <u>Options for the Teaching of English: The Undergraduate Curriculum</u>. Ed. Elizabeth Wooten Cowan. New York: MLA, 1975, pp. 70–76.

Translation

N   [9] Homer, <u>The Odyssey</u>, trans. Robert Fitzgerald (London: Panther, 1971), p. 101.

B   Homer. <u>The Odyssey</u>. Trans. Robert Fitzgerald. London: Panther, 1971.

Book in series

N   [10] C. V. Wedgwood, <u>The World of Rubens</u>, Time-Life Library of Art (New York: Time Inc., 1967), p. 123.

B   Wedgwood, C. V. <u>The World of Rubens</u>. Time-Life Library of Art. New York: Time Inc., 1967.

Something Extra

Articles signed and unsigned in encyclopedia

N   11 Walter E. Allen, ''Fielding, Henry,'' <u>Encyclopaedia Britannica</u>, 1980 ed., VII, 292.

B   Allen, Walter E. ''Fielding, Henry.'' <u>Encyclopaedia Britannica</u>. 1980 Ed., VII.

N   12 ''Japan,'' <u>The Random House Encyclopedia</u>, 1977.

B   ''Japan.'' <u>The Random House Encyclopedia</u>. 1977.

Article from monthly magazine

N   13 Michael Zeilek, ''The Birth of Massive Stars,'' <u>Scientific American</u>, April 1978, p. 113.

B   Zeilek, Michael. ''The Birth of Massive Stars.'' <u>Scientific American</u>, April 1978, pp. 110-118.

Article from weekly magazine

N   14 ''Battered Child,'' <u>Newsweek</u>, 30 June 1968, p. 68.

B   ''Battered Child.'' <u>Newsweek</u>, 30 June 1968, p. 68.

Review

N   15 Stanley Kanfer, ''The Shocking Entertainer,'' rev. of <u>Mencken: A Study of His Thought</u>, by Charles A. Fecher, <u>Time</u>, 29 May 1978, p. 98.

B   Kanfer, Stanley. ''The Shocking Entertainer.'' Rev. of <u>Mencken: A Study of His Thought</u>, by Charles A. Fecher. <u>Time</u>, 29 May 1978, pp. 98, 100.

Newspaper article signed and unsigned

N   16 Karen Rogus, ''Elderly 'Cannot Live on Bread Alone'; They Need Hot Lunches,'' <u>Houston Chronicle</u>, 4 June 1978, Sec. 4, p. 3.

B   Rogus, Karen. "'Elderly 'Cannot Live on Bread Alone'; They Need Hot Lunches." <u>Houston Chronicle</u>, 4 June 1978, Sec. 4, p. 3.

N   [17] "VFW Hospital Volunteers Honored," <u>Walla Walla Union-Bulletin</u>, 15 Oct. 1978, Sec. B, p. 11, cols. 1–5.

B   "VFW Hospital Volunteers Honored." <u>Walla Walla Union-Bulletin</u>, 15 Oct. 1978, Sec. B, p. 11, cols. 1–5.

In the past the Latin terms *ibid, loc. cit.,* and *op. cit.* were used when a reference that had already been mentioned was mentioned again. Increasingly, now, however, a short form of the first citation is being used because it is much clearer for the reader and easier for the writer.

Here are the short forms to follow:

1. If a source has already been cited and it is the only one by that particular author used in the research paper, merely repeat the author's name and the page number for the note.

    [18] Kanfer, p. 100.

2. If the author wrote more than one of the sources you are using, cite the author's name and the name of the particular source you are quoting.

    [19] Kanfer, "The Shocking Entertainer," p. 100.

3. If the source has no author, merely cite it the second time by title.

    [20] <u>Protect Your Pet Against Heartworm Disease</u>, p. 74.

    (You may also write simply *Protect Your Pet* or *Protect* instead of the full title, if desired.)

Check with your instructor to see what note forms are preferred for works previously cited.

Notes can be given in two places: the notes can appear at the bottom of the page where the note numbers themselves appear (the origin of the term *footnote*—at the foot of the page), or they can appear all together at the end of the research paper, as with the system Karen used in the sample research paper. When they appear together at the end, the page on which they appear is titled *Notes* or *Endnotes*. Either term is correct; the choice is up to you. Putting the footnotes at the bottom of each page is somewhat more convenient for the reader but much less convenient for the typist. Placing notes at the end of the paper seems to be the more prevalent practice today. Your instructor will tell you which placement he or she prefers.

Something Extra

DOCUMENTATION: APA STYLE

Another system of documentation, using the author-date method, has been devised by the American Psychological Association. Because it is used in psychology, education, and most of the social sciences, many of you will need to use it in your writing in college and later. For a full account of the APA system for preparing manuscripts, consult the *Publication Manual of the American Psychological Association,* 2nd ed. (Washington, D.C.: American Psychological Association, 1974).

Both the acknowledgment of sources in the body of a paper and the list of works appended to the paper are different from those we have shown in the sample research paper on pp. 207–222. Within the paper acknowledgments are made informally in the *text* of the paper, in *parentheses,* or in *both*. The information is brief, but sufficient to key each citation to the list of works at the end of the paper and to help readers find the cited material within a work.

A citation could be handled in any of these ways:

```
In 1981, Hibbard discovered three startling facts    Entirely in the text

In recent research on this topic (Hibbard, 1981)    In parentheses

Hibbard (1981) discovered    In text and in Parentheses
```

The examples above show ways to document a work by one author. Here are more examples, showing variations on this basic model:

Two or more authors

For two authors, use both names each time you cite their work.

```
Hibbard and Johnson (1981) discovered

In recent research on this topic (Hibbard & Johnson, 1981)
```

For more than two authors, use all names the first time you cite their work, but use only the name of the first author with "et al." after that.

```
Hibbard, Johnson, Korski, and Clark (1981) discovered
```

<u>first citation</u>

```
Hibbard et al. (1981) discovered
```

No author

For works with no identified author, use the first few words of the title of the work.

```
In recent research on this topic ("Research in Writing," 1981)
```

Multiple citations

For more than one work at a single point in your text, arrange the citations chronologically.

> In recent research on this topic (Hibbard, 1981, 1982)

For works by more than one author in a single citation, arrange the names alphabetically.

> In recent research on this topic (Hibbard & Johnson, 1981; Korski, 1980)

Citation of a part of a source

For specific pages or chapters, add page or chapter numbers after the date. Note that page numbers *must* be given for quotations.

> Hibbard (1981, pp. 3–4)
>
> Hibbard and Johnson (1981, chap. 5)

All works cited in your paper should be included in a list, entitled "References," beginning on a separate page at the end of your paper. (Do not include works you have not cited in your paper.) This reference list provides full identifying information, enabling your reader to find these works for further use.

A reference list prepared in the APA style is similar in many respects to a bibliography in the MLA style. To provide you with a variety of examples, and to make comparison possible, we will show you the list of works from the sample research paper on pp. 219–222, restyled according to APA.

References

Allen, W. E. Fielding, Henry. <u>Encyclopaedia Britannica</u> (Vol. 7). Chicago: Encyclopaedia Britannica, Inc., 1978.

Atkinson, B. Critic at large: 'Tom Jones' film version is a reminder to reread Fielding masterpiece. <u>New York Times</u>, November 8, 1963, Sec. 6, p. 28.

Battestin, M. C. (Ed.). <u>Twentieth-century interpretations of Tom Jones: A collection of critical essays</u>. Englewood Cliffs, N.J.: Prentice-Hall, 1968.

Something Extra

Cinema: John Bull in his barnyard. *Time*, October 18, 1963, p. 117.

Crowther, B. Cinematic 'Tom Jones': Fielding's classic novel made into great film. *New York Times*, October 13, 1963, Sec. 8, p. 1.

The current cinema. *New Yorker*, September 7, 1963, p. 98.

Fielding, H. *The history of Tom Jones, a foundling*. Mason Publishing, 1931.

Hilles, F. W. Art and artifice in *Tom Jones*. In S. Baker (Ed.), *Tom Jones: An authoritative text*. New York: Norton, 1973.

Johnson, S. Samuel Johnson on Fielding. In S. Baker (Ed.), *Tom Jones: An authoritative text*. New York: Norton, 1973.

Knight, A. *SR* goes to the movies: Richardson's England. *Saturday Review*, October 5, 1963, p. 52.

Maugham, S. (Ed.). In H. Fielding, *The history of Tom Jones, a foundling*. Philadelphia: John C. Winston, 1948.

Rogers, P. *The Augustan vision*. New York: Barnes & Noble, 1974.

Thomas, L. A very amazing entertainment. In S. Baker (Ed.), *Tom Jones: An authoritative text*. New York: Norton, 1973.

Tom Jones wins in a romp. *Life*, October 11, 1963, pp. 120–125.

Watt, I. Fielding as novelist: Tom Jones. In M. C. Battestin (Ed.), *Twentieth-century interpretations* of Tom Jones: A collection of critical essays.

Englewood Cliffs, N.J.: Prentice-Hall, 1968.

OUTLINE

A topic outline is made of words or short phrases. A sentence outline is made of complete sentences. The choice of which to use depends on how much specific information the writer wants to include in the outline. **DEFINITION**

Most outlines have 3 or 4 types of headings. Capital Roman numerals indicate the main divisions of the outline. Capital letters indicate the subparts of these main divisions. Arabic numerals indicate the breakdown of the information listed under the second-level headings. Lower-case letters indicate parts of the third-level heading. **DESCRIPTION**

I.
  A.
    1.
    2.
  B.
II.
  A.
  B.
  C.
III.
  A.
  B.
IV.
  A.
  B.
    1.
    2.
    3.
  C.
    1.
      a.
      b.
    2.

1. If you have a I, you must have a II; if an *A,* then a *B,* and so on. A single level of heading cannot appear by itself. **RULES**
2. The wordings of the headings of levels of the same type should be parallel. (I should be worded like II and II like III, for instance).
3. One level can have subdivisions in one section of the outline and no subdivisions in another section. This occurs because there is sometimes much to say about one topic and little or nothing to say about another. The outline, of course, shows the points made in the paper. And if there are

no points under a particular heading, nothing will appear there in the outline.
4. Capitalization of words in topic outlines is done two ways:
    A. Only the first word of each line is capitalized unless a word is a proper noun.
    B. Every word in the outline is capitalized except for prepositions, articles (a, an, the), and conjunctions appearing in the middle of a line.
    The choice is up to the writer.
5. No punctuation is needed after any head, no matter what level.
6. A period is placed after each Roman numeral, capital letter, Arabic numerals and lower-case letters in the outline.
7. Heads of the same level appear even with each other in the outline.
8. Double-space between headings in the outline.

PARAPHRASE

To *paraphrase* means to put in your own words. Here is a paragraph quoted from the *Encyclopaedia Britannica* followed by a paraphrase of the information.

Quote

> *The History of Tom Jones, a Foundling* was published on February 28, 1749. With its great comic gusto, vast gallery of characters, and contrasted scenes of high and low life in London and the provinces, it has always been the most popular of his works. The reading of this work is essential both for an understanding of 18th-century England and for its revelation of the generosity and charity of Fielding's view of humanity.

Paraphrase

> Three things made Henry Fielding's novel, *The History of Tom Jones, a Foundling,* published on February 28, 1749, popular. The book is full of blustering humor, there are a large number of characters in the novel, and Fielding gives pictures of upper-class and lower-class, everyday activities in England. When you read this book, you can see Fielding's attitude toward all people, rich and poor, especially how much he understood human nature.[1]

Notice that even though this quote has been completely paraphrased, it is still acknowledged in a note, because all the *ideas* came from this source.

PLAGIARISM

To *plagiarize* means to take someone else's words and/or ideas and put them into your writing as though they were yours. Some people deliberately steal other writers' work, but much plagiarism in students' research papers occurs through carelessness, uncertainty, or ignorance. Some simple rules will help you know how to avoid plagiarism.

1. Always put quotation marks around any direct statement from someone else's work. Also give a note for this quotation.
2. Note any paraphrase of another writer's ideas or statements.

3. Note any thoughts you got from a specific source in your reading.
4. Note any material, ideas, thoughts, etc., you got from your reading that can't be described as general knowledge.
5. Note any summary (even if in your own words) of a discussion from one of your sources.
6. Note any charts, graphs, tables, etc., made by others or any you make with others' information.

Study the three versions of a student's paraphrase of the following paragraph by Donald C. Pike.

Original Version, Quoted Directly from Source:

Two plausible explanations exist for the Anasazi departure from a homeland where life was full and complete: either life had ceased to be good and they were starved out, or they were driven out by someone else. There are strong indications that a severe drought extended over the plateau from 1276 to 1299, and quite possibly the Anasazi found agriculture as they had come to depend on it impossible. There are subtle inconsistencies to the theory, however, that tend to impeach its universality, giving rise to the second possibility. Wandering Shoshonean hunters—raiders by nature—had begun to roam the plateau somewhat earlier, and given the fortresslike quality of most Anasazi pueblos and cliff dwellings, it seems possible that these raiders had begun to make part, or most, or their living by preying on the vulnerable fields of the agriculturists. If this was the case, the Anasazi would in time be forced out. Whatever the answer, and it may be a combination of both, the Anasazi departed to other regions.
—Donald C. Pike

Student Version 1

Nobody really knows why the Anasazi, the cliffdwellers, left their homes, but two possible reasons are given. The drought of 1276–1299 may have destroyed agriculture as the Anasazi had come to depend upon it. The Shoshonean hunters, raiders by nature, may have also begun preying on the vulnerable fields and crops of the Indians. No one knows for sure, but these two explanations, perhaps even in combination, may explain the abandoned cliff dwellings.

The writer has clearly plagiarized. Here are the reasons this is true:

1. The writer uses information that is not common knowledge, information she got from reading the original paragraph, and yet she does not footnote it.
2. The writer uses many of the author's exact words and phrases—steals them, in fact—and she does not mention that the words and phrases are not hers. Even though she does use some of her own words occasionally, she owes credit to the author for the knowledge in the paragraph itself and for the author's direct words.

Student Version 2

Authorities often give two explanations for the departure of the Anasazi from their homeland. Either they were starved out, or they were driven out. There was a drought from 1276 to 1299, and it is possible that this drought affected

Something Extra

the farming drastically.[1] Also, there was a roaming band of raiders, the Shoshonean, who may have attacked the Anasazi.[2] Whatever the answer, and maybe it was a combination of both the drought and the invaders, the Anasazi departed to other places.

The student is still plagiarizing. Even though she footnotes the two facts, she is still passing off many of the author's words as though they were hers. Just footnoting the two facts does not give the student the license to use the author's phrases and words without giving credit.

Student Version 3

Anybody who has ever seen or read about the Indian cliff dwellings is perplexed by the question, why did the Anasazi leave? Their homes were very advanced in structure and design. They had good farms. There are two explanations generally given. The Indians may have left because of a severe drought that occurred in 1276–1299.[1] They may also have been forced out by the Shoshonean, a tribe of raiders.[2] Nobody really knows for sure. Whatever the reason—whether it was the drought, the invaders, or a combination of both—the Anasazi left their homes, and all that remains there now are the magnificent cliff dwellings that fascinate and intrigue everybody who sees them.[3]

Finally, the student has stopped plagiarizing. The first two sentences could be considered general knowledge or conclusions she came to after her preliminary general reading, therefore not attributable to any particular source. She clearly footnotes the two reasons given by Donald Pike in the original paragraph. And she even footnotes her last sentence because she has used Pike's idea that the reason might be a combination of both. Even though she has used her own words in that last paragraph, she gives credit to the author's idea because she didn't know it until she read it from him.

Reference Material

Atlases, Yearbooks, and Almanacs

Atlas of World History, Rand McNally, 1970
Britannica Atlas: Geography Edition, 1980
The CBS News Almanac, 1976–present
Demographic Yearbook, 1949–present
Facts on File, 1940–present
The Geographical Digest, 1963
Information Please Almanac, 1947–present
National Geographic Atlas of the World, 1981
The Negro Almanac, 1967–present
The New Cambridge Modern History, 1970
The New York Times Atlas of the World, 1981
The Oxford Bible Atlas, 1974
Rand McNally Commercial Atlas and Marketing Guide, 1876–present
The Statesman's Yearbook, 1864–present
Statistical Abstract of the United States, 1878–present
The Times Atlas of the World: Comprehensive Edition, 1980
Webster's New Geographical Dictionary, rev. ed., 1977
The World Almanac and Book of Facts; 1868–present

Yearbook of the United Nations, 1947–present
Yearbook of World Affairs, 1947–present

Biographical References

Biography Index, 1946–present
Chambers's Biographical Dictionary, 1974
Contemporary Authors: A Bio-bibliographical Guide to Current Authors and Their Works, 1967–present
Dictionary of American Biography, 16 vols. & supplements, 1944–1981
Dictionary of National Biography, 22 vols. & supplements, 1882–1953
Directory of American Scholars, 7th ed., 4 vols., 1978
International Who's Who, 1935–present
Twentieth Century Authors, 1942, supplement (1955)
Webster's Biographical Dictionary, 1976
Who's Who (Great Britain), 1897–present
Who's Who in America, 1899–present
Who's Who in [. . .] (Regions such as West, East, South, Midwest, etc., and professions such as theatre, football, jazz, insurance, etc.)
Who's Who of American Women, 1958–present

Bibliographies and Library Guides

Basic Reference Sources: An Introduction to Materials and Methods, Louis Shores, Chicago, American Library Association, 1954
Bibliographic Index: A Cumulative Bibliography of Bibliographies, New York, H. W. Wilson Co., 1937–present
Bibliography of Agriculture, Washington, U.S. National Agricultural Library, 1942–present
Guide to Reference Books, Eugene P. Sheehy, Chicago, American Library Association, 9th ed., 1976
Guide to the Use of Books and Libraries, Jean K. Gates, New York, McGraw-Hill, 4th ed., 1979
Historical Abstracts: Bibliography of the World's Periodical Literature, Eric H. Boehm, ed., Santa Barbara, Clio Press, 1955–present
MLA International Bibliography of Books and Articles on the Modern Languages and Literatures, MLA, New York, 1922–present
The Modern Researcher, Jacques Barzun and Henry F. Graff, New York, Harcourt, 3rd ed., 1977
The New Cambridge Bibliography of English Literature, George Watson, ed., Cambridge University Press, 4 vols., 1969–74
The New York Times Guide to Reference Materials, Mona McCormick, New York, Popular Library, 1978
Reference Books: A Brief Guide, Baltimore, Enoch Pratt Free Library, 7th ed., 1978
Science Reference Sources, Frances B. Jenkins, Cambridge, MIT Press, 5th ed., 1969
Sources of Information in the Social Sciences: A Guide to the Literature, Carl M. White et al., eds., Chicago, American Library Association, 2nd ed., 1973
The Use of Books and Libraries, Minneapolis, University of Minnesota, 10 vols., 1933–1963

A World Bibliography of Bibliographies, Theodore A. Besterman, Lausanne, Societas Bibliographica, 4th ed., 5 vols., 1963

Year's Work in English Studies, London, English Association, 1919–present

Booklists

Books in Print, 1948–present. All books currently in print in U.S. Author and title.

Cumulative Book Index, 1898–present. Author, subject, and title index of all books printed in English.

Paperbound Books in Print, 1955–present. All books in U.S. printed in paperback.

Subject Guide to Books in Print, 1957–present. All books currently in print in U.S. by subject.

Dictionaries

The American Heritage Dictionary of the English Language, 1970

The Basic Dictionary of Science, Macmillan, 1965

Dictionary of American Slang, 2nd ed., 1975

Dictionary of the Bible, John L. McKenzie, Macmillan, 1965

Dictionary of Geological Terms, rev. ed., 1976

Groves' Dictionary of Music and Musicians, 5th ed., 9 vols. and supplement, 1981

The Interpreter's Dictionary of the Bible, 5 vols., 1976

McGraw-Hill Dictionary of Modern Economics, 1973

McGraw-Hill Dictionary of Scientific and Technical Terms, 2nd ed., 1978

The Oxford English Dictionary, 12 vols. and supplement, 1933

The Random House Dictionary of the English Language (Unabridged Edition), 1966

Roget's International Thesaurus, 1977

Webster's Third New International Dictionary Unabridged: The Great Library of the English Language, 1976

Encyclopedias (General)

Chambers's Encyclopedia, 15 vols., 1973

Collier's Encyclopedia, 24 vols., 1981

Encyclopaedia Britannica, 30 vols, 1980

Encyclopedia Americana, 30 vols., 1981

New Columbia Encyclopedia, 4th ed., 1975

The Random House Encyclopedia, 1977

Encyclopedias (Specialized)

Cassell's Encyclopaedia of World Literature, rev. ed., 1973

Encyclopedia of Banking and Finance, 7th rev. ed., 1973

Encyclopedia of Religion and Ethics, 13 vols., 1961

Encyclopedia of American History, 5th ed., 1976

The Encylopedia of the Biological Sciences, 2nd ed., 1970

The Encyclopedia of Education, 10 vols., 1971

Encyclopedia of Educational Research, 4th ed., 1969

Encyclopedia of Painting, Bernard S. Myers, ed., 4th ed., 1979

The Encyclopedia of Philosophy, 4 vols., 1973

The Encyclopedia of Physics, Robert M. Besancon, ed., 2nd ed., 1974

Encyclopedia of Psychology, H. J. Eysenck et al., eds., 2nd ed., 1979

Encyclopedia of World Art, 15 vols., 1959–1968
An Encyclopedia of World History, 5th ed., 1972
International Encyclopedia of the Social Sciences, 17 vols., 1967
The Larousse Encyclopedia of World Geography, 1965
McGraw-Hill Encyclopedia of Science and Technology, 4th ed., 1977
The Mythology of All Races, 13 vols., 1932
The Negro in American History, 3 vols., 1972
The New Catholic Encyclopedia, 17 vols., 1981
New Larousse Encyclopedia of Mythology, 1974
The Oxford Companion to American History, 1966
The Oxford Companion to Music, 1970
The Reader's Encyclopedia, William R. Benet, ed., 2nd ed., 1965
The Reader's Encyclopedia of World Drama, 1969
Universal Jewish Encyclopedia and Readers Guide, 11 vols., 1944
Van Nostrand's Scientific Encyclopedia, 5th ed., 1976

Indexes (General)

Book Review Digest, 1905–present. Summarizes reviews of books from a large number of periodicals. Gives critical reception of books reviewed.
Humanities Index, 1974–present. Periodical articles about the humanities. Author and subject entries. (See *Social Sciences and Humanities Index* for 1965–1974. See *International Index to Periodicals* for 1907–1965.)
New York Times Index, 1851–present. Subject index in alphabetical order. Includes abstracts of newspaper articles. Every article appearing in this newspaper will be included by subject in the index.
Nineteenth Century Reader's Guide, 1890–1899. Periodicals for the last ten years of the 1800s.
Poole's Index to Periodical Literature, 1802–1906. Indexed by subject. Author index in supplemental volume.
Readers' Guide to Periodical Literature, 1900–present. An excellent guide for general purpose reading. Lists articles from a broad range of periodicals. Entries by author, subject, and cross listing. Most articles appearing in this index written for general public.
Social Sciences Index, 1974–present. Periodical articles in the social sciences. Indexed by author and subject. (See *Social Sciences and Humanities Index* for 1965–1974 and *International Index to Periodicals* for 1907–1965.)

Indexes (Specialized)

Accountants Index, 1921–present. Author and subject index of books, pamphlets, and periodical articles.
Applied Science and Technology Index, 1958–present. Subject index. (Before 1958, see *Industrial Arts Index.*)
Architectural Periodicals Index, 1972–present. Covers architecture and allied arts, constructional technology, design, landscape, etc. Indexed by subject and architect/project.
The Art Index, 1929–present. By author and subject. Indexes periodicals and museum bulletins.
Biographical Dictionaries Master Index, Gale Research Co., 1975. Subject index. Guide to *Who's Who* and collective biographies.

Biography Index, 1946–present. Indexes information about people, dead and alive. Indexed by biographee and profession.

Biological Abstracts, 1926–present. References, abstracts, and indexes to world's life sciences research literature. Indexed by subject, author, and keyword.

Biological and Agricultural Index, 1964–present. Subject index to periodicals in these and related fields.

Business Periodicals Index, 1958–present. Subject index. Covers many fields such as accounting, economics, advertising, public relations, etc.

Chemical Abstracts, 1907–present. Index to periodical articles, papers, conferences. Indexed by subject, keyword, author.

Congressional Information Service Index to Publications of the United States Congress, 1970–present. Lists all written material from Senate and Congress.

Dramatic Index, 1909–1949. Articles on theatre and plays.

Education Index, 1929–present. Indexed by author and subject. Articles in magazines, books, and other sources discussing the entire field of education.

Engineering Index, 1906–present. Subject index. Includes reports of technical societies, government agencies, laboratories, as well as engineering periodicals.

Essay and General Literature Index, 1900–present. Essays and articles which have appeared in books.

Film Literature Index, 1973–present. Indexed by title of movie and by director.

Index of Economic Articles, 1961–present. Subject and author indexes. (For 1886–1965, see *Index of Economic Journals.*)

Index to London Times, 1906–present. By subject.

The Monthly Catalog of the United States Government, 1898–present. Lists all government publications by title, date, and purpose. States availability of material.

Music Index, 1949–present. By subject and author.

The Newspaper Index, 1972–present. Subject listings from *The Chicago Tribune, The Los Angeles Times, The New Orleans Times-Picayune,* and *The Washington Post.*

Nuclear Science Abstracts, 1947–present. Indexed by personal author, corporate author, and report number.

The Philosopher's Index, 1967–present. By subject and author. Includes American and foreign periodicals and journals.

Psychological Abstracts, 1927–present. Author and subject indexes.

Public Affairs Information Service Bulletin, 1915–present. Subject index for areas such as government, international relations, economics, etc.

Religion Index, 1977–present. Indexed by author and subject. Index of book reviews by author. (See *Index to Religious Periodical Literature* for 1949–1976.)

Television News Index and Abstracts, 1972–present. Indexes subject by topic, institution, and personality.

Theatre, Film and TV Biographies Master Index, Gale Research Co., 1979.
  Subject index to biographical sketches of people in performing arts found in biographical directories and dictionaries.
Ulrich's International Periodicals Directory, new editions periodically.
  Lists all periodicals available in various fields.
Vertical File Index, 1932–present. Subject and title. Includes pamphlets, leaflets, mimeographed materials, etc.

Quotations

Dictionary of Quotations, Larousse, 1981
Familiar Quotations, John Bartlett, 14th ed., 1971
The Home Book of Quotations, Classical and Modern, 10th ed., 1967
The Oxford Dictionary of Quotations, 3rd ed., 1979

APPLICATION

1. Look at the following subjects. What would be two or three likely sources for information on them?

    a. Benefits of jogging.
    b. Solar energy for homes.
    c. Jane Fonda.
    d. Vegetarian diets.
    e. Problems in the Social Security System.
    f. How holograms are made.
    g. World hunger.
    h. Rodeos in America.

2. Choose four of these subjects, go to the library, and find three books, articles, or references that you would read if you were going to do a research project on the topics. Make bibliography cards for each source.

3. Go to the library and locate two indexes in the reference section that are not listed under *Reference Material* in this text. Write down the names of the indexes and a brief summary of what they contain.

4. Arrange each of the items below in the appropriate footnote and bibliography form.

    a. A book edited by S. H. Frost, M. P. Weiss, and J. B. Saunders.
       Title: *Reefs and Related Carbonates: Ecology and Sedimentology.*
       Publisher: American Association of Petroleum Geologists.
       Place of publication: Tulsa, Oklahoma.
       Date of publication: 1977.
       Reference from p. 276.
    b. Author: Allan G. Cameron and Brian A. Fox.
       Title: *Food Science: A Chemical Approach.*
       Publisher: University of London Press.
       Place of publication: London.
       Date of publication: 1970.
       Reference from pp. 150–151.
    c. Author: Carol T. Nadelson.
       Title: "The Woman Physician."
       Journal: *Journal of Medical Education.*
       Publication information: vol. 47, March 1972, pp. 176–183.
       Reference from p. 176.

d. Author: William Strunk and E. B. White.
   Title: *The Elements of Style*.
   Edition: second.
   Publisher: The Macmillan Company.
   Place of publication: New York.
   Date of publication: 1972.
   Reference from pp. 27–28.
e. Author: Robert E. Ornstein.
   Title: *The Psychology of Consciousness*.
   Publisher: W. H. Freeman and Company.
   Place of publication: San Francisco.
   Date of publication: 1972.
   Reference from pp. 129–130.
f. Author: David Viscott.
   Title: *How to Live with Another Person*.
   Publisher: Arbor House.
   Place of publication: New York.
   Date of publication: 1974.
   Reference from pp. 48–49.
g. Author: Joseph Fletcher.
   Title: "The New Religious Morality."
   Editors: A. K. Bierman and James A. Gould.
   Book: *Philosophy for a New Generation*.
   Publisher: The Macmillan Company.
   Place of publication: New York.
   Date of publication: 1970.
   Page numbers: 178–187.
   Reference from p. 180.
h. Title: "Hill Defends State's Death Penalty Statute."
   Author: none given.
   Newspaper: *Houston Chronicle*.
   Date of publication: March 31, 1976.
   Page: p. 1 and p. 4 in Section 1.
i. Author: Leo Bogart.
   Title: *The Age of Television*.
   Edition: second.
   Publisher: Frederick Ungar Publishing Company.
   Place of publication: New York.
   Date of publication: 1956.
   Reference from p. 99.
j. Author: Robert Keathly.
   Title: "The Hornet's Nest at Langly."
   Newspaper: *The Wall Street Journal*.
   Date of publication: February 11, 1976.
   Page: 16.

WRITING ESSAY TESTS

THE CREATING STAGE

By now you are probably accustomed, when approaching a writing assignment, to think first: "The *Creating Stage*—how can I find something to say?" **The *Creating Stage* for writing *essay answers* is actually a *Recovery Stage* and depends for its success on retrieving what you have put into your mind** while studying. The very purpose of the test is to determine whether you have learned and if you can discuss important concepts covered in class. Your instructor is setting up a situation where you can prove that you *have* learned and *what* it is you've learned. This means that the method of creating you use will be one that lets you recall the information you studied. You aren't really creating in this case to know what you *think* on a subject or to find out something you *didn't* know you knew. Your aim is to draw out and remember what you recently put into your head and make applications from this material. No amount of cubing or looping and the like will give you this material if it isn't already there. You either know something to say on the subject or you don't.

The *Creating Stage* is very short in writing an essay test answer and very closely tied to how much studying you have done. It will probably be as simple as making a list of what you remember, and from that, the points you want to cover. Put this list of points in the margin of your test paper so that you can see it from time to time as you write the answer. (Also, your instructor will be able to see the list if you run out of time and see where you had planned to go with the answer.)

THE SHAPING STAGE

Writing essay test answers is really a rather limited type of communication process. Instead of having to get the reader's attention, you can count—to a certain extent—on the good will of your instructor in reading your essay answers to the end. Instructors are, after all, paid to read the tests, and they are usually very conscientious about doing that.

You *can't* count, however, on the instructor's not getting tired or bored or confused or persuaded that you don't know a thing (all affecting your grade). So the Shaping Stage is extremely important in the presentation of your answer. What the instructor wants to know from your test answers is not the *information* itself—she or he already knows this—but rather whether *you* know the information. You should have these objectives:

1. To prove immediately that you know the material.
2. To be very clear.
3. To be as specific as possible.

You need not begin the answer with the same kind of lead-in, attention-getting opening you use in essays when you have to attract your reader's attention away from whatever he or she has been thinking about. What is paramount here is the *subject matter*. The instructor is by and large uninterested—at this time particularly—in your personality or individuality except as that plays off the subject matter. The instructor *is* interested in knowing that you know and understand the material, so you must make that clear immediately.

In shaping essay answers, begin immediately with a sentence that tells the instructor what you are going to discuss. This will be the topic sentence or thesis sentence of your answer. (In fact, your entire answer will probably be one long topic sentence paragraph or a series of topic sentence paragraphs.)

The next thing you must do in the essay answer is to give the information. If you can put it in a series of three to five points, give these swiftly and clearly. Then for each point give an example or two. *Be specific*. Quote as many facts, give as many examples, as you can in the time allowed. Finally the way your answer *looks* on the paper will be very important in your instructor's grading. Remember these facts of life:

1. The instructor will have many papers to grade.
2. The instructor likes order.
3. The instructor will respond much more favorably to neatness and correctness.

Be realistic. If a reader has to squint to read your writing, you're the loser. Therefore, be neat and write legibly.

WHAT TO DO IF YOU THINK OF A NEW POINT WHILE WRITING

As you know from the creating activities you have done, writing itself often generates new ideas, retrieves information you had forgotten, and stirs up, in general, your thinking apparatus. If this happens while you are writing an essay test answer, *put a quick note to yourself in the margin* (you can scratch it out later) and after you've finished the point you're making, look for a minute at your list and think where your new point might fit best. The important thing is not to run off with the new thought in the middle of what you are saying when you think of the new point. Instructors are no different from other humans—they like order. They, like the readers of your essays, need to be able to see where you are going. Rambling answers will confuse and perhaps even annoy your instructor. Keep him or her happy and calm! Having a definite *order* to your answer, where you clearly go from one point to another, is a huge step in this direction.

THE COMPLETING STAGE

Do everything in favor of yourself that you possibly can. Save yourself enough time to look over the paper:

1. Check spelling. If the words are misspelled, this can irritate your instructor immediately.
2. Be sure you have complete sentences.
3. Read over what you've written to be sure that it makes sense. Is a word left out? Too many words put in? Did you write one word when you meant another?

You will defeat your own purpose if you write frantically to the last minute and don't leave yourself enough time to look over the answer. You can do more by checking the answer than by giving one more point.

SUMMARY

This pattern may not feel right at first but do it anyway:

1. **Be in charge of yourself.** Don't let the test situation panic you or control you. Be calm, or you'll probably forget even the few facts that you think you do know. An essay test situation is simply a time for you to show your instructor something that he or she expects you to know. Be sure to take advantage of this opportunity. Organize; and write with the instructor in mind. Make it the aim of your answer to communicate to the instructor that you know the material.
2. **Read the question carefully to see what approach to take.** Almost every question reveals this approach.
3. **Take time to plan *before* you write.** Even if everyone around you is writing furiously, make a list of what you are going to say *before* you start writing.
4. **Have a straightforward thesis or topic sentence.** Let the instructor know exactly what you are going to say.
5. **Write in an orderly fashion.** Think of your points one by one, and go from point to point in a specific order. If you think of a new idea, put it in deliberately, not randomly.
6. **Give a lot of details, examples, and illustrations.** Fill your answer up with specifics.
7. **Finish in time to look over the answer.** You may find this difficult because of the temptation to write to the very end. But remember, the instructor doesn't want to know *everything* you know. If you select from what you know and present this selection in an orderly fashion, you'll get the grade you want.

APPLICATION

Here are two answers to examination questions written by students. Read each and write about or discuss the strengths and weaknesses of the answers.

Exam question: *Explain why the oceans are not filled in and the earth is not a slush on the surface.*

STUDENT'S LIST

a. Subduction
b. Plate tectonics
c. Deposition
d. Erosion

STUDENT'S ANSWER

With all the sediment from erosion flowing into the oceans, how come the oceans are not filled in and the earth surface a slush pot?

One reason is the simple idea called subduction. Subduction is a simple idea; the sheet of rock from one area is going or being forced under another. Along the west coast of South America this is evident. The Andes Mountains are a side effect of this.

Second, the way these rock plates can be explained is an idea called plate tectonics. This idea states that there are rockplates on the surface of the earth, and they are constantly colliding and something has to give. The Himalayas are a good example.

A third reason to examine is the fact that all around you are deposition of material from erosion and volcanic activity, not to mention thrust of mountains over time. Rivers are constantly flowing with large amounts of sediment. The Amazon River. The island of Hawaii is a volcanic mountain. You can see the accumulation, but the disappearance is not quite so apparent.

Fourth, erosion is happening at an unbelievable rate. With all this erosion, the oceans should be filled in. Take the Mississippi River for instance. In the last one thousand years it has built up a seven kilometer river delta. If you multiply this by one thousand times for the whole earth and take into account the depths, the oceans should have been filled in at least twenty-five million years ago. Subduction is the best guess.

Exam question: *List four major engineering achievements prior to the twentieth century and discuss their importance.*

STUDENT'S ANSWER
(NO LIST MADE)

The first major engineering project was the irrigation system. This idea enabled the Egyptians to farm many miles of nonproductive land. Secondly, and just as important, was the building of roads. The Romans built roads mainly for communication not transportation. Their army was constantly changing, and roads were vital to their success. The third development was the refinement of steel. This was a significant step to modern engineering, since it allowed production of machinery. The fourth design was a result of refinement of steel. It was the invention of the steam engine. This was very useful since it gave man an alternative energy source to slavery.

WRITING FOR BUSINESS

What marks the difference between *business* writing and the rest of the kinds of writing in the world? Well, *purpose,* for one thing. The purpose of business is to make a profit, and, therefore, we can think of business writing as being *specifically* related to buying or selling, dealing in commodities and services. Business writing communicates information that has consequences in the business world. Its purpose is to communicate information in the least complicated, most direct, most accessible form possible.

FEATURES OF BUSINESS WRITING

TONE

If there is a single quality that sets apart this particular style of writing, that quality is *tone*. One of the conscious choices writers have is what roles they will assume in a piece of public writing, and this text has everywhere emphasized how important it is for you as a writer to be genuine, not to sound "put on" or "artificial." Your question, then, is how you can be genuine and still put on a special costume for a special role.

The right tone for business writing is "businesslike"—crisp, efficient, orderly—sounding like someone who means business, who can really get the job done. To present that aspect of yourself doesn't require putting on any kind of mask or concealing your true qualities at all. It does mean using the composing process in order to pull together exactly the presentation you mean to make, in exactly the same way that you'd pose for a studio portrait in a different way than you'd pose for a snapshot during a picnic. What you want to do is show the strongest, most efficient side of yourself: serious, dependable, confident, capable, and effective.

ACCESSIBILITY

The second feature of business writing is its *accessibility*. Everything is peeled away that could possibly interfere with the message, slow it down, or conceal it. It is open, easy to get. This means **keeping sentences short and direct** rather than long and complex, **using familiar words** rather than exotic ones (*use* rather than *utilize*, for example), **avoiding unnecessary words,** and **avoiding jargon.** Writers often reach for such heavy phrasing because they want to sound impressive. What happens, in fact, is that the reader is pushed into insensibility by such swollen phraseology.

A version of jargon is the buzzword—something that will automatically tingle the reader. In fact, buzzwords are artificial technical language, and while they seem to lend great weight to an utterance, they actually are almost totally meaningless.

GERALD COHEN'S DIAL-A-BUZZWORD offers you a thousand impressive three-word combinations. Write your next proposal or technical manual in half the time. Directions:

1. Turn the dials to line up the words.
2. Select the most pleasing 3-word combinations.
3. Join the selected combinations into sentences.

[Dial-a-Buzzword wheel with three concentric rings of words:]

Outer ring: Multiple, Conceptual, Integrated, Overall, Modular, Dynamic, Incremental, Sequential, Operational, Functional

Middle ring: interactive, performance, communications, capabilities, parameters, facilities, applications, output, systems, input

Inner ring: support, area, interface, criteria, analysis, implementation, basis, approach, environment, compatibility

ACCURACY

Business writing always deals with information that matters, that has consequences. Therefore *accuracy* matters—a great deal. A sample business letter illustrates the point completely.

248 *Practical Applications*

SAMPLE LETTER: ORDER

```
                                   1401 Marble Hill
                                   Newton, Pennsylvania 99222
                                   October 10, 1982
Denver Auto Parts
16 Chambers Place
Denver, Colorado 22446

Dear Sir,

Please send me the following parts from your September catalog:

      one rear window gasket seal, part #3320756   (page 27) $19.75
      one "handy-jack" hydraulic lift, #740        (page 3)   98.00
      one VW Specialties Catalog                   (page 50)   3.95
                                              TOTAL: $121.70

Enclosed is my check for the full amount.  Please ship my order
as soon as possible to the address above.

                                   Sincerely,

                                   André Worth Vergara

                                   André Worth Vergara
```

See how many opportunities there are for accuracy to make a difference? In the return address or the name or address of the dealer; in the description of the parts or the page or price or number; in the arithmetic. Any error in any item might mean a delay, or an overcharge, or unnecessary correspondence back and forth to clear up the matter. Business writing must be accurate, or else it is completely valueless.

FORMAT

Because the message is so important, and because its accessibility is so important, there are several special devices of *format,* or presentation, that assist the writer in being accurate and complete and assist the reader in finding exactly the information sought. The sample letter just presented, a simple order, shows several of these format conventions.

As you can see, the whole letter has a kind of block form, and each block contains certain information. Because that convention (or agreement) always works that way, the reader doesn't have to look all through the letter to find, say, the return address: it's always in block #1. Here's a diagram of a **Standard Block Letter,** and the kinds of information it always contains in each block.

Features of Business Writing

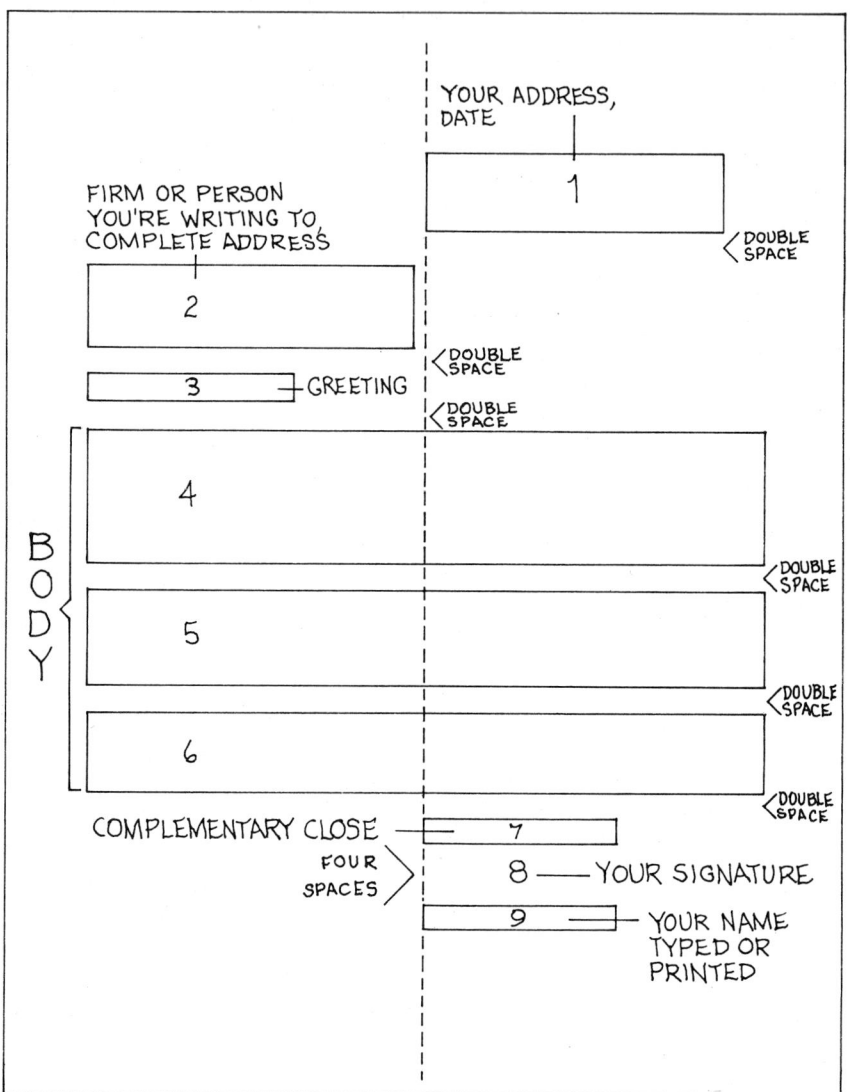

APPEARANCE

The *appearance* of business writing is slightly different from *format*. Appearance has to do with attention to such matters as details of margins at the top and bottom, the way a letter is placed on a page with proper balance on all sides, using a new typewriter ribbon (or black or blue ink if a letter is handwritten), and being free from foolish spelling or punctuation errors and also from smudges, strikeovers, and crossed-out words. *Appearance is visually what tone is verbally.* **It is the overall impression that greets the eye, quite apart from whatever is written.** And depending on the writer's care, it can create the initial impression of someone who is businesslike, orderly, and in control of matters, or it can suggest some kind of strolling disaster area. If a letter is a riot of smudges, strikeovers, cross-outs, and spelling errors, it won't get far in the business world, no matter *what* the content is about. First impressions do count, so you can expect to have business writing judged by its appearance.

BUSINESS LETTERS

THE "YOU" ATTITUDE

Compare these two statements:

1. "We are proud to open our new store, our third in Savannah."
2. "We are happy to open a new store in your neighborhood to serve you better."

The first is no doubt true—people have good cause to be proud of opening a new store, especially if it's their third. But that statement comes from the position of the *writer*—not the *reader*. We're glad they are proud—but what's that to us? The second, however, has the "You" Attitude. Their happiness (not pride) is about being in *your* neighborhood, and the store is there to serve *you* (not to add another store to the chain).

Of course there's no simple cure-all technique for business writing. But the point is to think in terms of the reader's benefit and then write in such a way that the reader's benefit is emphasized and highlighted. What are the reader's needs, concerns, interests?

REQUESTS

In a sense, *requests* and *orders* are similar in that both ask somebody to do something. Yet someone sending in an order is, in effect, merely responding to an invitation—an announcement, or an advertisement, or even a visit or call from a salesperson. A *request,* though, is usually something you generate on your own because of something you need or want. For example, it's not uncommon for students, doing research projects, to write to government agencies for special information. Most of us have had occasion to ask someone else for advice—a professor, a friend, an expert. When we handle requests in letter form, there are a few simple considerations that help things move along smoothly.

Be Clear and Specific. You won't get far writing to the state highway department and asking for "information about highways in this state." *What* about highways do you want to know? How the reduced speed rate has affected fatalities? What the plans are to finish paving that new stretch of Interstate? How many state parks are served by major highways? The more specific and precise you can be, the more likely you are to get what you want.

REQUESTS:
(1) Be clear and specific.
(2) Encourage an answer.

Encourage Response. Just because you ask doesn't mean that those you ask will oblige you with an answer. A request that's clear, specific, and polite will help to "enroll" them in your project, cause them to be sympathetic and to lend a hand. Other ways of encouraging response are by *telling who you are* and by *explaining how you'll use the information you're requesting*. The more "real" you are for them and the more understandable your request, the more likely they are to do what you're asking them to do.

The following page contains an example that will show you these elements in action. The requests are *clear* and *specific,* the writer *identifies herself* and explains her purpose in writing and tells how the information will be used.

JOB APPLICATIONS

When you're applying for jobs, you have two valuable tools: the letter of application and the résumé. Both have become well established over the years, so that there is an *expected form* to them, an *expected tone, appearance, order.* Yet because they are, in effect, devices by which you advertise yourself, it's very useful to look beneath the surface of the forms, to spend some extra time developing material that can be sorted into either the résumé or the application or both, and some time in working up the final appearance so that the letter will support the résumé, the résumé will back up the letter—and both will do the job for you that you want them to do: present you to the world of work as someone who is qualified, attractive, and definitely worth hiring.

JOB APPLICATION LETTER:
Highlights your qualifications, emphasizes particular achievements and abilities.

RÉSUMÉ:
Gives, in outline form, the data about your education, work experience, and activities that will be of interest to an employer.

AUDIENCE

Imagine the person who will be getting your letter—seated behind a desk piled high with incoming mail. Imagine, next, the first form letter—unimaginative, automatic, mechanical-sounding—then the second, the third, and so on to maybe the one hundred ninety-ninth. Imagine the boredom and the wearisomeness of it all. The reader just cannot stand one more form letter. But *she opens yours!* Ah-ha! It's original, personal, sparkling, scintillating. It has, of course, all the expected conventional material and information, but in addition to that, it carries your own unmistakable stamp, ring, quality.

SAMPLE REQUEST

This vignette may be a bit dramatic, but it happens often enough to be a fair representation of reality. And it does demonstrate that even in such a potentially impersonal information-moving situation as a job application letter, your ability to come up with an attractive presentation may provide just the edge that gets you past all those others. **It is to your advantage to get on top of the conventions of any set piece of business writing, and then to go** *beyond* **them.**

Dear Ms. Elk:

I am a sophomore education/psychology major at the University of Nevada and am writing a paper for one of my classes on the effect of TV commercials on children under 6.

I've had excellent luck with my library research, and now I want to add current information from our local TV stations, like Channel 3. I will share my report with other members of my class and I've written to the local TV magazine to see if they might publish all or part of it. I would of course be pleased to send you a copy if you would like to have one.

Would you please spend a few minutes answering these four questions?

1. Is there a person on your staff in charge of ads for children's programs? If so, could I please have the name?

2. Is there a network policy about the kind, number, subject, or treatment of commercials for children's programs? If so, may I have a copy?

3. Are there criteria that you at Channel 3 have developed (perhaps in addition to the network's) covering children's commercials?

4. Is there anything you think I sould know about children's commercials--any studies or guidelines or data which I haven't asked about? If so, would you please let me know what they are (and if available, please send me copies).

My paper is due in five weeks, so I would appreciate your response as soon as possible. Thank you for your assistance in this matter.

                                        Sincerely,

CONVENTIONS OF THE JOB APPLICATION LETTER

At the fundamental level, there are three:

MESSAGE

1. **What do you want to say?**
   I want this job.
   I'm qualified for it.
   You'd be well off to hire me.

AUDIENCE

2. **Whom are you saying it to?**
   Someone who does the actual hiring.
   Someone who screens applicants but doesn't do the actual hiring.

PURPOSE

3. **What do you want out of it?**
   I want my letter to look better than the others.
   I want to establish my qualifications.
   I want this job offered to me.

The way to say "I want this job" is to simply say so, although you can do some creating processes and come up with something a bit more individualized and effective. The way to say "I'm qualified" is by giving evidence (or information) about three areas of your life: school, work, and activities. You send all this to a real person (and take care to treat the person like a person, not a wall.) And you make your letter presentable by adhering to the conventions of Shaping and Completing.

CREATING

First, it is important to be clear about the areas in which you are going to develop information. By applying creating techniques to the conventional message of the job application letter, you will produce material usable in *both* letter and résumé, and you will increase your chances of expressing yourself in a special way that will make your letter stand apart from the crowd.

DO *CREATING* ON:
I want this job.
I'm qualified.
You should hire me.

I Want This Job. Notice that reference is to *this* job, not *the* job or *a* job; it's important to sharpen the focus. You're writing to a *particular company* in a *specific location* with a *unique product*—you don't want to tell them that you'd like to find *some* work *somewhere*.

Here are three creating activities for I Want This Job. Write as fast as you can for 3–5 minutes on each. These activities will help you get your ideas flowing and the job itself clearly focused. They also may trigger some original connections that will make your approach unique.

254 *Practical Applications*

1. List all the reasons you can think of for wanting *this* job.
2. List everything you can think of about *this* job.
3. Ask all the questions you can think of about this job.

I'm Qualified for This Job. Everyone who applies for the job will claim to be qualified; what's wanted is some *evidence* of this qualification. The three most common areas of qualification, usually, are *education, work experience,* and *interests.* Since almost every other letter will have a wooden, mechanical recitation on these points, your task is twofold: to come up with *your* **qualifications** and to **present them interestingly, even arrestingly.** That's a tall order, since the "rules" governing applications are a bit restrictive, with expected information in the expected places and in more or less the expected formats. Again, though, *creating* processes will help.

The following three activities will develop your sense of how you look as a candidate and add to the pile of ways in which you're qualified for *this* job:

  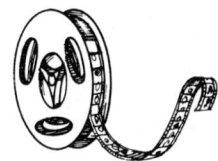

1. Do **cubing** on *my qualifications for this job.*
2. Do **looping** on *I'm qualified for this job.*
3. Review your life, like a movie, swiftly (about 10 minutes) and jot down every event that might have any bearing on your qualifications for this job.

You'd Be Well Off to Hire Me. Whenever we get to this spot in our own letters, we get a sinking feeling; after all, there are so many other applicants—who in the world would possibly want to hire *us!* But once again, *creating* processes come to the rescue. By doing the two following activities, you will clarify your intention to be serviceable on this job, and you'll begin to see the value you really do offer.

1. List all the things you might be able to do for the company if you had *this* job.
2. Complete this sentence at least 20 times (35 is even better): "On this job, I intend to . . ."

Now that you've done enough to be limber and to have the juices flowing nicely, here is a final assortment of things to make lists about. Spend 10 or 15 minutes on each of these—they are much more specific than the earlier creating activities—and they'll very likely provide information for the rough draft of your letter and résumé.

1. List all the *jobs* you've ever had, whether you were paid or not.
   What kinds of tasks did you do? How would that relate to what you might do on *this* job?
2. List all the times you've taken any *initiative,* taken the lead.
   Were you captain at team sports? Leader in organized activities—Scouts, Kiwanis, Bluebirds, Businesswomen of America?
   Think of childhood, grade school, high school, college.
3. List all the times you've been *successful*.
   What did you win? What awards? What acknowledgments? Prizes? Ribbons? Medals? Certificates?

When you finish these creating activities, you have a *lot* of material. Some of it may be worthless, some of it may be something you never would have thought of before, and some of it—much, probably—will be very useful indeed, once it is sorted out.

SHAPING

I'm Writing to _____. You've developed plenty of material so far, and you can sort it into the three basic groups: *education, work, interests*. The next question is: *what do you keep and what do you discard?*

To deal with that question, begin with a sense of audience. Remember that somewhere, on the other end of the mail route, there's a real person, sitting at a desk, holding a letter-opener, about to slit your—envelope. **The clearer you can visualize that person, the greater your chances of surviving the operation.** Having a specific person in mind will help you to (1) select and order the material at hand and (2) get the tone that will be most effective for that particular person.

Whom are you writing to? Essentially, it comes down to two types:

1. Someone who does the actual hiring.
2. Someone who screens all the incoming mail and then passes a few along for the "hiring" person to consider.

Unless you're writing directly to the head of the laboratory, the owner of the store, the foreman at the cannery, chances are that you won't be writing to the person who does the hiring. Instead, you'll be writing to a "screening person"—someone whose job it is to keep nearly everyone out (and thus to save the time of the person who will actually offer the job). Large corporations, businesses, and industries will almost always have a personnel department—

and if they do, you can be sure you'll be writing to the screening person. For the screening person, you'll need to be more distant, professional, cool, controlled. For the hiring person, you can probably afford to show a bit more personality, be a bit more direct and affable.

First Paragraph: Make It Hook and Hold. The first paragraph is the place to display your best and brightest credentials. It is probably *the* paragraph, of the whole letter, that counts the heaviest. To get it off to a fast start, be sure it contains everything it should: how you found out about this job (and which one you're applying for if there is more than one); your "hook"—the particular connection or claim, edge, or leverage you have that other applicants don't; and an instant, thumbnail summary of your qualifications.

FIRST PARAGRAPH:
How you heard;
which job;
your "hook";
your qualifications.

That first paragraph establishes who you are—and remember that a busy reader may very well take the short-cut of deciding everything on that one paragraph. You have four to seven lines to put forward your strongest (1) **reasons for wanting this job,** (2) **qualifications for this job,** (3) **connections with this job.**

You'll want to sort through those piles very carefully now—but don't take more than about 20 minutes.

The usual order for presenting this information is:

1. how you heard about the job;
2. which job you're applying for;
3. your "hook";
4. your qualifications.

However, there's no hard and fast rule about this. You can vary that order to put your own case most strongly. If you heard about the job from an influential person, put that information out early. If your training is particularly thorough, mention that right away. If your experience is especially rich, then that's what you want to put first.

If you are writing directly to the person doing the hiring, you are a bit freer to play up why you are applying for *this* job. If you know something favorable about the person, the job, the company, the product/services, work it in *if appropriate*. It's always legitimate to acknowledge a person or a laboratory or firm for their actual accomplishments, but it's more appropriate to do that to the person doing the hiring than to the person doing the screening. The first is more likely to respond than will the latter.

Paragraph on Education. For the body of the letter—after the introduction—you'll probably give one paragraph to each group of qualifications: a paragraph on education, another on work, and a third on interests. Of course your résumé will carry the full details: schools, degrees, courses, places where you worked, dates—all that. So all you want to do in the paragraph on education is to give the highlights, emphasize the points you want the reader to be sure to get.

EDUCATION
courses
research
honors
awards
distinctions
field trips
teachers

If you have taken any courses that are particularly relevant to this job, mention them. If you've had many courses related to this job, select only those that are most likely to make the best impression. And be sure to mention them by name, not by course number. *History 205* hardly tells anybody anything; *Colonial American History* tells a good deal more. If the relationship between the course and the job isn't completely obvious, explain the connection: "Because of the course in Colonial American History that I took last semester, I have developed a particular interest in working as a gunsmith in Williamsburg this summer."

If you have done special research projects in the area or related areas, mention them. Be sure to include any honors or awards, any distinctions that might demonstrate your particular qualities. Field trips? Work with a distinguished professor? Whatever it is, get it into this paragraph if it is connected to school and relevant to this job.

Paragraph on Work. Your work experience is evidence for the qualities that you hope to convince the reader you possess—qualities of employability. Any job—babysitting or pumping gas, volunteer nursing or carrying newspapers—shows that you are willing to hang in there day after day, steady and reliable. If you're a middle-aged adult, with many jobs over the years, you may need more than a paragraph to do justice to your career. If you've moved through a series of jobs to positions of increasing responsibility, say so. If you earned recognition or set performance records unusual for a person of your age and experience, don't keep it a secret.

WORK
jobs
responsibilities
positions
helping out
experiences
similarities

Most applicants will *say* they have certain qualities; you want to be sure to give *evidence* for *your* claims. Probably your creating activities have produced plenty of material, even though you may not actually have had a job that paid. Consider *anything* that might be related to work—activities, attitudes—*anything*. If you think it demonstrates the qualities you know you have of reliability, tenacity, and imagination—or whatever you think will be especially attractive in a candidate for *this* job—*mention it!* If you truly have absolutely nothing to say about work experience, you may want to leave this area blank and concentrate your energies in other directions.

As in the education paragraph, **be sure to arrange the material in some sensible order.** A jumbled hodge-podge won't do the job for you, won't impress the reader. Orderliness will. List the details chronologically, or in some other way that makes sense.

Paragraph on Interests/Activities. Finally, if you have any outside activities that might also be of interest or accomplishments not connected with either school or work, group those together. If you are writing to a screening person, you might want to leave this information for the résumé. If you're writing directly to the hiring person, it is more likely that you'd want to include it. Information about activities is almost always included on a résumé sheet; it is optional in the letter of application.

If, for example, you have an uncommonly large stamp collection, you might mention it; acquiring and arranging and keeping track of so much detail might well demonstrate exactly the qualities the employer is looking for. If you run five miles a day, rain or shine, that's probably evidence of a strong will and a healthy constitution. Being politically active or deeply religious may or may not help; keep in mind whom you're writing to and consider what the reaction might be. Just go ahead and sort through everything in the *activities and interests* pile. Whatever you come up with, be sure to relate it to *this* job.

Conclusion. With the body of the letter taken care of, you can now wrap the whole thing up. **Your conclusion is the final image you leave with your reader,** so you should take almost as much care with it as you did with your introduction. Keep it brief and crisp. Close with a snappy recapitulation of Why This Job and Your Qualifications and Your Desire for the Job. Then ask for a specific date for an interview or a response. Many applicants close weakly by saying they are "available" for an interview (who cares?) or that they "hope" they hear (who wants to waste away on hope?) or else they thank the reader for spending time with this letter (as though the letter weren't worth the time). Asking for a specific date for the interview is professional. It sounds strong, assured, and puts the burden on the reader *to respond*.

Completing

Once you have the content and form taken care of, give your draft a final going-over. Check that the balanced phrases are in parallel construction. Check for spelling, punctuation, capitalization, and other such mechanical errors. Check for odd or awkward phrases too. Be careful to eliminate "hoping," being "available," or thanking the reader for considering such a weak and unworthy candidate as your humble self. Be sure the addressee's name is spelled correctly. If you don't have the name already, the campus placement office can help you find it. Check the dates, the zip codes, and the punctuation for greeting and closing. Are there good clear indentions for the new paragraphs (5 spaces) or a double space between them? Is the conclusion strongly stated? Did you remember to type your name and leave room for the signature too?

When you've finished checking, your rough draft will probably really *look* rough. Rather than go straight to the finished copy, you may want to type the draft once more, this time to see how the margins will look, how the letter will balance on the page. With a clean "rough" draft in front of you, you won't have to make any decisions—or guesses—while you're typing the final copy.

Because the occasion is important (you *want* that job), you must be sure to **give the letter the best appearance you can.** Be sure the ribbon is fresh—crisp and black is what's wanted here. If you're not a very good typist, find somebody who is. This letter should be clean all the way through, with no typos, erasures, strikeovers, or dabs of correction fluid. Be sure to use good quality paper, too. The *appearance* of your letter gives off messages a mile wide. Are you flimsy dime-store stock or high quality bond? Are you right on target, complete and accurate, or are you covered with erasures, strikeovers, and paint-outs? Take pains to make the *appearance* of the letter say what you want it to say about you.

CHECKLIST FOR COMPLETING

Mechanics: names, dates, zip codes, punctuation.

Completeness: introduction, body, conclusion.

Style: tone positive and strong, phrases clear and natural, parallelism O.K.

Appearance: layout on page, margins, typing, paper.

SAMPLE LETTERS OF APPLICATION

Here are two sample letters of application. Each is well done; together they offer a modest range of variations while expressing their writers' particular qualities.

Return address

P.O. Box 8499
Richland Terrace
Digby, Georgia 30205
May 1, 1982

Internal address

Mr. Robert Pennington, Supervisor
Davidson's Personnel Department
817 Round Street
Atlanta, Georgia 30307

Dear Mr. Pennington: *Salutation*

mentions name, which job, and education

    Kim Bradley, Assistant Buyer of the Home Appliances department in your downtown store, referred your name to me. While conducting a tour of her department on January 15, Ms. Bradley informed me of Davidson's summer intern program for college students pursuing business degrees. As I live in the Atlanta area from May to September and am a marketing major at the University of Georgia, I would like to become an intern for Davidson's during those summer months.

work

    For the past three summers, I have been employed by the M. David Lowe Personnel Agency. As a temporary, I was exposed to a wide variety of jobs including receptionist to a Japanese steel company, receptionist to an advertising agency, law firm secretary, and mail sorter/deliverer for a major oil company. I learned how to adapt rapidly to the frequently changing job requirements of temporary work.

Activities

    Currently, I am taking marketing courses concerning consumer behavior, promotion, and retailing. My extra-curricular activities include membership in the Century Singers, a choral group at the University of Georgia. Through this organization, I met Ms. Bradley and assisted her in implementing the promotion efforts for the 1978 spring concert.

resumé

    The enclosed résumé will give you further information about my education and will provide a list of references.

Conclusion

    I will be in Atlanta from May 14 to May 23. Would it be possible for me to interview with you or another member of the personnel management on May 16? Prior to those dates, I can be reached by mail or by phoning 404-789-3333.

Sincerely, *Close*

Signature

Martha E. Schutt

Typed name

Practical Applications

404 James Street
San Diego, California 94567
April 24, 1982

Ms. Amilde Hadden
Beautiful Flowers, Inc.
890 University Drive
San Diego, California 94566

Dear Ms. Hadden:

Personal Contact — I spoke to you at our last AIFD meeting, and you suggested I write and apply for part-time work this summer and next fall. Jim Johnson and I both felt that working in your shop would give me the experience I need to compete for the better design jobs after graduation.

Activities — I have participated in many different activities in school which give me good qualifications to work for you. As you know, I am a member of AIFD, Student FTD, and California State Florists' Association. I have also worked with student floral concessions in the Floriculture Club, and this has taught me many basic skills and sales methods. I have competed in the California Allied Florists' design contest and scored high on my arrangement.

Employer — I am currently working in the admissions and records department of San Diego Community College, and this job has given me the public relations experience which is so important in the retail florist shop. I have spoken to my boss, Mr. Dave Workman, and he said that although he hates to lose a worker with three years of experience, he is enthusiastic about my getting a job related to my field of study. Feel free to contact him if there are any questions about my experience or work capabilities.

Conclusion — I would like to meet with you the week after final exams, May 12–May 19, if that is convenient. I can be reached after 5:00 at 932-4567 or at work at 932-7654. If I am not at the number when you call, please leave a message; I will return your call. I am looking forward to hearing from you.

Sincerely,

Kara O'Conner

Kara O'Conner

Enc: résumé

RÉSUMÉS

It will probably be good news and somewhat of a relief to learn that your résumé is much, much less demanding than the letter of application. What, then, is there to know about résumé sheets?

1. All of them look pretty much alike, and yours will need to look like the rest of them.

2. People reviewing them will expect information to be organized in the standard way so that they can easily and quickly find what they want to know.

3. They are used as a quick reference, and they'll probably be used during the interview also.

And that's pretty much it.

A résumé should have two important qualities: accuracy of information and aesthetic appeal.
The first of these—accuracy of information—is all but completely taken care of through the writing you've already done for the application letter. The aesthetic appeal is handled through carefully doing shaping work on the form provided—that is *don't try to get it all right the first time*. Use the first draft to get the material logged in accurately and the second draft to experiment with layout. When you're satisfied that the information is complete and accurate and the layout is accessible and crisp, then you're ready for the final draft that makes it all look so polished.

Once you know the basic formats, you have some latitude, so long as you keep the design clean and uncluttered. The basics about education and work experience must be there, with your name and address, and two to four references. Information about health and marriage, interests, and activities is optional.

Try to keep your sheet all on one page. Busy people don't want to be bothered with more than one page, so edit it down to that size if you possibly can and still do justice to your qualifications. Sometimes you can get more information in by adjusting the layout.

Remember that it is supposed to be a mere outline that gives only the most basic facts of your life—the facts an employer might find useful in deciding whether to hire you. And remember that the résumé sheet has a co-partner in the letter of application. The résumé gives the bare essentials; the application letter highlights and emphasizes, points up and interprets.

How, then, *should* it look—and what *does* go into a résumé? Take a look at the attached model—that's faster than a long essay of explanation.

Here is a second model together with a completed résumé. What is important for you to remember is that there is a variety of models. You have the choice of many, so just locate a résumé style that pleases you and follow that model. As this diagram shows, there is nothing mysterious or difficult about the résumé sheet. The subheads show the reader where to find the crucial information. All you need to do is take care to place the information in an attractive arrangement visually. What follows is a résumé sheet worked out on this model.

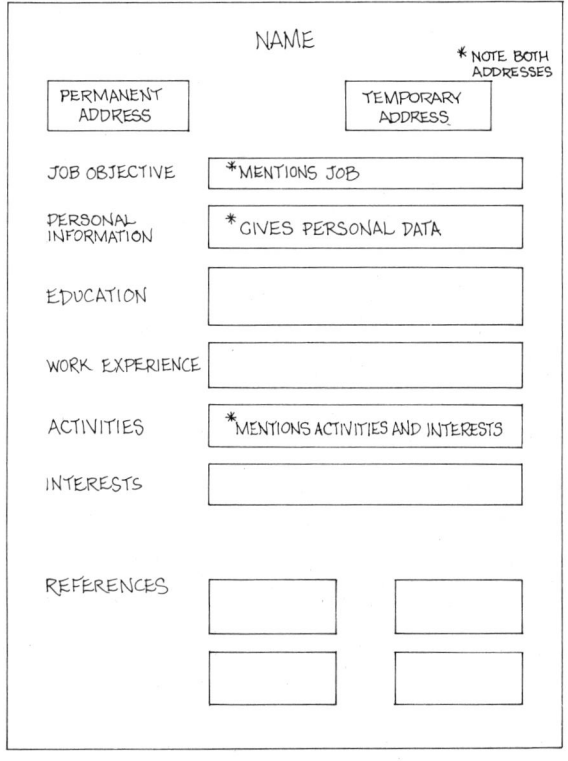

Résumé: Model 1

Résumé: Model 2

Résumés 263

James R. White   December 20, 1982

<u>Permanent Address</u>

1507 17th Street
Plato, Florida 32792
Telephone: 813-423-3326

<u>Temporary Address</u>

1602 Finfeather #28
Bryant, Florida 32816
Telephone: 904-822-6252

JOB OBJECTIVE	A position of responsibility in the Controller's or Treasurer's office of a large oil company, eventually qualifying for general management positions.
PERSONAL	Age 23, single, excellent health.
EDUCATION	1979-1983: Florida State University, Tallahassee, Florida. Candidate for B.B.A. degree in May 1983, with 3.0 average. Majored in accounting (emphasizing financial accounting) with courses in marketing, finance, management, business analysis, and economics. Received Dean's list honors for three semesters. 1975-1979: Plato High School, Plato, Florida. Graduated 18 out of a class of 456.
PREVIOUS EMPLOYMENT	1979-1982: Framed houses for four consecutive summers. 1982: Supervised work crew. 1981-1982: Subcontracted sheetrock and roofing work myself. 1978-1979: Worked as full-time cashier and stocker for the Kroger Company.
ACTIVITIES	Florida State University: Three-term treasurer of the FSU Sport Parachute Club. Member of FSU Accounting Society, Snow Ski Club, Pre-Vet Society, and the Brazos Valley Corvette Club. Plato High School: Member of the Plato Wildcat Marching Band, German Club, and National Honor Society.
INTERESTS	Jogging, Skydiving, current events
REFERENCES	Dr. Allen Bizzel Accounting Department Florida State University Tallahassee, FL 32816 Dr. Sid McDaniel Entomology Department Florida State University Tallahassee, FL 32816	John W. Harris, D.V.M. P.O. Box 1628 Bryant, FL 32816 Dr. Tom Oxner Accounting Department Florida State University Tallahassee, FL 32816

RÉSUMÉ

BARBARA WALKER
201 Lee Street
Walla Walla, Washington 99362
December 2, 1982

Education

    1980-82:
    University of Washington, Seattle
    Graduated with B.B.A. in Accounting, August 1982.
    Passed CPA Examination, November 1982.

    1978-80:
    Walla Walla Community College
    Graduated with A.A. degree, June 1980.

    1974-78:
    Walla Walla High School
    Graduated May 1978.

Work Experience

    1981-present:
    Seattle Student Finance Center
    --Handle daily deposits ranging from $2,000 to $50,000.
    --Verify checks written against the accounts.
    --Post transactions electronically and manually.
    --Balance all transactions at end of each day.
    --Assist in preparation of monthly financial statements.
    --Train new workers.

    1980-June to September and December:
    Accounting Assistant at Reserve Equipment Company, Olympia, Washington
    --Prepared employee payroll checks.
    --Reconciled monthly bank statements.
    --Performed duties of Accounts Payable Clerk.
    --Filed and answered telephones.
    --Posted and balanced various ledgers of parent company and its subsidiaries.

References

    Sue Young, Supervisor
    Seattle Student Finance Center
    P.O. Box Z
    Seattle, Washington 99330

    Jan Moore
    Reserve Equipment Company
    40 N. Bledsoe Avenue
    Olympia, Washington 99345

THE HANDBOOK

OVERVIEW

Parts of Speech
- Nouns
- Pronouns
- Verbs
- Adjectives
- Adverbs
- Prepositions
- Conjunctions
- Interjections

Sentence Errors
- Syntax Errors
- Punctuation Errors

Diction and Style
- Problems in Diction and Style
- Errors in Diction and Style

Punctuation

Spelling
- Spelling Rules

Mechanics
- Capitalization
- Abbreviations and Symbols
- Numbers
- Italics

A. B. C. Glossary of Usage

PARTS OF SPEECH

Why should you know what a part of speech is? If you had never learned that a noun is the name of a person, place, thing, or idea, wouldn't you still be able to speak and write English? You certainly would. You would have learned the rules for making English sentences and for using English words just by listening to others speak. Even a person who has never studied grammar formally can tell you that only certain words can occur in certain positions in a sentence. When you study parts of speech, you learn why this is so.

Words are assigned to a specific part of speech according to the functions they perform in a sentence. While many function as the same part of speech in every sentence (for example, *the, beside, of, Susan, he*), most may function as several parts of speech. Look at this list of words: *arm, finger, table, position*. Most of us would readily agree that they are all nouns since they all name things. But in actual use they can be several parts of speech, as these sentences illustrate:

> *Armed* with a yellow pad and a dozen sharp pencils, Mike decided to begin his theme.
> Mom plans to buy an *arm*chair for Dad.
> She *fingered* the imported silk blouse longingly.
> Pass me another *finger* sandwich.
> After a fruitless three-hour meeting, the frustrated committee voted to *table* the motion.
> I found an antique *table* lamp at the auction yesterday.
> Resigned to an afternoon of studying, she *positioned* herself under the oak.
> The administration has issued *position* papers on a number of issues.

If you were to insist that each of the words above could be used only as a noun simply because it names an object, you would give up some creative uses of the words. Understanding the function that each part of speech performs can help you use words imaginatively and purposefully. This is why studying parts of speech is valuable. To know how to use English creatively, you must understand how words work together to create meaning.

Words in English are classified into eight parts of speech: noun, pronoun, verb, adverb, adjective, preposition, conjunction, and interjection.

NOUNS

Although this is not a complete definition, a noun names a person, place, thing, or idea. Nouns can be divided into two broad categories: proper nouns and common nouns.

1. A proper noun names a specific person, place, thing, or idea; proper nouns are always capitalized.

William Shakespeare	King Tut	the Revolutionary War
The Queen Mary	The Netherlands	the Washington Monument
Chicago	Saturn	the Sphinx

2. A common noun names a person, place, thing, or idea that is one of many others in a class. Most nouns are common.

girl   railroad   pillar   universe   assumption
toy   honesty   sky   mind   development

Nouns have two basic functions in sentences: they may be subjects or objects. As a subject, a noun announces the topic of a sentence or a clause. In the sentences below, the nouns that function as subjects are italicized: **NOUN FUNCTIONS**

When the sudden *rainstorm* ended, the *swimmers* returned to the lake.

The *president* will make an important foreign-policy statement tonight.

The *desk* occupies most of my office.

As an object, a noun completes the meaning of a verb or verbal (verbals will be discussed in detail under *verbs*) or it joins with a preposition to form a prepositional phrase. The nouns used as objects are italicized in these sentences:

OBJECT OF THE VERB:	I finally finished my *term paper* at 3:00 A.M.
	The president vetoed the *tax reform bill*.
OBJECT OF A VERBAL:	Typing that *paper* was hard work.
	I still plan to write a *book* someday.
OBJECT OF A PREPOSITION:	During its last *session*, Congress gave itself a raise.
	I asked the movers to place the couch against the *wall* in the *living room*.

Nouns can be made *plural,* and they can be made *possessive.* (There are some exceptions, but this is a general rule.) Nouns are usually made plural by adding *s* or *es:*   **NOUN IDENTIFIERS**

taco/tacos; beach/beaches; radio/radios

Some nouns are irregular, and their plurals are exceptions:

ox/oxen; foot/feet; knife/knives

Usually, a noun is made possessive by adding an apostrophe and an *s:* '*s.*

fire/fire's warmth   writer/writer's desk

Making a noun possessive is one of the hardest things for beginning writers to get right. You have to decide if the noun is going to be plural possessive or singular possessive (this merely means that you have to know if you are talking

Parts of Speech

about one thing/person or more than one). The placement of the apostrophe in the possessive depends on whether the word is singular or plural.

> The lady's coat (singular possessive)
>
> The ladies' coats (plural possessive)

PRONOUNS

Pronouns are usually defined as noun substitutes because they frequently replace nouns mentioned earlier in a sentence or in a previous sentence. As noun substitutes, pronouns are important in reducing redundancy in sentences. Look at this sentence, for example:

John broke his leg as he was climbing down the mountain.

We know that each pronoun refers to *John,* but it would be frustrating and redundant to rename John each time we refer to him:

John broke John's leg as John was climbing down the mountain.

One of the most important functions of the pronoun, then, is to make communication more efficient by eliminating unnecessary repetition of nouns.

Pronouns are considered noun substitutes for another reason: they perform the same functions nouns do. They serve as subjects of sentences and clauses or as objects of verbs and prepositions.

> *This* is my favorite book.   (subject)
>
> *I* refuse to go to that class one more time.   (subject)
>
> You don't mean *that,* do you?   (object of the verb)
>
> My jeans are different from *those*.   (object of preposition)

Because of their close relationship to nouns, pronouns could be considered a kind of noun, and many grammarians and linguists classify them as nouns. However, they perform so many functions that they must be considered a separate part of speech which can be broken down further.

Personal Pronouns: **I, you, he, she, it, we, they, me, him, her, us, them.**

These occur in the same positions as nouns, but notice that the form of the pronoun changes with its function in the sentence. If it is used as a subject, the *nominative* form is used:

> *I* answered the telephone when *you* called.
>
> *They* plan to move into the new house across the street.

But when the personal pronoun serves as an object, the *objective* form is used:

I will accompany *them* on the trip to New Mexico.

Tell *us* all about the trip.

Mary will take the trip with John and *me*.

Possessive Pronouns: **my, mine, his, her, hers, its, our, ours, your, yours, their, theirs.**
As indicators of ownership or possession, these pronouns function just as possessive nouns do. Essentially, they modify the nouns with which they appear:

his books, *our* time, *my* story

Reflexive Pronouns: **myself, himself, herself, itself, yourself, ourselves, themselves.**
Reflexive pronouns occur only when they clearly refer to a noun or pronoun appearing earlier in the same sentence. This is why the pronoun is called reflexive: it is grammatically and semantically bound to the noun or pronoun it refers to.

Mary considers Mary a good person. → Mary considers *herself* a good person.

Johnny's mother had warned Johnny to behave Johnny's self before she spanked him. → Johnny's mother had warned him to behave *himself* before she spanked him.

Reflexive pronouns may also be used as *intensive pronouns* to provide emphasis to a noun or pronoun:

We painted the house *ourselves*.

I *myself* did all the work.

Notice that in each case, the intensive pronoun could be omitted without detracting from the meaning of the sentence—*I did all the work*. It simply makes the noun emphatic.

Relative Pronouns: **who, whose, whom, which, that, when, where, wherever.**
This set of pronouns replaces the noun in a relative clause. Like all other pronouns, relative pronouns are *referents;* that is, there is always a noun to which the pronoun refers:

The dress *which* I worked on yesterday is still not finished.

The street *where* Joan lives is hard to find.

I remember the man *who* told me how to get there.

In the first sentence, *which* refers to *dress;* in the second, *where* refers to *street,* and in the third, *who* refers to *man*. Notice that the relative pronoun is always the first word in the relative clause.

Demonstrative Pronouns: this, that, these, those.
Demonstrative pronouns function as nouns or as modifiers.

> NOUNS: *This* is not what I had in mind when I suggested we have a party.
> What did she mean by *that?*
> Which of *those* did you want?
> *These* are the best shoes I've ever owned.

Notice that demonstrative pronouns are somewhat vague when they are used as nouns. Out of context, you don't know what any of these pronouns refer to. In the context of longer passages of speech or writing, demonstrative pronouns always refer to a specific noun.

> MODIFIERS: *Those* flowers are the freshest ones in the shop.
> If you like exciting mysteries, read *this* book.

Interrogative Pronouns: who, which, what, whom, whose.
Interrogative pronouns are used in questions to represent the information that is unknown.

> *Who* is the woman you were talking to?
>
> *Whom* do you plan to go home with?
>
> *What* are you writing your term paper on?
>
> *Which* boys were caught in the department head's office?

Like relative pronouns, interrogative pronouns always appear at the beginning of the clause or sentence since it is the unknown information that is the focus of the sentence. Unlike relative pronouns, however, the referent for these pronouns is unknown.

Indefinite Pronouns: each, everyone, anybody, either, some, somebody, one, no one, several, everybody, any, all.
Indefinite pronouns may function as nouns or as modifiers:

> NOUNS: Give me three copies of *each*. (object of preposition)
> *Some* say she's the best chemistry teacher in the school. (subject)
> *No one* came to the party. (subject)
> *Anybody* can answer that. (subject)

Indefinite pronouns have no specific antecedent, but they are pronouns because they clearly function as noun substitutes. This set of pronouns is useful when specificity is not important to the meaning of the sentence.

MODIFIERS: *Several* boys were caught in the dean's office late last night.
One girl said she hated reading *all* the novels.

VERBS

The verb may be considered the heart of the sentence because it contributes to and affects meaning more than any other element in the sentence. It determines the number of nouns needed to make a sentence meaningful. It determines the time and the quality of the action. It sometimes focuses the reader's attention on a particular part of the sentence.

Verbs in English have four principal parts that form the basis of the tense system: present, past, past participle, present participle. Tense refers to the way we indicate when an action occurs. In English, we really have only two tenses, past and present, but we can add helping verbs and modals (to be discussed later) to make the time and quality of the action more specific and to give the illusion that there are more than two tenses.

Verbs may be regular or irregular depending on how the principal parts are formed. In regular verbs, the past and past participle are formed by adding *-ed* to the present:

PRESENT	PAST	PAST PARTICIPLE	PRESENT PARTICIPLE
dress	dressed	dressed	dressing
cross	crossed	crossed	crossing
pass	passed	passed	passing
alert	alerted	alerted	alerting

In irregular verbs, the past and past participle forms sometimes show changes in the main vowel, and sometimes these forms are entirely different from the present:

PRESENT	PAST	PAST PARTICIPLE	PRESENT PARTICIPLE
go	went	gone	going
lie	lay	lain	lying
write	wrote	written	writing
do	did	done	doing
is	was/were	been	being

Principal parts are important in understanding how time (tense) is expressed by the verb. *Present* expresses action going on right now:

I *pass* by his house every day.

Tom *is* sick today.

The past expresses completed action:

>He *crossed* the street without looking.
>
>Mary *wrote* me a long letter.

The past participle also expresses past action, but the addition of *have* as a helping verb changes the *aspect* (quality) of the past action. The tenses formed by combining *have, has,* or *had* with the past participle are called the perfect tenses. Helping verbs will be discussed in more detail under *Auxiliary*.

>He *has done* all he can do.
>
>I *have crossed* that street many times.

The present participle is used with a form of *be* to convey the sense of continuing action or future action:

>John *is going* home with me.
>
>She *is* upstairs *dressing* for her important job interview.

The Auxiliary (helping verb). As the sentences above show, the principal parts alone allow only limited distinctions of time and quality of action. To increase the range of action expressed by the verb, we use auxiliaries—special verbs that work with the main verb of a sentence. We have two kinds of auxiliaries in English: helping verbs and modals.

Helping verbs are forms of *have* and *be* used with the past participle and with the present participle to change the quality rather than the time of the action. Notice how a helping verb changes the quality of the past action in these sentences:

>PAST: I saw all I wanted to see at the museum.
>PAST PERFECT: I had seen all I wanted to see, so I went home.
>PRESENT PERFECT: Since I have seen all of these exhibits before, I will skip the museum tour.

Similarly, the addition of *be* to the present participle changes the *aspect* of the action:

>Since she moved to Dallas, she is writing home twice a week.
>
>We are now passing by the Capitol.

Helping verbs can be used together to further qualify the verb.

>Jack has been watching TV for three hours.

The meaning of the verb *has been watching* is quite different from the simple past—John *watched* TV for three hours. The expanded meaning occurs when we combine the perfect (*have* + past participle) and the progressive (*be* + present participle).

Modals are special kinds of verbs used with any of the principal parts to express the mode of the action. The modal indicates whether action is possible, permitted, required, or desired. The list of modals is short:

> can   may   must   will   shall
> could might ought would should

Things to remember about modals:

1. Modals always appear before the main verb:

   I *can* finish this tonight if I hurry.

   He *will* call me when he's ready.

2. When modals are used with helping verbs, the perfect or progressive markers (*-ed* or *-ing*) follow the modal:

   He *could* have *finished* if he had tried.

   You *should* have been *studying* instead of sleeping.

3. Modals must be used with other verbs; a modal alone does not express action. Try writing a sentence using only *shall* or *might* as the verb. You can't because by leaving out the verb, you leave out the heart of the sentence.

   Certainly, there are times when modals appear alone:

   Mary asked me if I was going to her party. I said I *might* if I finished all my work by then.

In context, we realize that *go* is the understood verb in the second sentence. Only when the context is understood do modals appear alone.

When we consider the possibilities allowed through combinations of principal parts, helping verbs, and modals, we see the versatility of English verbs:

He *writes* home every week.

Until this month, he *had been writing* home every week.

He *has written* more letters in two months than I have in two years.

We *should write* home more often.

I *will write* my parents tomorrow.

If I'm too busy, I *may write* the next day.

I *must have been writing* my paper in the library when you called.

Notice that the combinations reveal a rigid ordering of the main verb, helping verbs, and modals.

Parts of Speech 275

Subject–Verb–Complement Combinations. One of the most important functions of the verb is to indicate the number of nouns needed to complete the meaning of a sentence. We know that there must always be a noun to function as the subject for the verb, but some verbs require one noun, two nouns, or an adjective as a complement (completer of the action). Verbs are accordingly classified as *intransitive, transitive,* or *linking.*

1. When an action verb is complete without a complement, it is an intransitive verb.

    I *was talking* with my mother on the telephone.
    Our congressman *voted* against the bill.
    To get my exercise, I *walk* to school every day.

2. When an action verb requires a noun or nouns to complete its meaning, it is a transitive verb.

    He **hit** *the ball* farther than he ever had before.
    The president will almost certainly **veto** *the bill*.

The noun following the verb in these sentences is a direct object, but some verbs take an indirect object as well as a direct object:

                IO   DO
My mother taught me the alphabet when I was three.

        IO   DO
He gave me a beautiful corsage.

To test for an indirect object, simply reword it as a prepositional phrase that indicates at whom the action of the sentence is directed:

My mother taught the alphabet *to me*.
He gave a beautiful corsage *to me*.

A few verbs take an object complement along with a direct object. The object complement may be either a noun or an adjective:

In the last election, the American voters elected a Democrat *president*.
Mary considered Tom *a bore*.
We painted the hall *red*.

3. When the complement renames or modifies the subject, the verb is a linking verb. We have two kinds of linking verbs in English: *be* verbs and verbs that deal with the senses or with states of being. What makes the complement of a linking verb different from the complement of a transitive

verb is that it may be a noun (predicate nominative) or an adjective (predicate adjective). Furthermore, this complement carries most of the meaning in a sentence whose verb is a linking verb. The function of the linking verb is to show identity between the subject and the complement, so the verb itself carries little meaning and conveys little or no action. Notice how important the italicized complements are to the meaning of these sentences with *be* as a linking verb:

Mary was *sick* today.
The truth is *that I just didn't have time to do it*.
Truth is *evasive*.

Note the italicized complements of the linking verbs:

The heroine remained *unmarried*.
She became *despondent* when her lover died.
Professor Smith's clothes always look *wrinkled*.
In his baggy pants and narrow ties, he seems *unconcerned* about style.
I feel *awkward* every time I talk to him.

Active and Passive Voice. One way to provide focus in a sentence is to change the usual subject-verb-complement order. With an action verb, the subject functions as the doer of the action and the complement as the receiver of the action:

Bill (doer) threw (verb) the ball (receiver) powerfully to the second-baseman.
As my teacher looked over my paper, I revised several paragraphs.
The policemen chased the boys for two blocks.

Ordinarily, the doer is the focus of the sentence because he or she appears before the verb and the complement, but when you want to change the focus, you may change the *active* sentence into a *passive* sentence by putting the receiver of the action in the subject position:

The ball was thrown powerfully by Bill to the second-baseman.
The boys were chased for two blocks by the policemen.

The change from active to passive voice is a variation of the regular order of the sentence. The formula for this change is simple:

1. Transform the subject of the sentence into the agent of the action by rewriting it as a *by* prepositional phrase: by Bill, by the policemen.
2. Move the direct object (the receiver of the action) into the subject position.

3. Rewrite the verb using a form of *be (was, were, is, are)* and the past participle: threw → was thrown, chased → were chased.

Verbals. Although the verb usually functions as the predicate of a sentence, certain verb forms can serve as nouns and adjectives and adverbs. When a verb functions as a different part of speech, it is called a *verbal*. We have three kinds of verbals in English: *participles, gerunds,* and *infinitives*.

A *participle* is a verb used as an adjective. You can recognize participles when you note the use of the perfect form or the *-ing* form of a verb to modify some noun or pronoun in the sentence. In each of these sentences, the italicized phrases are participles that modify the noun serving as the subject:

The *evaporating* mist made the morning seem muggy.

Walking through the street, Tom could see the damage the flood had done.

The *tired* man trudged in to his last job interview.

A *gerund* is a verb used as a noun. You can recognize a gerund when you notice an *-ing* form (the same as the present-participle form) of a verb used in a position generally filled by a noun:

Studying makes me sleepy.

Going to the lake and spending the day fishing is my idea of a good time.

An *infinitive* is formed by adding *to* to the present verb form. Infinitives function as nouns, adjectives, or adverbs.

NOUN: *To quit* now would be unwise.
He plans *to read* the novel tonight.

ADJECTIVE: The best way *to write* is to isolate yourself from all distractions.

ADVERB: He is eating heavier meals *to gain* weight.
To sleep comfortably and soundly, drink warm milk before going to bed.

As these sentences illustrate, verbals may be either single words—*evaporating, studying, to quit*—or phrases that include an object or an adverb—*to gain weight, to read the novel, walking through the street, to sleep soundly and comfortably, going to the lake.*

ADJECTIVES

Adjectives are modifying words. Their function is to restrict the meaning of a noun by making it more specific, by describing it, or by indicating its characteristics. By adding adjectives to a noun, you make the subject more specific, which is desirable because the amount of information conveyed to a reader is increased.

Modification occurs on the level of words, phrases, and clauses:

    the *healthy* girl (word)

    the girl *with the rosy cheeks* (prepositional phrase)

    the girl *who sat in the dentist's office* (clause)

    the house *where I live* (clause)

Single-word adjectives usually occur before the nouns they modify:

    the *red* bird   the *ugly* house
    the *trickling* stream   *rush-hour* traffic

Adjective phrases and *clauses* occur after the nouns they modify:

    the tropical bird *with the brilliant red and blue feathers*

    the eccentric, old professor *whose clothes seemed at least 10 years old*

    rush-hour traffic *that wastes several hours of a worker's day*

Predicate adjectives occur after *to be* verbs and linking verbs:

    The meal was *delicious*.   I feel *fine* today.
    His clothes look *wrinkled*.   She remained *despondent*.

Although there are many words that we automatically qualify as adjectives—*fast, correct, brown, first, pretty, ugly, high*—the English language allows us to form adjectives in several ways.

Adjectival endings may be added to other parts of speech:

-y	sticky	gummy	sunny	chewy
-ful	beautiful	bountiful	colorful	awful
-ive	vindictive	instructive	conducive	restive
-al	verbal	colonial	proverbial	herbal
-ic	ironic	economic	metallic	gastric

Sometimes other parts of speech serve as adjectives without an added ending:

    college textbook   *wall* hanging
    food processor   *desk* top
    lawn mower   *lawn* chair

Frequently, when other parts of speech, especially nouns, are used as modifiers, the words tend to be perceived as a single unit. For instance, in most of the phrases above, it is difficult to determine whether the structure is an adjective plus noun or simply a compound noun. In either case, the phrases were originally formed by joining a noun used as an adjective to another noun in a modifying relationship.

As you saw in the discussion on verbs, *participles* are verb forms used as adjectives:

> the *grieving* parents the *condemned* prisoner
> the paint *peeling* off the walls the clothes looked *wrinkled*

The degree of modification can be altered through comparative and superlative forms:

> the *tallest* boy the *older* brother
> a *most fortunate* incident the *more appropriate* answer

ADVERBS

Adverbs, like adjectives, are modifying words, phrases, or clauses. They add specificity to the action in a sentence when they modify verbs, but they can also modify adjectives and other adverbs. The following sentences show the variety of functions and positions that adverbs (or phrases and clauses serving as adverbs) can take:

> *Finally,* my mother agreed to let me go.
>
> *Fortunately,* she also agreed to help me pay for my expenses.
>
> *During the party,* they threw me *in the pool*.
>
> *When I took Professor Smith's course* I learned much about literature.
>
> *To lose weight,* I plan to stop eating desserts.
>
> She didn't let her son ride the roller coaster *because she thought it was unsafe*.

These sentences show that adverbs may occur in many different positions in a sentence. Frequently, when an adverb occurs at the beginning, it is called a *sentence modifier* because it modifies the whole sentence rather than the verb alone. Notice the difference between the use of *finally* and *fortunately* in the sentences above. An adverb that modifies the verb can be moved closer to the verb without making the sentence sound awkward, but the sentence adverb sounds best in initial position:

> My mother *finally* agreed to let me go.
>
> She also *fortunately* agreed to help me pay my expenses.

Fortunately, the sentence modifier, sounds most natural in initial position but *finally,* which modifies the verb, may be moved to different positions without creating awkwardness. The sentence adverb comments on the action conveyed by the entire sentence.

Sentence adverbs also occur as transitional words, as in the following example:

> The wedding was scheduled to take place in her grandfather's garden. The reception, *however,* was to be held at the most elegant hotel in the city.

However links the two sentences by pointing back to the previous sentence and by signaling to the reader that the second sentence is a contrast to the first. This type of sentence adverb is a conjunctive adverb.

Adverb Forms. Adverbs occur in a variety of forms. Many words are considered adverbs simply because they convey the sense of time or place:

> still   now   today   only   there   south

But adverbs may be formed by adding *-ly* to an adjective. These are generally adverbs of manner because they tell how something is done:

> quickly   slowly   convincingly   colorfully   hopefully

Like adjectives, adverbs also express degree through comparative and superlative forms:

> most convincingly   more slowly   liveliest   lonelier

Finally, there are some adverbs which modify other verbs and adjectives by intensifying their meaning rather than by modifying them. Appropriately, these are called *intensifiers*. The words in italics in the following sentences are intensifiers:

> Everyone agrees that she is a *very* pretty girl.
>
> I'm *quite* sure I won't be able to devote *too* much time to this.

PREPOSITIONS

Prepositions are words or groups of words that indicate relationships between the object of the preposition and some other word(s) in the sentence. Prepositions function as indicators of time, place, cause, manner, agency, association, or other relationships. Usually, prepositions occur in phrases that function as adverbs or adjectives, as the following sentences illustrate:

> Tom lives *by* a noisy freeway.
>
> She sat *beside* me *at* the movies.
>
> *In* the summer, I'll be working full time *at* our local drugstore.
>
> *To* me, a summer job is a good way to prepare *for* a fulltime job *after* graduation.

In spite of her mother's refusal, Jane went anyway.

When the object of the preposition is separated from the preposition, the sentence may end in a preposition. For many people, this construction is one of the worst grammatical sins in the English language. There is really no logical reason for claiming that it is incorrect to end a sentence with a preposition. We hear and use sentences like these all the time:

Who are you going to the party *with?*

Who are you mailing that *to?*

That's something I won't put *up with.*

Notice how stiff the sentences sound if they are revised to avoid the preposition at the end:

With whom are you going to the party?

To whom are you mailing that?

That's something with which I won't put up.

The objection to ending sentences with a preposition is that it makes the sentence sound informal and casual. Ending a sentence with a preposition is not a grammatical but a stylistic matter.

Verb Particles. Certain prepositions have become so closely associated with certain verbs that the verb and preposition form a verb unit:

Would you *look up* this word for me?

Call me *up* when you want to talk.

I can't *make out* what number this is.

We took three prospective buyers to *look over* the property.

In these sentences, *up, out,* and *over* don't function as ordinary prepositions because they don't link an object noun to another part of the sentence. The prepositions are merely bound to the verb in such a way that they change its meaning. *Look* is quite different from *look up, make* is quite different from *make out,* and *look* is quite different from *look over.* Prepositions that are part of the verb are called verb *particles.*

However, not all prepositions that seem to be bound to the verb are particles. In the sentence we looked at above—*That's something I won't put up with*—*put up* is not a verb plus particle; it is an idiom, a frozen expression of the language. A true particle can be separated from the verb without affecting the verb-particle bond and without affecting meaning:

I *looked* the number *up.*

They spent three hours in *looking* the property *over.*

CONJUNCTIONS

Conjunctions join words, phrases, and clauses. *Coordinating conjunctions* join grammatically equal elements:

Mary **and** *her teacher* met to discuss her grades.

They argued *politely* **but** *earnestly*.

She tried to get her grade changed, **but** Dr. Allen refused to do it.

I love to sit on the patio *early in the morning* **and** *late in the evening*.

Notice that in each of the sentences, the conjunction joins elements of the same grammatical rank: two nouns, two adverbs, two independent clauses, two prepositional phrases.

There are only a few words that function as coordinating conjunctions:

and   but   for   or   nor   (sometimes *so* and *yet*)

When coordinating conjunctions occur in pairs, they are called *correlative conjunctions*:

Neither Tom *nor* Mary is going.

Not only did he fail his chemistry test, *but* he *also* missed the deadline for turning in his English paper.

Correlative conjunctions include *either . . . or, neither . . . nor, not only . . . but also, both . . . and, not . . . but.*

Subordinating conjunctions join unequal elements. In fact, the function of these conjunctions is to show a dependent relationship between two clauses:

Because I was late three times, I was penalized one letter grade.

Although I worked hard to make the canoe waterproof, it flooded *when we were in the middle of the lake.*

The occurrence of a subordinating conjunction is a clue that the clause following it must be linked to an independent clause. Therefore, knowing that subordinating conjunctions signal dependence should help you recognize and avoid sentence fragments.

The following are some of the words that function as subordinating conjunctions:

after	so (that)	even though
although	before	until
as	how	unless
as if	whenever	through
if	wherever	when
when	while	that (when introducing noun
because	though	clauses)

Parts of Speech   283

Conjunctive Adverb

> He had studied until 2 A.M. However, when he saw the test, he realized he hadn't studied enough.

In this sentence, *however* does not indicate a grammatical relationship between the two sentences. It could be left out without affecting the fundamental meaning. Conjunctive adverbs are communication aids; they make logical (not grammatical) relationships between sentences that would be only implicit otherwise. They are aids to coherence.

INTERJECTIONS

When you interject something, you interrupt the usual flow of a thought or sentence or conversation. That is exactly what interjections do—they interrupt the usual grammatical flow of the sentence. Interjections are not grammatically bound to the sentences they appear in, but they do add expressions of surprise, emotion, or anger. In the following sentences, the interjections are italicized. Notice that the commas set them off from the rest of the sentence both grammatically and semantically.

> *Oh,* I didn't know you were waiting for me.
>
> *Good grief,* Charlie Brown, won't you ever learn?
>
> *Alas,* I was doomed to fail my first college math course.

Interjections should be used sparingly in writing. Although they emphasize speech effectively, they sometimes seem overdramatic, archaic, or out of place in writing.

SENTENCE ERRORS

Checking over your sentences to catch careless syntactic and grammatical errors is an important part of the Completing Stage. You want to ensure that your reader gets your message without any distractions from awkwardly constructed sentences. What follows is an examination of some common errors that crop up in everybody's writing.

SYNTAX ERRORS

Agreement. Rules of agreement affect the relationship between subject and verb and between pronoun and antecedent. Agreement simply means that a singular subject must have a singular verb and that a pronoun must match its antecedent (the word it refers to) in number (singular or plural), in gender (masculine, feminine, or neuter) and in person (first, second, or third). Usually, agreement occurs automatically when you speak and write. For example, when you say, "John likes to have doughnuts for breakfast," you know that since *John* is a singular noun, the verb must be singular too. However, if you had said, "My roommate and I like to have doughnuts for breakfast," you would have used a plural verb, *like,* to match the compound subject, *my roommate and I.*

Problems in agreement between subject and verb occur when it's not clear whether the subject is plural or singular. Notice how subtle agreement errors can be:

The chef's salad and the baked chicken looks good.

At first, the sentence sounds correct. The sentence communicates your message, but in writing, it's hard to overlook that compound subject—chef's salad *and* baked chicken. The verb should be plural—*look*—to agree with the plural subject.

Compound subjects joined by *or* and *nor* often cause agreement problems:

Neither John nor my brother are going to camp this summer.

The sentence sounds acceptable, but the conjunctions *nor* and *or* suggest singularity: not *both,* but one or the other is going. The verb, therefore, must be singular:

Neither John nor my brother is going to camp this summer.

Indefinite pronouns—*each, every, any, anybody, one*—cause similar agreement problems, especially when there is a prepositional phrase between the subject and verb:

Each of the boys want to try out for the team.

Only one of the chairs need to be reupholstered.

What has happened in these sentences is that the object of the preposition has influenced the verb choice. *Boys* and *chairs* are so close to the verb that they seem to be plural subjects. To avoid this error, simply remember that *each, none, any,* and other indefinite pronouns are singular.

Prepositional phrases affect other kinds of subjects as well:

The decreasing number of college students have been attributed to the declining birth rate over the past twenty years.

If you take out that prepositional phrase, you notice that the subject—*decreasing number*—is singular, so the verb should be *has been attributed.*

Agreement can also be a problem with **pronoun reference.** Remember that a pronoun is a noun substitute. Usually, the sentence contains a noun to which the pronoun refers, and the pronoun must reflect the grammatical features of that noun. If the noun is plural, the pronoun must be plural; if it is feminine, the pronoun must be feminine. Most of the time, pronoun agreement presents no problems, but some sentence constructions make pronoun agreement difficult to achieve. As in subject-verb agreement, indefinite pronouns cause problems here too:

Everybody finished *their* themes in 50 minutes.

Someone left *their* umbrella here.

Does *everyone* want *their* coffee in the living room?

You hear constructions like this all the time. There is really no problem in communicating meaning; the problem is grammatical. Indefinite pronouns like *everybody, anyone, anybody, someone, no one, one, each* are always singular, so they must be matched by singular pronouns. Since speech is much less rigid than writing, pronoun agreement is not distracting then. However, in writing, communication is much more formalized, and lack of pronoun agreement may distract the reader. To achieve agreement in each of these sentences, *their* should be replaced with *his* or *her*.

Pronouns cause problems in sentences for one other reason. Sometimes it's not clear what the antecedent of the pronoun is. Remember, a pronoun must refer to a specific noun. Sometimes, however, you may be misled by a word or phrase that appears to be an antecedent but actually isn't:

The *Swiss* have not been at war for many years. *It* is a neutral country.

It clearly refers to *Switzerland,* but notice that the only possible antecedent is *Swiss*. To correct this, you would rewrite the sentence as follows:

Switzerland has not been at war for many years. It is a neutral country.

In this sentence, notice how the writer easily makes a pronoun reference error:

He was opposed to gun control because he felt every citizen should have one for self-defense.

Any reader would know that *one* is a substitute for *gun,* but the antecedent is *gun control*. Again, revision is necessary to correct the error:

He was opposed to gun control because he felt every citizen should be allowed to own firearms for self-defense.

Predication. Faulty predication, a mismatch between the subject and the verb and the object, is a common sentence error. The subject, verb, and complement not only have to be grammatically compatible but also have to fit together logically. This error is hard to detect. Even though something seems to be wrong with the sentence when you read it, the meaning may come across anyway. In the following sentences, you can understand what the writer means, but the subject-verb-object relationship is illogical in each.

> Any person absent on the final day of classes would have meant that the end-of-school picnic could not be held.

Here, the subject-verb base is *person would have meant*. The relationship is illogical because *person* is a concrete noun, but the verb and noun clause complement clearly call for an abstract subject. The sentence should be rewritten:

> Any person's *absence* would have meant that the end-of-school picnic could not be held.

In this sentence, a superfluous *about* causes faulty predication:
> The subject of his talk was about employment after graduation.

What has happened in this sentence is that the meaning of *subject*—what something is about—and the prepositional phrase *of his talk* have merged to produce an awkward sentence. You can say *The subject of his talk was employment* or *His talk was about employment,* but not both, as the original sentence does.

Some errors in predication occur when an adverb phrase is forced to function as a noun phrase:

> An allegory is where characters symbolize virtues and vices.
>
> The reason I'm not going is because I don't like the girl who is hosting the party.

Frequently, the verb *be (is, was, were, am)* signals equality between the noun and the complement, so the complement must be grammatically equivalent to the noun. These sentences should be rewritten so that a noun or noun clause after *is* shows equivalency between the subject and the complement:

> An *allegory* is a *story* in which characters symbolize virtues and vices.
>
> The reason I'm not going is *that I don't like the girl who is giving the party.*

Sometimes the subject-verb relationship is simply illogical:

> When air fares are reduced, there will no longer be so many cars driving people to vacation spots.

The actual subject is *cars* and the verb is *will be driving*. The verb needs a human subject rather than an inanimate one:

> There will no longer be so many people driving cars to vacation spots.
>
> or
>
> There will no longer be so many cars driven to vacation spots.

Sentence Errors

Modification. Modification, one of the means of expanding the basic sentence pattern, sometimes causes sentence errors. It should always be clear to the reader what sentence element a modifier refers to. As in most sentence errors, there may be no great loss of meaning when misplaced modifiers occur, but the resulting awkwardness or ambiguity may distract the reader or may create an unintentionally comical sentence. Most sentences with misplaced modifiers can be corrected through slight revision.

> DANGLING PARTICIPLE: Having many heroic qualities, George Washington's life was colored by a handful of fables.

The problem here is that the participial phrase modifies *George Washington* instead of the subject *life*. Revision can correct the error:

> Having many heroic qualities, George Washington lived a life colored by a handful of fables.

> INTRODUCTORY PHRASE: Through the use of polls, it is evident that the majority of the American public doubts the findings of the Warren Commission.

The problem here is that the introductory adverbial phrase doesn't seem to go with any part of the sentence. Again, slight revision can correct the sentence:

> Through the use of polls, we have learned that the majority of the American public doubts the findings of the Warren Commission.

> PREPOSITIONAL PHRASE: We have, for example, people who have done something that most of us will never do, such as the astronauts, Arctic explorers, mountain climbers.

Here, the reader is led to expect examples of what it is that most of us will never *do*. Instead, we find examples of *people,* a word which occurs much earlier in the sentence. To avoid this sort of awkwardness, the sentence should be rewritten so that the prepositional phrase is closer to the word it modifies or so that it accurately modifies the word it follows:

> We have people such as the astronauts, Arctic explorers, mountain climbers, who have done something that most of us will never do.

or

> We have people who have done something that most of us will never do, such as journey to outer space, explore the Arctic, climb mountains.

To avoid errors in modification, always place the modifier as close as possible to the word it modifies. And you should always make sure that there is a word to be modified. Your goal in effective modification, as in all parts of writing, should be to make your meaning and intention clear to the reader, so you shouldn't force your readers to decipher your meaning or to correct mentally the sentences they are reading.

Parallelism.   The key to effective parallelism is the matching of grammatical parallelism with logical parallelism. When those parts don't match, we have the problem of faulty parallelism. Your thoughts may fit together nicely and the repetition available through parallelism may provide the emphasis you want, but unless the parallel elements are grammatically parallel, the pattern is more distracting than it is emphatic.

Notice how grammatical and logical parallelism combine effectively in this sentence:

> A university turns out people who have matured greatly, who have respect for others, and who have developed great responsibility.

The parallel relative clauses modifying *people* are the heart of the sentence. Each clause describes the kind of person a university turns out, thereby creating logical parallelism. Grammatical parallelism is achieved by repeating the relative pronoun *who* and similar predicates in each clause (although *respect* is not a verb, it still reinforces the pattern since the verb in that clause is *have*):

> *who have matured* greatly
>
> *who have respect* for others
>
> *who have developed* great responsibility

Such parallelism in form and content has a pleasing effect on the reader. Unfortunately, when there is parallelism in content but not in form, the effect is not as pleasing.

Problems in parallelism can usually be traced to faulty *coordination* between the elements that are supposed to be parallel. Remember, coordination and parallelism link grammatically equivalent sentence elements. When the coordinated parts are not grammatically equal, the sentence sounds awkward:

> He admired Mary's arrangement of yellow roses and daisies on the piano and how she had brightened the room with smaller arrangements.

Here, the writer has coordinated a noun—*arrangement*—with a noun clause—*how she had brightened the room*. The sentence should be revised so that both elements are nouns or noun clauses:

> He admired the arrangement of yellow roses and daisies on the piano and the smaller arrangements that brightened the room.

> or

> He admired how Mary had arranged the yellow roses and daisies on the piano and how she had brightened the room with smaller arrangements.

Faulty parallelism is a serious sentence error because it can be very distracting. The pattern sets up expectations for the reader, who anticipates that parallelism in thought will match parallelism in grammatical structure. If a parallel series starts with one grammatical category and shifts to another, the effect of parallelism is destroyed, and the reader is disappointed.

PUNCTUATION ERRORS

Some sentence errors occur when you fail to use punctuation marks to indicate relationships between sentences. You will see later that punctuation is a system for marking sentences so that the reader can follow the writer's thought, stopping and pausing in the appropriate places. When these marks are missing or when they are misused, meaning may be lost or misunderstood.

Comma Splice. A comma splice occurs when you join two independent clauses with a comma:

> As a child, the alcoholic did not learn the things a child needs to learn, thus his life was destined to go bad.

Remember that an independent clause demands a punctuation mark that signals completion, so independent clauses should always end in a period, a semicolon, or a comma followed by a coordinating conjunction.

You can correct a comma splice in one of the following ways:

1. Rewrite the sentence as two independent sentences:

> As a child, the alcoholic did not learn the things a child needs to learn. Thus, his life was destined to go bad.

2. Assuming the ideas of the sentences are closely related, replace the comma with a semicolon:

> As a child, the alcoholic did not learn the things a child needs to learn; thus, his life was destined to go bad.

3. Make one sentence dependent on the other through subordination:

> Since the alcoholic did not learn as a child the things children need to know, his life was destined to go bad.

4. Join the independent clauses with the appropriate coordinating conjunction:

> As a child, the alcoholic did not learn the things a child needs to learn, and so his life was destined to go bad.

A comma splice is a serious punctuation error for two reasons: (1) it suggests that you are unable to distinguish between independent clauses, which should be marked with a period or semicolon, and dependent clauses, which may be marked with a comma, and (2) it sends the reader conflicting signals. The comma signals only a pause, but the s-v-c pattern of the two independent clauses signals completion and indicates a need for terminal punctuation.

Run-on Sentences. Run-on sentences are much like comma splices except that here, all punctuation is omitted between the independent clauses:

> Universities are an important part of our world it is their teaching of our children that should someday bring about a better world.

A run-on sentence misleads the reader. With no period or semicolon to mark the end of one sentence, she reads the attached sentence as if it were part of the first one. When she discovers the writer's mistake, she must reread the sentences, mentally inserting the needed punctuation.

Run-on sentences send loud signals to the reader. They suggest that the writer is a careless editor, and they reveal the writer's failure to indicate closure in a sentence through appropriate terminal punctuation.

You can correct run-on sentences in several ways:

1. Rewrite the run-on sentences as two separate sentences:

> Universities are an important part of our world. It is their teaching of our children that should someday bring about a better world.

2. Insert a semicolon between the fused sentences if the two sentences are closely related in content:

> Universities are an important part of our world; it is their teaching of our children that should someday bring about a better world.

3. If the sentences are joined by a coordinating conjunction, they must be separated by a comma:

> Universities are an important part of our world, for it is their teaching of our children that should someday bring about a better world.

4. Use subordination to make one sentence dependent on the other:

> Universities are an important part of our world since their teaching of our children may someday bring about a better world.

Sentence Fragments. A fragment is the opposite of a run-on sentence: a run-on sentence occurs when two sentences are run together without punctuation, but a fragment occurs when part of a sentence is punctuated as a complete sentence.

Fragments may suggest to the reader that the writer does not know the difference between a complete sentence and a clause or a phrase. Usually, this isn't the problem, though. When you write your first draft, fragments slip in unnoticed during the pressure of composition. Your thoughts are coming fast, and you don't take time to consciously make each sentence perfect and grammatical the first time you write it. That's perfectly all right—for the first draft. During the Completing Stage you should catch and correct fragments.

Look at the sentences below. Try to figure out how the fragment occurred.

> Many people look down on conformity. They see those who are always following blindly as fools who are too scared to think for themselves. Perhaps not having to think is why they conform. That and the fact that there is safety in numbers.

The last sentence is a fragment. It probably occurred when the writer got so caught up in getting her thoughts down that she didn't notice the grammatical form of her sentence. You could correct this fragment in several ways.

1. Link it to the previous sentence:

> Perhaps not having to think is why they conform, or perhaps they feel there is safety in numbers.

or

> Perhaps not having to think is why they conform—that, and the fact that there is safety in numbers.

2. Make it a complete sentence:

> Perhaps not having to think is why they conform. The feeling that there is safety in numbers may also explain why people conform.

Although you should try to get rid of fragments in your writing, you should know that they are not always grammatical errors. Frequently, writers use fragments intentionally for emphasis, as an afterthought, or as a transitional device. The following passage is from an article in which a writer describes his impressions and his memories as he comes back home to care for his dying mother. Notice that the fragments are necessary to create the illusion that the writer is allowing us to look into his mind:

> For his mother is, in fact, near death, though lingering, and that is why he has spent three restless weeks in her house—a thousand miles west of his own, in a suburban town on the Hudson. Waiting. A duty.
>
> From Robert Henderson, "Colloquy," *The New Yorker,* July 17, 1978, p. 25.

Intentional fragments are okay. It is the accidental ones that disturb the reader and that you want to be sure to get rid of during editing and proofreading.

DICTION AND STYLE

PROBLEMS OF DICTION AND STYLE

Deadwood. Deadwood is any word or expression that contributes nothing to your meaning and is therefore superfluous. This sentence is full of deadwood:

> Because of the fact that America's oil reserves are slowly running out, it is to be expected that the country will have to find other methods of supplying energy.

"Of the fact that" and "it is to be expected" are examples of deadwood. They can be scratched out without detracting from the meaning:

> Because America's oil reserves are slowly running out, the country will have to find other methods of supplying energy.

Whenever you find one of the following phrases in your writing, scratch it out. In most cases, your sentence will survive without it, and usually it will be a much clearer sentence that it was before:

due to the fact that
it happened that
there are/is

> Clutter is the disease of American writing. We are a society strangling in unnecessary words, circular constructions, pompous frills and meaningless jargon. Our national tendency is to inflate and thereby sound important.
> —William Zinsser

Deadwood also occurs when you use more words than necessary. Notice how these expressions can be trimmed down to a single word or to a shorter phrase:

make an attempt to	try
reach a decision	decide
it is the belief of	believes
is in the process of being	is being
the question as to whether	whether
in a hasty manner	hastily
owing to the fact that	since/because
in spite of the fact that	though/although/despite
the fact that I had arrived	my arrival
the fact that he had not succeeded	his failure
of great importance	important
in connection with	with

For beginning writers, deadwood is hard to detect and difficult to get rid of. Those empty phrases and superfluous words seem to make writing more impressive. Truly impressive writing communicates cleanly, directly, and efficiently.

Redundancy. Redundancy also leads to wordiness. Redundancy—unnecessary repetition—occurs when words are used carelessly and thoughtlessly. When a person refers to a "new innovation" he is not listening to what he is saying. *Innovation* already means "new," so the phrase is redundant. Watch for phrases that show needless repetition of the same meaning in two words:

fellow colleague	colleague
surrounding environment	environment
impending failure that will eventually occur	impending failure
carelessly discarded litter	litter
necessary prerequisite	prerequisite
long in size	long
blue in color	blue
of an indefinite nature	indefinite
by means of	by

Circumlocution. Circumlocution—the deliberate use of roundabout expressions—creates wordiness and obscurity. Again, the objective of writers who use circumlocutions is to sound impressive, not to communicate efficiently and directly. Ironically, when you recognize circumlocutions in a piece of writing, you are struck not by its impressiveness, but by its absurdity. In the passage below, circumlocutions are italicized. Notice how they obscure meaning and make communication difficult.

(1) As silent tears *flowed down my cheeks in diamond-filled rivulets,* I reflected on the presumptuous attitudes of *society's "young adults."* (2) Of course, generalization during *a period of severe depression is opted for,* and I consider myself no failure!

(3) It appeared to me that the feelings of *humans aged eleven to nineteen* toward the *humans that had survived on this planet for the longest number of years* ranged from bothersome to useless. (4) *Sporting a different opinion,* and *allowed to exclude myself* from this degrading category *for the sole reason* that *I was the inventor* of the horrible thought, I began to defend this misconception *possessed by the multitudes.*

(5) My attitude, *I must admit,* ran the gamut from bothersome to surprisingly capable and extremely helpful, so I cannot debate the reasoning behind the depicting of "old people" as bothersome. (6) *In order to clear my records, I must reveal* that I consider almost every age of our species bothersome! (7) I believe that to be a predominant human characteristic, perhaps even a prerequisite!

The writer reveals other problems—the use of trite diction and errors in denotation, but circumlocution is the problem that interferes with communication the most. The roundabout expressions confuse the reader. Sentence (3) is particularly obscure. It seems that it is the feelings of young people that are bothersome and useless, but it becomes clear later that "bothersome and useless" refers to older people. In sentence (4), circumlocutions reverse the author's intended meaning. The writer says he will *defend* the misconception when he actually means that he will prove it wrong.

By rewriting the circumlocutions as direct expressions, the writer's message becomes clearer, shorter, and much easier to understand:

> As I sat crying, I reflected on the presumptuous attitudes of young people. We all tend to generalize when we are depressed, and that's what I was doing then. As I saw it, teenagers consider older people bothersome and useless. I, of course, excluded myself from this generalization, and I tried to prove that prevalent attitudes toward older people were founded on misconceptions.
>
> I believe older people can be productive, but I admit that I sometimes consider them bothersome. I cannot defend that attitude; however, I consider people of almost any age bothersome, and I think most people feel this way at one time or another.

Wordiness that results from using circumlocutions, redundancy, and deadwood can be difficult to get rid of. Writing is hard work, and many writers are reluctant to scratch out a single word that represents the effort behind their writing. Don't let yourself make that mistake. Remember that the quality of communication is more important than the quantity of composition. Think of words as a resource too valuable to waste. Write as if you had to pay for each word you put down on the page. You don't have to go to the extreme of making your writing telegraphic. Simply train yourself to question the function of every word in your writing, and scratch out any word that doesn't add to your meaning.

Jargon. Jargon sometimes refers to the vocabulary characteristic of a particular group; for example, medical jargon, educational jargon, legal jargon. In this sense, the word carries no negative connotations. It merely refers to the set of words that professional or social groups use to communicate among themselves efficiently. In a different sense, jargon is a serious problem in writing. Anytime a writer is more interested in impressing the reader than in communicating effectively, his writing may be labeled jargon.

No single problem turns writing into jargon. Instead the problem is really an accumulation of problems—wordiness, pretentiousness, abstractness, overuse of the passive voice—but the biggest problem is the motivation in using jargon. Usually, it reflects an attempt to sound intelligent and impressive. Ironically, jargon produces bad writing, and readers who recognize jargon realize that the writer is insecure and pompous rather than intelligent and impressive.

You can avoid jargon by remembering that the object of writing is communication. Because it obscures meaning, jargon interferes with communication. The following guidelines, based on what we've discussed about effective use of words, should help you avoid the problems that contribute to jargon:

1. Make your writing as clear and as straightforward as possible. Avoid "big" words and pretentious language simply to impress your reader. Be merciless in editing your writing. Strike out any word that adds nothing to your meaning, regardless of how impressive the meaningless phrase seems. Remember the term for meaningless phrases: DEADWOOD.

2. Strive to make your writing vivid. Whenever possible replace *is* and other *to be* verbs with a stronger verb. Avoid too many abstract nouns (*-tion* and *ment* endings). Remember: these nouns can frequently be replaced by a verb to make a stronger sentence.
3. Be natural. Don't avoid a first-person pronoun simply because you fear it may make your writing too casual. Don't use the third person (*one, a person, the student*) in an attempt to sound impersonal. Don't rely on passive voice as a means of sounding impressive.

Trite Diction. Vividness in writing is reduced by trite diction. Trite phrases and clichés were once fresh and original, but they have lost their vividness through overuse. Trite expressions slip into our speech very easily without causing problems. In writing, however, triteness is something to avoid. One writer has described clichés as blank checks that a writer gives to the reader hoping the reader will fill in the meaning himself. Trite diction has a lulling effect on the reader. Since the expressions are familiar to everyone, the reader exerts less effort in following the writer's thoughts. Furthermore, since the expressions are predictable and overused, the reader may conclude that the thought is also unoriginal.

Avoid such clichés and trite expressions as:

out of the horse's mouth	rude awakening
pretty as a picture	nip in the bud
whistling in the dark	apple of his eye
well-rounded education	can't judge a book by its cover
in this day and time	fresh as a daisy
in the nick of time	blind as a bat
giant step	easy as pie

Trite diction is not always the result of using clichés. Sometimes triteness is due to the use of nouns and verbs or nouns and adjectives in well-worn combinations. In the following sentences, the italicized words are examples of these combinations:

1. The sun was *glaring down* on all our *greased bodies* and giving us the most professional tan we had ever had. The water was *refreshingly cool* and a *gorgeous shade of blue*. *All good things must end*, and we decided to go to our rooms, clean up, and enjoy some *night life*.
2. While the *figures* are *staggering*, there are still a few ways to *soften* the college tuition *crunch*.

ERRORS IN DICTION AND STYLE

The problems we've been considering—wordiness, redundancy, jargon—are not errors. You should avoid them because they reduce the impact of your writing and sometimes confuse your message for the reader. However, there are some problems in diction that we do consider errors because they involve mistakes in meaning, context, and associations.

Wrong Denotation. The denotation of a word is its dictionary meaning. Sometimes, when writers hurry or use words carelessly, they misuse the denotation of a word. For example, a sports announcer covering a college football game may describe the beginning of the game as "a bombastic opening." If you look in a dictionary, you'll find that no meaning of *bombastic* fits the context. *Bombastic* means "high-sounding, high-flown, pretentious," a meaning that has nothing to do with the opening of a football game. Clearly, the announcer has made a mistake. He wanted a strong word to describe the opening minutes of the game, a word that conveyed the excitement, unexpectedness of the underdog's surprise touchdown. No doubt, he chose *bombastic,* thinking that it was somehow related to the meaning of *bomb.*

Probably no other error makes you look as foolish before your reader as an error in denotation. You can avoid making these embarrassing errors by understanding why they occur:

1. When a writer attempts to use a new, unfamiliar word that he may have heard before, he may use it in the wrong context.
2. Sometimes a writer inadvertently uses a word similar in sound to the one he wants:

    They faced the *aspect* of spending a night in the woods.

    The correct word is *prospect*.

3. Some errors in denotation occur when a writer confuses homophones:

    Our football team should *fair* better this season than it did last year.

    The correct word is *fare*.

Errors of this kind are hard to detect since they occur as you transfer an oral expression into writing, but you can avoid wrong denotation by being a careful listener, by using a new word only when you are positive you have used it correctly, and by reading carefully so that you learn to use words like *bombastic, aspect, fare* in the correct contexts.

Unidiomatic Expression. All languages have certain groupings of words that native speakers recognize as idiomatic expressions. This means that throughout the development of the language certain words have been used together consistently so that they now form an idiom, a unit of speech that is what linguists call "frozen." This means that only certain words can be used in the expression; if the words are changed, the phrase loses its idiomatic quality and frequently its meaning as well.

Frequently, carelessness in speaking or writing leads to the use of unidiomatic expressions as in the following sentence:

The senator agreed to the proposal for a compromise, but when the bill was rewritten, he *disagreed to* most of the points.

"Agree with," "agree to," and "disagree with" are idiomatic expressions, but "disagree to" is unidiomatic.

Mixed Metaphors. You've already seen that figurative language makes writing vivid and concrete. However, when a metaphor is misused, the result is an error in diction. Metaphors and many other figures of speech are based on analogy. This means that there must be some basis of comparison between the literal and figurative meanings you are trying to convey. Furthermore, that comparison must be appropriate and consistent throughout the unit of writing in which the metaphor occurs. When you introduce incompatible images to describe a single idea or object, you produce a mixed metaphor:

> Men, I'm asking you to put your shoulders to the wheel and help bail us out of this financial quagmire.

The speaker has given the reader the opportunity to visualize a ludicrous image: workers with their shoulders to the wheel simultaneously in a sinking boat and in a quagmire.

A mixed metaphor is an error in diction because it defeats the purpose of figurative language. It obscures meaning by distracting the reader through an unintended comical or incongruous image. Therefore, when you use figurative language, make sure that it clarifies rather than obscures your message and that the image you present is consistent at least through the sentence in which it appears.

PUNCTUATION

Punctuation can be one of the most difficult and frustrating parts of editing. The rules that govern this part of writing sometimes seem arbitrary, and that makes it difficult to use punctuation correctly. However, when we study punctuation, we discover that it is as systematic as syntax. Furthermore, we realize that punctuation marks are very important in indicating the writer's purpose.

We can approach punctuation on two levels: on a mechanical level and on a functional level. On the mechanical level, punctuation is a series of rules that are applied automatically, almost mindlessly, when certain conditions occur in sentences. All your life, you've heard rules like the following:

- Place a comma before the coordinating conjunction in a compound sentence.
- Use commas to set off nonrestrictive clauses.

A mechanical approach to punctuation is fine, if you can remember what terms like "compound sentence" and "nonrestrictive" clause mean; but you may not remember them. That is when a functional approach may be more rational.

On the functional level, punctuation is a system in which marks and symbols signal to the reader the writer's intentions about how a sentence should be interpreted. In speech, you "punctuate" your sentences with pauses, voice pitch, intonation, modulations in speed of utterance, facial gestures, hand motions. In writing, punctuation compensates for the absence of these visual and vocal clues to meaning. Commas, periods, semicolons, dashes, parentheses, underlining, and other marks of punctuation help the reader follow your train of thought. Effective use of punctuation tells the reader much about your intentions in your sentences. Punctuation, then, is primarily for the reader.

ELEMENTS OF PUNCTUATION

ELEMENT	FUNCTION	EXAMPLES
PERIOD **.**	A period indicates a full stop at the end of a sentence.	Boysenberry ice cream is good.
	A period is used with an indirect question instead of a question mark.	She asked if I liked the opera.
	A period is used after an *acceptable* sentence fragment.	Did you enjoy the festival? Very much.
	A period always goes inside the quotation marks.	The horticulturist said, "Daffodils often grow on hills."
	Use periods after initials in names.	John F. Kennedy, Dr. E. K. Hambrick
	Use periods between dollars and cents.	$54.98
	Use periods with abbreviations.	Inc., Ms., M.D.

	Use periods following the numbers or letters in lists or outlines.	I.
		  A.
		  B.

COMMA **,**	A comma can link, enclose, separate, and show omissions.	
	To link: Place a comma before a coordinating conjunction *(and, but, or, nor, for, so, yet)* when it combines two sentences (independent clauses).	The tacos were good, and the sangria was even better.
	(Some handbooks suggest that the comma can be omitted if the sentences are short, if there is no complicated puncutation in them, and if the sentences won't be misread. You will always be safe, however, if you insert the comma. This will obviate your having to make an individual decision each time.)	
	To separate: Commas separate introductory elements from the rest of the sentence.	During the first game of the series, we had four runs, six hits, and no errors. Finally, I'm finished.

ELEMENT	FUNCTION	EXAMPLES
	The comma may be omitted if the introductory clause or phrase is short and does not cause confusion without the mark of punctuation. You will never be wrong, however, to insert the comma.	When you go I will go.
	Commas separate items in a series.	Cigarettes harm your lungs, my lungs, and everybody's lungs. I learned how to be a leader, how to take orders, how to control my temper, and how to work with others. I ate the big, juicy, wormless, delicious red apple.
	The comma before the final item in a series is optional.	We had stories to tell of Indian pueblos, spicy food and hot summer nights.
	No comma is needed if all items in a series are joined by *and*.	We saw Porsches and Jaguars and Mercedes Benzs on the lot.
	A comma joins two coordinate modifiers. (To identify coordinate modifiers, see if they can be switched and the meaning stays the same.)	Her romantic, optimistic view of life encouraged us.
	A comma separates a nonrestrictive element that comes at the end of the the sentence.	They all like the fall of the year, especially if they are in the mountains.
COLON ● ●	A colon is a punctuation mark of anticipation that halts the reader, then connects the first statement to the following one.	
	A colon can connect a series or list to the sentence.	I have four classes: math, biology, English, and history.
	A colon can link one statement to another to develop, illustrate, explain, or amplify it. When used in this way, the colon can even link two sentences.	Any large cafeteria can have two related problems: it must fix enough food but not too much, and it must keep the food from spoiling.
	A colon can introduce a stacked list.	The following courses will be offered in the fall: Math 103 Math 209 Math 308 Math 104 Math 210 Math 309

ELEMENT	FUNCTION	EXAMPLES
	A colon adds emphasis to a phrase that completes a sentence.	Only one thing can make me happy: a new camera.
	Colons can separate chapters and verses as well as hours and minutes.	Genesis 1:1 9:30 A.M.
	In proportions, colons mean ratios.	$8:4 = 12:x$
	A colon can follow salutations in letters.	Dear Sir: Dear Karma: Dear Ms. Geoffry:
	When using colons with quotations, capitalize the first letter of the first word of the quotation if the quote originally began with a capital letter.	The sign stated: ''No shoes, no shirt, no service.''
	A colon always goes outside quotation marks.	These are qualities he calls ''good'': honesty, generosity, and bravery.
	If you quote a statement that ends with a colon, drop the colon and add ellipses.	''Any large cafeteria can have two related problems . . .,'' an author contends.
QUESTION MARK	Use a question mark at the end of a sentence that asks a question.	What do you think you're doing?
	With quotations, when the writer who is doing the quoting is asking the question, the question mark goes outside of the quotation marks.	Did she say, ''I wouldn't marry you if my life depended on it''?
	When the quotation is a question, the question mark goes inside the quotation marks.	She asked, ''What do you think you're doing?''
SEMICOLON ;	A semicolon can join two sentences that are close in meaning. It indicates a greater pause than a comma but not as great a pause as a period. Semicolons can also add clarity to involved sentences.	
	Place a semicolon to join closely related sentences.	I want to go; he doesn't.
	Use a semicolon to join closely related sentences combined with a conjunctive adverb.	I want to go; however, he doesn't.

Punctuation

ELEMENT	FUNCTION	EXAMPLES
	Use the semicolon to divide series in sentences that have several series.	This year I'm taking math, English, weightlifting, and biology; next year I'm taking history, chemistry, drafting, and swimming.
	Use a semicolon to separate sentences joined by a coordinating conjunction if the sentences already have commas.	In most cases, I would order steak, baked potato, and salad; but today I think I'll order fish.
EXCLAMATION POINT	Exclamation points are used at the end of sentences to show surprise, anger, or emphasis.	She's married! Hell, no, I'm not giving in! I'll never do that again!
QUOTATION MARKS	Quotation marks enclose direct repetition of words.	
	When you quote anything word for word from another source, enclose those words in quotation marks.	The report said, "Too many high school graduates are going to college."
	If a quotation is longer than five lines, indent all of the lines of the quotation five spaces from the left margin, single-spaced. Don't use quotation marks with indented quotations.	

	If a quotation is more than one paragraph (and it is not indented because it's not more than five lines), put quotation marks at the beginning of every paragraph but at the end of only the last paragraph.	"I can't pay the rent; I can't pay the rent.
		  "My kids are hungry.
		  "My house is cold.
		  "My husband left me.
		  "I can't pay the rent."

	If you have a quotation within a quotation, use single quotation marks (the apostrophe key on a typewriter) on the inside quote.	Regan asked, "Did I hear him say 'Get lost'?"
	Use quotation marks to indicate titles of short stories, magazine and newspaper articles, songs, and essays.	"Home on the Range" "A Modest Proposal"

ELEMENT	FUNCTION	EXAMPLES
	Always put periods and commas inside closing quotation marks.	"I'll go," he said.
	Always put colons and semicolons outside closing quotation marks.	The hero said, "I'll pay the rent"; that surprised me. These are my favorite "classes": lunchtime, study hall, and rest period.
	For all other punctuation: If the punctuation is a part of the quotation, place it inside the quotation marks; if the punctuation is not a part of the quotation, place it outside the marks.	
	See *question marks*.	
	Words used in a special way or words to which the writer wants to draw attention for some reason are put in quotation marks.	"Teasing" your hair is bad for it.
APOSTROPHE '	Use the apostrophe to show possession, to mark the place where letters are omitted, and to indicate the plural of numbers and letters.	
	Possession:	
	An apostrophe is used with an *s* to form the possessive case of some nouns.	Barbara's lifestyle
	With compound nouns, the last noun takes the possessive to show that they both own something.	Quick Draw and Huckleberry's capers
	When each noun possesses something (individually), then both nouns are possessive.	Jack's and Jill's pails
	With singular nouns that end in *s,* you can form the possessive by adding only an apostrophe or by adding an apostrophe and an *s*.	a waitress' job, an actress' costume a waitress's job, an actress's costume
	Use only an apostrophe for plural nouns that end in *s*.	a secretaries' meeting, students' reports

Punctuation 303

ELEMENT	FUNCTION	EXAMPLES
	Add only an apostrophe to nouns that end in multiple consecutive *s* sounds.	Charles' tricks, Jesus' parables
	Don't use an apostrophe with possessive pronouns.	yours, its, his ours, whose, theirs
	Omission: An apostrophe marks where letters or numbers have been left out of a word or date.	I'm, I'll, can't, back in '43
	Plurals: Apostrophes indicate the plural of numbers.	6's, 70's, seven 1,000's
	An apostrophe with an *s* can show the plural of a word as a word	You had seventeen *you's* in that paragraph.
	If a term is all capital letters or ends in a capital letter, you don't need an apostrophe for the plural.	I'll have six B.A.s before it's all over. Eight ADDs are enough for that computer program.
HYPHEN —	Use a hyphen between parts of compound words. (If you are not sure whether a compound word should be hyphenated, check your dictionary.)	all-night, attorney-general, son-in-law, able-bodied men
	Use a hyphen between a prefix and the main word in the following cases:	
	Hypenate words formed from a prefix and a proper noun.	all-American, anti-Soviet
	Hyphenate to avoid two identical vowels next to each other.	re-entry, anti-intellectual
	Hyphenate prefixed words to distinguish them from words spelled the same but without the hyphen.	re-create/recreate, re-dress/redress, re-cover/recover
	Hypenate to join *ex-* to a word when you mean *former*.	ex-wife, ex-student
	Use a hyphen to indicate word division at the end of a line, but observe these guidelines:	

304   *The Handbook*

ELEMENT	FUNCTION	EXAMPLES
	Divide the word only between syllables. (Check your dictionary if you are not sure where the syllables of a word divide.)	help-fully, not helpf-ully; some-thing, not someth-ing
	Do not divide words of one syllable.	forced, though, calmed
	Do not separate a suffix or syllable of less than three letters or a one-letter prefix or syllable.	-ed, -le a-, e-, o-
	Separate hyphenated words only at the hyphen.	sister-in-law, well-known, semi-retired
	Do not divide a word on the last line of a page.	
DASH	When typing, use two hypens (--) to indicate a dash.	
	A dash can indicate a sharp turn in thought.	That marks the end of that class—unless I failed the last test.
	A dash can add emphasis to a pause.	I'll get the job done—after I take another break.
	Dashes can set off an explanatory series or an appositive series.	Two of the applicants—Steve and Lisa—will be offered jobs.
	Dashes can add emphasis to a parenthetical element (an item inserted in the sentence that isn't essential to meaning).	Only one person—you—can control what you say.
PARENS (PARENTHESES) ( )	Recently we discovered that the punctuation marks were called parens and the information inside the parens, along with the parens, was called parenthesis. This news is not earth-shattering, but it is interesting.	
	Parens suggest a closeness between the writer and the reader and imply that you two know something that the rest of the world might not know. Parenthetical information is played-down and de-emphasized: it may not be essential to a sentence, but it may be interesting or helpful to the reader.	Many American presidents (for example, Dwight Eisenhower) were military leaders. CUNY (City University of New York) offers a variety of programs.

Punctuation 305

ELEMENT	FUNCTION	EXAMPLES
	Punctuation:	
	Parenthetical material does not affect the punctuation of a sentence. If a parenthetical clause comes at the end of a sentence, for example, the period to end the sentence would go outside the parens.	I like some history courses (American), but hate others (ancient Greek).
	When numbering a series of items in a sentence, use two parens, not one.	I'll eat (1) potatoes, (2) meat, (3) carrots, and (4) gravy.
	When a complete sentence is parenthetical, the end punctuation goes inside the parens.	I want to know (You can tell me if you want to.) what I've got to do to improve.
	If you have an item that you need to set off with parens inside of a parenthetical idea, use brackets.	I want to know (You can tell me [if you want to].) . . . .
ELLIPSIS • • •	Ellipsis is a puctuation mark that shows you've left out some words.	
	When you quote only part of a statement, insert elipsis to show where you've left the information out.	"Work . . . is the privilege of all citizens," the politician explained.
	It's not fair to leave any important information out of a quotation or to pull words from a quotation and change the meaning.	
BRACKET [ ]	Brackets are used to set off material that is your own inside quotation marks which surround someone else's words.	"The trio [Kingston Trio] will appear at the Bottom Mark Sunday, November 12," read the announcement in the paper.
VIRGULE/SLASH /	A virgule or slash is used to separate two things which belong together as choices or to separate lines of poetry that have been run together.	Do you know the either/or rule? Roses are red/Violets are blue/Sugar is sweet/And so are you.

SPELLING

Spelling errors are among the most difficult errors to detect when you are editing your work. In detecting punctuation errors and sentence-structure problems, you at least know when an error is likely to occur, and you can train yourself to watch for it. For instance, you can watch for structures that might lead to comma faults. But how are you supposed to know whether you've misspelled a word? Many textbooks suggest that you check every word you are not sure of. If you think that advice is illogical, you're right. It is based on the assumption that we can intuitively guess which words may be spelled incorrectly. Sometimes, that is true. That advice works with difficult words or with words that you are so uncertain about that you can't even attempt to spell them. But it's not just difficult words that are misspelled. It is the everyday, ordinary words that are misspelled most frequently. Unfortunately, misspelling often reflects carelessness or a failure to observe usage rules. When you spell *all right a-l-r-i-g-h-t* or the possessive pronoun *their t-h-e-r-e*, the problem is not really spelling—it is usage. Misspelling difficult words and misspelling words because of a failure to observe rules are two extremes of the spelling problem; fortunately, both are relatively easy to correct. You can find difficult words in the dictionary, and you can check the usage section of most grammar textbooks for the others.

The spelling errors that are most troublesome and most difficult to correct are those that you don't suspect are errors. When you spell *aggravate a-g-g-r-i-v-a-t-e* or *separate s-e-p-e-r-a-t-e*, the words slip right by in proofreading because it doesn't occur to you that you might have misspelled them. Don't expect your reader to be understanding and to say, "Oh well. He probably doesn't know that *aggravate* is spelled with an *a* not an *i*." No! What the reader will say is, "What a dummy! Everyone knows that *aggravate* is spelled with an *a* not an *i*!"

The reader's reaction to spelling errors is the strongest argument for learning to spell correctly. Misspelling, like punctuation and syntax errors, distracts the reader. How can you expect the readers to hear and accept your message when your misspellings are making more noise than they can ignore?

You may think it's a little late to be learning how to spell. After all, you may think, if you didn't learn to spell correctly in twelve years of schooling, you certainly won't learn in one or two semesters of college English. You *can*, however, learn to spell now, despite past failures, if you approach the problem methodically.

First, you should understand why some spelling errors occur.

1. When you experience the pressure of writing, you sometimes omit, add, or substitute letters in words that you know how to spell. In the rush of writing down your thoughts, words, sounds, and letters get jumbled up as your brain sends signals to your hand. So, you write *it* instead of *is, then* instead of *than, to* instead of *the*. Errors like these are comparable to typos on the typewriter. Fortunately, you can catch every one of these errors when you proofread. They should jump right out at you.

2. Homophones—words that sound alike or nearly alike but have different meanings and spellings—are another common cause of spelling errors. Again, you know that *weather* and *whether* mean entirely different things; yet occasionally you write a sentence like this:

   My decision on weather to go to our local junior college or the state university was one of the most difficult in my life.

   Even though the error is explainable, it is not excusable. Readers have no patience with writers who make careless mistakes like this. Your reliability and authority as a writer suffer when you habitually confuse homophones. Train yourself to be sensitive to homophones.

3. When you confuse words like *accept—except, affect—effect, allusion—illusion,* the problem is more than just a simple confusion of homophones. There is more than misspelling involved here. To use these words correctly, you must learn the distinctions in meaning which make one member of each pair entirely inappropriate in a given context.

4. Finally, there are those words that cause spelling errors simply because, for some reason, they are difficult to spell. You may have heard people say that inconsistencies in spelling and pronunciation make English a hard language to learn as a second language. To a certain extent this is true. Imagine what it must be like for a non-English speaker to learn to spell *rough, though,* and *fought,* where *ough* is pronounced differently in each. Native speakers are plagued by similar problems:

   a. Distincions between
      -ent, -ant—dependent, existent, dominant
      -al, -el, -le—barrel, battle, nobel, noble, political
      -ly, -ally—basically, publicly, politically
      -able, -ible—acceptable, permissible, excitable, eligible

   b. Indistinct vowels in
      privilege definite separate grammar sponsor
      primitive sacrifice pursue calendar divine

Unfortunately, there is no trick to help you remember which is the correct spelling. However, it is unlikely that you misspell every one of these, so make a special effort to learn those that do give you trouble. Don't guess at the spelling. If you're not sure whether the word is spelled *insoluable* or *insoluble*, take a few minutes to look it up.

COMMONLY MISSPELLED WORDS

accept, except	embarrass	occurred
access, excess	emigrant, immigrant	past, passed
accommodation	environment	personal, personnel
acquire	equipped, equipment	perform
adapt, adopt	exceed	precede
affect, effect	excite	presence, presents
all together, altogether	existence	principal, principle
altar, alter	fare, fair	privilege
angel, angle	formally, formerly	proceed
believe	forth, fourth	prophecy, prophesy
benefited	forty	quiet, quite
berth, birth	grammar	receive
born, borne	guarantee	referring
calendar	hear, here	respectively, respectfully
capital, capitol	holy, wholly	right, rite, write
censor, censure	hungry	schedule
choice, choose, chose	independent	separate
cite, sight, site	instance, instants	similar
coarse, course	irrelevant, irreverent	sophomore
complement, compliment	it's, its	staid, stayed
congratulations	knew, new	stationary, stationery
correspondence	know, no	success
council, counsel	knowledge	suit, suite
counselor	laboratory	superintendent
dairy, diary	later, latter	than, then
decent, descent	lead, led	their, there, they're
definite	loose, lose	threw, through
description	luxurious	to, too, two
desert, dessert	maintain, maintenance	vain, vane, vein
desperate	moral, morale	weak, week
dining, dinning	necessary	weather, whether
dyeing, dying	ninety	who's, whose
elicit, illicit	occasion	worse, worst
		writing

Final advice to help you improve your spelling:

1. Notice the kinds of spelling errors you make habitually. Keep a list of the words that are marked as misspelled in your graded papers. Learn to spell them correctly, and resolve that you won't make that error again. There is no excuse for misspelling *separate, receive, achieve, definite* more than once.

2. When you read, pay attention to the spelling of unusual words or words that you use in speech all the time but rarely in writing—for instance, *facetious*.
3. Learn the spelling rules that will clear up habitual errors.

SPELLING RULES

Despite the inconsistencies in English spelling, there are some rules that show spelling isn't as haphazard as it sometimes seems to be. You should learn these, not simply because they are rules, but because they can help you avoid errors that distract your reader's attention away from your message.

-ie/-ei

If you don't already know this rule, memorize it and use it:

I before *e*

Except after *c*

Or when sounded as *a*

As in *neighbor* or *weigh*

Unfortunately, there are many exceptions to this rule—*weird, leisure, height, foreign*—but it's helpful in remembering the spelling of many commonly misspelled words—*receive, deceive, achieve*.

FINAL e + SUFFIX

1. When the suffix begins with a vowel, drop the final *e:*

    stare + ing   staring
    note + able   notable

    Except when the word ends in *-ce/-ge:* courageous, singeing, noticeable, knowledgeable.
2. When the suffix begins with a consonant, keep the final *e:* wasteful, shameful, likeness, engagement, pavement, careful.
Important exception: argument.

FINAL CONSONANTS

1. When a suffix beginning with a vowel is added to short words or short accented syllables ending in a consonant, double the final consonant:

    deferral   bugged   handicapped
    fitted   stirring   beginning

2. If the final syllable ends in a consonant but is not accented, don't double the final consonant:

   bigoted   riveter   murderer

3. When a suffix beginning with a consonant is added to a word ending in a consonant, the final consonant is not doubled:

   deferment   fitness   capful

FINAL y + SUFFIX

Change *y* to *i,* except when the suffix is *-ing:*

   beautiful   satisfied   But: flying, dying,
   died   lied   satisfying

FINAL c + SUFFIX THAT BEGINS WITH A VOWEL

Change *c* to *ck:*

   picnicking   trafficked
   panicky   frolicking

There are many more rules of English spelling, but these are the ones that will help you prevent the misspellings that occur most frequently.

MECHANICS

Mechanics are rules that standardize certain things in writing. In some cases they function as signals to the reader; but, in most cases, mechanics are simply conventions that standardize things like capitalization, the use of numbers, and abbreviations. It is important that you observe these rules, though, because readers expect you to observe conventions even on things that don't substantially affect your message.

CAPITALIZATION

1. Capitalize the first word of every sentence.
2. Capitalize proper nouns:

   NAMES OF PERSONS   MONUMENTS, MUSEUMS, BUILDINGS, ETC.
   James Frank Harper   the Smithsonian Institute
   Herman Melville   the Library of Congress
   Jesus Christ   the Lincoln Memorial

NAMES OF PLACES	EVENTS AND PERIODS	NAMES OF VESSELS
Washington, D.C.	the Civil War	*The U.S.S. Constitution*
Luxembourg	the Stone Age	*Apollo 8*
	the Renaissance	*Old Ironsides*

3. Capitalize names of deities:

   Jehovah   Krishna   Jupiter

4. Capitalize titles before and after names:

   Dr. John Smith   Professor Barbara Walker
   Mrs. Jack McHenry   the Rev. Bill Baker
   Ms. Rita Kneipp   Susan O'Casey, Ph.D.
   Capt. John Smith   Queen Elizabeth II

5. Capitalize the first word and all other words except prepositions, conjunctions, and articles in the titles of literary works, movies, and works of art:

   The Catcher in the Rye   *Casablanca*
   For Whom the Bell Tolls   *Romeo and Juliet*
   the *Mona Lisa*   "Ode to a Nightingale"

6. Capitalize names of recognized groups and organizations:

   Republicans   Christian Science
   Democrats   Daughters of the American Revolution
   Jaycees   National Organization for Women

7. Capitalize *specific* course names:

   Math 130
   Psychology 441

8. Capitalize directions when they refer to specific geographical areas:

   Gone with the Wind is set in the South.
   She's from West Texas.

9. Avoid unnecessary capitalization:

   I am taking a *history* course this semester.
   Dallas is *northwest* of Houston.
   They consider themselves members of the *upper* class.
   John will be a *senior* next year.

ABBREVIATIONS AND SYMBOLS

You should use abbreviations and symbols sparingly and carefully in your writing. There are few abbreviations and symbols that are acceptable for the kind of writing you do in an English class, but if you notice the writing you are exposed to every day—newspapers, magazines, textbooks—you will see that abbreviations and symbols are rarely used there too. In general, writers avoid abbreviations because they make writing seem casual and unpolished. That's why you should avoid abbreviations like *dept., apt., Mon., assoc.,* in the context of your writing. Don't write:

   I have an appointment with the head of the math dept. tomorrow.

In some cases, abbreviations are permissible. The following guidelines should help you use abbreviations properly:

1. Abbreviate titles when they are part of a name: Mrs. Sue Young Stewart, Dr. James Smith, Lt. Col. James T. Anderson.

2. Organizations that are more commonly known by initials than by the full name may be abbreviated: AFL-CIO, NASA, NATO, SALT, OSHA, NOW. When you are not sure whether your audience will recognize the acronym, be sure you write out the whole name the first time you refer to it; you can use the initials for subsequent references.

3. Abbreviate the names of states only when they are part of an address. If you are referring to Fresno, California, in the text of your paper, do not write Fresno, Calif.

4. Latin abbreviations—etc., e.g., i.e.—are permissible in most writing.

5. Other acceptable abbreviations include the following: A.M., P.M., A.D., B.C., rpm, mph.

6. Many abbreviations have become common through everyday use: TV, CB, hi-fi, stereo, C.O.D. Use them only if they fit the tone of the particular piece you are writing.

7. Use the dollar sign ($) only for exact sums or for estimates of very large sums—$4.83, $1.6 billion—but write "about three dollars."

8. Do not use the ampersand (&) as a substitute for *and* in your writing unless it is part of an organization's name, as in Harper & Row.

9. Spell out percent (%) and cents(¢):

   The survey shows that only 9.6 *percent* of all college freshmen are financially independent.

   The price of ground beef has gone up 50 *cents* a pound in one month.

Mechanics

NUMBERS

Figures used in the text of your writing should be spelled out most of the time. Follow these guidelines for using numerals correctly:

1. Spell out numbers from one to ten. In very formal writing, spell out all two-digit numbers.

    We have read *five* books this semester; we may choose from a list of 25 novels.

2. Use figures to indicate exact sums, time, large figures, dates: 2:30 A.M., $8.65, 203,431, 1961, 500 B.C.

3. Avoid beginning a sentence with a figure. If you can't rewrite the sentence so the figure is not at the beginning, then spell out the number.

    Avoid: 1963 marked the beginning of an important era in American life.

    Rewrite: In 1963, Americans began an important era in politics.

4. Numbers from 21 to 99 are hyphenated when spelled out: thirty-five, ninety-seven. Make sure you learn how to spell these: forty (not fourty), ninety (not ninty).

ITALICS

Indicate italics in handwritten and typed work by means of underlining. Use italics in the following instances:

1. To indicate foreign words: writ of *habeas corpus, in absentia.*

2. To indicate emphasis:
    What do you mean *he* did it?
    It was Brad, *not* Dan, who wrote the winning essay.

3. To refer to words as words: *Penultimate* is one of my favorite words, but I hardly ever get to use it.

4. To indicate titles of literary works, works of art, movies, ships: *The Queen Mary, The Agony and the Ecstasy, Starry Night.*

A.B.C. GLOSSARY OF USAGE

THE ITEM...	EXPLAINED...	AND IN ACTION!
a/an	Use *a* before words that begin with a consonant and *an* before words that begin with a vowel (a, e, i, o, u). Words beginning with pronounced *h* take *a;* words with the *h* not pronounced take *an*.	**a** bartender, **a** juggler, **a** Fiat; **an** onion, **an obnoxious oaf; a** humble team; **an** hour.
above/below	Sounds too legal in phrases like "the above reasons, the ideas listed above, and in view of the above." If you can, substitute a word or phrase like *therefore, because of these reasons, for these reasons,* etc. The same is true for *below*.	
absolute/absolutely	Because these words are used so often, they have lost some of their punch. Instead of "I am absolutely exhausted," "I am exhausted" sounds more confident and sincere.	
accept/except	*Accept* is a verb meaning "to receive." *Except* is a preposition meaning "with the exclusion of."	I **accept** your explanation. **Except** for the fact that she can't type, she'd make a good secretary.
access/excess	*Access* means "approach" or "permission." *Excess* means "more than the usual or specified amount."	I don't have **access** to the record. An **excess** of money is one thing I'll never have.
adapt/adopt	*Adapt* means "to change something to fit a new purpose." *Adopt* means "to accept something as one's own without change."	Shawn **adapted** his old dance steps to the new beat. We **adopted** the neighborhood's stray dog and named it Useless.
admit/confess	*Admit* is not quite as serious as *confess*. A *confession* is considered legally binding. We might *admit* that we could be wrong, but we're not going to *confess* anything until we're certain we're wrong.	I **admit** that you could be right. I'll never **confess** to stealing that popsicle.
adopt/adapt	See *adapt*.	

THE ITEM...	EXPLAINED...	AND IN ACTION!
advice/advise	*Advice* is a noun.	Her **advice** was good, but it wasn't what I wanted to hear.
	Advise is a verb.	She **advised** me well, but I didn't want to listen.
affect/effect	*Affect* is a verb that means "to influence."	I'm not sure how this new drug will **affect** you.
	Effect is a noun that means "a result."	The **effect** of that loss will never be known.
again/back	If you use these after words that begin with *re-*, you're just repeating yourself and wasting ink. Instead of "resume again," just say "resume."	
aggravate	You can only aggravate a condition that is already bad, so avoid using *aggravate* in sentences like "That aggravates me" when you mean that something annoys or irritates you.	
ain't	The use of *ain't* is controversial. Yes, it's used by some educated speakers in casual conversation. However, it's not appropriate in formal and classroom writing unless it's deliberately used for a particular effect.	
all/all of	Use *all of* only when referring to items that you could actually count. If you're not referring to items that could be counted, use *all*.	**All of** the fish were active. **All** I wanted was some peace and quiet.
all . . . not	Statements with *all . . . not* are often not clear. "All the bums in the world are not worth saving" leaves the reader confused. Does this say that none of the bums, or only some of them, are worth saving? Try using *not all* when you mean only *some*.	
all right	*All right* is always two words.	
all that	Avoid *all that* in sentences like "I didn't care all that much."	
all together/altogether	*All together* means "everybody is together."	We were **all together** at the party.
	Altogether means "entirely."	She is **altogether** too snobbish.

The Handbook

THE ITEM...	EXPLAINED...	AND IN ACTION!
allusion/illusion	*Allusion* means "a reference."	I certainly didn't recognize those **allusions** to the Bible.
	Illusion means "deceptive impression."	The magician's **illusions** fooled me.
almost/most	*Almost* means "nearly." *Most* is used to draw comparisons. Don't shorten *almost* to *most* when you mean "nearly" as in "I like most everybody."	
already/all ready	*Already* is an adverb that means "by this time" or "prior to" (some designated time).	Have you finished those jalapeños **already**?
	All ready is an adjective phrase that means "everything is ready."	We were **all ready** to go to the concert when we discovered that the car had a flat tire.
among/between	*Among* generally refers to at least three items.	I never expected to find you **among** this group of people.
	Between refers to two items.	He couldn't decide **between** playing football and studying sociology.
angry/mad	See *mad*.	
ante-/anti-	*Ante-* means "before."	**ante**-bellum, **ante**cedent
	Anti- means "against."	**anti**-establishment, **anti**social
anybody/any body nobody/no body somebody/some body	*Anybody, nobody,* and *somebody* are all indefinite pronouns.	**Nobody** will every know what I've gone through.
	Any body, no body, and *some body* are adjectives and nouns paired together.	**No body** was found after the crash.
anyways	Use *anyway,* not *anyways*.	She won't go **anyway.**
anywheres	Use *anywhere,* not *anywheres*.	I can't find it **anywhere.**
area/field/subject	Try not to overuse these words as in "Her hardest courses are in the field of economics." Say, "Her hardest courses are in economics" instead.	
as/like	*As* is a conjunction, so it will introduce a clause.	They didn't do their homework **as** I asked them to.
	Like is a preposition.	I want a pair of jeans **like** Mary's.
as/such as	You can't substitute *as* when you mean *such as*. Instead of saying "I love all green vegetables as broccoli, spinach, and turnips," say "such as broccoli...."	

A.B.C. Glossary of Usage

THE ITEM...	EXPLAINED...	AND IN ACTION!
as good as/as much as	Don't use these phrases to mean "practically" as in "She as good as ordered me to say it."	
aspect	*Aspect* literally means "a position facing a particular direction." Try not to use the word when you mean view in general because the word loses some of its meaning and most of its punch.	After I considered what you said, I could see a new **aspect.**
assure/ensure/insure	*Assure* means "to promise." *Ensure* and *insure* both mean "to guarantee" or "make sure." Because *insure* reminds us of insurance, some writers use it only in that sense and use *ensure* to mean "make sure" in other senses.	She **assured** me she'd be here. I **ensured** my job security when I got tenure. He **insured** his personal property for $100,000.
at the same time that	When all you mean is "while," don't waste so many words and so much space by saying *at the same time that!*	
at this (that) point in time	This phrase is just a wordy way of saying "now" or "then."	
aware/conscious	*Aware* usually refers to circumstances or happenings. *Conscious* usually refers to your own feelings.	I'm **aware** that the game starts at 7 I **consciously** made the decision.
awhile/a while	*Awhile* is an adverb. *A while* is a noun plus the article *a*.	I laughed **awhile**; then I cried **awhile.** I laughed for **a while.**
back/again	See *again*.	
background	Try not to use this word when you actually mean "reason." *Background* is a contrast to *foreground* and should be used as such.	
bad/badly	*Bad* is an adjective *Badly* is an adverb.	I feel **bad** about forgetting you. He performed **badly** last night.
balance	See *emphasis*.	

THE ITEM...	EXPLAINED...	AND IN ACTION!
basically/on the basis of	These words are often used when they add nothing to the sentence. Try leaving them out.	
	We were judged *on the basis of* appearance.	We were judged on appearance.
	The chair is *basically* sound.	The chair is sound.
being	*Being* can often be eliminated from a sentence when it's not a part of the main verb.	
	With the majority of the vote *being* neither for or against, the bill will probably be dropped.	With the majority of the vote neither for or against, the bill will....
being as/being that	Avoid using these phrases when you mean "because" or "since."	
	Being as she's always late....	Because she's always late....
below	See *above*.	
bemused	*Bemused* means "bewildered," not "amused."	
beside/besides	*Beside* means "at the side of." *Besides* means "in addition."	I sat down **beside** her. I'll have three tacos **besides** the order of enchiladas, guacamole, rice, tamales, refried beans, and tortillas.
better than	Don't use *better than* when you mean "more than."	
between/among	See *among*.	
between you and I	Since between is a preposition here, you need to say "between you and me."	
born/borne	*Born* refers to birth. *Borne* refers to carrying.	I was **born** November 10, 1952. I've **borne** this burden long enough.
both	Avoid pairing *both* with words like *alike, together,* etc.; that just repeats the same idea.	
	Use *and*, not *as well as*, to connect two words with *both*.	**Both** Rita and I want to learn to ski.
bring/carry/take	*Bring* means "to transport something so that it is nearer."	**Bring** me that paper.
	Carry means "to transport something in any direction."	**Carry** that coin with you everywhere.
	Take means "to transport something so that it is farther away."	**Take** this book back to the library.

A.B.C. Glossary of Usage

THE ITEM...	EXPLAINED...	AND IN ACTION!
but however/ but nevertheless/ but yet	All of these phrases add nothing to a sentence because there is no need for two transitions when one will do just as much. I want to go, *but yet* I want to stay.	I want to go, **yet** I want to stay. I want to go, **but** I want to stay.
but that/but what	These phrases are also unnecessary. Try *that* instead. There's no question *but that* we'll win.	There's no question **that** we'll win.
can/may	*Can* refers to an ability or power. *May* refers to permission, opportunity, or willingness.	They **can** finish that article tonight if they hurry. They **may** not finish—ever.
carry	See *bring*.	
case/instance	Often these words are used when they're not needed. Who was involved *in the instance* of the car theft?	Who was involved in the car theft?
cause/reason	A *cause* makes something happen or produces an effect. A *reason* is a statement of explanation or justification.	The **cause** of death is not known. The **reason** I failed that test?—I didn't study.
cause is due to	In case you feel an urge to use this clause—don't. It's wordy and does nothing for your sentence.	
censor/censure	A *censor* is a person who decides if something will be allowed. A *censure* is the criticism of that thing.	The **censor** won't let such words be used on the radio. The administration heaped **censure** on our broadcast.
center around	*Center on* or *center upon* sounds more accurate.	
character	Don't use this word needlessly. She was *of a generous character*.	She was generous.
cite/sight/site	*Cite* means "to quote an authority or example." *Sight* refers to landmarks or things to see as well as vision. *Site* refers to buildings or a piece of land.	He **cited** the coach's instructions as the reasons for his success. Did you see all the **sights** in South Dakota? I hope he regains his **sight** after the surgery. Construction **sites** are dangerous.

THE ITEM...	EXPLAINED...	AND IN ACTION!
climactic/climatic	*Climactic* refers to climaxes. *Climatic* refers to climate and weather.	The experience was **climactic**. **Climatic** conditions should improve.
compare to/ compare with	*Compare to* usually emphasizes similarities. *Compare with* emphasizes relative values which can be alike or different.	He **compared** the classroom **to** a jail. He **compared** smoking cigarettes **with** smoking marijuana.
complected	Use *complexioned* or just say, "Her complexion was dark."	
complement/compliment	*Complement* refers to anything that completes the whole. *Compliment* refers to praise.	That scarf **complements** your dress perfectly. I don't know how to take a **compliment**.
compose/comprise	*Compose* means "to make up the whole or to create." *Comprise* means "to include."	Mozart **composed** music. The library is **composed** of one million volumes. The library **comprises** one million volumes.
concept/conception	A *concept* is a thought or idea. A *conception* is the sum of ideas, or concepts, on a subject.	My **conception** of a good life was formed from all of the **concepts** I was taught.
concern	Instead of saying "The subject of the book concerns good against bad," say "The subject of the book is good against bad." If you mean *is,* say it.	
confess/admit	See *admit*.	
conscience/conscious	*Conscience* is a noun. *Conscious* is an adjective.	His **conscience** bothers him. She is **self-conscious.**
conscious/aware	See *aware*.	
consensus	*Consensus* means "general agreement," so statements like "a general consensus of opinion" are repetitious. Just say "the consensus" or "the general opinion." A consensus is very close to being unanimous.	
consist of/consist in	*Consist of* means "to be made up of." *Consist in* means "to lie in" or "exist in."	An omelet **consists of** eggs, milk, and garnishes. Unity **consists in** standing together.

A.B.C. Glossary of Usage

THE ITEM...	EXPLAINED...	AND IN ACTION!
contemptible/ contemptuous	If something is *contemptible*, it deserves contempt. If you're *contemptuous*, your contempt is showing!	Cheating is **contemptible**. Her **contemptuous** feelings are inexcusable.
continual/continuous	*Continual* means "recurring at intervals." *Continuous* means "nonstop" or "uninterrupted."	I don't even have a tan yet because of the **continual** rain this summer. Snow fell **continuously** for two hours this afternoon.
contributing factor/factor	A *factor* is something that actively *contributes* to the production of a result, so *contributing factor* is repetitive. Just say *factor*.	
convince/persuade	*Convince* means "to win agreement."	I **convinced** Jared that the movie was worth watching.
	Persuade means "to move to action."	I **persuaded** Jared to watch the movie.
cope	You usually *cope with* some problem, so try not to use *cope* without *with*. Avoid saying "She just couldn't cope."	
correspond to/correspond with	If you *correspond to* something, you match it. If you *correspond with* it, you write it a letter.	
could of	Actually, you mean *could've (could have)*. Instead of saying "I could of won hours ago, but I wanted to give you a chance," say "I could have (or could've) won hours ago..."	
council/counsel	A *council* is an assembly or meeting. *Counsel* is advice or a lawyer to give advice.	She was elected to city **council**. The accused murderer's **counsel** said to plead not guilty.
criteria/criterion	*Criteria* is plural. *Criterion* is singular.	Those **criteria** will be hard to meet. That **criterion** is unreasonable.
crucial	*Crucial* means "essential to resolving a crisis." It shouldn't be used as a substitute for *important*; *crucial* means much more critical than just *important*.	

THE ITEM...	EXPLAINED...	AND IN ACTION!
data	*Data* is generally considered as plural. *Datum,* singular, is rarely used. You could say *fact* for *datum* and sound just as smart.	
deduce/deduct	*Deduce* means "infer." *Deduct* means "subtract."	How did you **deduce** that fact? I'd like to **deduct** the car on my income tax form.
defective/deficient	*Defective* means "faulty." *Deficient* means "lacking in some ingredient."	That rear axle is **defective.** My background in writing was **deficient.**
definite/definitive	*Definite* means "without question" or "positive." *Definitive* means "final."	I'm going to Florida this summer, and that's **definite.** We've got to find a **definitive** answer to the parking problem.
depend	Don't just say, "It *depends.*" It must *depend on* something or *upon* something.	
desert/dessert	*Desert* is the dry land. *Desert* means "to leave." *Dessert* is what some of us eat too much of.	If Las Vegas is the **desert,** send me! Don't **desert** me. I'll have three helpings of **dessert.**
device/devise	*Device* is a noun. *Devise* is a verb.	This **device** should save time and trouble. I must **devise** a way of convincing the prof that I know what I'm talking about.
dialogue	Avoid using *dialogue* in a sense of trading ideas. It means "conversation" in a strict, literary sense.	
differ from/differ with	*Differ from* means "to have some things that are different." *Differ with* means "to disagree."	
different	You sometimes use this word when it's obvious. Why say "I have three different excuses for being late?" If the excuses weren't different, then you wouldn't have three, would you?	

A.B.C. Glossary of Usage

THE ITEM...	EXPLAINED...	AND IN ACTION!
different from/different than	*Different from* is considered correct.	These jeans are **different from** the ones I wanted.
	Different than is appropriate in special cases.	That sandwich tasted **different than** I had expected.
discreet/discrete	*Discreet* means "modest" or "with good judgment."	She was **discreet** about her success.
	Discrete means "distinct."	We're talking about two **discrete** topics.
disinterested/uninterested	Both are used to mean *not interested,* but most educated speakers use *disinterested* to mean "impartial" and *uninterested* to mean "indifferent."	
due to the fact that	If all you mean is "since" or "because," that's all you have to say. *Due to the fact that* is much too wordy for such a simple meaning.	
during the course of	*During the course of* is the longest way we can think of to just say "during." Why waste all that energy?	
effect	See *affect.*	
e.g.	In footnotes or in information within parentheses, *e.g.* can be used to mean "for example."	Don't substitute a noun for a verb (**e.g.,** *job* for *run*).
egoism/egotism	*Egoism* is an ethical doctrine of self-interest.	We studied **egoism** in sociology.
	Egotism is an exaggerated view of yourself, or conceit.	She's so **egotistic** that she won't ever admit that she could be wrong.
elicit/illicit	*Elicit* means "to bring forth" or "evoke."	I can't **elicit** a response.
	Illicit means "not permitted."	This affair isn't **illicit;** we're married!
emigrant/immigrant	An *emigrant* has left a country. An *immigrant* has arrived in a country.	

324   *The Handbook*

THE ITEM...	EXPLAINED...	AND IN ACTION!
eminent/imminent/immanent	*Eminent* means "outstanding" or "distinguished."	She is an **eminent** scientist.
	Imminent means "about to happen."	Success is **imminent**.
	Immanent means "inherent" and is used mostly in religion and philosophy.	Is God **immanent** in all things?
endeavor	*Try* sounds better, if that's what you mean.	
enhance	*Enhance* means "to increase desirability" or "to make more attractive."	
	You can't use *enhance* to increase everything. For example, you can't enhance your reading skills.	
ensure	See *assure*.	
enthuse	Although *enthuse* is widely used, many experts think it's too informal for classroom writing. It's all right to use *enthuse* in your conversations, but go ahead and use *enthusiastic* in your writing.	Response to the call for aid was **enthusiastic**.
equally as	*Equally as* means "as," so there's no need to say both.	
especially/specially	*Especially* means "distinctively" or "outstandingly."	She is **especially** talented in dance.
	Specially means "with a certain purpose in mind."	That steel was **specially** formed for support.
et al.	This abbreviation stands for "and others." It is mostly used in footnotes and bibliographies. *Et al.* refers to people.	
etc.	*Etc.* means "and other things." Don't use unless it can't be avoided. Also, don't use *etc.* for people.	
	See also *et al*.	
ever so often/every so often	*Ever so often* means "very often."	I think of you **ever so often**.
	Every so often means "once in a while."	I remember to take that medicine **every so often**.

A.B.C. Glossary of Usage

THE ITEM...	EXPLAINED...	AND IN ACTION!
every day/everyday	*Every day* refers to something that you do every single day.	I have to work **every day.**
	Everyday means "commonplace."	Your temper is becoming an **everyday** problem.
except	See *accept*.	
excess	See *access*.	
facet	*Facet* can't be substituted for "part" because facets mean that the perspective has shifted.	I see a new **facet** of the problem every time I approach it from a different angle.
factor	See *contributing factor*.	
fantastic	*Fantastic* is overworked today. Only use it in the sense of fantasy.	
farther/further	*Farther* is an adverb which actually talks about distance.	How much **farther** to the next town, Dad?
	Further means "additionally" or "more."	We'll have to discuss this **further.**
fatal/fateful	*Fatal* refers to death.	That accident could have been **fatal.**
	Fateful refers to destiny or fate.	The **fateful** act caused me to wonder about fortune telling.
few/little	Use *few* when you're talking about things or people that you can count. Use *little* when you are talking about things that are measured.	**few** hours, **few** failures, **few** kids, **few** radishes, **few** aardvarks **little** trouble, **little** time, **little** success, **little** interest
fewer/less	*Fewer* and *less* are like *few* and *little*.	
	Fewer compares amounts that can be counted separately.	I have **fewer** marks on my paper than he does.
	Less compares amounts that can't be counted separately.	I've got **less** sense than anybody.
field	See *area*.	
figure/calculate	Avoid using these words when you mean "guess" or "suppose." If you *figure* or *calculate* something, it should be certain.	
final	A conclusion, finding, result, ending, outcome is *final*. So you don't have to say "final ending."	

326 *The Handbook*

THE ITEM...	EXPLAINED...	AND IN ACTION!
for free/for the purpose of/for the simple reason that	All of these expressions are wordy and can be eliminated.	
	The bike was *for free*.	The bike was free.
	We are gathered *for the purpose of* raising money.	We are gathered to raise money.
	I'm tired *for the simple reason that* I haven't slept in three days.	I'm tired because I haven't slept in three days.
foreword/forward	A *foreword* is an introduction to a book.	Nobody reads **forewords**.
	Forward means "up front."	Put your best foot **forward**.
formally/formerly	*Formally* means "according to form."	I haven't asked **formally**.
	Formerly means "previously."	She was **formerly** the president.
framework	Try not to overuse *framework* when it's not referring to a definite structure. The structure can be abstract, but it must be a structure.	
fulsome	*Fulsome* means "disgusting" or "insincere," not full of something.	
funny	*Funny* refers to laughter. If you mean "strange" or "odd," say it.	
further	See *farther*.	
gap	Just about everybody is tired of hearing "generation gap," "credibility gap," "communications gap." Try to use *gap* only when you literally mean a physical hole.	
gender	Although *gender* identifies and classifies words according to sex, don't use the word when you're referring to anything but grammar.	
general public	The public is a general group of people, so you can just say *public*.	
good/well	*Good* is an adjective.	This pie tastes **good**.
	Well is an adverb.	You all did **well** on that assignment.
	When you're talking about health, you can use either one.	Aren't you feeling **good**? Aren't you feeling **well**?

A.B.C. Glossary of Usage

THE ITEM...	EXPLAINED...	AND IN ACTION!
had better	*Had better* can't be shortened to "better." Don't say "I better win the race," say "I had better win the race."	
hanged/hung	Back in the Wild West, men were hanged almost every day. Everything else (including the dirty laundry and the jury) was hung.	
hang-up	We all have *hang-ups,* but try to call them "problems" or "biases" or "inhibitions" in writing.	
has reference to	*Refers to* is simpler.	
head up	If you've hit a wild shot in golf and you want your partner to get her head up, that's fine. But if you want your partner to *head up* the foursome, use "direct" or "lead" instead.	
historic/historical	*Historic* refers to events that helped shape history. *Historical* refers to events that pertain to history but didn't necessarily shape it.	The **historic** influence of the French Revolution can't be measured. What does that **historical** marker say about St. Simon's Island?
hopefully	In formal writing, avoid using *hopefully* to mean "I hope." In personal writing and everyday speaking, *hopefully* is fine.	**I hope** that these concepts are clear. **Hopefully,** the referee will call a technical foul before this game gets too rough.
host	Avoid *host* as a verb. Some people say "entertain" sounds better.	
human/humane	*Human* means "having to do with mankind." *Humane* means "having the good qualities of a human, especially kindness, compassion, or mercy."	Act like a **human!** Saving that dog from the traffic was **humane.**
idea/ideal	An *idea* is a conception or thought. An *ideal* is a principle.	What a brilliant **idea** you had! Your **ideals** are not the highest.
i.e.	This abbreviation means "that is."	

THE ITEM...	EXPLAINED...	AND IN ACTION!
if and when	You probably mean *if,* or you mean *when.* Use one or the other.	
ignorant/stupid	An *ignorant* person hasn't been taught much; a *stupid* person couldn't learn something if he were taught.	I may be **ignorant** in math, but I'm not **stupid;** if you'll teach me, I'll learn.
illicit	See *elicit.*	
illusion	See *allusion.*	
immanent	See *eminent.*	
immigrant	See *emigrant.*	
imminent	See *eminent.*	
imply/infer	*Imply* refers to what a statement means; an implication is not always stated in the original, but the idea is included in the meaning.	Your criticism **implies** that she's not worth seeing.
	Infer refers to an interpretation—a listener's or reader's judgment based on the statement.	From what you said, I **inferred** that it would be a waste of money to eat at the Greasy Spoon.
in to/into	These are different in that *in to* is usually part of an infinitive (*to* form of a verb). *Into* means *inside of.*	I'm going **in to do** my laundry. I'm going **into** that cave soon.
in a very real sense/ in all probability/ in all likelihood/ in order to/ in back of/ in regards to/ in terms of/ in connection with/ in excess of/ in spite of the fact that/ in this day and age/ in number/ in length/ in size/ in area/ in volume/	Avoid all such phrases. They are wordy and can cause confusion.	
incident/incidence	An *incident* is an event or occurrence. *Incidence* refers to how often something happens or rate of occurrence.	That was an unforgettable **incident.** The **incidence** of unwanted pregnancies is dropping in the Boston area.

A.B.C. Glossary of Usage

THE ITEM...	EXPLAINED...	AND IN ACTION!
incredibly	Don't overuse this word to try to make another word stronger. "He's incredibly strong" could just be "He's strong."	
individual	Don't use *individual* when you just mean "person." Todd is an incredible *individual*.	Todd is an incredible person.
infer	See *imply*.	
input/output	These words are almost dead from overwork. Try using them only when you're talking about mechanically putting something in and out.	
inside of/outside of	*Inside* and *outside* mean the same as *inside of* and *outside of*. So why use the extra words?	
instance	See *case*.	
insure	See *assure*.	
irregardless	*Irregardless* is actually *regardless*.	**Regardless** of the time, I'm going to wait for my friend.
join together	You can just say "join" or "together." They both mean the same thing, so it's a waste to say both.	
kind of/sort of/type of	If you feel the urge to write these phrases, don't. They're not necessary, and you shouldn't lose any meaning if you leave them out of your sentence. So pick up your pencil, mark through them, and go on writing.	
large number of/ large part/ large portion/ large share	If you mean *many,* just say *many*.	
later/latter	*Later* means "after a while." *Latter* relates to the second of two things being referred to.	See you **later,** alligator. If I had to choose between spaghetti or lasagna, I'd choose the **latter.**

330 *The Handbook*

THE ITEM...	EXPLAINED...	AND IN ACTION!
lay/lie	*Lay* means "to place" or "set down" (lay, laid, laid).	Please **lay** the book on the table carefully. Yesterday, you **laid** it on the edge and it fell off. I should have **laid** it down myself.
	Lie means "to recline" (lie, lay, lain).	I want to **lie** down when I get home. Yesterday, I **lay** in bed until 9:00. I haven't **lain** in bed that late for a long time.
leave/let	As a verb, *leave* shouldn't mean "to allow."	**Let** me have your packages.
lend/loan	In formal writing, avoid *loan* as a verb.	The bank will **lend** money at 12%.
	In informal writing and conversation, *loan* as a verb is accepted.	**Loan** me a quarter.
less	See *fewer*.	
let	See *leave*.	
let's us	*Let's* means "let us," so you don't need to say *let's us*.	
lie	See *lay*.	
like	See *as*.	
little	See *few*.	
loan	See *lend*.	
loose/lose	*Loose* is an adjective that means "not fastened" or "unrestrained."	That screw is **loose**.
	Lose is a verb that means "the opposite of win" or "to be deprived of."	I hope you didn't **lose** your checkbook.
lot(s) of	These expressions, although common in informal writing, should be avoided in formal writing. Try to be more specific.	
mad/angry	Although *mad* is used to mean angry, *mad* goes one degree further to imply insane.	
may	See *can*.	

A.B.C. Glossary of Usage

THE ITEM...	EXPLAINED...	AND IN ACTION!
media/medium	*Media* is plural	The **media** are concerned with being objective.
	Medium is singular.	India ink is the **medium** for that sketch.
mighty	*Mighty* means "imposing in size or extent." Don't use it to mean "very."	**Mighty** Mouse
more preferable	Just say *preferable*.	
most	See *almost*.	
myself	Use *myself* only as a reflexive pronoun, not as a substitute for "I" or "me." Don't say, "If you want a ride, call either Jane or myself."	I told **myself** that I had to be a complete idiot. If you want a ride, call either Jane or **me**.
nature	When used to mean "sort" or "kind," *nature* is often unnecessary and vague. Instead of saying "The nature of the disease caused discomfort," say "The fever connected with the disease caused discomfort."	
near future/not too distant future	*Soon* would probably work just as well, and it would certainly be simpler.	
nobody	See *anybody*.	
nor/or	*Nor* will follow *neither* in a sentence of comparison. *Or* will follow *either*.	**Neither** rain **nor** snow will dampen my spirits. **Either** rain **or** snow could interfere with the barbeque.
not too/not that	If you mean "not very," say it. *Not too* and *not that* sound sluggish. She's *not that* interested in going. She's *not too* interested in going.	She's **not very** interested in going.
of between/of from	Don't use two prepositions when one will do the job.	I'll give you a list of ten to 12 people.

332   *The Handbook*

THE ITEM...	EXPLAINED...	AND IN ACTION!
oftentimes	*Oftentimes* sounds great when you're sitting on the front porch swing telling tales. Otherwise, you should use "often."	
on the part of	How did we ever get in the habit of saying *by* with so many words?	
orient/orientate	Both of these words mean the same thing, so use the shorter, simpler one—*orient*.	
output	See *input*.	
outside of	See *inside of*.	
owing to the fact that	Such a long string of words might put the reader to sleep. Try "since."	
past/passed	*Past* is something that has already happened. *Passed* is the past action of *passing*.	My **past** record isn't too great. He **passed** the ball.
per	*Per* sounds a bit stiff for everyday classroom writing. Try to use it only when you're referring to math formulas.	
percent/per cent	Either spelling is accepted. Spelling the word out rather than using the symbol is preferable in writing.	
persecute/prosecute	*Persecute* means "to harass because of a belief." *Prosecute* means "to follow to the end," or "to seek legal action for a crime."	Hitler **persecuted** the Jews. Allied Nations **prosecuted** those in Hitler's regime for persecuting Jews.
personal/personnel	Your own belongings are your *personal* things. If you want a job, write to the company's *personnel* director.	
persuade	See *convince*.	
phenomena/phenomenon	*Phenomenon* is singular.	
plan on	You *plan to* do something, not *plan on* doing it.	
poorly	Avoid *poorly* when referring to health.	

A.B.C. Glossary of Usage

THE ITEM...	EXPLAINED...	AND IN ACTION!
precede/proceed	*Precede* means "to go ahead of" or "to surpass." *Proceed* means "to continue on."	The secret servicemen **preceded** the president into the room. We **proceeded** on course.
predominate/predominant	*Predominate* is a verb. *Predominant* is an adjective.	
prejudice/prejudiced	*Prejudice* doesn't always mean that you are against something; you could be prejudiced for something. Notice that the adjective is *prejudiced,* not *prejudice.*	I was **prejudiced** in favor of lowering bus rates.
pretty	*Pretty* is overused. Don't use it to mean "very."	
principal/principle	A *principal* is a leader, chief, or head. *Principle* is a noun that means "theory, concept, rule."	My brother thinks he's the **principal** character in that story. That **principal** is a push-over. Should moral **principles** be taught in school?
proceed	See *precede.*	
prophecy/prophesy	*Prophecy* is the noun. *Prophesy* is the verb.	That **prophecy** will never come true. You **prophesy,** but your prophecies don't come true.
prosecute	See *persecute.*	
quote	For most writing, *quote* is just fine. But if you want to be formal, use *quotation.*	
raise/rise	*Raise* means "to lift up." *Rise* means "to get or go up."	He **raised** that chair with his finger. I saw it **rise** above his head.
rarely ever	Just say *rarely.*	
rather than	When you use *rather than,* be careful that your comparisons are parallel. Rather than eating lunch, we decided to eat breakfast.	Rather than eat lunch, we decided to eat breakfast.
real/very	These words are overworked. Try to give them a rest as often as you can.	

The Handbook

THE ITEM...	EXPLAINED...	AND IN ACTION!
reason	See *cause*.	
reason is because	*Because* means the same thing and saves energy.	
reckon	*Reckon* is another one of those front porch words. It's fine for a down-home, yarn-spinning effect, but that's about all.	
in regard to/with regard to	If you can just say "about" or "concerning," prefer one of those.	
relevant	Don't use *relevant* by itself. Your topic must be *relevant to* something.	
reticent	*Reticent* doesn't mean "reluctant." It means "inclined to be secretive or silent."	
rise	See *raise*.	
same/the same	The words aren't pronouns. Don't say "I did the same."	
scene	Try to avoid using *scene* in the sense of "drug scene." A *scene* is "a place where something has happened or will happen."	
semi-	See *bi-*.	
sensual/sensuous	*Sensual* means "carnal" or "having to do with sex." *Sensuous* refers to the senses.	
set/sit	*Set* means "to put something down." *Sit* means "to occupy a place."	**Set** the book on the table. **Sit** down.
shall/will/ should/would	Once, people insisted on using *shall*. Now, it's considered very formal, and *will* is considered perfectly all right.	I **shall** return. (formal) I **will** return. (normal)
sight	See *cite*.	
similar to	If you mean *like,* say it; it's shorter and clearer.	
sit	See *set*.	

A.B.C. Glossary of Usage

THE ITEM...	EXPLAINED...	AND IN ACTION!
some time/sometime/sometimes	*Some time* means "an amount of time."	I'll need **some time** to think.
	Sometime means "at any time."	Bring it to me **sometime**.
	Sometimes means "once in a while."	I **sometimes** forget to go to class.
somebody	See *anybody*.	
something	*Something* is usually overused and not clear. Avoid it.	
sort of	See *kind of*.	
specially	See *especially*.	
stationary/stationery	*Stationary* means "fixed."	That fixture is **stationary**.
	Stationery is the paper.	What cute **stationery!**
stupid	See *ignorant*.	
subject	See *area*.	
such as	See *as*.	
suppose	If you mean *supposed* be sure you add the *d*.	We were **supposed** to go fishing, but the wind was blowing too hard.
surely	*Surely* is the adverb, but *certainly* sounds better.	
take	See *bring*.	
that/which/who	*That* and *which* generally refer to nonhuman objects. *Who* refers to people.	
theirselves	Use *themselves* instead.	
thusly	*Thus* is correct.	
till/until	These words are correct. Don't use *til* or *'til*.	
to/too/two	*Too* means "also."	I want to go, **too.**
	Two is the number.	I'll take **two** helpings.
	To is everything else.	I plan **to** drive **to** town.
totally	Don't use *totally* just to mean "very"; it means entirely or completely.	
type of	See *kind of*.	
under water/underwater	*Under water* is the prepositional phrase.	Ralph performs **under water.**
	Underwater is the adjective or adverb.	Aquarena Springs has Ralph, the **underwater** pig.

THE ITEM...	EXPLAINED...	AND IN ACTION!
uninterested	See *disinterested*.	
until	See *till*.	
use to/used to	Make sure you say "used to."	She **used to** weight 237 pounds. Her car **used to** have heavy-duty shocks, didn't it?
very	See *real*.	
ways	If you mean "distance," *way* is the right word.	I've got a long **way** to go.
weather/whether	*Weather* is what's going on outside the window. *Whether* is the conjunction.	What's the **weather** like? **Whether** you go or not, I'm going.
well	See *good*.	
which	See *that*.	
who	See *that*.	
will/would	See *shall*.	
would like for	Save space; say "want"	

INDEX

A/an, 315
Above/below, 315
Abbreviations and symbols, use, 313
A. B. C. guide to usage, 315–37
Absolute/absolutely, 315
Accept/except, 315
Access/excess, 315
Acknowledgment of sources. *See*
    Documentation: APA style;
    Documentation: MLA style
Action verbs, 176
Adapt/adopt, 315
Adjectival endings, 279
Adjective, 278–80
    defined, 278–79
    how to use, 279–80
    phrases and clauses, 278
Admit/confess, 315
Adopt/adapt, 315
Adverb, 280–81, 284
    conjunctive, 284
    defined, 280
    forms of, 281
    sentence modifiers, 280–81
    as transitional words, 281
Advice/advise, 316
Affect/effect, 316
Again/back, 316
Aggravate, 316
Agreement of subject and verb, 284–86
Aims, definition, 49
Ain't, 316
Alexander, Shana, 104
All/all of, 316
All . . . net, 316
All right, 316
All that, 316
All together/altogether, 316
Allusion/illusion, 317
Almost/most, 317
Already/all ready, 317
Among/between, 317

Analogy, pattern of essay organization, 77
Analysis, how to use in essay writing, 171
Analysis, pattern of essay organization, 71, 75
Angry/mad, 317
Ante-/anti-, 317
Anybody/any body 317
Anyways, 317
Anywheres, 317
Apostrophe, 303–4
Application assignments:
    analyzing a thesis, 68–70
    checking conclusions, 107
    checking essay for flow, 151
    checking essay for paragraph development, 136
    checking essay for relatedness, 130
    checking essay for thesis, 94–96
    checking essay for topic sentence paragraph, 123
    checking paragraph for topic, 129–30
    classical invention, 34
    coordination, 163
    creating techniques, 12–13, 20
    double creating technique, 36
    finding topic sentence, 126–28
    function paragraph, 143–45
    including the reader, 63–65
    introductions, 87–89
    limiting by adding, 122–23
    looping, 20
    method of paragraph development, 133–38
    paragraphs stay on topic, 129–30
    patterns of organization, 79–80
    preliminary agreements, 52
    promise and delivery system, 108–9
    reference material, 241–42
    revising for coordination, 163
    revising for subordination, 165

    revising for variety, 158
    topic sentence paragraphs, 137–38
    transition and reminder signs, 151
    verbal communication, 45–46
Application, letter of, 260–61
Area/field/subject, 317
Arden, Harvey, 144–45
Aristotle, 25–26
    common topics, 25–26
As/such as, 317
As good as, as much as, 318
As/like, 317
Aspect, 318
Assert, definition, 186
Assertion-with-proof essay, 186–87
    characteristics of, 186
    contexts, 186–87
Assure/ensure/insure, 318
Atlases, yearbooks, almanacs, 236–37
At the same time that, 318
At this (that) point in time, 318
Audience. *See also* Reader
    definition, 42
    determines form, 70
    giving value to, 54–55
    invent and know, 50
    specific, 50
Author card, 198
Aware/conscious, 318
Awhile/a while, 318

B*ack/again*, 318
Background, 318
Bad/badly, 318
Balance, 318
Bare bones outline, 97–100
Basically/on the basis of, 319
Basic essay arrangement, 57–58
Being, 319
Being as/being that, 319
Below, 319

Bemused, 319
Better than, 319
Between early and late shaping, 60–84.
 See also Form; Patterns of organization; Reader; Thesis
 checklist for reader, 63
 checklist for thesis, 63
 form determined by message, 71
 knowing the reader, 60–65
 organizing principle, 79
Between/among, 317
Between you and I, 319
Bibliographical entries: APA style, 230–33
 citation of part of source, 231
 multiple citations, 231
 one author, sample card, 230
 reference list, sample, 231–33
 works with no author, 230
 works with two or more authors, 230
Bibliographical entries: MLA style, 224–229
 article from encyclopedia, 228
 article from magazine, monthly, 228
 article from magazine, weekly, 228
 article from newspaper, 228–29
 book, essay or chapter from, 227
 book with four or more authors, 226
 book of more than one volume, 227
 book, no author cited, 226
 book with one author, 226
 book in series, 227
 book with translator, 227
 book of two or three authors, 226
 editions, 226
 editors, 226
 review, 228
 second references, 229
Bibliographies, 237
Bibliography, 191, 196, 225–28
Bibliography cards, 197
Bibliography, sample entry, 225
Biographical references, 237
Bird, Isabella, 138–39
Boettinger, Henry, 142
Booklists, 238
Born, borne, 319
Both, 319
Bracket, 306
Brainstorm, definition, 10
Brainstorming, 10–11
Break-down order, pattern of essay organization, 71
Bring, carry, take, 319
Business letters, 249–61
 of application, 260–61
 Format: standard block, 249–50

 order, 249
 request, 253
 responses, 252
Business writing, 247–65
 appearance, 250–51
 Gerald Cohen's Dial-a-Buzzword, 248
 purpose, 247
 tone, 247
But however/but nevertheless/but yet, 320
But that/but what, 320
Buzzword, 248

Cabin building and essay writing, 1–5
 collecting ideas, 1–2
 finishing, 3–5
 planning and building, 3–4
Campfire dance, 89–92
Can/may, 320
Capitalization, 311–12
Card catalog, 196
 author's card, 196
 call number, 196
 Library of Congress call number, 196
 subject headings, 196
Carry. See Bring
Case/instance, 320
Casstevens, David, 177–78
Cause/effect pattern of organization in essay, 71, 73
Cause/reason, 320
Cause is due to, 320
Censor, censure, 320
Center around, 320
Center of gravity sentence, 15, 18–19
Cerf, Bennett, 169
Character, 320
Circumlocution, 294–95
Cite/sight/site, 320
Citing sources, 229
Climactic, climatic, 321
Coleridge, Samuel Taylor, 92
Colon, 300–301
Comma, 299–300
Comma splice, 290–91
Communication, verbal, 43–46
 encoding aids, 44
 listener, 44
 re-creation aids, 44
 Ross Model, 45
 support system, 44–45
Compare to/compare with, 321
Comparison and contrast in paragraph development, 133
Comparison/contrast pattern of essay organization, 71, 76
Complected, 321

Complement/compliment, 321
Completing, 114–187
 dissecting sheet, 179–82
 final considerations, 182–85
 overview, 115
 purpose, 116–18
 revising for energy: sentences, 156–71
 revising for flow: paragraphs, 119–45
 revising for punch: words, 172–78
 rules of correctness, 117–18
 transition and reminder signs, 145–51
 symbolic value, 118
Compose/comprise, 321
Concept/conception, 321
Concern, 321
Conclusion of essay, 105–9
Concrete words, 175
Confess/admit, 321
Conjunctions, 283
 coordinating, 283
 correlative, 283
 defined, 283
 subordinating, 283
Conjunctive adverb, 284
Conscience/conscious, 321
Conscious/aware, 321
Consensus, 321
Consist of/consist in, 321
Contemptible/contemptuous, 322
Contexts. *See* Preliminary agreements
Continual/continuous, 322
Contributing factor/factor, 322
Convince, persuade, 322
Conventions, writing, 47
Coordinate, definition, 161
Coordinating conjunctions, 162, 283
Coordination, 161–64
 clauses, 162
 phrases, 162
 sentences, 162
 words, 162
Cope, 322
Correspond to/correspond with, 322
Could of, 322
Council/counsel, 322
Create, definition, 8
Creating, 6–39
 overview, 7
 personal writing, 42
 purpose, 8, 42
Creating techniques, 9–36
 brainstorming, 10–11, 35
 classical inventions, 25–35
 cubing, 21–24, 35
 discussion questions, 36
 double technique, 36
 list, 11–12, 35

looping, 13–20, 35
  reporter's formula, 10, 35
  student samples, 19–20, 24, 33
  summary, 34–36
Criteria/criterion, 322
Crucial, 322
Cubing, 21–24
  practice in, 22–23
  purpose, 21
  rules, 21
  student sample, 23–24
Cubing, definition, 21

Development, paragraph, 130–36
  adding to general statement, 131–32
  chart, 136
  comparison and contrast, 133
  definition, 133
  description, 133
  explanation and analysis, 133
  facts and figures, 133
  illustrations, examples, details, 132–33
  narration, 133
  principles, 123, 128, 130
Development, thesis, 100–104
  analysis, 102
  bare bones outline, 98–99
  cause/effect, 102
  classification, 103
  comparison and contrast, 101
  definition, 103
  description, 100
  details, 101
  examples and illustrations, 100
  narration, 101
Dash, 305
Data, 323
Deadwood, 293
Deduce, deduct, 323
Deduction, pattern of essay organization, 71, 75
Defective, deficient, 323
Definite, definitive, 323
Definition, use in
  classical invention, 25–26
  paragraph development, 133
  pattern of essay organization, 71, 74–75
Deliver, definition, 85
Demonstrative pronoun, 272
Depend, 323
Description, use in
  paragraph development, 133
  pattern of essay organization, 71, 73
Desert/dessert, 323
Develop, definition, 96

Device/devise, 323
Dialogue, 323
Dickens, Charles, 170–71
Diction and style, 293–98
  errors in, 296–97
  problems in, 293–96
Dictionaries, 238
Differ from/differ with, 323
Different, 323
Different from/different than, 324
Discover, definition, 8
Discreet/discrete, 324
Disinterested/uninterested, 324
Dissecting sheet, 179–81
Documentation, 192
Documentation: APA style, *See*
  Bibliographical entries
Documentation: MLA style. *See*
  Bibliographical entries
Double creating technique, 36
Draft, definition, 56
Due to the fact that, 324
During the course of, 324
Durrell, Lawrence, 125–26

Early shaping. *See also* How-to-essay;
  Preliminary agreements; Trial draft
  contexts, 52
  invent and know audience, 49–50
  message, 51
  purpose, 49
  writing conventions, 47
Effect, 324
E.g., 324
Egoism/egotism, 324
Elbow, Peter, 14
Elicit/illicit, 324
Ellipsis, 306
Emigrant/immigrant, 324
Eminent/imminent/immanent, 325
Encyclopedias, 238–39
Endeavor, 325
Energy, definition, 159
Enhance, 325
Ensure, 325
Enthuse, 325
Equally, 325
Essay assignments;
  assertion-with-proof, 186–87
  evaluation, 152–55
  explanation, 110–12
  how-to, 53–60
  personal experience, 37–39
  problem/solution, 81–84
Especially/specially, 325

Essay conclusions, 105–109
  closure principle, 106
Essay conclusion
  give something new, 105–6
  reminder to readers, 105
  spin-off, 105–6
  summarizing main points, 105
Essay patterns of organization. *See*
  Patterns of organization
Essay tests, 243–46
  completing, 245
  creating, making a list, 243
  shaping, check list, 244
  summary, 245
Et al., 325
Etc., 325
Evaluate, definition, 152
Evaluation essay, 152–155
  characteristics, 153
  checking development, 155
  choosing context, 153
  completing, 155
  creating, 154–55
  shaping, 155
  standards, external, 152
  standards, internal, 152
Ever so often/every so often, 325
Every day/everyday, 326
"Everything You've Always Wanted to Know About Energy but Were Too Weak to Ask," 141
Examining your paper, 179–85
Example, pattern of essay organization, 71, 77–79
Except, 326
Excess, 326
Exclamation point, 302
Expand, definition, 96
Explain, definition, 110
Explanation and analysis in paragraph development, 133
Explanation essay, 110–12
  characteristics of, 110
  choosing a context, 110–12
  creating techniques, 112
  final check, 112
  shaping, 112

Facet, 326
Factor, 326
Facts and figures in paragraph development, 133
Fantastic, 326
Farther/further, 326
Fatal/fateful, 326
Few/little, 326

Fewer/less, 326
Field, 326
Figure/calculate, 326
Final, 326
Final considerations, 182–85
   editing, 182–83
   manuscript form, 183–85
Finding ideas, classical invention, 25
Flow, checking essay for, 151
Flow, definition, 119
Flow, ways of achieving, 142
Footnotes, 191, 225
For free/for the purpose of/for the simple reason that, 327
Foreword/forward, 327
Form. *See also* Patterns of organization
   determined by audience, 70
   determined by message, 70
   determined by purpose, 70
Formally/formerly, 327
Fragments, 291–92
Framework, 327
Fulsome, 327
Function paragraph, 138–51
   to accommodate author's style, 141
   add detail, 142
   add drama, 138–39
   add emphasis, 142
   analyzing choices, 144–45
   characteristics, 119, 138
   checking for flow, 144
   contexts for, 142
   definition, 139
   describing the function, 143–44
   to develop an example, 142
   identifying, 143–44
   as a transition, 139
   as psychological break, 140
   purpose of, 138
   to set off dialogue, 140
Funny, 327
Further, 327

Gap, 327
Gender, 327
General public, 327
General-specific order, pattern of essay organization, 71, 74–75
Going public; writing for audience, 42
Good/well, 327
Gross, Theodore, 159
Guthrie, Woody, 172–73

Had better, 328
Handbook, The, 266–314
   overview, 267
Hanged/hung, 328
Hang-up, 328
"Hanging" indentation, 225
Has reference to, 328
Hayden, Naura, 141
Head up, 328
Historic, historical, 328
Hopefully, 328
Host, 328
How-to-essay, 53–60
   characteristics of, 53
   choosing context, 53–54
   creating techniques for, 54
   final check, 55
   knowing audience, 54, 58
   rules for, 55
   trial draft, 56–60
Human/humane, 328
Hyphen, 304–5

Idea/ideal, 328
I.e., 328
If and when, 329
Ignorant/stupid, 329
Indefinite pronouns, 272
Indexes, 239–41
Interrogative pronouns, 272
Illicit, 329
Illusion, 329
Illustrations, examples, details, in paragraph development, 132
Immanent, 329
Immigrant, 329
Imminent, 329
Imply/infer, 329
Incident/incidence, 329
Incredibly, 330
Individual, 330
Induction, pattern of essay organization, 71, 75
Infer, 330
Input/output, 330
In regard to/with regard to, 335
Inside of/outside of, 330
Insider, writer as, 51, 55
Instance, 330
Insure, 330
Interjection, 284
In to/into, 329

Introduction, 86–89
   analyzing, 87–88
   aspect/perspective of, 86
   to make promise clear, 86
   get reader's attention, 86
   reveal intended message, 86
   reader's responses to, 88–89
Invent, definition, 8, 25
Irregardless, 330
Italics, 314

Jargon, 295
Job application letter, 252–261
   completing, 259
   conclusion, 259
   content, 252
   conventions, 254
   cubing, 255
   list, 254–55, 256
   looping, 255
   introduction, 257
   paragraph on education, 257–58
   paragraph on interests, activities, 258–59
   paragraph on work, 258
   samples of letters, 260–61
   shaping, 256–59
   visualizing audience, 252
Join together, 330

Kennedy, X. J., 175
Kettering, Charles, 34
Kind of/sort of/type of, 330
King, Martin Luther, 140–41

Lagniappe, 224
Large number of, 330
Late shaping. *See also* Conclusion; Introduction; Thesis
   agreement with reader, 85
   conclusion, 105–9
   developing thesis, 89–107
   introduction, 86
   promise and delivery system, 108–9
   rewriting the essay, 85–109
Later/latter, 330
Lay/lie, 331
Leave/let, 331
Lend/loan, 331
"Letter from Birmingham Jail," 140–41

Less, 331
Let, 331
Let's us, 331
Library resources. *See also* Reference
    material
    Card catalog, 196
    Reader's Guide, 198
Lie, 331
Like, 331
Lincoln, Abraham, 167
List, definition, 11
List-making, example, 11–12
Little, 331
"Living Dead Sea, The," 144–45
Loan, 331
Looping, 13–20
    application, 20
    definition, 13
    using in how-to essay, 54
    practice in, 15–17
    purpose of, 13
    rules, 14–15
    student example, 17–20
Loose/lose, 331
Lot(s) of, 331

McCarthy, Mary, 166
mad/angry, 331
Mailer, Norman, 168
Malcolm X, 166
Maslow, Abraham, 171
Master storyteller, 92–94
May, 331
Mechanics, 311–14
    abbreviations and symbols, 313
    capitalization, 311–12
    italics, 314
    numbers, 314
Media/medium, 332
Mighty, 332
Mixed forms, pattern of essay
    organization, 77
Mixed metaphors, 298
Modes, definition, 49
Modification, 288–89
More preferable, 332
Most, 332
"Motherliness," 104
Myself, 332

Narration
    in paragraph development, 133
    pattern of essay organization, 71, 72

Nature, 332
Near future/not too distant future, 332
New York Times index, 198
Nietzsche, 176
Nobody, 332
Nor/or, 332
Not too/not that, 332
Note card, 200, 225
Note, sample, 225
Notes, MLA style, 224–25
Noun, 268–70
    common, 269
    defined, 268
    identifiers, 269–70
    proper, 268–69
Numbers, 314

Of between/of from, 332
Oftentimes, 333
Olsen, Tillie, 169–70
On the part of, 333
Orient/orientate, 333
Orwell, George, 174–75
Outline, 233–34
    sentence, 233
    topic, 233
Output, 333
Outside of, 333
Overview
    completing stage, 115
    creating stage, 7
    "Handbook, The," 267
    practical applications, 189
    shaping stage, 41
Owing to the fact that, 333

Paragraph. *See* Function paragraph;
    Topic sentence paragraph
Parallel, definition, 167
Parallelism, 289–90
    identifying examples, 168–69
    transforming sentences, 168
Parallelism, definition, 165
Parallel sentences, use of
    add style, 166
    establish rhythm, 166–67
    give sense of order, 167
Paraphrase, in research paper, 234, 235–36
Paraphrase, student samples, 235–36
Paren (parentheses), 305–6
Parts of speech, 268–284

Past/passed, 333
Patterns of organization
    break-down order; analysis, 71, 75;
    classification, 71, 76; example, 71, 77–79
    general-specific order: definition, 71, 74–75; induction, 71, 75; deduction, 71, 75
    mixed forms, 77
    relationship order: analogy, 71, 77; comparison/contrast, 71, 76
    recognizing patterns, 79–80
    review, 79
    spatial order: description; 71, 73
    thesis determines form, 80
    time order: narration, 71, 72; process, 71, 72; cause/effect, 71, 73
Patterns of organization essay, 71–78
    "Freshman to Freshman: Surprises in English," student essay, 77–78
Per, 333
Percent/per cent, 333
Period, 299
Persecute/prosecute, 333
Personal experience essay, 37–39
    creating techniques, 38–39
    purpose, 37
    writing contexts, 37–38
Personal/personnel, 333
Personal pronouns, 270–71
Personal writing, characteristics, 42–43
Persuade, 333
Phenomena/phenomenon, 333
Pike, Donald C., 235
Plagiarism, 234–36
Plan on, 333
Point, definition, 99
Poorly, 333
Possessive pronouns, 271
Precede/proceed, 334
Predication, 286–87
Predominate, predominant, 334
Prejudice, prejudiced, 334
Preliminary agreements, 48–52
    contexts, 52–53
    determining purpose, 49
    inventing audience, 49–51
    matching audience to context, 52
    message, 51–52
    why, what, to whom, 49–51
Prepositions, 281–82
    defined, 281
    functions, 281–82
Pretty, 334

Index 343

Principal/principle, 334
Principles of topic sentence paragraph, 123–38
Private, definition, 42
Problem/solution essay
  characteristics, 81
  choosing context, 82
  choosing problem, 83
  creating techniques for, 83
  final check, 84
  rules, 84
  shaping, 83–84
Proceed, 334
Process, pattern of essay organization, 71–72
Promise, definition, 85
Promise and delivery system, 108–9
Pronouns, 270–73
  defined, 270
  demonstrative, 272
  indefinite, 272
  interrogative, 272
  personal, 270–71
  possessive, 271
  reflexive, 271
  relative, 271
Proof, definition, 186
Prophecy/prophesy, 334
Prosecute, 334
Psychic distance, 60
Public, definition, 42
Public writing
  characteristics, 43
  writer's objectives, 43
Punctuation, 298–307
  mechanical level, 298
  functional level, 298
  apostrophe, 303–4
  bracket, 306
  colon, 300–301
  comma, 299–300
  dash, 305
  ellipsis, 306
  exclamation point, 302
  hyphen, 304–5
  paren (parentheses), 305–6
  period, 299
  question mark, 301
  quotation marks, 302–3
  semicolon, 301–2
  virgule/slash, 306

Question mark, 301
Quotation mark, 302–3
Quote, 334

Raise/rise, 334
Rarely ever, 334
Rather than, 334
Reader. *See also* Audience
  agreement with, 85
  checklist for, 63
  comparing response to essays, 63–65
  interests of, 60–63
  as person, not wall, 60, 63–65
  reaction, 61–62
Reader's Guide, 198
  cross index, 203
  subject headings, 198
  title of article, 198
  title of magazine, 198
Real/very, 334
Reason, 335
Reason is because, 335
Reckon, 335
Recursive, definition, 47
Redundancy, 294
Reference material, 236–40
  application, 241–42
  atlases, yearbooks, almanacs, 236–37
  bibliographies and library guides, 237–38
  biographical references, 237
  booklists, 238
  dictionaries, 238
  encyclopedias, 238–39
  indexes, 239–41
  quotations, 241
Reflexive pronouns, 271
Relatedness, checking essay for, 130
Relationship order of essay organization, 71, 76, 77
Relative pronouns, 271
Relevant, 335
Reminder signs
  pronouns used as, 150
  refresh reader's memory, 150
  repetition of key words, 150
  synonyms used as, 150
Repertory, definition, 13
Reporter's formula, 10
Research paper, 190–242
  bibliography cards for, 197, 199
  card catalog, 196
  credibility of sources, 205
  equipment needed, 195
  finding a topic, 200–204
  library aids, 194–206
  nonwriting skills, 190–92
  notecards for, 199–200
  outline, 205–6, 233–34
  questions about, 223

Reader's Guide, 198, 202–3
  student diary, 193–206
  student sample essay, 207–22
Résumés, 262–65
  aesthetic appeal, 262
  information included, 262
  definition, 252
  model 2, 263
  samples, 264–265
Reticent, 335
Revising for energy: sentences. *See also* Sentence combining
  balance and repetition, 169–70
  combining sentences, 159–71
  combining words, phrases, clauses, 162
  coordination, 161
  identifying balanced structures, 170–71
  imitating sentence patterns, 171
  parallelism, 165–69
  stylistic changes, 169–70
  subordination, 165
  variety, 156–58
Revising for flow. *See* Topic sentence paragraph: Function paragraph
Revising for punch: words, 172–78
  active verb forms, 176–77
  exactness, specifics, pictures, images, 172–79
  finding vivid words, 177–78
  flabby words, 176
  identifying problem words, 178
  rules for, 175
  specific words, 175–76
Review exercises, imitating patterns, 171
Rise, 335
Roethke, Theodore, 120
Rogers, Carl, 139
Ross model, 44–45
  area of mutual influence, 44
Ross, Raymond S., 45
Rough, definition, 56
Rules in classical invention, 27–28
Run-on sentences, 291

Same/the same, 335
Scene, 335
Seeds of Man, excerpts, 172–73
Semicolon, 301–2
Sensual/sensuous, 335
Sentence combining, 159–71
  for emphasis, 161
  of equal parts, 163
  for variety, 159
  revise choppy sentences, 160
  subordination, 164–65

Sentence errors, punctuation, 290–92
    comma splice, 290–91
    fragments, 291–92
    run-on sentence, 291
Sentence errors, syntax, 284–290
    agreement of subject and verb, 284–86
    modification, 288–89
    parallelism, 289–90
    predication, 286–87
Set/sit, 335
Shall, will, 335
Should, would, 335
Shaping. *See also* Between early and late shaping; Early shaping; Late shaping
    overview, 41
    promise and delivery system, 108
    purpose of, 42
    writing conventions, 47
Shaping, definition, 40
"Shooting an Elephant," 174–75
Sight, 335
Silences, excerpts from, 169–70
Similar to, 335
Sit, 335
Slash, 306
Somebody, 336
Something, 336
Something extra, 224
Some time/sometime/sometimes, 336
Sort of, 336
Sources. *See* Bibliographical entries
Spatial order, pattern of essay organization, 71, 73
Specially, 336
Spelling, 307–10
    reasons for errors, 307–10
    spelling rules, 310–11
Stage 1. *See* Creating
Stage 2. *See* Shaping
Stage 3. *See* Completing
Stationary/stationery, 336
Stupid, 336
Subject, 336
Subordinate conjunctions, 164
Subordinate, definition, 161
Subordination, 164–65
Such as, 336
Suppose, 336
Surely, 336

Take, 336
That/which/who, 336
Theirselves, 336

Thesis, 66–70, 89–104
    aids for formulating, 67
    campfire dance, 89–92
    checking essays for, 94–96
    checklist for, 68
    criteria for, 66–68
    definition, 66, 67
    fulfilling agreement, 89–96
    as magic string, 66
    master storyteller, 92–94
    summary of, 68
Thesis development, 96–104
    analysis, 102–3
    bare bones outline, 97–100
    cause/effect, 102
    classification, 103
    comparison and contrast, 101–2
    definition, 103–4
    delivering what is promised, 96–97
    example: "Motherliness," 104
    examples/illustrations, 100
    description, 100
    narration, 101
    specific details, 101
Thought-producing techniques, 9–13
Thusly, 336
Till/until, 336
Time order, pattern of essay organization, 71–73
To/too/two, 336
Topic sentence paragraph, 119–138
    application assignments: 122–23, 126–28, 129–31, 133–38
    characteristics, 119
    checking essay for, 123
    definition, 119, 120, 122
    function of, 119
    how it operates, 120–22
    principle 1: state main idea, 123–28, 137
    principle 2: stay on topic, 128–30, 137
    principle 3: supply enough information, 130–38
    promise and delivery system, 119
    topic sentence placement, 124–26
    topic sentence understood, 125–26
Topic sentence paragraph development, 132–33
    adding to general statement, 131–32
    comparison and contrast, 133
    facts and figures, 133
    illustrations, examples, details, 132–33
    narration, 133
    specific details, 131
Topoi. See Aristotle's common topics
Totally, 336

Transitions and reminder signs, 145–51
    checking for flow, 151
    to explain function, 151
    identifying signs, 151
    purpose, 150
    transitions, concept of, 145
    transitions as connectors, 146–48
    transitions, examples, 146–48
    transitions, signal words, 149
Trevelyan, G. M., 150
Trial, definition, 56
Trial draft, 56–60
    basic essay arrangement, 57
    characteristics, 56–57
    check for topic sentence, 128
    conclusion, 59
    cooling period, 59
    getting started, 58
    preliminary steps, 57
    reader's response, 59
    rules for, 56
Trite diction, 296
Type of, 336

U*nder water/underwater,* 336
Unidiomatic expressions, 297
Uninterested, 337
Until, 337
Use to/used to, 337

Verb, 273–278
    active and passive voice, 277–78
    auxiliary, 274
    combinations, 275
    intransitive, transitive, 276
    irregular, 273
    linking, 276
    modals, 275
    principal parts, 273
    regular, 273
    subject/verb/complement, 276–77
    tense system, 273
Verbals, 278
Verb particles, 282
Very, 337
Virgule/slash, 306

Ways, 337
Weather/whether, 337
Well, 337
Which, 337
White, E. B., 66, 126–27
Who, 337

Index 345

Will/would, 337
Would like for, 337
Writer's objectives, public and private, 43
Writing assignments, *See* Essay assignments
Writing to communicate, 42–112
Writing conventions, 47
Writing essay tests, 243–46
   application, 246
   completing, check list, 244
   creating, list for, 243
   shaping and summary, 243–45
Wrong denotation, 297

Z

Zinsser, William, 293

ACKNOWLEDGMENTS

DEDICATION

"i carry your heart with me" by E. E. Cummings. Copyright 1952 by E. E. Cummings. Reprinted from his volume *Complete Poems 1913–1962* by permission of Harcourt Brace Jovanovich, Inc.

STAGE ONE

"Looping" material from *Writing Without Teachers* by Peter Elbow. Oxford University Press, 1975. Reprinted by permission.

"Aristotle's Common Topics" from *The Little Rhetoric* by Edward P. J. Corbett. Copyright © 1977 by John Wiley & Sons, Inc. Reprinted by permission.

STAGE TWO

"All through *The Elements of Style* . . ." from *The Elements of Style,* Third Edition, by William Strunk, Jr. and E. B. White. Copyright © 1979 by Macmillan Publishing Co., Inc. Reprinted by permission.

"The key to getting and holding attention . . ." and "Purpose is the greatest influence on form." from *Moving Mountains* by Henry Boettinger. Copyright © 1969 by Henry Boettinger. Reprinted by permission of Macmillan Publishing Co., Inc.

From "Motherliness" from *Talking Woman* by Shana Alexander. Copyright © 1976 by Shana Alexander. Reprinted by permission of Delacorte Press.

STAGE THREE

Excerpt from "I Knew a Woman" copyright 1954 by Theodore Roethke from *The Collected Poems of Theodore Roethke.* Reprinted by permission of Doubleday & Company, Inc.

"Everywhere the white arcades . . ." from "The Cyclades" from *The Greek Islands* by Lawrence Durrell. Copyright © 1978 by Lawrence Durrell. Reprinted by permission of Viking Penguin Inc.

"I think the stature of humor . . ." from p. 245 in *Essays of E. B. White.* Copyright 1941, © 1956 by E. B. White. Printed by permission of Harper & Row, Publishers, Inc.

"I think this is the fourth spring . . ." from pp. 34–35 in *Essays of E. B. White.* Copyright 1941, © 1956 by E. B. White. Reprinted by permission of Harper & Row, Publishers, Inc.

S. I. Hayakawa, *Language in Action and Thought.* New York: Harcourt Brace Jovanovich, 1978.

"I shall not soon forget my first night here . . ." from p. 114 of *A Lady's Life in the Rocky Mountains* by Isabella Bird. Copyright © 1960 by The University of Oklahoma Press. Used by permission of the University of Oklahoma Press.

"Thus far I have tried to describe . . ." from *On Becoming a Person* by Carl R. Rogers. Copyright © 1961 by Carl R. Rogers. Reprinted with the permission of Houghton Mifflin Company.

From "Letter from Birmingham Jail" (pp. 90–91) in *Why We Can't Wait* by Martin Luther King, Jr. Copyright © 1963 by Martin Luther King, Jr. Reprinted by permission of Harper & Row, Publishers, Inc.

"If you were to ask people what they would like . . ." from *Everything You've Always Wanted to Know About Energy but Were Too Weak To Ask* by Naura Hayden. Copyright © 1976 by Naura Hayden. Reprinted by permission of E. P. Dutton, Inc. (A Hawthorn Book).

Excerpts from pp. 241–2 "Try to remember . . . image you had made up?" and p. 92 "The past is completely eliminated . . . no way of knowing." in *Four Arguments for the Elimination of Television* by Jerry Mander. Copyright © 1977, 1978 by Jerry Mander. Reprinted by permission of William Morrow & Company.

"Style is organic to the person . . ." and "Clutter is the disease of American writing . . ." from Chapter 2, "Simplicity," and p. 19 from *On Writing Well* by William Zinsser (Harper & Row). Copyright © 1976 by William K. Zinsser. Reprinted by permission of the author.

From "The Living Dead Sea" by Harvey Arden from *National Geographic Magazine,* February 1978. Copyright © 1978 by National Geographic Society. Reprinted by permission.

"Giving What You Say a Sense of Wholeness" from *Together: Communicating Interpersonally* by John Stewart and Gary A. D'Angelo. Copyright © 1975 by Addison-Wesley, Reading MA. Reprinted by permission.

"But what will America look like . . ." from *Cannibals and Christians* by Norman Mailer. Copyright © 1966 by Norman Mailer. Reprinted by permission of the author and the author's agents, Scott Meredith Literary Agency, Inc., 845 Third Avenue, New York, New York 10022.

From *Seeds of Man* by Woody Guthrie. Copyright © 1976 by Marjorie Guthrie. Reprinted by permission of the publisher, E. P. Dutton, Inc.

From "Shooting an Elephant" in *Shooting an Elephant and Other Essays* by George Orwell. Copyright 1950 by Sonia Brownell Orwell; renewed 1978 by Sonia Pitt-Rivers. Reprinted by permission of Harcourt Brace Jovanovich, Inc., the estate of the late Sonia Brownell Orwell and Martin Secker & Warburg Ltd.

From "Who Killed King Kong" by X. J. Kennedy from *Dissent* Spring 1960. Copyright © 1960 by the Dissent Publishing Corporation. Reprinted by permission.

PRACTICAL APPLICATIONS

Material from *Readers' Guide to Periodical Literature* is reproduced by permission of The H. W. Wilson Company.

"Two plausible explanations exist . . ." from *Anasazi: Ancient People of the Rock* by David Muench and Donald G. Pike. Copyright © 1974 by American West Publishing Company. Used by permission of Crown Publishers, Inc.

"Gerald Cohen's Dial-A-Buzzword" Chart courtesy Gerald Cohen.

A000030569320e

DATE DUE

#47-0108 Peel Off Pressure Sensitive

DISSECTING SHEET

Look at the essay you have written. Look at its anatomy. Fill in the questions below to see if your writing "works."

1. What is the idea in your paper that was in your head that you now want to get into your reader's head?

2. Read your first two sentences. (Remember, you have about that much space to get and keep your reader's attention.) Would *you* read past these two sentences? Mark the appropriate line below:

   ____ first two sentences extremely interesting; I can hardly wait to read on.

   ____ first two sentences OK, and I'm mainly counting on my reader's good will.

   ____ first two sentences crummy. I wouldn't read another word.

3. Look at your opening paragraph. Do you have any pronouns in it? (Not that there's anything especially wrong with pronouns, but they often signal that generalizations have been made, and generalizations *unless specifically planned by a writer* are often death to your message.) If you have any pronouns, write them here. If not, write *none*.

4. Do you use any words like *people, everyone, society,* etc.? If so, what specific purpose do these words serve? (These words often signal nonperson writing, no personal interest in the subject.) If you used none of these words, write *none* here.

5. Have you been *very* clear in your opening paragraph to state exactly the message you are taking the trouble to write to another person? Write the sentence here that comes directly from your paper showing your purpose in writing the paper. (If this isn't in the first paragraph, tell where it is and how it happened to be in that place. If the purpose of your paper is found in more than one sentence, write as many of the sentences from the paper as are necessary to show what the purpose is.)

6. What is the connection between your first and second paragraphs?

7. Read over the rest of your paper. How many separate points do you make in order to get your message across? List them here:

   (1.)   (3.)   (5.)
   (2.)   (4.)

(If you made more than five, you probably tried to cover too much territory in a single writing; people usually do not remember over five pieces of information at one time.)